Education, Democracy and Development

Education, Democracy and Development

Equity and Inclusion

Edited by
N.V. Varghese
Madhumita Bandyopadhyay

NIEPA

SHIPRA

Rs. 1600; US$ 64

ISBN: 978-93-88691-37-6

First Published in India in 2020

Education, Democracy and Development: Equity and Inclusion

Published by:
SHIPRA PUBLICATIONS
LG 18-19, Pankaj Central Market
I.P. Ext., Patparganj, Delhi 110092, India
Tel.: +91 11 2223 5152/6152, 9650028065
E-mail: info@shiprapublication.com
www.shiprapublication.com

Preface

Equality is an idea embraced by all political formations rooted in democratic traditions. While inequalities in traditional societies were the result of unequal share in the ownership of landed property and wealth, inequalities in modern societies are mainly emerging from variations in earnings from professions. Education is a necessary passport for entry into professions. Unlike landed property and wealth, education can not be inherited. Therefore, distribution of educational opportunities and individual access to education determine the nature and extent of inequalities in the present and in the future.

There are unending debates on whether or not democracy promotes economic and social development. At times these debates are inconclusive. It is argued that the electoral democracies are hesitant to take hard decisions to foster faster development when such decisions may not have a mass appeal. Therefore the question is posed more as either promoting economic growth or distribution than facilitating both. In general, the democratic regimes are associated with egalitarian policies and they are the least tolerant to inequalities in society.

The experience in the recent past has shown that inequalities are widening in many of the countries following democratic form of government. The evidence shows that the democratic states following progressive state policies have successfully combined the objectives of growth and equity. Many of them followed positive discriminatory policies to level off the existing inequalities. Those states which embraced market principles did not pay adequate attention to egalitarian polices and were responsible for uneven progress among different segments of population.

Ever since education is considered as a fundamental right, its universal provision became a national concern and a social imperative. Equality of educational opportunity is an inclusive notion and it forms a cornerstone to equality in social progress in our efforts to reach the sustainable development goals. This book on "Education, Democracy and Development: Equity and Inclusion" provides an opportunity to review and reflect on these themes both globally and in India.

More specifically, this volume provides deeper insight into the issues related to the role of education in promoting democracy and sustaining the achievements made by several countries. Since equity is one of the core issues in linking education with democracy and development, it is important to create strong, inclusive and effective institutions for promoting just as well as humane society.

I hope that this volume will make good contribution to analysing and understanding important issues challenging the progress of education in global context and it will be a useful reading for policy makers and researchers interested in the contemporary issues pertaining to educational development in the current context.

New Delhi
September, 2019

N.V. Varghese
Vice-Chancellor
NIEPA, New Delhi.

Acknowledgements

The National Institute of Educational Planning and Administration (NIEPA) organised an International Seminar on "Democracy, Education and Development: Issues Relating to Inclusion, Equity and Sustainability." The seminar attracted a large number of participants from abroad and India. The participants consisted of academics and policy makers. This volume is based on selected papers presented in the seminar.

Our heartfelt greetings to all authors who have contributed different thematic papers to the seminar and these are Volker Wedekind, University of Nottingham, UK; Aslam Fataar, Stellenbosch University, South Africa; Shireen Motala, University of Johannesburg, South Africa; Crain Soudien, University of Cape Town, South Africa; Sandra Schmidt, Columbia University, USA; Caroline Dyer, University of Leeds, USA; Judith E. Parker, Columbia University, USA; H.S. Bhola, Indiana University, USA; Thomas F. Luschei, Claremont Graduate University, USA; Teboho Moja, New York University, New York; Radhika Iyengar, Angelique R. Mahal and Fatima Ahmad, Columbia University, New York; Kenneth King, University of Edinburgh, UK; Keith Lewin, University of Sussex, Falmer, Brighton; Roger Jeffery, University of Edinburgh, UK; Praveen Jha and Pooja Parvati, Tata Trust; Satadru Sikdar, NIPFP, New Delhi Jawaharlal Nehru University, New Delhi; Santosh Mehrotra, Jawaharlal Nehru University, New Delhi; A. Mathew, NIEPA, New Delhi; S. Irfan Habib, New Delhi. Vimala Ramachandran, ERU, New Delhi; and Badri Narayan, Jawaharlal Nehru University.

In addition, faculty from NIEPA and other universities, research scholars, policy makers also actively participated and contributed to the deliberations and discussions in the seminar. It is also mention-worthy that the seminar could also engage young scholars of NIEPA as well as other universities, international and national NGOs in intense dialogue and discussions in the seminar. We express deep gratitude to all the educationists, social scientists, policy makers and development practitioners who contributed in the seminar significantly as chair and presenters though their papers have not been included in this volume. These are A. Vaidyanathan, Honourary Fellow, Centre for Development Studies, Kerala; P. Balakrishnan, Centre for Development Studies, Kerala, K. Sujatha, Department of Educational Administration, NUEPA; Sachidanand Sinha, Jawaharlal Nehru University, New Delhi; Geetha B. Nambissan, Jawaharlal Nehru University, New Delhi; Kuldeep Mathur, Former Director, NIEPA, New Delhi; Daniel A. Wagner, University of Pennsylvania, USA; Ratna Ghosh, McGill University, Canada; Karuna Chanana, Former Professor, Jawaharlal Nehru University,

New Delhi; S.K. Thorat, Former UGC Chairperson and Director, ICSSR; A.R. Vasavi, Nehru Memorial Museum and Library, New Delhi; Sudhanshu Bhushan, NIEPA, New Delhi; and A K Singh, Department of Educational Policy, NIEPA. We also thank all rapportures from NIEPA, such as Aarti Srivastava, Neeru Snehi, K. Biswal, N.K. Mohanty, Y. Josephine, Suman Negi, Rashmi Diwan, Sunita Chugh, Savita Kaushal, P. Geetha Rani, Naresh Kumar, Kashyapi Awasthi, R.S. Tyagi, Subhita G.V, Veera Gupta, Sangeeta Angom, Mona Sedwal, Shreya Tiwari, V.P.S. Raju, A.N. Reddy, S.K. Mallik, and L. Binita Devi.

We thank all the contributors to this volume. We would also like to thank the then Vice-Chancellor, NUEPA, Prof. R. Govinda for all his support in organising the seminar. NIEPA administration played an important supportive role in organising the seminar. We are also thankful to the publication department for processing the manuscript for publication.

We gratefully acknowledge the suggestions and comments received from experts and participants who have attended the seminar. The core team developed for conducting the seminar comprising Mr. Basavaraj Swamy, Registrar; Mr. P.N. Tyagi, Training Cell In-charge; Mrs. Usha Thyagarajan, Finance Officer; Shri Chander Prakash, SO, Accounts Section at NIEPA took up all challenging as well as mundane task to ensure successful completion of the seminar and therefore, deserves special acknowledgement. This book would not have been able to reach this stage, without support provided by Dr. Vaishali, Ms. Anupriya Kholia, Dr. L. Binita Devi, Ms. Meenakshi Khandari, Mr. Ankur Singh and Ms. Poonam for conducting the seminar as well as compiling the chapters included in the book.

New Delhi
September, 2019

N.V. Varghese
Madhumita Bandyopadhyay

Contents

List of Abbreviations

ACE	Advanced Certificate in Education
ACER	Australian Council for Educational Research
AICTE	All India Council for Technical Education
AIE	Alternative and Innovative Education
AIES	All India Educational Survey
AIIMS	All India Institute of Medical Science
AISES	All India School Education Survey
ANA	Annual National Assessments
ANC	African National Congress
ASER	Annual Status of Education Report
BPL	Below Poverty Line
BJP	Bharatiya Janata Party
BSP	Bahujan Samaj Party
CABE	Central Advisory Board of Education
CAPS	Curriculum and Assessment Policy Statement
CCs	Community Colleges
CERD	Committee on the Elimination of Racial Discrimination
CLER	Configurations-Linkages-Environment-Resources
CP	Community Polytechnics
CREATE	Consortium for Research on Educational Access, Transitions and Equity
CTE	Continuing Technical Education
CGS-LGA	Conditional Grants Scheme to Local Government Areas
DBE	Department of Basic Education
DEE&L	Department of Elementary Education and Literacy
DFID	Department for International Development
DHET	Department of Higher Education and Training
DISE	District Information System for Education
DM	District Magistrate
DNTs	Denotified and Nomadic Tribes
DoE	Department of Education
EAU	Escuela Activa Urbana
EDI	Educational Development Index
EFA	Education for All
EGS	Education Guarantee Scheme
FARC	Revolutionary Armed Forces of Colombia
FET	Further Education and Training
GDP	Gross Domestic Product
GEFI	Global Education First Initiative

GER	Gross Enrolment Ratio
GMC	General Medical Council
GMR	Global Monitoring Report
GNP	Gross National Product
GO	Government Order
GOI	Government of India
GSHDR	Gujarat State Human Development Report
GUNI	Global University Network for Innovation
HCT	Human Capital Theory
HLP	High Level Panel
ICT	Information Communication Technology
IHDR	Indian Human Development Report
IHDS	Indian Human Development Survey
IIM	Indian Institute of Management
IIT	Indian Institute of Technology
IMC	Indian Medical Council
IMS	Indian Medical Service
INSRAW	International Research and Training Institute for the Advancement of Women
MDGs	Millennium Development Goals
MHRD	Ministry of Human Resource Development
MLA	Member of Legislative Assembly
MP	Member of Parliament
MSEP	Mathematics and Science Education Project
MSET	Mathematics, Science, Engineering, and Technology
NAAC	National Assessment and Accreditation Council
NABARD	National Bank of Agricultural and Rural Development
NAPCC	National Action Plan on Climate Change
NAEP	National Assessment of Educational Progress
NAS	National Achievement Survey
NASSCOM	National Association of Software and Services Companies
NCAER	National Council of applied Economic Research
NCDNSNT	National Commission for Denotified, Nomadic and Semi-Nomadic Tribes
NCE	National Coalition for Education
NCERT	National Council of Educational Research and Training
NCF 2005	National Curriculum Framework 2005
NCV	National Certificate (Vocational)
NCS	National Curriculum Statement
NCWP	National Certificate for Work Preparation
NDA	National Democratic Alliance
NGOs	Non-Governmental Organisations
NMIS	Nigeria MDG Information System
NNSSF	National Norms and Standards for School Funding
NPC	National Planning Commission
NPEGEL	National Programme for Education of Girls at Elementary Level
NQF	National Qualifications Framework
NREGA	National Rural Employment Guarantee Act
NSDS	National Skills Development Strategy
NSF	National Skills Fund
NSNP	National School Nutrition Programme

NSQF	National Skills Qualification Framework
NSSO	National Sample Survey Organisation
NUEPA	National University of Educational Planning and Administration
OBCs	Other Backward Castes
OBE	Outcomes-Based Education
OECD	Organisation for Economic Cooperation and Development
OSAGI	Office of the Special Adviser on Gender Issues and Advancement of Women
OWG	Open Working Group
PBL	Problem-Based Learning
PCI	Principal Component Index
PTAs	Parent-Teacher Associations
PTR	Pupil-Teacher Ratios
RNCS	Revised National Curriculum Statements
ROME	Re-Orientation of Medical Education
RTE Act	Right to Education Act
SACE	South African Council for Educators
SACMEQ	Southern and Eastern African Consortium for Monitoring Education Quality
SAP	Structural Adjustment Programme
SAQA	South African Qualifications Authority
SCs	Scheduled Castes
SCR	Student Classroom Ratio
SDGs	Sustainable Development Goals
SDU	Schools Development Unit
SDSN	Sustainable Development Solutions Network
SEMCs	School Education Management Committees
SETAs	Sector Education and Training Authorities
SG	Secretary General
SP	Samajwadi Party
SMT	School Management Team
SSA	Sarva Shiksha Abhiyan
STs	Scheduled Tribes
SUBEB	State Universal Basic Education Board
TEQIP	Technical Education Quality Improvement Programme
TIMMS-R	Third International Mathematics and Science Study Repeat
TIMSS	Trends in International Mathematics and Science Study
TVET	Technical and Vocational Education and Training
UDHR	Universal Declaration of Human Rights
UEE	Universal Elementary Education
UGC	University Grants Commission
UHCI	Universal Health Coverage for India
UKIERI	UK-India Education and Research Initiative
UNESCO	United Nations Educational Scientific Cultural Organisation
UNSTT	UN System Task Team
VET	Vocational Education and Training
WCED	Western Cape Education Department
WDEFA	World Declaration on Education for All

1
Introduction

N.V. Varghese and *Madhumita Bandyopadhyay*

Democracy and Development: The Debate

Democracy implies an egalitarian approach to and framework for development and it questions unequal distribution of opportunities, income and wealth. The idea of redistributive justice forms the core value to mobilise people for democracy (Ansell and Samuels, 2014). The presentation of 'democracy as Robin Hood' holds well in the debates on the virtues of democracy. The argument that economic equality will follow political equality gives hope to people to vote for those subscribing to democratic values and practices.

The debate on whether or not democracy promotes economic development is inconclusive. There are arguments and theoretical models that show that democracy facilitates development, democracy acts as a hindrance to development, and that democracy has little or no relationship with development (Przeworski and Limongi, 1993). Some argue that democracy promotes economic development and democratic institutions are compatible with effective economic development.

There is also an argument that democratic regimes are less capable of managing development than authoritarian regimes. It is argued at times that a strong authoritarian state is better able to engineer a successful process of economic development than an electoral democracy (see for a review of theoretical models Sirowy and Inkeles 1990). The electoral democracies will be hesitant to take hard decisions which may be necessary for fostering faster development, but are unpleasant and not appealing to the masses. The authoritarian regimes, on the other hand, may be decisive in implementing policies.

It is argued by Professor Huntington that while the idea of compatibility perceived progress towards any of the development goals is reinforced by movement towards achievement of other goals, the conflict notion pointed to the contrary experience and the reconciliation policies tried to prioritise and sequence the move towards development goals (Huntington, 1993; 1996). While some of these development goals may be compatible, all such goals need not be considered for policy planning as well as implementation.

Development implies change which is not welcomed by all at all times. Development also implies fairness in distribution of resources and benefits of growth. It can be argued that democratic governments are associated with more egalitarian policies. If development implies sharing the benefits by all segments of society, then democratic forms of government have an advantage over other forms of government. This is also an argument which needs further empirical validation. For example, the decades of 1990s and 2000s have seen transition of largest number of countries to democracy. This period also witnessed widening of inequalities. The OECD review shows that the gap between rich and poor in most OECD countries has widened over the past two decades. Inequality of incomes was higher in most OECD countries in the mid-2000s than in the mid-1980s (OECD, 2008).

It is very difficult to reconcile with the fact that spreading of democracy is also associated with widening inequalities. It seems the public policies vary among countries which results in widening or narrowing down of inequalities in democratic regimes. For example, some of the most equal societies, such as Denmark and Norway are democratic. Similarly, countries, such as France and Spain moved toward more equality while inequalities were widening in the OECD countries which are also democratic countries.

The politics of aspiration plays an important role in democratic societies and political parties compete to inspire voters through aspirational ideas. The idea of redistributive justice is a core theme to keep aspiration levels of the people high. Democratic egalitarianism is a value promoted in the democratic frame of analysis and supported through legislative measures. While developed countries emphasise more on individual freedom, the less developed countries focus more on group based rights. The basis of group based rights may vary in different contexts. It may be based on religion, ethnicity, economic and social backwardness.

A faster progress of the deprived groups is necessary to level-off the differences among social groups. The advancement of the deprived groups is seen as an indicator of success of democracy. The egalitarian principles need to be seen not only at the entry level (equality of opportunities) but also at the outcome level. Many countries had the chance to have people from the deprived groups in high offices, even when these countries did not succeed in meeting the challenges of extending democratic egalitarianism to all segments of their population.

One of the challenges of promoting the idea of democratic egalitarianism is that the aspirations of the public outstrip the surplus generating capacity of the state. The group rights and a concern for the deprived at times slip into the domain of competitive populism resulting in discourses and dispensations focusing more on distribution than on growth and equitable distribution. The argument for indiscriminate subsidies borders on competitive populism.

Education and Democracy

Empirical evidence shows that one of the most important factors contributing to economic growth in the recent decades is human capital (Engelbrecht, 2003). The human capital theory postulates a positive relationship between education and economic growth and the empirical evidence generated under this framework supports and validates this hypothesis (Schultz, 1961; Becker, 1964). In most societies income from landed properties as a share of national and personal income declined and the share of earnings from professions increased. Education is an important factor influencing job recruitment and income. Those who possess higher qualifications and degrees stand better chances to be selected to higher paying jobs. In other words, education can be a source of better jobs and income, an unequal distribution of educational opportunities can also be a source of inequalities.

Education produces positive democratic effects. The relationship between mass education, literacy and democratic development is strong. Education as a social requisite plays a role in political socialisation. An empirical analysis of 108 countries for a period of 1960-2000 (Drackner and Subramanyam, 2010) shows that a more equal access to education accelerates transition to democracy and a large share of educated population boosts chances of maintaining democracy. It seems adult literacy is the single most predictor of level of democratisation. Therefore, investment in primary education is highly rewarded from this point of view. Further, commitment to democratic ideas appears to increase with levels of education and it is expected that higher education may result in top-down pressures for democracy.

Democratic societies are more egalitarian and inclusive, as they not only respect the will of the majority but also protect the fundamental rights of individuals and minority groups. Education is a universal human right and is also a mean of achieving other human rights. Therefore, an effort to achieve education for all (EFA) is a logical extension of the democratic principles. The RTE from this perspective is crucial in extending democratic ideals through distribution of educational opportunities. However, the idea of democracy in education becomes meaningful when one ensures not only equity in access to education but also equity in outcomes, at least in terms of learning outcomes.

The EFA efforts, no doubt, show that countries have succeeded in bringing children to schools, but, evidences on the extent of learning that take place in the classrooms are still disturbing and discouraging. Children fail to learn what they are supposed to learn even when they continue to stay in schools. GMR report (2014) characterises this phenomenon as a manifestation *global learning crisis* – a situation of "extreme inequalities in achieving the most basic learning requirements, both between and within countries add up to a global learning crisis that needs urgent action" (GMR 2013-14: 191). The empirical evidence suggests that the cognitive skills acquired during education are more strongly related to individual earnings, income distribution and economic growth than mere access to education. In some of the regression based studies, years of schooling as a variable for predicting individual earnings is replaced by indicators for cognitive skills (Hanushek and Woessmann, 2015). It is shown by these authors that variations in economic growth are better explained by the quality of education and cognitive skills acquired by the students. The implications of children not learning adequately at the primary level is alarming, if one looks at it distribution among countries. Nearly 40 per cent of the primary school children worldwide are not learning the basics in reading and mathematics. However, in the developed countries, such as in North America and Western Europe, nearly 96 per cent of the primary school children attain minimum levels of learning. The situation in the developing countries is very unfortunate. For example, only one-third of primary schools children in South and West Asia and only one-fifth of children in Sub-Saharan Africa attain minimum levels of learning at the end of primary cycle. In other words, while we are narrowing down variations in regional enrolment, but the ahievement continue to be considerable and concentrated in the deprived regions in the world (GMR, 2014).

The learning deficit is also unequally distributed among different socio-economic groups within a country. Even in the developing countries, children living in wealthy regions do better than those from poorer regions. Similarly, children in urban areas learn more than their counterparts in the rural areas. In developed countries poorer children learn less than the rich children (GMR, 2014: 192). Children from rich families in poor countries on average learn more than those from poor families. Girls from poor families are more disadvantaged in this regard than boys from similar background (GMR, 2014: 195).

The learning deficits at the primary level are transmitted to the secondary level and they have a cumulative effect leading to underperformance and eventual dropping out of poor performing children at the secondary and tertiary levels of education. The dismissal of a large number of students from IIT, Roorkie in the recent past is an example of students failing to perform due to the cumulative learning deficit created by the system.

The challenge of improving learning while expanding access is compounded in developing countries, since many of the new entrants are from marginalised households and first generation learners. There are examples of countries which tried to overcome the challenges posed by the learning deficits. For example, Kenya and Tanzania represent a situation of increased enrolment accompanied by enhanced levels of learning. The case studies of these countries indicate that cumulative learning deficits can be reduced through public policy and targeted interventions.

The learning deficits are often concentrated in poorly resourced localities, among children from disadvantages groups, among those who speak minority languages and hail from immigrant families. Any efforts towards reducing inequalities in learning outcomes need to focus on providing complementary education or additional support for catching up of these children. There are instances where poor perform well when programmes to promote equity in learning are designed and effectively implemented.

Questions are asked about it possibilities of sustaining progress while maintaining equity is concerned. In countries, such as the USA and UK, the question of sustainable development acquires an altogether different dimension with almost universal secondary education and institutions of higher education already achieving a critical stage of knowledge generation. As opposed to individual as the unit of analysis in Western academic discourse, many developing countries have communitarian approach to social justice which, might prove to be problematic because within the community there are differences that may be perpetuated. This poses a great challenge to inclusive policy of education adopted by the state. As the state finds its resources exhausted, private capital in education is favoured and this often comes into conflict with equitable development and inclusive state policy.

What then is the optimal mix of policy that could support inclusive development? In India and possibly in South Africa, the path of democratisation, though not free from pitfalls, has led to upward mobility of social classes though it will require for both countries to travel a long way to establish an inclusive and egalitarian society in every respect. It is widely recognised that, education is key in establishing an inclusive society. This requires new approaches and understanding of the manner in which education can relate to economic development with considerable implications for policy and planning for creating a democratic society as well. As it has been mentioned in a recent document of OECD, a well-educated population is essential for a country's economic and social development as higher level of education means higher earnings, better health and a longer life. So, it is in society's interest to ensure that all children and adults have access to a wide variety of educational opportunities (OECD 2012: 72).

It is acknowledged that socio-economic background of children has an impact on the access to education as well as academic achievement. It is observed that children from disadvantaged background such as low socio-economic status or from an immigrant background or parents with low educational level, etc. are more likely to perform poorly and leave school early. Almost all countries have paid attention to promote equity by providing education to deprived section of population, who have been denied educational opportunity for ages. The policy brief of OECD (2008) on "Ten Steps to Equity in Education" provides an overview of such initiatives by different countries across the world which includes education of people affected by migration, minorities, children showing poor performance because of low economic background and so on.

It has been realised that expansion of education could not bring equity automatically unless immense efforts are not made to bridge the gender and social gaps in enrolment, participation, learning outcome, completion and transition to next level. It has also been mentioned that governments often allow parents a choice of schools, partly in the interests of equity. But this may in fact increase the risk of inequity because better-educated parents make better- informed choices. In many OECD countries, greater choice in school systems is associated with larger differences in the social composition of schools. The conclusion is that school choice requires careful management from an equity perspective, particularly to ensure that it does not result in increased differences in the social composition of schools" (OECD 2008: 3). It has also been suggested to provide adequate resources to deal with equity issues particularly in some special situation, such as where immigrants and minorities are attending schools to promote their participation in early childhood education, improving their learning level at school as well as at the territory level, teacher's professional development, etc.

The socio-economic and cultural factors also have been discussed by other researchers (Marks, Cresswell, Aniley, 2010). In their research they have found that cultural and material resources are important for students' achievement across the country (under study). It has also been found that the school plays an important role in strengthening impact of socio-economic inequalities on the education of children.

According to Dewey's perspective, education has immense impact on societal development as "connections between education and civil society and proposed not just engagement by formal means such as voting but by developing a well-informed population who would be able to understand and act in society." Dewey has mentioned "school as a special environment" because the school has the function of "coordinating within the disposition of each individual and the diverse influences of the various social environments into which he enters."

Drawing reference from John Dewey that the aims of education should be oriented towards preparing young people to be full and active participants in all aspects of democratic life, Christopher Koliba (2000), has tried to examine how democracy and education are linked to each other and what is the role of school to promote the democratic process in society. It has been observed that, "the conception of schools as democratic institutions leads to an entirely new set of assumptions regarding governance and the role of students in their own learning."

According to Mitter (1993), the present global scene raises questions about the socio-economic, political and cultural framework laying the ground for a constructive interaction between the three forces which greatly determine people's existence and survival, namely Development, Democracy and Education. Drawing reference from Dewey's fundamental study, Democracy and Education (1916), Mitter has emphasised on "voluntary disposition and interest" which is very important for democracy and can only be created by education. As Mitter explains, "Dewey also finds in the essential quality of democracy as a mode of associated living, of conjoint communicated experience" (Dewey 1916b: 93). Dewey has focused his attention on the structure of the social system in another book, *The School and Society* (1899) within which education and democracy can interact successfully. It is because of this, it has been stressed that, education must pass through an equally complete transformation, and for this purpose, each school should be an "embryonic community life," active with types of occupations that reflect the life of the larger society which is worthy, lovely and harmonious"(Dewey 1916a: 19-20). However, as mentioned by Mitter, it has necessary preconditions which can be considered as virtues, i.e. "on the one hand, the will, readiness, and ability to shape and organise one's life independently and responsibly, and on the other, the willingness of all citizens to develop and consolidate the education system in order to pass these preconditions on to the next generation."

Mitter has also emphasised on school autonomy where head teachers, teachers, pupils, as well as parents and the members of the community all can have the opportunity to make choices and decisions. For linking education, development and democracy, the author has stressed on adoption of new approaches to development, but also, at the same time, to democracy. Finally, author concludes that "Unless these are developed, the task of linking development to fundamental values, focused upon human rights and human dignity will remain incomplete" and in the final analysis, as opined by author, "development and democracy must both depend upon the effectiveness of an education which supports both of them and also links their functions to the fundamental human value."

While highlighting the political aspects of citizenship, Ruitenberg (2015) has argued that democratic citizenship education must include the education of equality. As Ruitenberg says, "Equality is inherently primary and central in democracy and politics" and citizenship education needs to emphasise on egalitarian aspects of citizenship to promote equity in school which shapes the lives of people.

Education is also considered as an important ingredient for achieving the goals of human development in sustainable manner. It also plays an important role in successful globalisation as well as sustainable development as argued by Little & Green (2009). The authors have defined successful globalisation as "economic growth combined with equality and social peace" and they have examined how education is linked with successful globalisation in different country contexts. Drawing reference from a comparative study of China, India, Kenya, Sri Lanka, and East Asia, Japan, Hong Kong, Singapore, South Korea, Taiwan authors have shown that "while economic and political policies have usually been the mere important drivers of development for all countries for all times, education has been a necessary, if not sufficient component. Authors have also mentioned five sets of policy which include achievement of mass education; planned expansion of secondary; technical & higher education; development of communication skills; equitable expansion of education; awareness of the potential of both the official and hidden curriculum of educational institutions. Linking education with sustainable development, authors have mentioned that it is required to change the way of educating children as well as adults to ensure sustainable development which is seen in three spheres of environment, society and economy. Authors have recommended for interdisciplinary approach for further research in this area.

It is widely known that adequate investment of financial resource is the key to educational development and promoting equity in education by providing education to all irrespective of their socio-economic background. Gomes (1993), comparing the situation between Latin America and South Korea, has raised the issue of low investment on education in Latin America, though there has been some evidence of concern for basic education of poorer children. The situation became worse because of debt crises in last decade, as Gomes states, "Every opportunity needs to be taken to obtain support for the improvement of education. Access, equity, quality and efficiency all are necessary conditions to the breakdown of Latin America's isolation."

Buch (1975) in his article "Democracy, Development and the Administrative System" has stressed on effective functioning of administrative democracy in the federal system of India. Despite being a "centre-oriented polity", in India, state intervention has been adopted to deal with state level disparities and regional imbalances to ensure equity in development" (1975: 346). There are three distinct levels of administrative unit functioning in India: Central Government, State Government and Local Government, which is the "starting point for the projection of the aspirations of the people, the sum total of which is national policy" (1975: 348). Buch has concluded finally, "Development in a democratic society insists on interaction at all levels and a correction of errors through public exposure and debate. But a democracy in turn can be even more ruthless in the implementation of plans because it is the people, rather than a faceless bureaucracy, who act as watchdogs" (1975: 355).

The Papers

The papers focussing on the related themes are organised under four themes in this volume:

I: Education and Democracy

Education holds the key to both democracy and development. It is instrumental in developing a democratic society while supporting the development process. Generally, education is considered as a potential enabler for promoting a democratic society in line with the principle of equal opportunity which, in turn, may give a big impetus to development in a comprehensive sense.

The papers in the section on democracy and education show that education is instrumental in developing a democratic society while supporting the overall development process. This section has papers based on national and international experiences.

The paper by Crain Soudien focusses on South Africa's experiment with democracy and its implications for education. It reviews the cumulative impact of the policy interventions on educational development in South Africa during the past 20 years to provide quality education and to improve learning levels among the disadvantaged groups. The paper by Thomas Luschei analyses the Columbian experience of proving education under conflict and violence. The innovative education programme of "*Escuela Nueva*" had positive impact on access, participation and learning outcome of children. The paper by Bhola focuses on inter-linkages between literacy, education and democracy with development which is inclusive and sustainable. Kenneth King in his paper extends these country experiences to global context and to post 2015 period. He argues that education plays an important role in achieving other development goals and in developing "global citizenship" which is gaining increasing importance in the post 2015 development agenda.

The last paper included in this section shows the experiences of different groups in education and democracy. The paper by Badri Narayan has focused on the comparative experience of democracy by *Dalit* groups such as "*Mushars*" with other castes to show the extent of deprivation experienced by groups in comparison with other groups.

II: Education and Development

The chapters included in this section show the importance of education in development which is inclusive and all encompassing. These papers collectively show that investment on education not only contributes to accelerate the process of development but also for sustaining it.

The chapter by Teboho Moja is on the poor access of higher education in African countries and its effects on economic development, employment, equity and social justice. Higher education promotes employment and contributes to democracy, political stability and sustainability in many developing countries. In Africa higher education systems remain largely elite and hence not in a position to play these positive roles. Similar concerns are expressed in another paper by Judith E. Parker in the context of the USA. The focus in this paper moves from access to achievement. The paper describes different models and examples of initiatives taken for achieving the goal of sustainable learning in the USA. Based on the experience of different education programmes of the USA, the paper argues for developing a sustainable learning culture and elaborates on the role of technology in facilitating sustainable and inclusive learning environment. Another paper by Volker Wedekind links development with Vocational Education in South Africa. The paper shows that the dominance of human capital theory has resulted in focusing on economic and social issues and the issue of skill shortages has become a central concern of national development strategies.

The paper on a similar theme by Santosh Mehrotra argues for a radical restructuring to vocationalise secondary education in India. Improving employability is important to take advantage of the growing youth bulge and the country's demographic dividend. The paper shows that since only two per cent of India's workforce had acquired any form of formal vocational training and an additional 8 per cent of the workforce had acquired vocational training informally on the job, the task involved to provide vocation training to nearly 136 million youthful new entrants to the labour force will be a challenge. Another paper by Roger Jeffery addresses the issue of development of professionally skilled manpower in India. The competition for admissions to medical colleges is very high; the rates of tuition fees are high and the language of instruction, very often, is English. These factors make it difficult to implement policies related to inclusiveness in professional education in India.

III: Education and Equity

Equity is one of the core issues in linking education with democracy and development. In a specific historical context, democracy appeared as a liberating experience as it provided an opportunity for realising the ideal relationship between state and society mediated through citizenship with its principle of equality, liberty and justice. In the current context, the emerging contestations of democracy coming from a variety of sources — ranging from multi-culturalists, feminists and proponents of new social movements to neo-left theorists call for new vision, approach and practices of democracy. The paper by Keith Lewin argues in favour of public funding to promote equity in the distribution of educational facilities. The education of the poor cannot be left to the private sector and will be best served by public investments. The paper by Praveen Jha, Pooja Parvati and Satadru Sikdar raises issues pertaining to marketisation, commodification and public funding and argues that with the rise of neo-liberalism in recent decades public services such as education, health, etc. have increasingly been subjected to the logic of the market. S. Irfan Habib in his paper focusses on the role and contributions by national leaders like Maulana Abul Kalam Azad and Dr. B.R. Ambedkar towards building an egalitarian society. The paper by Vimla Ramachandran explores how the education system has created hierarchies and forms of social exclusion thereby challenging the very foundations of equality and equal opportunities. The paper shows that the education system has created new hierarchies and forms of social exclusion and inclusion.

IV: Right to Education

Education is a fundamental human right and essential for the exercise of all other human rights. It promotes individual freedom and empowerment and yields important development benefits. The advancement of the rights-based approach to education creates sites of inclusion and exclusion that are socially and politically determined. Hence, there appears to be an education-development trajectory that is mediated through contestations in a democracy. Further, inclusiveness is generally advocated as a rights-based and affirmative policy. However, it is often argued that inclusiveness has its own limits as core policy or as a right, and may have a trade-off with growth, implying that resources necessary for inclusion of different sections of society cannot be mobilised without a positive economic growth trajectory.

The paper by R. Govinda and A. Mathew focusses on differential provision for school education which has affected children living in smaller habitations located in disadvantaged areas. Drawing references from different reports and surveys, authors have made an effort to understand the process of exclusion in such schools that lead to low quality primary education which has affected education of socio-economically marginalised sections living in smaller habitations. Shireen Motala argues in her paper that unlike other countries in Sub-Saharan Africa, South Africa has near universal access up to the end of the compulsory phase. The universal access has not translated into improved learning since learning levels continue to be low. The paper by Radhika Iyengar, Angelique R. Mahal and Fatima Ahmad is on alternative ways of implementing EFA in the most populous country in Africa (Nigeria) and the second most populous country in the world (India). The paper discusses among many things, the mode of participation of local people in planning and budgeting of educational development as an important element to sustain and strengthen democracy at grassroots level. The paper by Sandra Schmidt explores the contemporary challenges to democratisation associated with space and diversity with the special focus on African immigrant youth who are forced to create identity in the United States while simultaneously being positioned as outsiders within the USA. The issue of migration from a different point of view is discussed in another paper by Caroline Dyer where she analyses the extent of formal education deprivation among mobile pastoralist children in India, especially in the context of the RTE. The analysis shows that a sizeable, but largely invisible, segment of the Indian population continues to experience denial of access to formal education provision.

Aslam Fataar argues that the youth are often placed at the margins of the public sphere and major political, socio-economic, and cultural processes explores the possibilities of young people organising to shape their livelihood and education. The paper points out that there are specifiable interactive relationships between students' living contexts and how they construct and position their educational subjectivities within these contexts.

It seems that it is difficult to establish neither a linear relationship nor a conclusive positive association between democracy, education and development. The deliberations in the seminar brought these varying viewpoints in the papers included in this volume. The themes identified for deliberations in the seminar bear this out. The themes include education and development, right to education, inclusion, equity and democracy, teaching and learning, and democracy and education. The present volume presents selected papers presented at the seminar.

References

Ansell, and Samuels, (2014): *Inequality and Democratisation: An Elite Competition Approach*, New York, Cambridge University.

Buch, (1975): Democracy, Development and the Administrative System. *India International Centre Quarterly*, 12 (4) (December 1985): 345-55 Indian International Centre. Accessed at: http://www.jstor.org/stable/23001575

Dewey, John (2010): *Education as a Social Function.* In Arthur, James and Davies, Ian (Ed), Education Studies Reader, Routledge, 183-91.

Drackner, Mikael and Subrahmanyam, Gita (2010): Educational Investment and Democratic Development: A Theoretical and Empirical Overview, Sweden: SIDA, Stockholm.

Engelbrecht, Hans-Jurgen (2003): Human Capital and Economic Growth: Cross-Section Evidence for OECD Countries. *Economic Record,* 79 (Special Issue, June): 40-51.

Gomes, Candido (1993): Education, Democracy and Development in Latin America. *International Review of Education,* Springer, 39 (6): 531-540.

Assessed at: http://www.jstor.org/stable/3444979

Hanushek, Eric and Woessmann, Ludger (2015): *The Knowledge Capital of Nations: Education and the Economics of Growth,* Cambridge, MA: MIT Press.

Huntington, Samuel P. (1993): Clash of Civilisations. *Foreign Affairs,* 72 (3): 22–49.

Huntington, Samuel P. (1996): *The Clash of Civilisations and the Remaking of World Order,* New York: Simon & Schuster.

Koliba, Chirstopher (2000): Democracy and Education Schools and Communities Initiative Conceptual Framework and Preliminary Findings, assessed on 24/06/2015, http://www.uvm.edu/-dewey/articles/Democonc.html

Little, Angela W. & Green, Andy (2009): Successful Globalisation, Education and Sustainable Development, *International Journal of Educational Development,* 29: 166-74.

Assessed at: http://www.sciencedirect.com/science/article/pii/S0738059308001028#

Marks, Gary N., Cresswell, John & Aniley, John (2010): Explaining Socio-economic Inequalities in Student Achievement: The Role of Home and School Factors. In Arthur, James and Davies, Ian (Ed): *Education Studies Reader.* Routledge, 98-119.

Mitter, Wolfgang (1993): Education, Democracy and Development in a Period of Revolutionary Change, *International Review of Education, Springer,* 39 (6), (November): 463-71. Assessed at: http://www.jstor.org/stable/3444973.

OECD (Organisation for Economic Cooperation and Development (2008): *Growing Unequal? Income Distribution and Poverty in OECD Countries,* Paris: OECD.

OECD (2008): Ten Steps to Equity in Education, *Policy Brief,* OECD Publishing. Assessed at: http://www.oecd.org/education/school/39989494.pdf

OECD (2012): What is Equity in Education?, *Education at a Glance 2012: Highlights,* OECD Publishing Assessed at: http://dx.doi.org/10.1787/eag_highlights-2012-29-en.

Przeworski, Adam, and Limongi, Fernando (1993): Political Regimes and Economic Growth. *Journal of Economic Perspectives,* 7 (3):51-70.

Ruitenberg, (2015): The Practice of Equality: A Critical Understanding of Democratic Citizenship Education, *Democracy and Education,* 23 (1), Article 2/ Assessed at: http://democracyeducationjournal.org/home/vol23/iss1/2

Sirowy, Larry and Alex, Inkeles (1990): The Effects of Democracy on Economic Growth and Inequality: A Review. *Comparative International Development,* 25 (1): 126-57.

UNESCO (2005): EFA Global Monitoring Report: The Quality Imperative, *Chapter 2: The Importance of Good Quality: What Research Tells Us,* UNESCO Publishing, pp. 40-78. Assessed at: http://unesdoc.unesco.org/images/0013/001373/137333e.pdf

2

South Africa's Experiment with Democracy and Its Implications for Education

The Balance Sheet after 20 Years

Crain Soudien

Of all the challenges confronting the post-apartheid government in South Africa, education appears to be the most difficult. Positively, the World Bank reports that in South Africa, it is very likely that only half of the children who start school in 2014 will make it to Grade 12. Many of these children won't make it past grade 10 and will leave school without any recognised educational qualification. At the same time unemployment among young people between the ages of 18 and 24 years is 50 per cent, twice the national average. The national senior certificate pass rate, the exit point of the schooling system, in 2013 probably would have been 24 per cent if the pass mark was set at 50 per cent rather than 30 per cent.

This chapter attempts a critical evaluation of the impact of democracy on the school system in South Africa. What has South Africa democracy meant for education? Have the initiatives of the new government and its partners in the non-governmental sector had any impact on the educational system? If they have, what is the nature of this change?

Apartheid Legacy

South Africa inherited an educational system that was profoundly discriminatory. This discrimination took its character from the National Party's vision of apartheid, which effectively institutionalised *inequality* as an operational principle. This inequality was of a racial and socio-economic-class nature. People who were classified white were privileged, while those who were classified coloured, Indian and African were discriminated against but also treated differentially. African people were disadvantaged most severely. There were thirteen separate departments of education, one each for whites, coloured and Indians, and nine for the supposedly distinct ethnic groupings identified by the apartheid state.

The major consequence of racial inequality was the development of distinct quality regimes in the educational system. While these regimes were the direct product of the differential privileging and neglect that issued out of the workings of the apartheid system, it is necessary to emphasise that they came to evolve into relatively autonomous and distinct formations. Important about these quality regimes, as formations, is that they were, and still are, simultaneously pedagogical and psycho-sociological in their character. With respect to the pedagogical dimensions of their character, they manifested the ill-effects of resource neglect such as poor infrastructure and material provisioning, poor teacher preparation and simply poor oversight. More complex about them, however, was, and remains, the psycho-sociological. Twenty years into the democratic era it has become more and more clear that scant attention has been paid to this dimension of quality.

The most serious manifestation of this psycho-sociological situation was the habituation in the schooling system of a mind-set of disaffection. The school habitus of the 1980s was one of intense alienation from the very idea of school. Morale levels among pupils and teachers in black schools but particularly in African schools were extremely low. This led, as Wilson and Mamphele (1989: 144) argued, to breakdown in schools "with teachers often drunk, absent from work, and (in some instances) assaulting – even raping – pupils." Compounding this disaffection, and giving it a dangerous political legitimacy, was the student uprising of the 1970s which introduced into the schools complex new power configurations in which pupils in many instances came to determine the effective character of the school in terms of how teaching and learning could take place in schools. It is now widely accepted and yet hardly addressed, for whatever reason, that the affective aspect of formal education when the new government came into power in 1994 was in systematic disarray. Teachers' demoralisation about their work and learner disaffection were clearly in evidence in 1994 and were the most marked features of the system that was inherited by the new state.

What is clear with reference to this recent summary is that the post-apartheid state and non-governmental agencies have moved to address this legacy but what is argued here is that they have done so in uneven and insufficiently coherent ways. While the state, as the major agency, has taken important steps to confront the twin challenges of inequality and quality it has done so in ways which have not adequately addressed their inter-relationship. The poor quality of black schools, in general, and African schools in particular, is a racial artefact, and cannot be addressed through strategies that focus, separately, on racial and other forms of inequality on the one hand, and the degraded quality of teaching and learning in the classroom on the other. What has evolved in South Africa is a problem with its own dynamics.

The Change Agenda

Looking back we see that the focus of the new South African government in its first ten-year tenure was that of policy development. It had to undo the extraordinary edifice of structured inequality bequeathed to it by the apartheid state. In education the policy agenda was framed by a succession of White Papers, six in all. The central objective of this policy platform was to create a single, non-racial and equitable system of provision. The South African Schools Act was the foremost instrument in achieving this. It dissolved the separate education authorities and organised them behind a new single Department of Education. The Act established the principle of compulsory education. With this South Africa quickly reached its enrolment goals in terms of primary universal education.

Important regulations were introduced aimed at shaping (i) the learning environment and (ii) the organisational and bureaucratic infrastructure. With respect to learning, the most important changes were the introduction of Curriculum 2005, and its revision, the Revised National Curriculum Statements (RNCS) in 2002. Alongside of these changes, the Department of Education (DoE) sought to put in place new quality assurance mechanisms for appraising teacher development and school improvement. In terms of the formal management of the system, the DoE established the South African Council for Educators (SACE), a statutory body for the regulation of the profession and the development of the educator corps. In the provinces, as the work of Fleisch (2002) showed with respect to Gauteng Province, a great deal of restructuring activity was taking place to develop administrative structures which were thought to be appropriate for the developmental needs of the system. In the provinces, as the work of Fleisch (2002) showed with respect to Gauteng province, administrative structures which were thought to be appropriate for the developmental needs of the system were established. A key administrative innovation was the establishment in most provinces of districts. The objective of the district was to devolve authority and to bring delivery of services closer to schools.

At the national level, the DoE developed a set of measures aimed at redressing the imbalances in teacher-pupil ratios inherited from the apartheid order. These attempted to establish norms that would hold for the system as a whole and to provide for the re-deployment of teachers from schools where the ratio was deemed to be too low to schools where this figure was considered to be high. In the Western Cape, where many schools were deemed to be over-staffed, over 6000 teacher posts were closed down.

After 2004 the system went into a second phase of development (see *Annual Report 2003-2004*, Department of Education, 2004). The most important feature of this development was a focus on the institutionalisation and refinement of the reforms and innovations — consolidating the managerial capacity of the system, strengthening its personnel, and improving oversight and monitoring mechanisms. In this period no major new policies were introduced. The most significant activity in the system included the splitting of the DoE in 2009 into the DBE and the Department of Higher Education and Training. The DBE deals with all schools from Grade R to Grade 12, and adult literacy programmes. Also important was the introduction of the Further Education and Training (FET) band, itself the long but anxiously awaited elaboration of the system's outcomes-based curriculum of Grades 10, 11 and 12 (see *Cape Times,* 19 July 2005 and *Cape Argus,* 19 July 2005). Refinement was evident in the introduction in 2008 of a new National Curriculum Statement (NCS) with a different structure for managing the exit matriculation examination. This was accompanied by the introduction of a Curriculum and Assessment Policy Statement (CAPS) intended to be fully implemented by 2014.

The earlier emphasis on consolidation was also to be seen in the following: an agreement concluded between the DoE and the unions around an integrated quality management system; the launch in 2003 of what it called the "National Recruitment Drive" to encourage young people to consider teaching as a profession; the funding of in-service study for the Advanced Certificate in Education (ACE) for over 2000 teachers in subjects such as mathematics, science and technology and, most importantly in some ways, the initial roll-out of the RNCS and "Common Tasks for Assessment for the General Education Training Phase." Along with the introduction of the NCS in 2008, the DoE introduced a new inspectoral system, which the then Minister of Education described as an attempt to see how well teachers were doing their jobs (Naidu & Govender, 2008: 13). It also instituted a teacher education advisory committee drawn from leaders in the teacher trade unions and academic community to advise it on how to monitor the efficacy of the reforms that had been instituted to improve the teaching profession.

Accompanying the work of the state throughout this period was a very activist-oriented NGO sector. The size and scale of these initiatives were substantial. *Getting Learning Right* (Taylor & Vinjevold, 1999) provided a sense of this in 1999 in its large assessment of the quality of school improvement studies. The authors reported that the general approach of these initiatives was based on both whole-school and INSET approaches. The earlier trend was towards INSET work: "Thus, in 1995, the National Teacher Education Audit.... identified over 90 INSET programmes (aimed at classroom level activities) and only a few "whole school development" projects. By contrast, at the present time (1999), stand-alone INSET programmes are few and far between" (Taylor & Vinjevold, 1999: 34). While Taylor and Vinjevold (1999) estimated that donor and NGO activity, despite increasing in number, reached only some 5 per cent to 7 per cent of South African schools, the empirical work of Swilling and Russell (2002) showed that the education non-profit or civil society sector was extensive in the early years of the new millennium.

Understanding the Reform Agenda

In terms of this reform and improvement agenda it is important to understand what philosophical approaches underpin them. As Reeves (2005: 38) has said, herself drawing from a study conducted by Muller (with Roberts, 2000), two main approaches emerged in South Africa – the "outside-in" and "inside-out" approaches.

The first, the outside-in approach, is essentially the standardised approach of government. It uses the classic levers of compulsion and inducement. The inside-out approach, on the other hand, broadly represents the approach of the NGO movement. In contrast to the accountability orientation of the state, it focusses primarily on "support activities" (Taylor *et al*, 2003:5), "issues of the organisational culture of schools: shared values, vision and teamwork" (Taylor *et al*, 2003: 4). Where the outside-ins take a system-wide view, the inside-outs are much more interested in individual schools.

As in the international experience, the inside-outs have two orientations. They belong to, generally, either the school effectiveness or the school improvement movements. A general critique of "the "inside-outs," particularly those in the school improvement camp, is the emphasis they place on the whole school and their relative neglect of the pedagogical" (Taylor *et al*, 2003: 11). In concentrating on teachers, parents, and students "buying-in" or coming to "own" the process of reform they have been criticised for emphasising the "soft" and the cultural dimensions of the teaching and learning process, rather than the process itself (Taylor *et al*, 2003:11). The emphasis in these programmes tended to fall on teacher professionalisation: developing the individual teacher's deportment and approach to his or her work. As Reeves has commented, "over time those involved in school development efforts began to question "whether training programmes for individuals offered by such interventions can have an impact on the (instructional) system if they are not linked to institutional development." Development activities soon shifted to second generation "whole school" approaches (Reeves, 2005: 38-39), albeit with a continued focus on the dispositional dimensions of teaching, such as teaching methods, these programmes came to include the questions and challenges of educational management (Reeves, 2005). Quoting Muller, Reeves commented that leadership and school organisation were firmly placed on the agenda but that the focus still fell "on persons rather than systems" (Reeves, 2005: 39).

As a result of this critique, third generation programmes sought to bring a systemic focus into view with a shift from support to accountability. Two waves of this development occurred by 2008. A first attempt to institutionalise a system-wide perspective came in the form of the Integrated Quality Management System from the state itself, which effectively placed emphasis on collegiality. While a system of monitoring was instituted and arrived in the school as an outside-in initiative, it depended on a peer-review approach for its essential functioning. A second approach saw a shift away from collegiality with the introduction of the new inspectoral system described above – the National Education, Evaluation and Development Unit. The primary task of this new unit would be to put in place a system to evaluate teachers and principals: It was reported that by 2009 it would be possible "to fire useless teachers and principals" (Naidu & Govender, 2008: 13). One fix also suggested would be to introduce school inspectors. The South African Democratic Teachers Union (Sadtu), the country's largest teaching union, remains opposed to such a plan. Their stance harks back to a time when inspectors from the white National Party government were viewed with suspicion in black schools. "They were just there to find fault, policing teachers without playing a development role," said Mugwena Maluleke (Holborn, 2014: 2), Sadtu general secretary, in December 2012 when President Jacob Zuma proposed re-introducing inspectors.

Impact of the Reform and Improvement Process: A Macro View

We might ask questions about the impact of state and NGO intervention. How well, in light of the twin problems of equality and quality, has the change strategy of the state and its partners in the NGO world worked? Assessments of what has been achieved have been mixed (*See*, *inter alia*, Pendlebury & Enslin, 2004; Chisholm, 2004; Fiske & Ladd, 2004; Nelson Mandela Foundation, 2005; Lam, Ardington, Branson & Leibbrandt, 2012; Spaull, 2013). It has been argued that the failures in South Africa's education system reflect the problems that have beset governance in the country more generally since 1994. While the system has figures which show that Gross Enrolment Ratios (GER) already exceeded 103 per cent in 2001 in the compulsory phase of schooling (see DoE, 2003: 11), and that that the country had gone beyond its gender balance targets (see Bloch, 2005: 9), a lack of skills, monitoring and accountability have led to poor policy implementation, inferior training of teachers and bureaucrats, and a system many people have lost hope in. Those who can afford to are increasingly sending their children to private schools. With respect to equality, Fiske and Ladd

(2004), Chisholm (2004) have shown that disparity remains the order of the day in relation to social class, language, gender, race and location (with province, urban and rural, township and suburb featuring strongly as distributive indicators). It is true, by and large, that the question of access to education at one level has been resolved. Legislation is in place (DoE, 1996) stipulating that every child has a right to school access, even if the child cannot pay the fees of that school. Work carried out by Soudien and Sayed (2003) in three provinces, the work of Fiske and Ladd (2004), and the large study commissioned by the Nelson Mandela Foundation on education in rural communities (2005) make it clear that the state has effectively succeeded in winning the struggle for access in the primary school, but distinctly less so in the secondary school. Spaull has shown (*See* UNISA, 2012 below) that in fact apart from many small gains like access to schooling and gender equality (DBE, 2013c)

South Africa still faces the reality of two different education systems, a dysfunctional schooling system (75 per cent) and a functional schooling system (25 per cent), which are miles apart in their respective performance. Despite the high spending and many interventions which were made by the government over the past twenty years the system remains virtually unchanged. Our government spends 20 per cent of total government expenditure on education, of which 78 per cent goes to teacher salaries. Yet, the education system continues to propagate, rather than mitigate, inequality. If you are born into a family which is poor, your prospects for social mobility are very slim. Education is the main driver of social mobility but the system continues to reproduce inequality because there are so few good schools, which are also geographically and financially inaccessible to the poor.

With respect to social class, the Soudien and Sayed (2003) study suggested that there was a domino-effect playing itself out within the school system. When the apartheid system began breaking down, previously excluded African, coloured and Indian children began to move in large numbers into schools from which they had been kept out as one of the schools participating in the research programme is an example of. African children began to move into formerly Indian and coloured schools and black children in general made their way into formerly white schools. Naidoo's (1996) work suggests that the process of integration followed distinct socio-economic paths in KwaZulu-Natal in both the former Natal Education Department (previously white) and the former House of Delegates (previously Indian) schools.

Fiske and Ladd (2004) also write extensively of the "classed" nature of the social change, with the high costs of travelling to the more stable schools really only being an option for more affluent people. Significant about the process of integration has been its distinct class character, with the poor not having the same access to the "openness" of the new system in the same way as their more financially stable counterparts. For African and coloured people, in particular, there has been a flight of the more economically stable elements from their communities, leaving those schools largely with the poorest and most vulnerable members of the community. The DoE's response to this has been to create "no-fee" schools for the poorest communities. In lieu of the fees that they would have collected the Department has suggested the possibility of subsidising these schools to the extent of R400 per learner (DoE, 2003). It needs to be emphasised, however, that the benefits of these developments have not yet impacted on the schools of the poor that have come acquire distinct socio-economic characteristics. As the relatively better-off families have left their communities, the schools have fallen into what one might call sink-hole syndromes and become the dumping grounds of the larger system. In the Western Cape where principals have battled to keep criminality out of their schools (*Cape Argus,* 2005) it has been emphasised how strong the impact of poverty in the community has been on these schools. It continues to be the case that for every 100 children who began Grade 1, only 52 make it to Grade 12. There is a large dropout rate in poorer rural communities (Nelson Mandela Foundation, 2005). These anomalies, relative to some official statistics that suggest full enrolment in the system, suggest that children are in fact dropping out of the system. There have been, as Figure 2.1 below makes clear, distinct improvements in enrolments at the Grade 10 level in the period under review, but decidedly less so at the Grade 12 level.

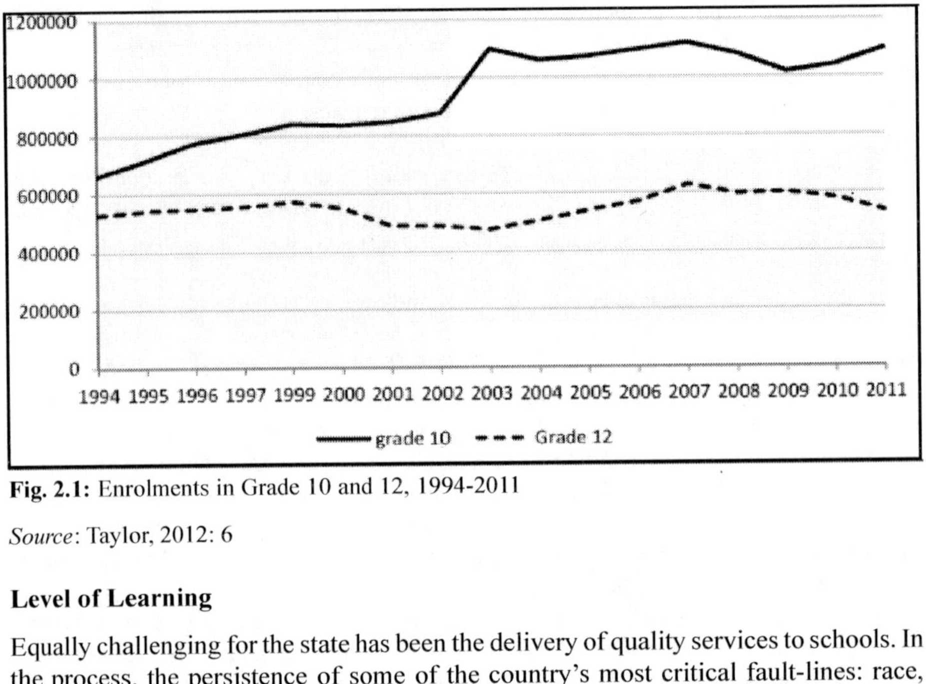

Fig. 2.1: Enrolments in Grade 10 and 12, 1994-2011

Source: Taylor, 2012: 6

Level of Learning

Equally challenging for the state has been the delivery of quality services to schools. In the process, the persistence of some of the country's most critical fault-lines: race, class, gender and social location, has been revealed. These fault-lines manifest themselves most starkly in the serious backlogs which remain in delivery. Similarly, if not more problematic, and bearing on the question of quality, there is substantial evidence to show that, while formal access has been achieved, substantial access, or what has sometimes been referred to as "epistemological access," is still some way off.

The findings of the various tests have all consistently shown exceedingly low levels of competence across the nation for both mathematics and reading. The 2001 national Grade 3 systemic assessment (the final report appeared in 2003) reported an average score of 30 per cent for numeracy and 54 per cent for literacy (DoE, 2003: 24).

The Third International Mathematics and Science Study Repeat (TIMMS-R) placed Grade 8 South African learners at 44 per cent, below the mean scores of all participating countries.

South African pupils, moreover, came last in the list of 39 countries and attained a mean score of 275 out of a possible total of 800 marks (Howie, 2001: 18). Significantly, the best performing pupils in South Africa scored at the level of the mean of pupils in leading countries in the list such as Singapore. Less than 0.5 per cent of South Africa's pupils featured in the international top 10 per cent benchmark (Howie, 2001: 19). In the Monitoring Learner Assessment (MLA) study for Grade 4 students, South African learners attained an average numeracy score of 30 per cent, placing it last amongst the 12 participating African countries (Taylor *et al*, 2003: 19-27). Between 1995 and 2002 the study showed that no improvement had occurred in learners" attainment in Mathematics and Science in Grade 8. It was decided in 2002 that the Grade 8 tests were too difficult for the Grade 8s and so they were given to the Grade 9s. As Spaull says (2013: 4), "Comparing the performance of the Grade 9 pupils between 2002 and 2011 showed that there was a noticeable improvement in Maths and Science performance amounting to approximately one and a half grades of learning." He cautions against celebrating this achievement because the "post-improvement level of performance..... is really low..... the average South African Grade Nine child perform(s) between two and three grade levels lower than the average Grade Eight child from other middle-income countries" (*ibid*). (*See* Figure 2.2)

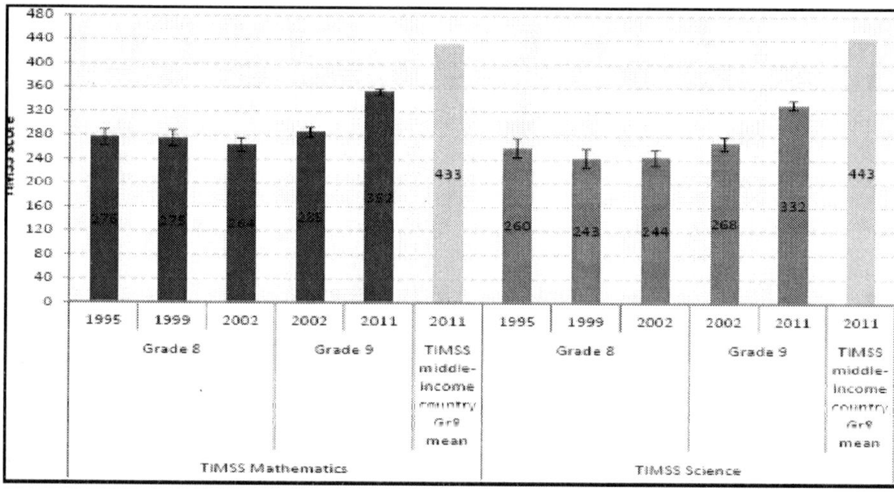

Fig. 2.2: South Africa TIMMS Maths and Science Grade 8 and 9 Performance 1995 to 2011

Source: Spaull, 2013: 13.

The broad profiles of these scores were repeated in the SACMEQII evaluation for grade 6 which showed that relative to the pre-determined mean of 500 points as a benchmark for the project, South African learners scored below this value for both Mathematics (486.2) and Reading (492.4) (Moloi and Strauss, 2005: 65). The study found that the modal competence level for reading for Grade 6 learners in South Africa essentially stood at Level 3 (Basic Reading). This was only achieved by 19.1 per cent of the learners in the study (Moloi and Strauss, 2005: 67). Only 26 per cent of the learners could read above a Level 4 standard (independent reading). In mathematics the modal level of attainment for Grade 6 learners was Level 2 (Emergent Numeracy), which was attained by 44,4 per cent of the learners; "(i) in addition, there were 7,8 per cent of the learners who achieved only Level 1 (Beginning Numeracy). Altogether this left less than 50 per cent of the learners reaching competence levels higher than Emergent Numeracy" (Moloi and Strauss, 2005: 68-69). In SACMEQ III (2007), South African pupils ranked 10th out of the 14 systems in the region, below significantly poorer countries such as Tanzania, Kenya and Swaziland. The study found that 27 per cent of South African Grade 6 learners were illiterate. They could not read a short and simple text and were not able to extract any meaning from it (Spaull, 2013: 4).

The Macro indicator report (DBE, 2013c) showed, in particular, that incomplete coverage of the curriculum and inadequate teacher subject knowledge are examples of the problematic "inputs" to education quality. The quality, moreover, is differentially distributed, with children who learn in the former white sector of the system being provided with much better education than those in the former coloured and former African systems. This is evident in the Australian Council for Educational Research (ACER) benchmarked tests conducted in the independent (i.e. private) schools in South Africa. As the test results reflected below make absolutely clear, the country's privileged schools are, in contrast to the disadvantaged schools, doing well in terms of levels of attainment reached in Mathematics and English. These ACER tests, administered through the Independent Examinations Board of South Africa, show that the learners in these schools are operating above international averages.

Impact of the Reforms: A Micro View — The MSEP Case-Study

Looking a scale lower in the system, it is helpful to highlight the research of the Maths and Science Education Project (MSEP) (see Clark, 2013) at the Schools Development Unit of the University of Cape Town. This work was done between 2008 and 2013 in five schools in the greater Cape Town area in collaboration with the Western Cape Education Department and with the support of the Royal Dutch Government. The project came into being on the back of a baseline study of learner performance in Mathematics and Physical Science in Grades 10-12 in the province (MSEP, 2007). With a budget of R18.1m its primary goal was to assist the schools in improving their performance in Mathematics and Science.

The five schools were all secondary schools selected in consultation with the Western Cape Education Department (WCED). The selection process was by and large part informed by performance in two of these areas, namely: "Functionality of the school" and "Learner achievement." In consultation with WCED officials, it was agreed that what were called Type I schools which were deemed to be too dysfunctional were to be avoided at all costs. Instead, schools classified as "under-performing", Type II, and schools that were performing well, Type III, should be selected. The five schools are described below as A, B, C, D and E. Schools A, C and E, were allocated in townships with African populations and would have fallen under the Department of Education and Training in the apartheid era. One of the schools was a post-1994 school. School D was a school that would have been classified as "coloured" during the apartheid era and School B was a former Model C school but drew its learners largely from the former "coloured" and African townships. Its learners, however, were from largely lower middle class families.

The approach for managing MSEP was undertaken by a team of academics in the School of Education. Responsibility for project implementation was given to the Schools Development Unit (SDU), a school intervention unit of the School of the School of Education. The project was essentially based on an "evidence-bound" approach. The idea was to manage the project on the basis of ongoing research.

At the point of entry at the start of the school year in 2007, a comprehensive baseline of learner performance in Mathematics and Physical Science in Grades 10-12 was undertaken. In total, over 2,700 learners across the five schools (and a number of control sites) were tested. An analysis of results confirmed the extent of the weaknesses in many learners' foundational knowledge and the gaps which existed in their understanding of key concepts in both subjects across the three grades of the FET phase of schooling. This proved the stimulus for the establishment of an extensive learner intervention programme, focusing strongly on support for Grade 12s.

A teacher baseline study was also undertaken. Many mathematics and science teachers participated in the survey which included classroom observations (some of which were video recorded) and interviews. This classroom level engagement provided useful insights about teachers' everyday pedagogic practices.

From the outset, the mathematics team had adopted a strongly research-led approach with a focus on what had come to be constituted as school mathematics. The intention was to analyse the way in which the subject was taught and learnt in the classroom, thereby identifying the problems that might emerge and in response, developed a set of intervention strategies to attempt to overcome these problematic teaching and learning practices.

Reviewing the project in 2010, in the middle of its period of implementation, it was felt that by and large MSEP objectives had been met at three schools – C, D and E; whilst at the other two (A & B) progress was held up to varying degrees by a range of contextual factors. In the case of School A, there was clearly a leadership crisis developing at the school. This unfortunately extended down into the School Management Team (SMT), which appeared divided and without direction. In the face of growing organisational incoherence, the situation grew increasingly unstable and (amongst other things) instructional time became a commodity in short supply at the school. This had a negative impact on performance and based on the 2010 matric examinations, School A was judged to be losing the battle to hold on to its academic gains of the mid-2000s. In response to this worsening state of affairs, at the end of the year the project began actively engaging with the district's education officials, in the hope that in 2011 the school could be assisted to develop and then implement elements of an effective turn-around strategy.

In the case of School B, one of the factors taken into account when choosing the school was that it was an example of an ex-model C school which had (and was still) experienced a quite dramatic shift in the demographics of the learner body. At the outset, the school presented itself as being open to engagement in whatever professional development activities MSEP had to offer. Unfortunately as subsequent events were to show, teachers at the school were not be so forthcoming and the principal in particularly played a somewhat negative "gate-keeping" role.

In what follows impact is assessed through the schools' NSC results and their performance in the three subjects: mathematics, physical sciences and life sciences over the five years of the intervention. As the report shows, impact has been variable. Significant interventions at either the teacher and/or student level were made in these subjects in the course of the project. Further to subject-level performance, consideration is also given to participation rates[1] in each subject. In mathematics and physical sciences this is viewed as a significant performance indicator, particularly in the light of the imperative imposed by the *Dinaledi* project, namely, that schools increase or retain high levels of enrolment in these two subjects in the FET.[2]

An important way of assessing the schools' progress over the duration of the MSEP project is to see how the schools in the province fared generally over the same five-years period. As the graph below shows, the past 10-years have seen a general *downward* trend in matriculation and NSC performance across the province's secondary schools. It is also important to note that this trend was evident in the country as a whole for the period. This trend was only reversed in 2009 (in the second year of the NSC). NSC pass rates have yet to reach the same levels as those achieved at the turn of the century. It should be noted here that the "pass" standard against which schools and the system are measured is essentially the lowest level of attainment required for the award of an NSC. In terms of this a candidate has to offer seven subjects. Of these seven subjects, a mark of at least 40 per cent is required for home language, a minimum of 40 per cent for two other subjects and a minimum of 30 per cent for three subjects. For admission into higher education to qualify for certificate, diploma and degree level study, the requirements are more stringent. In the graph below (Figure 2.3) it should be noted that the pass profile reflects both the old matriculation system and the newer NSC system which was introduced in 2008. The two systems are different but the aggregated mark derived for each to determine an outcome of pass or fail amounts to the same.

What this Figure 2.4 shows is that there was a clear decline in the province from 2003 to 2009. After that the rate began to improve. It had not by 2012 reached the level at which it had been in 2003.

Significant about the MSEP project schools is the variation in their performance from one year to the next. Dealing then first with the three township schools:

Significant about School A (*refer* Fig. 2.4) was how much more poorly than the province average it performed. The MSEP project would have started in 2008 but it was only in 2010, when its pass rate stood below 50 per cent that its performance began to improve. For the project, a major issue was an ongoing leadership crisis, centred on the school principal. This undoubtedly impaired the school's functionality in the five-years period from 2006 through to 2010. An indication of the extent of this decline is the fact that in 2005, the school's pass rate stood at 82.3 per cent, significantly

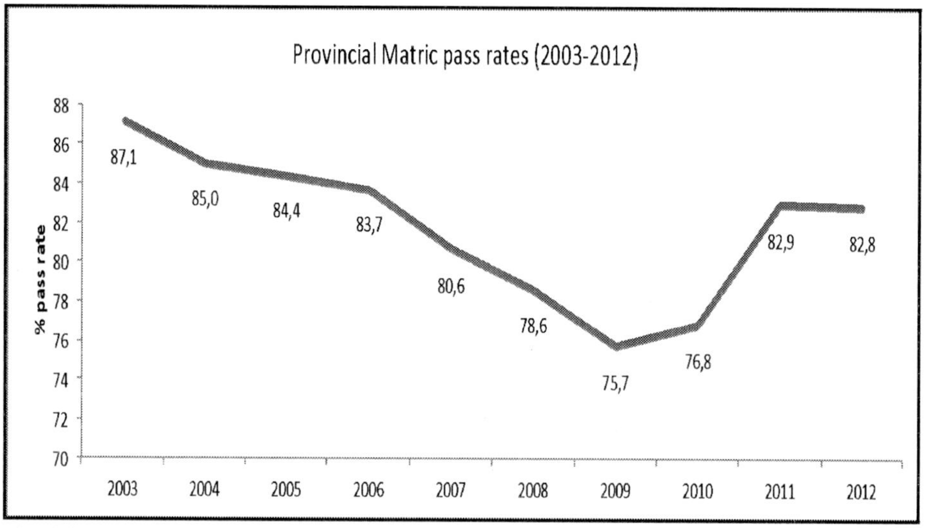

Fig. 2.3: WCED Matric/NSC Pass Rate for the Period 2003 to 2012.

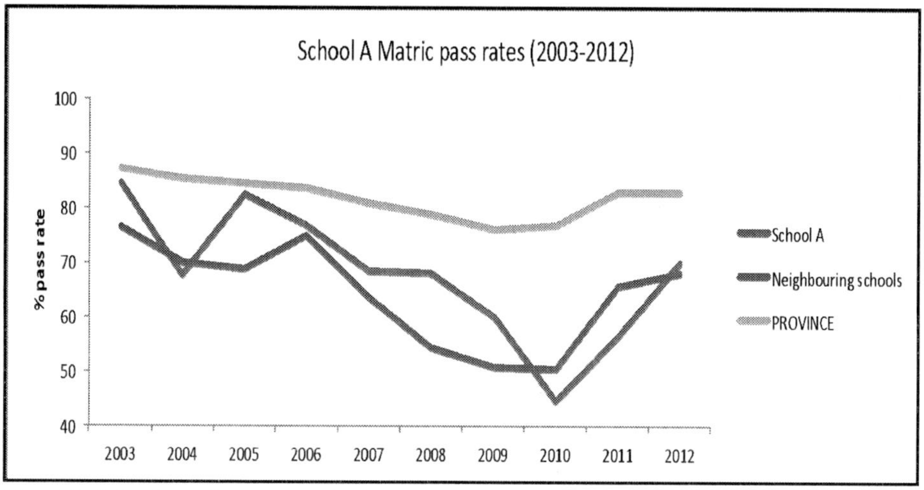

Fig. 2.4: School A: *"Bottoming Out"*

higher (+13.7 per cent) than the average in neighbouring township schools[3]. By 2010, the school was under-performing (-5.9 per cent) relative to its neighbours. With a pass rate that had dipped well below the 60 per cent threshold level, it was deemed by the local education department to be at high-risk and was effectively placed "on report." One further consequence of which was that it had its membership of the *Dinaledi* project curtailed.

In response to the crisis the MSEP project put considerable effort during the final two years of its implementation (2011 & 2012) into strengthening school organisational management in collaboration with District officials. And with what is seen as some success – by 2012, the NSC performance returned to the level of the local average and appeared to be on an upward trajectory.

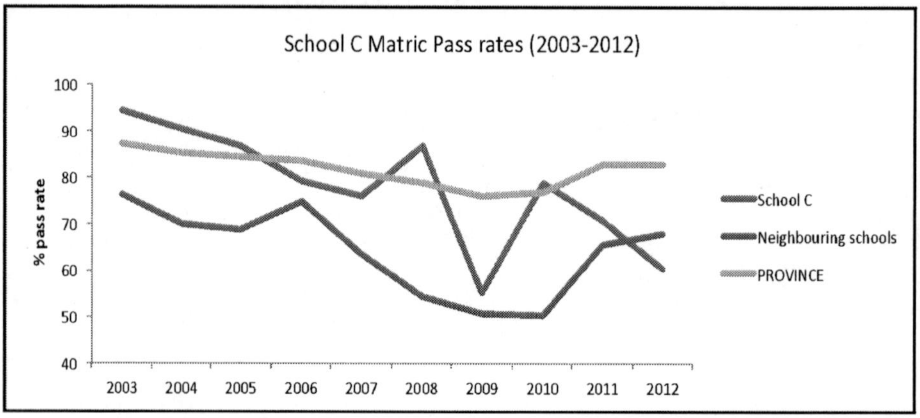

Fig. 2.5: School C: "*Growing Instability*"

In contrast to School A, School C (*refer* Figure 2.5), also a township school, was much closer to the provincial average. When the Project started working at the school in 2008 it had just experienced a calamitous fall in its pass rate. This may, as with the other schools, have had something to do with the switch from the matric to the NSC. In 2009 it saw a significant increase in its NSC performance (from 76.0 per cent in 2007 to 86.9 per cent). Strikingly, since then, in 2010, it saw a fall from approximately 80 per cent down to nearly 60 per cent in the course of one year and was performing more poorly than its neighbouring schools. These swings in performance were a continual concern for the principal and his management team during the course of the four years the Project worked at the school. However, given its context and limitations in (particularly human) resources, it may well be that School C is on a downward trajectory which will not easily be arrested without a significant shift in the way in which school management functions.

School E (*See* Figure 2.6 below), also a township school because of its demographic make-up, was able to perform well above comparable township schools. Like other schools it also experienced a fall in its average pass rate in 2009. It improved in 2010 and 2011 but deteriorated in 2012.

School D (*refer* Figure 2.7), it should be remembered, is a former "coloured" school. Its performance also dipped in 2009. It improved in 2010 and then declined in 2011 but then improved again 2012. Significant about the school is the annual fluctuation in a range of almost ten percentage points each year.

As reflected in the above graph (Figure 2.8), with the exception of one year (2008) the school's academic performance over the past decade has been on the decline. As the profiles for the schools show their NSC performance levels for the period indicated very little consistent improvement. But what did their performance in the subjects of focus of the MSEP project look like? The Figure below (Figure 2.9) summarises the situation across the five schools. In mathematics, in three schools (A, B & C)

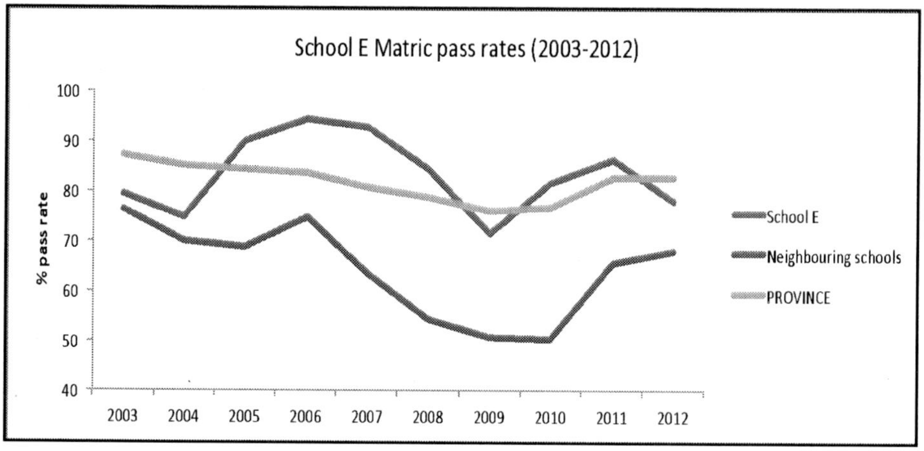

Fig. 2.6: School E: *"Holding On"*

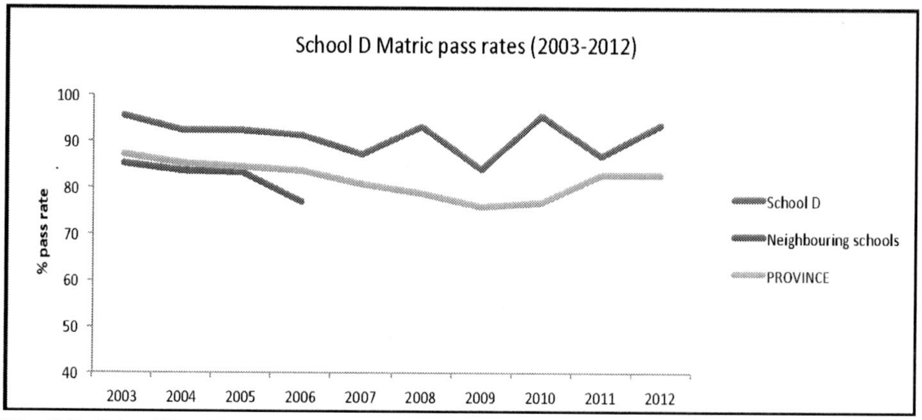

Fig. 2.7: School D: *"Running Slightly Ahead"*

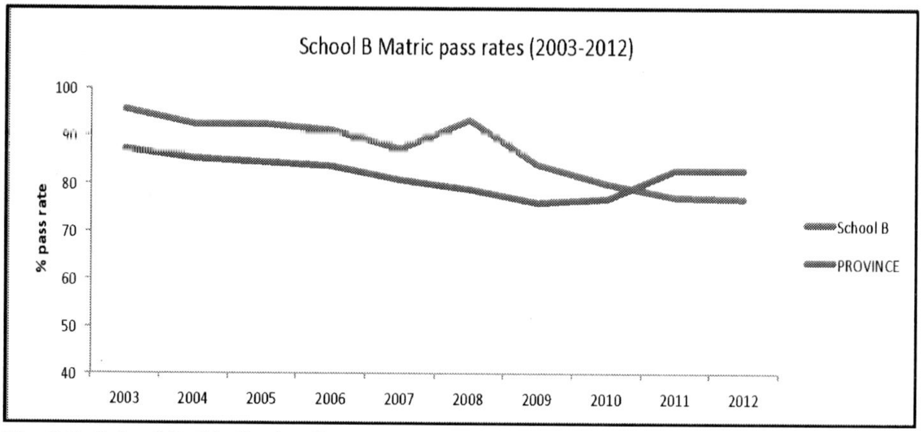

Fig. 2.8: School B: *"In Decline"*

performance declined by more than 10 per cent between 2008 and 2012, and at School E by between 6-10 per cent. It was only at School D where performance levels were essentially unchanged, with only a small decline over the five years.

Matric Trends 2008-2012

		Subject perfomance	Subject participation rates
School A	Mathematics	- -	- -
	Physical Sciences	- -	++
	Life Sciences	0	++
School B	Mathematics	- -	+
	Physical Sciences	- -	0
	Life Sciences	- -	+ +
School C	Mathematics	- -	- -
	Physical Sciences	- -	0
	Life Sciences	- -	-
School D	Mathematics	0	+ +
	Physical Sciences	+ +	+ +
	Life Sciences	0	+ +
School E	Mathematics	-	- -
	Physical Sciences	-	- -
	Life Sciences	-	- -

KEY	
0	no significant change (+/- 5%)
+	improvement (6-10%)
+ +	improvement (>10%)
-	decline (6-10%)
- -	decline (>10%)

Fig. 2.9: Matric Trends 2008-2012

Source: Clark, 2013.

When it comes to mathematics participation rates,[4] the overall number of learners enrolled for this subject in 2012 (439) was marginally higher than the number enrolled in 2008 (433). At three of schools (B, C & D) there were significant increases: at School D from 47.5 per cent (57 learners) in 2008 to 60.8 per cent (104 learners) in 2012. At School B, there was a smaller yet significant increase from 49.3 per cent (66 learners) to 57.3 per cent (98 learners). Whereas significant declines were experienced at both Schools A & C (17.7 per cent and 22.2 per cent respectively); the most dramatic decline was at School E, where the participation rate of 99.2 per cent in 2008 had dropped to only 41.4 per cent in 2012.

A somewhat different picture emerges, however, when one looks at performance at the 50 per cent+ level in each subject. This is presented graphically in Figure 2.10.

Clearly, over the past five years in both physical and life sciences the trend is upward. There has been over the period a marked improvement in the numbers of learners scoring 50 per cent or higher. In physical sciences, the increase from 53 to 83 learners represents a 57 per cent growth; in life sciences, the number has almost doubled (from 108 to 204). What this suggests is some impact in the schools. When this

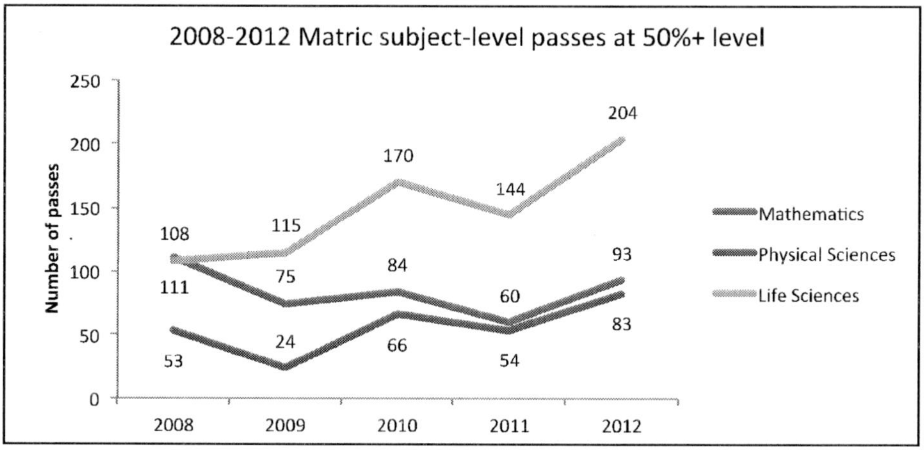

Fig. 2.10: Matric Subject Level Passes at 50 Per Cent+ Level 2008-2012

improvement is taken together with the increased participation rates, there is some basis for suggesting that the project influenced performance in the school. There is also a positive to take away in the increased numbers of learners doing these subjects in the project schools.

But it is, in conclusion, still the fluctuation which is the more important feature with which to be working here. Why is the performance in all of the schools so unpredictable? Why are schools able to reach relatively good levels of attainment in one year and then in the very next to be several point scores "down"?

How does one, in light of this unpredictability, come then to make sense of the nature of the impact of this project work in the schools? Towards making this assessment it is important to draw together the insights and learnings from the project. These are gathered together below in point form to present the outlines of a narrative for what is happening in the schools as they experience the interventions that are taking shape around them:

1. *Learner's Poor Foundations.* A critical point of departure with which to work is the persistence of learner weaknesses in their subject knowledge. An analysis of these early results confirmed the extent of the weaknesses in many learners" foundational knowledge as well as gaps that existed in their understanding of key concepts in both subjects across the three grades of the final phase of their schooling.
2. *Teachers' Subject Knowledge.* Alongside of the learners' weak grasp of their subjects, telling was the extent of weak teacher subject knowledge. Their teaching tended to be textbook-bound, with a heavy reliance on a fairly limited range of worked examples and illustrations from these texts. Teaching tended to be strongly teacher-centred and particularly in mathematics was procedural and rote-determined, with little attention being paid to developing deeper conceptual understanding. This narrow framing meant that in many instances

learners were unable to apply their newly acquired understanding into unfamiliar contexts. In the sciences, there was virtually no experimentation being undertaken, even where equipment was available and as in mathematics, teaching tended to be superficial and lacking depth. A further difficulty experienced, particularly in Grades 10 & 11, was with curriculum pacing. In several schools teachers were struggling to keep up with the official "pace setters." In consequence sections of curriculum were at risk of being left out, with potentially negative consequences for learners during their subsequent years of study. Particular issues arose in the way mathematics was taught. A research paper generated by the project, titled "Failure by example" (Davis & Johnson 2010), referred to the way in which examples were often used as the method of teaching, providing the learners with little chance of being able to think mathematically affecting the way that learners came to understand many ideas in mathematics (*See* also Davis, 2010; 2011; Davis & Gripper, 2012a; Davis & Gripper, 2012b).

3. *Insufficient Assessment Capacity.* Compounding teachers' weak subject knowledge was the difficulty they demonstrated in assessing appropriately. Teachers articulated a concern with not having the expertise and/or experience to set assessment activities at a suitable level for the NCS curriculum.
4. *Teachers' Dispositions.* Evident in the work of the Project was the fact that teachers, in addition to their academic challenges, had personal and professional difficulties in responding to the situations in which they found themselves. At the level of both the classroom and the staff room they demonstrated a diffidence to engage with the complexity of the situation in which they found themselves. There was, for example, reluctant co-operation with the project. For MSEP, without a strong advocacy role from the principal there was little inducement for staff to engage with the Project in any meaningful way. Indeed many teachers at two of the schools displayed what Hargreaves (1993) characterises as *rampant individualism;* which sees them answerable for their actions to no one but themselves. Teachers were often unlikely to be predisposed towards the type of professional development that MSEP was offering, which required a degree of classroom interaction. There was generally a deep reluctance, which many South African teachers display, in allowing outsiders access to their classrooms. There was mostly poor attendance at training seminars provided by the project. As with any school and its staff it was found that teacher who were observed routinely enacted practices that were deeply entrenched, difficult to disrupt and the tug of habituated ways of doing things very often overwhelming.
5. *Leadership and Management.* How leadership responded to these circumstances was also critical. In four of the schools on the programme there were weak accountability structures, which in effect left many teachers never having to answer for their actions or inactions. It soon emerged that there was often a leadership crisis at most of the schools involved in the programme. The MSEP trainers observed a high level of contestation around authority

and in the absence of well-functioning management structures, particularly at the level of subject department heads, there were high levels of unregulated teaching practices. The curriculum was poorly managed at all levels and instructional time was limited. When coupled with underlying shortfalls in many teachers' content, pedagogic and classroom management skills, what went on in classrooms seemed quite limited indeed.

6. *Union Influence.* The main teachers' union, the South African Democratic Teachers Union, appeared to take a deeply ambivalent stance towards authority and control, exerting undue influence in some schools a significant and negative role in determining the nature of the engagement between the school and district officials. Officials are sometimes denied access to teachers' classrooms and their involvement limited to fairly narrowly defined regulatory roles.

Taken together these factors are crucial for understanding how schools come to perform so erratically and unpredictably. In neither the learners' nor teachers' knowledge and professional foundations are there sufficient resources to be able to withstand the challenges the circumstances throw at them. There isn't either in the managerial and administrative environment, whether one is talking about the formal edifice of the state or the alternative membership structures with their own authorities such as the trade unions, sufficient regulatory authority, legitimacy and power to consistently hold teachers to account. There are, in other words, insufficient affordances, internal and external, within the system to hold it even in a state of minimal equilibrium. It does not have sufficiently bedded down practices or principles to guarantee the minimal realisation of the educational promise of the school. It is too susceptible and vulnerable to any form of disturbance.

Conclusion

In reflecting then on where the country is after twenty years of democracy, aside from the not inconsiderable right of access to education, the criticism can easily be made that little else has been achieved. It can even be said that the DoE and the subsequent DBE has contributed to what many see as the degradation of the fabric of the teaching and learning landscape and particularly the dire demoralisation of the teaching corps (*See* Phurutse, 2005; Hall with Altman, Nkomo, Peltzer& Zuma, 2005; Shisana, Peltzer, Zungu-Dirwayi & Louw, 2005). It must be conceded, however, that the state has assiduously addressed the resource needs of the system. It has each year, for example, substantially increased the volume of resources it has placed at the disposal of the system. In the current financial year it will be spending R253.8b on education, the single biggest commitment on the part of the state. Similarly the NGO movement has not lessened the volume and intensity of its work in schools.

But the problem, it is widely agreed, is not one of resources. Many countries achieve more with distinctly less. It is, instead, what the country is doing with its resources — the *what* and the *how*. This question is key. A Thabo Mbeki biographer, Brian Pottinger (2008: 11), has commented with respect to the government's broad reform approach to the legacy of apartheid that, "the ANC (African National Congress) indulged in an orgy of legislative and policy over-reach during (Mbeki's) term. Maddened by a compelling view that everything could be righted by legislative fiat, the ANC built a body of regulation and expectation that the state's fragile resources could never meet.... It was defeated by the terrifying logic of the unintended consequence." The position that Pottinger is critiquing is quintessentially what I referred to earlier as the outside-in approach. What he is taking aim at is the social engineering intention embedded inside the policy. The first major critique to make therefore is that the social engineering approach of the education policy platform is almost by definition that of imposition. It is true that the state has moderated some of the outsider elements of its policy by granting more agency to those inside the school insofar as policies such as the peer-evaluation of teachers of each other's work brings them greater control of their working environments. But it is the outside-in elements of the policies that have carried the greater weight. It is as a consequence of this that the second, and the more pertinent, comment to make is that the new reforms and the measures intended to carry them, because they emanate from outside, themselves misunderstand and misidentify the scope and the gravity of the challenge. This is also evident, I want to suggest, in the fluctuations one sees in the outcomes of important interventions such as that of MSEP.

What is this misunderstanding? The major problem, it is suggested here, is that the state was and remains unable to confront its inherited and what one might describe as the *legacy* nature of the quality problem. The most revealing illustration of this misunderstanding is evident in the way that the state has gone about approaching the complex of people, practices and the structures in which their practices take form. In its outside-in approach it has come to fundamentally under-estimate the complexity confronting it. It has assumed that this complexity is amenable to managerial manipulation. Harley and Wedekind (2004: 211) make this point clear with respect to the state's understanding of the teacher. They critique the change assumptions inherent in Curriculum 2005 which reconstituted the role of the teacher from that of the central figure of authority in the classroom to that of a facilitator in a learner-centred classroom. This was at odds pedagogically with the practice of the majority of teachers (*See* also Matobako, 2012). At issue here is the constructivist philosophy of the curriculum with its pervasive middle-class conceptions of professional teacher identity. In this conception teachers are self-sufficient and able to operate with enhanced levels of independence. At the height of the process of implementing the curriculum, they were even encouraged to do away with their textbooks and to develop their own resources. Their pupils, to compound this, were projected as resourceful young learners who would make it an article of learning to take responsibility for what they and the teacher together would study in the class. Reviewing these ideals, Harley and Wedekind (2004: 212) suggest that the visionary aspects of the curriculum allowed its protagonists to "overlook the profound inequalities in South African schools and to despatch teachers on a..... voyage of faith" (2004: 212), where failure was the only possible outcome. They argue, further, that "the single mindedness of the very pursuit of the social vision has undermined itself..... [because] commitment to a vision of *what ought to be* has undermined the ability of policy to consider seriously *what is*" (204: 213).

In work with department officials who were involved in the training of teachers, it became clear how strongly these trainers felt that teachers had been let down (Robinson & Soudien, 2009: 475). Teachers made it clear that "[w]e did not have a full grasp of the issues involved." It is what "grasp" means that is at issue.

The essential approach of the state in its managerial emphasis, particularly now in scripting practice for teachers, assumes that it is teachers' subject knowledge which is the major problem. This is confirmed in the analysis of observers such as Spaull (2013). Spaull's recommendations for the reform of the crisis. He suggests that the system should "implement a nation-wide system of diagnostic teacher-testing and training", and "provide a clear articulation of who is responsible for ensuring pupil learning, and to whom, with clear consequences for non-performance" (Spaull, 2013: 7). I would like to suggest, in response to this conclusion, that the "grasp" which teachers are referring to is not simply technical. It is subject knowledge which they need but it is significantly more. It is, as the MSEP project found, about helping teachers come to a more informed sense of how they could be responding to the circumstances in which they find themselves. This informed-ness is not simply political "empowerment" in a clichéd sense of teachers taking control. It is not the control inherent in the politics of teacher unionism where teachers will decide who will or will not enter their classrooms. It is not the control over their salaries. It is about a complex awareness of their own strengths and weaknesses and the capacity to be able to act simultaneously in their own and their learners' interests. This is a different kind of politics. It is about a politics of the self which speaks to their professionalism beyond the limits of the instrumental relationship with knowledge of subject. They need, clearly, to be helped to act with confidence in the classroom with respect to what they know so that they can use the resources at their disposal with confidence.

Notes

1. These are expressed as a percentage of learners in the grade taking the subject.
2. Further Education and Training Phase: Grades 10-12.
3. Performance was calculated from a total of 20 township schools.
4. Calculated as the percentage of learners in the grade who took the subject.

References

Cape Argus, 19 July 2005.

Cape Times, 19 July 2005.

Chisholm, L. (2004): *Education and Social Change in South Africa,* HSRC Press, Cape Town.

Christie, P.; Butler, D. & Potterton, M. (2007). Schools that Work: Ministerial Committee Report. Pretoria: Department of Education.

Christie, P. (2008): Changing Schools in South Africa: Opening the Doors of Learning, Heinemann, Sandton.

Clark, J. (2013): Report on the Maths and Science Project. Schools Development Unit, University of Cape Town. Unpublished report.

Clark, J. & Linder, C. (2006): Changing Teaching, Changing Times: Lessons from a South African Township Science Classroom, Rotterdam: Sense Publishers.

Crouch, L. & Vinjevold, P. (2006): South Africa: Access Before Quality, and What to Do Now? *Profesorado. Revista de Curriculum y Formaciondel Profesorado.* 10 (1): 1-16. http://www.ugr.es/~recfpro/rev101ART6ing.pdf. Retrieved 24 February 2014.

Davis, Z. (2010): Researching the Constitution of Mathematics in Pedagogic Contexts: From Grounds to Criteria to Objects and Operations. In V. Mudaly (Ed.), *Proceedings of the 18th Annual Meeting of the Southern African Association for Research in Mathematics, Science and Technology Education*, UKZN, 18-21 (January 2010): 378-87.

Davis, Z. (2011): Orientations to Text and the Ground of Mathematical Activity in Schooling. In Venkat, H. and Essien, A. (Ed.), *Proceedings of the 17th National Congress of the Association for Mathematics Education of South Africa*, University of the Witwatersrand, Johannesburg 11-15 July 2011: 310-22.

Davis, Z. & Gripper, D. (2012a): An Investigation of the Use of the Notion of Equality in the Mathematical Activity of Two Groups of Grade Ten Students. In: Nampota, D. & Kazima, M. (Ed.) *Proceedings of the Twentieth Annual Meeting of the Southern African Association for Research in Mathematics, Science and Technology Education,* Volume 1: Long Papers, 16- 19 January 2012, University of Malawi, Cross Roads Hotel, Lilongwe Malawi, pp. 51-63.

Davis, Z. & Gripper, D. (2012b): A Few Remarks on the Teaching of Inequalities to Grade Ten Students. In: Nieuwoudt, S.; Laubscher, D. and Dreyer, H. (Ed.) *Proceedings of the 18th National Congress of the Association for Mathematical Education of South Africa (AMESA)*, University of the North-West, Potchefstroom, 25-28 June, pp. 157-68.

Davis, Z. & Johnson, Y. (2007): Failing by Example: Initial Remarks on the Constitution of School Mathematics, with Special Reference to the Teaching and Learning of Mathematics in Five Secondary Schools. In Setati, M.; Chitera, N. & Essien, A. (Ed.), *Proceedings of the 13th Annual National Congress of the Association for Mathematics Education of South Africa: The Beauty, Utility and Applicability of Mathematics*, 2-6 July 2007, Uplands College, Mpumalanga, Volume 1, pp. 121-36.

Department of Basic Education (South Africa) (2013a): *Progress made on Basic Education Outcome*, published by the Department of Basic Education in October 2013.

Department of Basic Education (South Africa) (2013b): *Education for All (EFA) 2013 Country Progress Report: South Africa,* published by the Department of Basic Education in October 2013.

Department of Basic Education (South Africa) (2013c): *General Education System Quality Assessment: Country Report South Africa,* published by the Department of Basic Education in October 2013.

Department of Basic Education (South Africa) (2013d): *Macro Indicator Report,* published by the Department of Basic Education in October 2013.

Department of Education (South Africa) (1995): *White Paper on Education and Training (Notice 196 of 1995)*, Government Printer, Pretoria.

Department of Education (South Africa) (2001): *The National Policy on Whole-School Evaluation*, Department of Education, Pretoria.

Department of Education (South Africa) (2003): A Report to the Minister: A Review of the Financing, Resourcing and Costs of Education in Public Schools, Department of Education, Pretoria.

Department of Education (South Africa) (2004): *Annual Report 2003-2004*, Government Printer, Pretoria.

Department of Education (South Africa) (2005): *Minister Naledi Pandor Budget Speech*, Available at: http://www.education.gov.za/mainmedia.asp?src=mvie&xsrc=873. Accessed 28 March 2006.

Fiske, H. & Ladd, E. (2004): Elusive Equity: Education Reform in Post-Apartheid South Africa, HSRC Press, Pretoria.

Fleisch, B. (2002): Managing Educational Change: The State and School Reform in South Africa, Heinemann, Sandown.

Hargreaves, A. (1993): *Changing Teachers, Changing Times,* London: Continuum.

Harley, K. & Wedekind, V. (2004): "Political Change, Curriculum Change and Social Formation, 1990-2002." In Chisholm, L. (Ed.): *Education and Social Change in South Africa,* Cape Town: HSRC Press, pp. 195-220.

Holborn, L. (2013): Education in South Africa: Where did it Go Wrong? Published in *Africa in Fact, Journal of Good Governance*. Available at: http://allafrica.com/stories/201309020840.html Accessed 15 February 2014.

Mail & Guardian (2014): 10 Things about Education, article by the *Mail & Guardian* correspondent, published 17 Jan 2014. Available at: http://mg.co.za/article/2014-01-16-10-things-about-education

Mathematics and Science Education Project (2007): *MSEP Baseline Survey Report*. University of Cape Town.(Prepared for MSEP by: Lydia Abel, Achmat Adams, Norman Davies, Zain Davis, Cynthia Fakudze, Dave Gilmour, Yusuf Johnson, Rüdiger Laugksch, Emmanuel Mushayikwa, Anthea Roberts & Crain Soudien.) Mimeo.[Embargoed].

Matobako, S. (2012): Forms of Social Solidarity and Teachers' Evaluations of Students' Acquisition of Criteria for the Reproduction of School Mathematics. In: Nampota, D. & Kazima, M. (Ed.): *Proceedings of theTwentieth Annual Meeting of the Southern African Association for Research in Mathematics, Science and Technology Education,* Volume 1: Long Papers, 16 - 19 January 2012, University of Malawi, Cross Roads Hotel, Lilongwe Malawi, pp. 157-70.

Naidoo, J. (1996): Racial Integration of Public Schools in South Africa: A Study of Practices, Attitudes and Trends, Education Policy Unit, University of Natal, Durban.

Naidu, B. & Govender, P. (2008): "School Inspectors Return, but They'll be Nicer This Time, *Sunday Times,* 28 September, p. 13.

Nelson Mandela Foundation (2005): Emerging Voices: A Report on Education in South African Rural Communities, HSRC Press, Pretoria.

Pendlebury, S. & Enslin, P. (2004): Social Justice and Inclusion in Education and Politics: The South African Case, *Journal of Education,* 34: 31-50.

Pottinger, B. (2008): So Mbeki's Failures are not Visited upon the Next Generation, *Business Day,* 21 October, p. 11.

Phurutse, C. (2005): *Factors Affecting Teaching and Learning in South African Public Schools*, Report published for the Education Labour Relations Council.

Reeves, C. (2005): Literature Review: Contextual, Institutional, Classroom and Systemic Level Factors That Impact on the Success of Black Learners in High School Mathematics and Science. Unpublished report produced for the Mathematics, Science Education Project (MSEP), University of Cape Town, Cape Town.

Robinson, M. & Soudien, C. (2009): Teacher Development and Political Transformation: Reflections from the South African Experience. In Somekh, B. & Noffke, S. (Ed.), *Handbook of Educational Action Research,* Sage, Thousand Oaks, CA, pp. 467-80.

Soudien, C. & Sayed, Y. (2003): Integrating South African Schools? Some Preliminary Findings, *Institute for Development Studies Bulletin*, 34(1): 29-42.

South Africa History Online (n.d.). Hendrik Frensch Verwoerd. http://www.sahistory.org.za/people/hendrik-frensch-verowerd

Swilling, M. & Russell, B. (2002): *The Size and Scope of the Non-Profit Sector in South Africa,* Graduate School of Public and Development Management, University of the Witwatersrand and the Centre for Civil Society, University of Natal, Johannesburg.

Taylor, N. & Vinjevold, P. (1999): Getting Learning Right: Report of the President's Education Initiative Research Project, Joint Education Trust, Johannesburg.

Taylor, N.; Muller, J. & Vinjevold, P. (2003): *Getting Schools Working: Research and Systemic School Reform in South Africa,* Maskew Miller Longman, Cape Town.

Terreblanche, S. (2002): *A History of Inequality in South Africa,* University of Natal Press, Pietermaritzburg.

UNISA (2012): South African Education: Unequal, Inefficient and Underperforming. *Report from the College of Education, University of South Africa.* Available: http://www.unisa.ac.za/cedu/news/index.php/2012/07/cedu-microwave-presentation-south-african-education-unequal-inefficient-and-underperforming/Accessed: 15 Feb 2014

Western Cape Government (2013): *Education Update,* December 2013, Edition 18. http://www.designinfestation.com/WCEDNEWSindex.php?option=com_content&view=article&id=45 per cent3. Accessed 24 February 2014.

Wilson, F. & Mamphela, R. (1989): *Uprooting Poverty.* Cape Town: David Philip.

3

Building Peace and Democracy amidst Conflict and Violence

Lessons of Colombia's *Escuela Nueva* Model

Thomas F. Luschei

How did Colombia achieve a transition to peace and democracy? Three factors seem to the important. First, the practical leadership of Presidents Alvaro Uribe and Juan Manuel Santos who consistently campaigned against or worked to achieve dialogue with guerrilla groups. Second, economic prosperity: the country attained sustained economic growth during the 2000s. Third, education may have played a role in shepherding Colombia toward peace and democracy. Colombia's Escuela *Nueva* rural school improvement programme, which was founded in 1975 to confront failure in Colombia's rural, multi-grade schools, may have contributed to more peaceful social interactions among children.

Escuela Nueva was designed to address the conditions of small, multi-grade rural schools through a systemic approach of curricular support for teachers and students, cooperative and student-centred learning, flexible student promotion, democratic governance, and community participation. Starting as a small pilot programme in 1975 in Colombia's poorest rural regions, *Escuela Nueva* expanded to tens of thousands of schools. In 1985, the Colombian government adopted *Escuela Nueva* as official policy for all of its rural schools.

Escuela Nueva has been consistently recognised as one of the most successful educational programmes in the developing world (Benveniste & McEwan, 2000). Most of the research on *Escuela Nueva* has focused on the model's success in increasing student test scores. However, evidence also suggests that *Escuela Nueva* has had positive impacts on girls' participation, children's self-esteem, peaceful interactions among children, and democratic behaviour. In a study of one of Colombia's most violent regions, Forero-Pineda *et al* (2006) found that the implementation of *Escuela Nueva* is positively related to democratic behaviour and peaceful interactions among children.

This paper attempts to analyse the role of *Escuela Nueva* in building peace and democracy. This paper examines two questions: (i) What does current evidence tell us about the role of *Escuela Nueva* in promoting democratic behaviour and peaceful interactions among children and communities? (ii) What are the key features of the *Escuela Nueva* model that contribute to the development of democratic behaviour and *Convivencia* among children?

The Escuela Nueva Approach

Escuela Nueva approach features cooperative, flexible, and individualised learning that places the student at the centre of instruction. According to a report issued by a group of Colombian scholars known as the "Mission of the Wise Ones," the essence of *Escuela Nueva* includes self-study learning materials used by children to work at their own pace, active and co-operative learning groups, and student government (FEN, n.d.). As students work in small groups according to their learning needs, the teacher works individually with students or groups. In contrast to a traditional teacher-centered approach, *Escuela Nueva* is active and participatory. Given the autonomy to work at their own pace, children have the opportunity to develop confidence in directing their own learning and classroom environment. One of *Escuela Nueva's* most important features is the involvement of students in classroom and school decision-making. Students in each class elect their own student government representatives to carry out key school activities and represent student opinions. *Escuela Nueva* schools also involve parents in real and important ways. For example, parents in rural areas often help in the design and maintenance of school gardens and provide important agricultural lessons to students.

Within Colombia, the *Escuela Nueva* model has also been applied in urban education contexts and to integrate migrant and displaced children into the formal school system. *Escuela-Activa Urbana* (EAU), *Escuela Nueva*'s urban cousin, which was introduced in 1987, has expanded to the Colombian departments of Antioquia, Boyacá, Caldas, Cundinamarca, Norte deSantander, and Valle del Cauca. Out of necessity and by design, *Escuela Nueva* began in small schools with children of many ages and grades. EAU, which operates in urban settings with single-grade classrooms, applies the same flexible and co-operative approach to classrooms with only one grade. Yet the legacy of *Escuela Nueva* demands that even in single-grade classrooms, teachers attend to the individual needs of students. In applying the philosophy and approach of multi-grade teaching to the context of single-grade urban classrooms, EAU brings to bear a powerful tool to address children's individual learning needs. And by bringing children together in small cooperative learning groups and encouraging them to take charge of their learning—as well as their classrooms and schools—both *Escuela Nueva* and EAU can also construct among students both *Convivencia* and non-cognitive skills like leadership and responsibility.

Escuela Nueva's Impact on Educational Outcomes

The *Escuela Nueva* has provided many of the world's most marginalised children with relevant and high-quality learning opportunities. UNESCO study showed that rural schools outperformed urban schools, except in very large cities and this success was directly attributed to *Escuela Nueva* (UNESCO/LLECE, 2002). This success is remarkable given the extremely difficult conditions in which *Escuela Nueva* functions. Many other studies have shown that the *Escuela Nueva* shows higher student creativity and self-esteem, higher test scores, greater participation of girls, and stronger civic and democratic behaviour (Benveniste & McEwan, 2000; Chesterfield, 1994; McEwan, 1998; Psacharopoulos, Rojas, & Velez, 1993; Rojas & Castillo, 1988).

Ernesto Schiefelbein (1992a, 1992b), an ex-Chilean Minister of Education and former Director of UNESCO, has described consistent and compelling evidence of *Escuela Nueva*'s success. For example, a 1987 evaluation compared a sample of multigrade *Escuela Nueva* schools with large rural schools with one teacher per grade and found that the *Escuela Nueva* schools had lower repetition and drop-out rates in every grade except the first grade. In a test given to *Escuela Nueva* students and students of traditional rural schools, *Escuela Nueva* third graders outperformed students in graded rural schools by 19 per cent in Maths and 12 per cent in Spanish. Schiefelbein also reports that *Escuela Nueva* was able to accomplish superior results with only a five to ten per cent increase in costs over traditional rural school programmes. Additionally, a 1988 study found that 89.3 per cent of Colombian teachers believed that *Escuela Nueva* was superior to other rural school programmes (Schiefelbein, 1992a, 1992b).

There are also studies that support the success of adaptation of EAU. A 1999 study of Escuela Activa Urbana schools in Bogotá found that children in these schools participated more in school activities and parents perceived that their children worked more collaboratively (IDEP-FVG, 1999). A 2002 study by Colombia's National University found that urban schools adopting EAU had superior results to traditional schools after two years of implementation (FEN, n.d.). Such results apply to schools with a range of educational and socio-economic contexts. For example, in 1998 one of the poorest and lowest-performing public schools in Bogotá began implementing the EAU methodology, with a focus on interactive and collaborative reading and writing projects. In 2003, the school's fifth grade students scored at the top of all public schools in the city in interpreting and explaining language (Constanza Jerez, 2003). In the Colombian city of Medellín, the InstituciónEducativa Octavio CalderónMejía, which uses the EAU methodology in Grades 1 through 11, has been recognised several times as one of the top public schools in the city (Holguín & Ospina, n.d.). Principals at both of these schools attributed their successes to the adoption of the EAU model.

Expansion of Escuela Nueva in Colombia and Beyond

Due to *Escuela Nueva*'s considerable success in Colombia, international organisations like Save the Children, UNESCO, UNICEF, and the World Bank have promoted the introduction of *Escuela Nueva*'s strategies to other countries in Latin America and the Caribbean (Luschei, 2004). In 1990, the World Conference on Education for All featured *Escuela Nueva* as one of its two roundtable sessions from Latin America (Colbert, Chiappe; Arboleda, 1993). In 2013, Vicky Colbert, co-founder of the *Escuela Nueva* model and executive director of the Fundación Escuela Nueva Volvamos a la Gente (FEN), a Colombian non-governmental organisation that supports the *Escuela Nueva* model, was recognised with the Qatar Foundation's WISE Prize for innovation in education. The WISE Prize was designed to recognise outstanding global educational achievements, similar to the recognition of the Nobel Prize in other fields (Qatar Foundation, 2014). Altogether, representatives of more than 40 countries have visited Colombia to see the *Escuela Nueva* model in action and 16 other countries have adopted the *Escuela Nueva* model. These include Brazil, Chile, Dominican Republic, East Timor, El Salvador, Guiana, Guatemala, Honduras, Mexico, Nicaragua, Panama, Paraguay,

Peru, Philippines, Uganda, and Vietnam. Estimates suggest that *Escuela Nueva* has reached an estimated five million children worldwide (FEN, 2014).

Conceptual Framework: Education, Peace, Democracy, and Convivencia

In his book *Wars, Guns, and Votes: Democracy in Dangerous Places,* Collier (2009) argues that education can be used as a tool to unite disparate social elements and reduce the likelihood of political conflict or civil war. Collier (2007) has also argued that countries with greater educational attainment are much less likely to engage in civil conflict (Collier, 2007). In other words, the more time that children and adolescents spend in school, the less likely they are to resort to conflict to resolve disputes. The evidence also suggests that education can encourage individuals to participate more in civic behaviour, which can lead to more democratic societies. In their review of social science research examining the influence of educational expansion, Hannum & Buchmann (2005) find evidence of a positive relationship between educational expansion and both democratic behaviour and political participation. Benavot (1998) found that tertiary level educational expansion from 1980 to 1988 had a positive influence on measures of national political democracy. However, he did not find similar evidence of a positive impact of expansion at the primary and secondary levels.

At the individual level, evidence also suggests that access to education has a positive influence on political participation. For example, studies suggest that more educated citizens are more likely to vote and express more tolerant and democratic values (Hannum & Buchmann, 2005). Yet according to Hannum and Buchmann (2005: 346), "the assumption is that schools are responsible for transmitting these outlooks, but exactly how schools promote these outlooks is unclear."

Evidence of the Impact of Escuela Nueva on Peaceful Interaction and Peer Cooperation

Although substantial evidence supports the existence of positive relationships among education, peace, and democracy, there is less evidence about the actual classroom- and school-level mechanisms that instill more peaceful and democratic behaviours in children. It is important to examine these processes and relationships within their contexts and at the classroom and school levels. Research on *Escuela Nueva* both in and outside of Colombia provides some evidence of how this model may lead to such important outcomes. For example, in a comparison of *Escuela Nueva* and traditional rural schools in Colombia, Pitt (1999) found that *Escuela Nueva* schools had more positive school climates and higher levels of democratic behaviour. However, the author did not find significant differences in civic participation across the two school types.

In a study of one of Colombia's most violent regions, Forero-Pineda *et al* (2006) found that the degree of implementation of *Escuela Nueva* is positively related to democratic behaviour and peaceful interactions among children. Specifically, the authors compared the impact of *Escuela Nueva* schools to traditional public schools in six municipalities of the Coffee Region of Colombia. According to data provided by the authors, the homicide rate (number of homicides per 100,000 inhabitants) was significantly higher in the Coffee Region relative to national homicide rates. For example, in 1980 the homicide rate across Colombia was below 40 homicides per 100,000 inhabitants, while the rate was nearly 50 per 100,000 inhabitants in the Coffee Region. By 2000, the homicide rate had climbed to just over 60 nationally but to over 100 in the Coffee Region.

Forero-Pineda *et al* (2006) examined the relationship between the *level of implementation* of the *Escuela Nueva* model and various student outcomes and behaviours.[2] The authors chose this approach because *Escuela Nueva's* history and pervasiveness across rural areas in Colombia mean that most schools employ at least some aspect of the *Escuela Nueva* methodology. Moreover, due to high levels of teacher mobility in Colombia, many teachers who work in non-*Escuela Nueva* schools have received training in *Escuela Nueva* methodologies and may use some of the methods.

The results of Forero-Pineda *et al*'s research (2006) lend substantial support to the possibility that *Escuela Nueva* has positive influences on peaceful and democratic behaviour of children. They found a positive relationship between the level of implementation of *Escuela Nueva* and *Convivencia,* or the peaceful social interaction of children, which is comprised of four key dimensions: "active respect for others, universal solidarity, fair play, and equity" (2006: 275). The authors found a positive and significant relationship between *Convivencia* among children and the teacher-level implementation of *Escuela Nueva,* a measure of the degree of *Escuela Nueva*-related training that a teacher has received.

The authors also found a positive relationship between *Convivencia* and classroom implementation of *Escuela Nueva,* but this relationship was not statistically significant. In addition to exploring impacts on *Convivencia* of children, the authors also applied questionnaires to parents and alumni. They found that greater overall implementation of *Escuela Nueva* (combining both classroom and teacher implementation measures) is positively associated with parents' encouragement of children to become school leaders. Teacher-level implementation of *Escuela Nueva* was also positively related to parents' positive answers regarding whether children's learning at school influences family decisions about their communities. Classroom level implementation of *Escuela Nueva* was positively associated with parents' participation in monitoring projects and resources in the community. Finally, the authors found that alumni of the schools studied were more likely to participate in voluntary organisations if they were graduates of *Escuela Nueva* schools.

In addition to research in Colombia, there is also evidence that applications of the *Escuela Nueva* methodology in other settings can have an important impact on children's democratic behaviour. For example, Chesterfield (1994) compared behaviours of first and second grade students in 20 Guatemalan rural schools. Half of these schools used the *Escuela Nueva* methodology while half used traditional pedagogical models. Chesterfield used direct observation of children to examine democratic behaviours and attitudes such as taking turns and assisting classmates in various activities, expressing opinions and attitudes, and participation in student government and leading fellow students. Although Chesterfield did not find differences across school types in terms of assisting others in academic work or in political and social involvement (results he attributed to the young age of the students), he did find that a large majority of turn taking (80 per cent) occurred among *Escuela Nueva* students. Additionally, while turn taking in traditional schools was associated with waiting for teachers to review student work, turn taking in *Escuela Nueva* schools occurred more spontaneously.

Convivencia

In their study of the impact of *Escuela Nueva* in Colombia's Coffee Region, Forero-Pineda *et al* (2006: 275) define *Convivencia* as "peaceful social interaction of children." The authors note that this term is a "concept of common use in Colombia to identify the conditions associated with non-violent human relations" (2006: 275). According to the authors, *Convivencia* is theoretically composed of active respect for others, universal solidarity, fair play, and equity (2006: 275). The authors used a student survey to operationalise each of these elements as follows:

- *Active respect for others*: Forero-Pineda measure this dimension of *Convivencia* through seven questions related to children's propensity to work and play with others, regardless of differences in gender, race, or geographical origin. As an example, one survey question asks students to respond to the statement, "I help my classmates with their homework, independently of who they are" (2006: 293).
- *Universal solidarity*: Forero-Pineda *et al* (2006: 293-94) measure universal solidarity with four questions related to students' empathy and generosity with others. For example, one question asks students how they would react if a student in their class could not afford pencils.
- *Fair play*: Forero-Pineda *et al* (2006: 294) measure the concept of fair play with four questions related to children's opinions of breaking rules. For example, one question asks students to respond to the statement, "If my best friend asks me to let her copy my answers during a test, I let her copy."
- *Equity*: Forero-Pineda *et al* (2006: 275-76) measure the concept of equity with three questions related to sharing and the distribution of resources. These questions may capture elements of both equity and generosity. For example, one question asks students *what* they would do with a sec*ond* piece of bread after eating the first: give it to a friend, give it to a poor child who does not have any lunch, or save it for later (2006: 294).

In sum, Forero-Pineda *et al* (2006) found the implementation of *Escuela Nueva* to be positively associated with *Convivencia.* They also found positive relationships between levels of implementation of *Escuela Nueva* and parental involvement and participation. Consequently, the outcome of *Convivencia* as proposed by Forero-Pineda appears to be amenable to change through the schooling approach and experience provided to students. Yet these broad patterns do not shed much light on how this change actually occurs. To understand what *Convivencia* looks like and how it is influenced by the *Escuela Nueva* approach, we must look inside schools and classrooms. Below I describe the methods employed to conduct a more school-focussed approach.

Implementation of EscuelaNueva in Urban Areas

This research was originally guided by two principal questions:

(1) What have been the successes and challenges of implementing EAU in urban areas of Colombia?
(2) How do teacher-, school-, and community-level factors influence the adoption and implementation of EAU?

Based on the implementation framework of McLaughlin (1987), which shows that implementation of educational reforms depends on the capacity and will of local actors, especially teachers, this research study explores how capacity, will, and other factors influence the successful implementation of EAU. The empirical evidence of the study is based on six EAU schools in five Colombian states. Data were collected through semi-structured interviews of principals and teachers of their schools. Further, three interviews were conducted with representatives of the Fundación *Escuela Nueva* Volvamos a La Gente (FEN), a non-governmental organisation that has worked to strengthen and expand the *Escuela Nueva* model in Colombia. These were supplemented by many informal conversations with representatives of FEN and interviews with several researchers examining the impact and success of *Escuela Nueva* in Colombia. The interviewees were identified through both purposive and "snowball" sampling and included school principals, teachers, representatives of the NGO Fundación *Escuela Nueva* Volvamos a La Gente, and researchers. Altogether, I interviewed 37 participants in six schools and five states. Table 3.1 provides details regarding interview locations and participants.

Table 3.1: Interview Participants and Locations

Sr. No.	*State*	*Participants*	*Participant Roles*
1.	Cundinamarca	3	NGO Representatives
2.	Cundinamarca	1	Researcher
3.	Cundinamarca	2	NGO Representatives
4.	Cundinamarca	3	Researchers
5.	Cundinamarca	1	Researcher
6.	Cundinamarca	2	NGO Representatives
7.	Boyacá	2	Principal and Coordinator, primary school
8.	Boyacá	1	1st grade teacher, primary school
9.	Boyaca	1	4th grade teacher, primary school
10.	Boyacá	1	2nd grade teacher, primary school
11.	Antioquia	1	Principal, primary and secondary school (grades 1-11)
12.	Antioquia	1	2nd grade teacher
13.	Cundinamarca	2	Principal and 5th grade teacher
14.	Quindío	4	1 coordinator, 1st grade teacher, 2nd grade teacher, 5thgrade teacher from primary school
15.	Caldas	4	1 principal, 1 coordinator, 2 teachers from Grade 1-11 school
16.	Caldas	8	1 principal, 1 coordinator, 6 primary teachers
	Total	**37**	

Interviews probed several areas related to participants' knowledge of and history with EAU, opinions regarding the effectiveness of EAU, challenges and experiences of implementing EAU, and specific questions related to school-level capacity and will to implement EAU. Data collected through recorded interviews, which I conducted in Spanish, were transcribed and coded according to the key themes of capacity and will. Other key themes and codes emerged from the interviews, particularly the impact of EAU methodologies on students' academic success, self-confidence, cooperative behaviour, and leadership abilities. Interview respondents shared many important insights regarding successes and challenges in implementing EAU, as well as important observations related to capacity and will to implement the model. Yet respondents" enthusiastic insistence on discussing EAU's impact on student outcomes related to *Convivencia* compelled me to focus primarily on this theme for the present study.

Although the interviews conducted for this study were designed primarily to probe the challenges and successes of implementing the *Escuela Nueva* model in urban contexts, interview respondents spoke consistently and enthusiastically of the model's impact on their students' cooperative and civic behaviour, as well as autonomy, self-confidence, and leadership skills. Over time, I realised that these responses pointed to a new and compelling story of the impact of EAU. This story relates primarily to *Convivencia,* but also to civic and democratic behaviour and other non-cognitive skills that are likely to have an important impact on children's academic success and lives.

Convivencia

The literal translation of *Convivencia* is coexistence or living together. The term combines the Spanish word "*con*" (with) with "*vivencia,*" which can be translated as lived experience. As discussed above, Forero-Pineda's (2006) framework of *Convivencia* includes active respect for others, universal solidarity, fair play, and equity. Although their findings provide a helpful framework, they do not completely align with my interview findings. Instead, I organise the discussion of *Convivencia* primarily according to the concept of getting along with others. This dimension of *Convivencia* manifested itself most clearly through descriptions of daily interactions and relationships among students. Interviews of school leaders and teachers consistently expressed the positive influence of EAU on cooperative and harmonious behaviour. For example, in one fifth grade classroom in the state of Cundinamarca, a teacher asked students to identify changes in their classroom that had occurred since they first began participating in EAU at the beginning of the school year. Several students offered themselves as examples, indicating that they treated their classmates better as a result of the new approach employed by their teacher. Other students indicated that their classmates had also become friendlier and more cooperative. This school was a particularly interesting case because the teacher was alone in applying the EAU approach, so the contrast with traditional pedagogical approaches in other classrooms in the same school was very striking.

A principal in a primary school in the state of Boyacá noted that the "friendship mail." Allows students to send messages to each other through a class mailbox and "if there are problems between students, as there is anywhere, a student sends a note about it, and the students come to an agreement and they work it out. It's very interesting."

Similarly, a coordinator in a primary school in the state of Quindío offered the example of a student group developed to solve conflicts called "Constructors of Peace." As the coordinator observed, "Our institution like so many others faced problems of aggression, but through the student government we created committees according to the needs and interests of the children. One need was healthy *Convivencia,* so they created a committee called "Constructors of Peace." The coordinator continues:

This committee has leaders with certain characteristics, the most difficult children. So it is surprising to see those children with the most problems, how they appropriated that role, that they are the constructors of peace. Imagine if they are the most difficult and they are changing, they carry more and more children and everyone takes on that role. The idea of the project is that not only the leader is going to behave well, but that we are all going to be constructors of peace.

A principal in a large urban school with grades 1 through 11 contrasted her school with others in the city: "While out there they kill each other and there's bullying, there are many things, here no. Here I have just small things like forgetting to follow the dress code. Here there haven't been problems. Here the problem can be more intense with the adults, but not with the students. The students are very respectful." A second grade teacher at the same school observed, "This school does more than form humans, we try to have them develop a healthy *Convivencia.* This school has very little space for play, but look, there are never fights among the children, you don't see them. Look at them with their tranquility and *Convivencia,* so many values, so much sharing."

In addition to getting along as friends and classmates, interviews also suggested that children in EAU schools work together cooperatively to complete their classroom work, which enhances student learning. A first grade teacher in the state of Boyacá observed that because the EAU model is cooperative, it transforms individual work into group work and teaches students to share and get along. According to this teacher, this model also helps children learn because "if a child does not understand a concept, his friends explain it to him and helps him and he learns more than if just one person tries to explain it to him."

Perhaps the foundation of *Convivencia* is empathy and caring about others. As a first grade teacher in the state of Boyacá observed, "The children at our school develop independence, they are leaders, they collaborate; but above all else, they think about others, not just themselves, but in others."

Civic and Democratic Behaviour

Although children's attitudes and behaviours related to *Convivencia* are linked to civic and democratic behaviour, the dimensions of *Convivencia* discussed above do not completely capture these important behavioural elements that are likely to contribute to social harmony and civic participation. Given *Escuela Nueva's* emphasis on student governance and community participation, as well as the key role that democratic behaviour will play in Colombia's continued emergence from civil conflict, below I discuss evidence from interviews regarding these important behaviours and attitudes.

In my interviews, many principals and teachers emphasised the importance of student government in developing children's ideas about and involvement in democratic behaviour. For example, a principal of an EAU school in the state of Boyacá described an activity in which older children acted as "godparents" of the younger children and were responsible for their well being in school: "if someone has a problem, the godparents fix it by meeting with the student government, with the president, the vice president and secretary and the committees, and they resolve the problem depending on the grade. So they meet and they fix whatever problem that comes up." A second grade teacher in the same school observed:

"Here a nice thing is that there are many resources like the committees. All the children participate in committees and there is the *Convivencia* committee, the sports committee, the academic support committee, and each one has its function and its leader. So the *Convivencia* committee is responsible for, when there is some problem in getting along, the children resolve it. So if a classmate treats another child poorly, the leader of the *Convivencia* committee looks for him and talks to him and tells him that isn't done and he teaches him about peace and *Convivencia,* about values."

A principal in a large urban Grade 1-11 school made similar observations about student government in his school:

This school has a class government and a school government. The class government, like all of them, has a president, vice president, committees. The student government in this moment has a student rector, a student coordinator for secondary and a student coordinator for primary. Every 15 days these students organise the "day of institutional autonomy." They lead the school, while the teachers and administrators are in training meetings. The student leaders manage the school, and it is very nice because if you walk by a classroom, the other students are paying attention, the primary coordinator is managing the young student teachers, they are exercising that autonomy, the leadership that they learn with this model. It is a very significant experience.

The experience of student government and leadership, in addition to generating democratic knowledge and behaviour, can also lead to further development of *Convivencia.* As a second grade teacher in an EAU school in the state of Antioquia observed, in explaining student government:

There is a leader in everything, in cleaning up, the environment. They check how things look, they see who threw trash on the ground. So everyone feels happy to be involved. It's very important to be able to help each other in *Escuela Nueva.* It's very important the treatment we give each other here, we have all the elements, we mold ourselves and our students.

Several interview respondents noted that the opportunity for all children to participate inleadership and governance activities resulted in improved leadership skills and confidence of allstudents. For example, a second grade teacher in an urban primary school in the state of Boyacá observed that students had become much more autonomous since the school adopted EAU. They also developed important leadership skills through daily interactions in class and through participation in student government. As an example, this teacher explained how students took turns being the leaders of their tables. As leadership was not always concentrated among one child, all children were able to develop leadership skills and confidence.

Several interview participants noted the positive reactions of parents to the growing leadership skills of their children. In particular, a second grade teacher in Antioquia observed:

"The parents have received this very well. We can tell this by the number of children who come here every year, it is not a small number. Yes the parents like it, they like that their children are leaders, that they stand out, the principles that they have, the values of *Escuela Nueva.* It's because that is what life is now. What do we look for in terms of competencies now? A young leader, a child who is not tempted by others, who takes responsibility for his own work, who uses the tools around him. I just spoke to a parent who said, "teacher, I like the way you work with my child."

Autonomy, Independence, and Other Non-Cognitive Skills

The most important of the key results not discussed above is the impact of EAU on non-cognitive skills like independence, work ethic, self-discipline, and pro-social behaviour. One of the key skills indicated by participants in my interviews in Colombia relate to development of autonomy among students as a result of EAU's self-directed model. Through daily self-directed work, students in EAU schools read, conduct research, discuss, write, and present important information to classmates. As a fifth grade teacher in the state of Cundinamarca observed:

> "Here (in an urban setting) the family is much more dysfunctional because everyone works, the children are alone, the parents return at night, so it is important for the children to learn among themselves. We use a level of self-learning and that has awoken a lot of curiosity in learning; here the children have many dreams".

In addition to developing curiosity and independence, a third grade teacher in the state of Boyacá noted that through autonomous and independent work, students learned not only how to learning dependently, but also develop important reading comprehension skills.

Finally, when asked why teachers in an urban school would want to implement a programme developed for rural areas, a primary school principal in the state of Caldas observed:

> "This model gives the children a more active education, of having an education where there is autonomy and where they can participate in work with a team, where there is research, where there is responsibility, and where there they themselves assume the roles that must be assumed. We have an active model of construction and participation. Where the child participates and researches and the teacher stops "blah blahblahblah," instead it's the student who asks, analyses looks for his own answers, shares with his classmates and arrives at different conclusions."

Discussion and Conclusion

My findings suggest that daily interactions among children taught with the *Escuela Nueva* methodology help them to develop empathy and agency that promote school-wide *Convivencia.* These outcomes interact with authentic student government to build a sense of efficacy among children that they can and should intervene positively in their communities.

Given Colombia's violent history, these results should have important implications for other societies coping with conflict and violence. The evidence presented in the paper indicates that *Escuela Nueva* methodology can have a positive impact on *Convivencia,* cooperative behaviour, and civic and democratic skills and knowledge. There is also limited evidence about the actual mechanisms or aspects of the *Escuela Nueva* methodology that lead to such positive outcomes. Participants in my interviews consistently indicated the important influence of cooperative, autonomous group work and student governance. Each of these components of the *Escuela Nueva* model, which also feature prominently in the urban model of EAU, provides students with both the tools and the need to solve problems together and to work toward consensus.

Finally, what are the lessons from *Escuela Nueva* for building peace and democracy in other areas of the world? The primary lesson is that children's behaviour and relationships inside the classroom significantly affect their behaviours and attitudes outside of the classroom. Children who are treated as passive subjects in isolation from each other will be less likely to work collaboratively to solve problems and will, as a result, be less likely to develop empathy, leadership skills, or autonomy. These are very tentative conclusions and have not been tested or observed outside of Colombia. There are currently versions of *Escuela Nueva* in at least 16 countries outside of Colombia. The potential for studies on the successes of these programmes in other contexts — especially those with difficult histories of conflict and violence — provides rich ground for future research.

Notes

1. The author received support for this research from a United States Fulbright Core Fellowship. The author acknowledges the extremely valuable advice and support of representatives of the *Fundación Escuela Nueva Volvamos a la Gente*and the *Centro de Investigación y Formaciónen Educación* (CIFE) at the *Universidad de los Andes*, Bogotá. I would also like to thank all of the interview participants who generously shared their time andinsights with me. Finally, I am grateful for the excellent research assistance of Giselle Navarro.
2. Forero-Pineda *et al* (2006) constructed two indices to measure the level of implementation of *Escuela Nueva,* a classroom index and a teacher index. The classroom index includes physical and organisational elements: desk ortable organisation, presentation of subjects, use of study guides, frequency of group work, use of classroom libraries and learning corners, and curricular flexibility. The teacher index measures the relevant training a teacher has received. The two are combined into a global index that ranges from 0 to 100.

References

Benavot, A. (1996). Education and Political Democratisation: Cross-National and Longitudinal Findings. *Comparative Education Review,* 40, 377–403.

Benveniste, L.A. & McEwan, P.J. (2000). Constraints to Implementing Educational Innovations: The Case of Multigrade Cchools. *International Review of Education,*46(1/2): 31-48.

Chesterfield, R. (1994). *Indicators of Democratic Behaviour in Nueva Escuela Unitaria (NEU) Schools.* Research Report. Guatemala: Academy for Educational Development, Juárez and Associates, Inc., and IDEAS Ltd USAID.

Colbert, V.; Chiappe, C. & Arboleda, J. (1993). The New School Programme: More and Better Primary Education for Children in Rural Areas in Colombia. In Levin, H.M. & Lockheed, M.E. (Ed.), *Effective Schools in Developing Countries*, London: The Falmer Press, pp. 52-68.

Collier, P. (2007). Economic Causes of Civil Conflict and Their Implications for Policy. In Crocker, C.A.; Hampson, F.O. & Aall, P. (Ed.), *Leashing the Dogs of War: Conflict Management in a Divided World.* Washington, DC: USIP Press Books.

Collier, P. (2009). Wars, Guns, and Votes: Democracy in Dangerous Places. New York: Harper Collins.

Constanza Jerez, A. (2003). Los colegiosquesaben. *El Tiempo,* June 8, p. 3-5.

Forero-Pineda, C.; Escobar-Rodríguez, D. & Molina, D. (2006). *Escuela Nueva*'s Impact on the Peaceful Social Interaction of Children in Colombia. In Little. A. (Ed.), *Education for All and Multigrade Teaching: Challenges and Opportunities*, Dordrecht, Netherlands: Springer, pp. 265-99.

Fundación Escuela Nueva Volvamos a la Gente [FEN]. (n.d.). Escuela Nueva Activa Urbana: Modelo para mejorar la calidad de la educación y construirciudadanía.Bogotá, Colombia: FEN.

Fundación *Escuela Nueva* Volvamos a la Gente [FEN]. (2014). *Escuela Nueva in the world.* Retrieved from http://www.escuelanueva.org/portal/en/escuela-nueva-model/escuela-nueva-in-the-world.html.

Grupo de Memoria Histórica [GMH]. (2013). *Basta Ya! Colombia: Memorias de Guerra y Dignidad.* Bogotá, Colombia: Imprenta Nacional.

Hannum, E. & Buchmann, C. (2005). Global Educational Expansion and Socio-Economic Development: An Assessment of Findings from the Social Sciences. *World Development,* 33(3), 333-54.

Holguín, C., & Ospina, M. (n. d.). El podertransformador de la Escuela Nueva — Escuela Activa Urbana en la I.E. Octavio Calderón Mejía. Bogotá: Fundación Escuela Nueva Volvamos a la Gente.

Instituto para la Investigación Educativa y el Desarrollo Pedagógico y Fundación Volvamos a la Gente [IDEP-FVG]. (1999). Construcción de unmodelo de Escuela Activa Urbana y de formación para la convivenciaciudadana a partir de la estrategia de Escuela Nueva y suexperienciaen el Distrito Capital. Bogotá, Colombia: Autor.

Luschei, T.F. (2004). Timing is Everything: Brazil's Borrowing of *Escuela Nueva.* In Steiner-Khamsi, G. (Ed.), *The Global Politics of Educational Borrowing and Lending*, New York: Columbia University Teachers College Press, pp. 154-68.

McEwan, P.J. (1998). The Effectiveness of Multigrade Schools in Colombia. *International Journal of Educational Development,* 18(6): 435-52.

Psacharopoulos, G.; Rojas, C., & Velez, E. (1993). Achievement Evaluation of Colombia's Escuela Nueva: Is Multigrade the Answer? *Comparative Education Review,* 37(3): 263-76.

Qatar Foundation. (2014). WISE: Building the Future of Education. Retrieved from http://www.wise-qatar.org/.

Pitt, J. (1999). Civic Education and Citizenship in *Escuela Nueva* Schools in Colombia. Unpublished thesis, University of Toronto, Canada.

Rojas, C. & Castillo, Z. (1988). *Evaluación del Programa Escuela Nueva* [Evaluation of the New School Programme]. Bogotá: Instituto Ser de Investigación.

Rothstein, R. (2004). Class and Schools: Using Social, Economic and Educational Reform to Close the Black-White Achievement Gap. Washington, DC: Economic Policy Institute.

Schiefelbein, E. (1992a). In Search of the School of the XXI Century: Is the Colombian Escuela Nueva the Right Pathfinder? Santiago, Chile: UNESCO/UNICEF.

Schiefelbein, E. (1992b). Redefining Basic Education for Latin America: Lessons to be Learned from the Colombian Escuela Nueva. Paris: UNESCO, International Institute for Educational Planning.

UNESCO/LLECE.(2002). First International Comparative Study of Language, Mathematics, and Associated Factors for Students in the Third and Fourth Grade of Primary School. Second report, Santiago, Chile.

United Nations Office on Drugs and Crime [UNODC] (2011). *Global Study on Homicide.* Vienna: UNODC.

4

Painting Profiles of National Futures with Six Artful Brushes[1]

Democracy, Development, Education, Inclusion, Equity and Sustainability

H.S. Bhola

Policy Borrowing and Lending in Education as a cross-national transaction has been traced back to as early as the year 1900. To begin with, it was basically a European phenomenon. Since the beginning of the New Millennium, however, Policy Borrowing and Lending has seen a heightened interest among the Education Policy elite around the Globe and, concomitantly, among students and scholars of International Comparative Education (Phillips and Ochs, 2004; Steriner-Khamsi and Waldow, 2012). The International Seminar on "Democracy, Development and Education as Related to Issues of Inclusion, Equity and Sustainability," organised by the National University of Educational Planning and Administration (NUEPA) in collaboration with UK-India Education and Research Initiative (UKIERI) that has brought us all to New Delhi, India during this March 6-8, 2014, also has a similar objective: that of promoting Educational Policy Borrowing and Lending among policy-makers, planners, implementers and evaluators participating in this event (*See* Note 1 under Notes and References).

Policy Borrowing and Lending, however, is not just a matter of listening to Stories narrated by fellow participants and to go home inspired to re-direct and reproduce the Stories of interest in the new settings. Stories do indeed end in wise sayings, maxims, metaphors, morals, proverbs and parables, which after careful analysis can lead to generalisations, and which in turn can be synthesised into principles for writing scripts for future interventions in the real world. After careful testing and re-testing, these principles can lead to theoretic statements and models for praxis, for future use in different settings of time and place. In the following, we present a Model, namely – The Epistemic Triangle – that may be useful in such cross-national transfers of Experiences.

The Epistemic Triangle Presented and Elaborated

The Epistemic Triangle first presented in a paper (Bhola, 1996) was by no means, a grand new departure in Epistemology – the philosophy of Knowledge Production. It was only meant to be seen as an integration of three seminal aspects of Epistemology: Constructivist Thinking, Dialectical Thinking and Systems Thinking – also called Systemic Thinking, distinguishing it from merely Systematic Thinking. All of the three angles of the Epistemic Triangle had decades of robust traditions of philosophic examination, but the bane of academic specialisation may have resulted in profound discussions of each, but without regard to the other two angles of the triangle. Systems Thinkers had not said much about Dialectics, or about Constructivism. Indeed each of the three in the trio was quiet about the other two. (*See* Figure 4.1) The Epistemic Triangle as conceptualised (Bhola 1996) suggested a Synthesis of the three separate conceptual traditions — Constructivist Thinking, Dialectical Thinking and Systems Thinking (Bhola, 1996, 1998, 2002, 2013).

A picture is worth a thousand words. The graphic representation of The Epistemic Triangle included on the next page could lend itself to a whole volume (*See* Figure 4.1 below). To begin with, we will discuss the easily discernable and the essential image of the Epistemic Triangle formed by Systems Thinking, Dialectical Thinking and Constructivist Thinking. Additional bits of conceptualisations placed in the heart of the Triangle, among them: Epistemological/Ideological Filters; Post-Modernity; Critical Theory; and the Feminist Critique must await any detailed discussions.

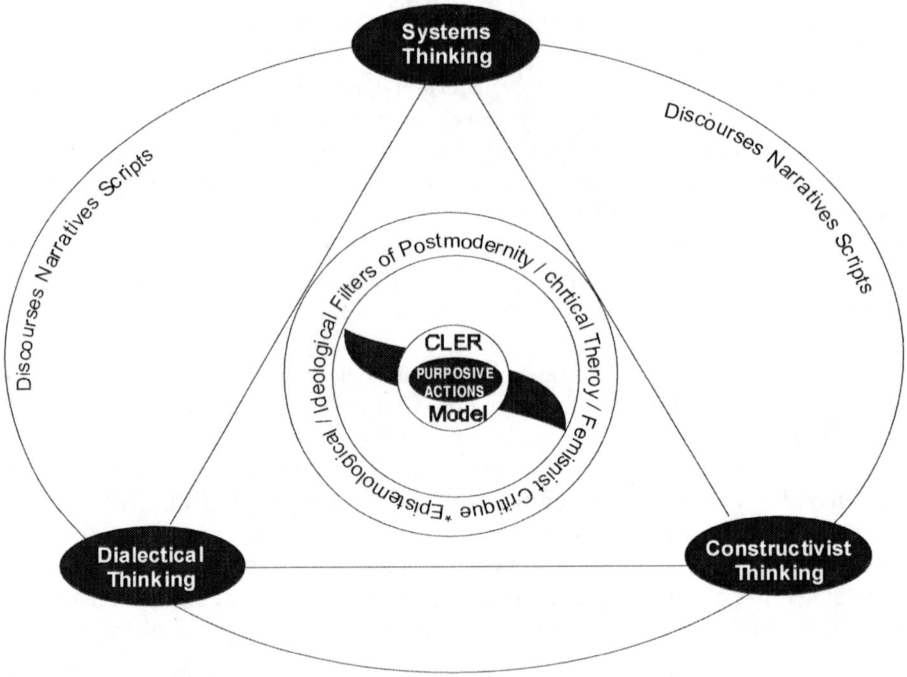

Fig. 4.1: The Epistemic Triangle: Toward New Integrations, Expanding Syntheses

Constructivist Thinking

Epistemologists – philosophers who study the nature of knowledge production and justified beliefs – assert that Reality is not an Open Book, just lying out there for everyone to read that same one *Text*, and to make the exact same *Meanings* out of that text. Reality is indeed a mirror reflecting multiple versions of reality each *individually* and *socially* constructed. This process continues in never-ending cycles of construction, de-construction, and re-construction (Berger and Luckman, 1966).

Dialectical Thinking

A second important contribution from Epistemology comes in the conception of Dialectical Thinking. Dialectical Thinking informs us that *Cause-and-Effect Relationships* in the Real world are not one-directional – "A" as a Cause creating an Effect "B." Indeed, the real social world is one of "Mutual Shaping." In the very social process pertaining to Agent "A" effecting Agent "B," "A" at the same time is effected by "B." Only in controlled laboratory situations could cause-and-effect relations be simplistically viewed as one-directional that could be called positivist interventions (Jameson, 2010; *Kovel, 2008;* Bhola 2011, Bhola 2013).

Systems Thinking

Thirdly, there is Systems Thinking – or Systemic Thinking – which is much more than mere Systematic Thinking. Systemic Thinking asserts that there is *no such thing as clearly-bounded, self-contained, and self-sufficient independent social entities* but that these social entities as systems may have several sub-systems within them – interfacing, overlapping and interacting, each with the other. These Systems, in turn, may be part of overlapping supra systems – political, economic, social, cultural, technological and educational – multi-layered, tent over tent, right from the Local to the Global. These systems and sub-systems and supra-systems, of course, in themselves are not natural or God-given; these are in fact all humanly-invented individual and social constructions (Bertalanffy, 1968; Checkland, 1999; Meadows, 2008, Midgley, 2002).

Serendipities of the Epistemic Triangle

The Epistemic Triangle has provided several serendipities – enabling us "to make some happy and unexpected discoveries by accident." For example, Constructivist Thinking has generated a full-fledged Theory of Discourse and methodology of discourse analysis: providing us with the discipline of "minding our language" – carefully distinguishing between, or combining, "individually held meanings" with more or less "generalised meanings" – invented by particular groups, in particular social-cultural settings, at a particular time and place (Wetherell, Taylor and Yates, 2001, reprinted in 2002, 2003) Another important spin off from the Discourse Theory is the Standpoint Theory – asserting that "Where you "Sit" is where you "Stand" – thereby pointing to the fact that individuals" worldviews are defined by their location in the complex of power relations and social and cultural standings. The Standpoint Theory is most associated with the Feminists who have talked of the unique Feminist Epistemology. Critics have called this Epistemological relativism (Harding, 2004).

The Epistemic Triangle for Praxis

Viewing the challenges of planned activity from within the Epistemic Triangle, compels assumptions of Interdisciplinary Perspectives to be able to deal with the ever-present multiple Contexts of History, Political Economy, Culture, Society, Technology and new phenomenon of Globalisation. It also follows that in defining Research Questions, Policies, Programme Designs and Evaluations, using Interdisciplinary Perspectives, both Quantitative and Qualitative methodologies, will have to be used in tandem.

The education and research initiative (UKIERI) seen through the tri-focal lens of the epistemic triangle.

Viewing UKIERI through the lens of the Epistemic Triangle, will compel some particular viewpoints: First and Foremost, the Constructivist Angle of the Triangle would compel us to pay attention to The Language of Our Discourse, which in the following Discourse includes the language of: Democracy, Development, Education, Inclusion, Equity, and Sustainability. All of these terms have indeed been Constructed, De-Constructed and Re-Constructed over *History*, subject to *Political Economies* of Nations, and in responsiveness to the over-arching phenomenon of *Globalisation.*

Democracy has come to be a national virtue and nearly all nations claim to be Democratic – with their self-defined "particular characteristics." Development, first defined in terms of the world-wide colonial experience, was *Economic Growth*, soon twinned with *Modernisation*, which later came to face "*Limits of Growth*," and then came to preach the necessity of *Human Capital*. Education too, it came to be realised, was easily definable. While old categories of Education by *Sectors* and *Levels* persist, new categories and descriptors have taken over — *Formal, Non-Formal, and Informal Education*, are themselves in process of mutual adaptations. *Literacy* at one end and *Lifelong Learning* on the other end, have gone through scores of constructions in-between.

Inclusion, literally meaning "including much or all" today has acquired highly politicised connotations: e.g., what will be the criteria of Inclusion — *Gender, Caste, Class, Ethnicity or Race?* Equity, which in common parlance meant *Fairness* was now joined with *Justice* – while neither Equity nor Justice has universal definitions. Finally, with the new Sensibilities towards *Global Warming*, has come the new vocabulary of *Sustainable Development*, requiring that Development Projects had to engage with *Protection*, *Mitigation* or *Adaptation* to Global Warming as appropriate to particular Environmental realities in each location, and in each country or region.

Instrumental Processes		Categories of Objectives
DEMOCRACY	⟷	INCLUSION
DEVELOPMENT	⟷	EQUITY
EDUCATION	⟷	SUSTAINABILITY

Fig. 4.2: The Education and Research Initiatives: A Frame for Calculus of Means and Ends

In the following we will remark on the relationships, among and between Democracy, Development, Education, Inclusion, Equity and Sustainability, with references, here and there, to UK, USA, India, South Africa, and occasionally, to other Developing and Developed Countries.

Instrumental Processes

Democracy: Democracy has come to be a national virtue and nearly all nations claim to be Democratic – with their self-defined "particular characteristics." Democracy, "a political system in which all members of a society have an equal share of formal political power," can be traced back to classical Athens of the sixth century B.C. In the context of "modern representative democracy, formal equality, is embodied primarily in the right to vote..... In U.K. the seeds of Democracy were sown in 1215 Charter – Magna Carta – that King John signed a proclamation to the effect assuring "certain liberties..... including freedom of individual against arbitrary authority of the Despot..... From a protracted historical process [it] *became the source of constitutional law in the English-speaking world* [Italics added]. It is also noteworthy that Magna Carta itself has "undergone change of meanings – and has been called names from "capitalist" to "communist" document – an example of the process of *reconstructions*" (Wikipedia, 12/31/13).

That Magna Carta over historical time became a source of constitutional law in the English-speaking world, is worth pondering upon. It was truly historic that the British influence on Americans came to be the source of the American Revolution of 1775. The British did not and still do not have a formal "Constitution" but they do have a whole set of proclamations and precedents that serve as an "Unwritten Constitution" and were liberally used as the Founding Fathers in America searched for "A More Perfect Union (Library Thinkquest, 12/31/13)."

The Constitutional Precedents of UK and the American Constitution as Codified and Adopted have influenced the writing of Constitutions of nation states that on Independence from colonial rule sought to write and adopt their own Constitutions. Both India and South Africa in their own ways provide interesting examples of the process of writing of each nation's first Constitution.

The Indian Constitution: The Indian Constitution of 1949 was written by an International Committee of constitutional scholars and constitutional lawyers from America, England and other European countries and, of course, from within India, to provide a framework for creating a Democratic Socialist state. A noteworthy feature of the Indian Constitution was seeking "Affirmative Action" on behalf of certain castes and tribes – earlier called untouchables in the Hindu caste hierarchy, or depressed classes by the British, and now have been given a somewhat neutral descriptor of "Scheduled Castes and Tribes" and lastly in our times, Dalits. The Indian Constitution is easily the most amended Constitution of the world, having been engaged in the never-ending process of responding to newer and newer caste, and class interests and India's Supreme Court Judgements. Another important feature of the Indian Constitution is to provide an interface between the Central Government and the Planning Commission – an example which has now been followed by several other nations around the world.

About the South African Constitution

The Constitution of the Republic of South Africa (1996) as adopted by the Constitutional Assembly was jointly influenced by Britain, America and other Western nations. The new Republic of South Africa as a sovereign democratic state proclaimed to uphold the values of: (a) Human dignity, the achievement of equality and the advancement of human rights and freedoms; (b) Non-racialism and non-sexism; (c) Supremacy of the constitution and the rule of law; and (d) Universal adult suffrage, a national common voter roll, regular elections and a multi-party system of democratic government, to ensure accountability, responsiveness and openness. With one stroke of pen, on Tuesday, December 10, 1996, by signing the South Africa's new constitution into law, Nelson Mandela lit up the new nation's skies with the promised brightness of a Just Future, and at the same moment buried the old Apartheid regime deep in the ground (Mandela, 1994).

In a masterly essay on the ups and downs of democracy (*The Economist*, March 21, 2014), the question is raised as to why "the most successful political idea of the twentieth century..... has run into trouble?" In answer it is said, that the wounds are self-inflicted.

Development: Development, unsurprisingly, first defined in terms of the colonial experience, was *Economic Growth*, soon twinned with *Modernisation* (Inkeles and Smith, 1974). Then, the "*Limits of Growth*," (Meadows, and others, 1972) became part of the economic discourse, accompanied by emphasis on Human Capital and Social Justice (Ekanga, 2005; Sen 2009)). The latest is Sustainable Development – signifying not merely a development project that is sufficiently funded and has the support of beneficiaries, but one that serves all the peoples without destroying the Local and the Global Environments; and engages in the processes of Protection, Mitigation or Adaptation, as appropriate to particular Environmental realities of Global Warming (United Nations 2002; Bhola and Gomez, 2008).

The very idea of Development has been questioned – dismissed as Lumpen-bourgeoisie and lumpen development (Andre, 1972). Ali Mazrui, an academic and political writer originally from Mombasa, Kenya and now a well-known figure on the world stage, talked of "Colonisation of the Mind" being part of Development processes of the once colonised nations (Wikipedia, accessed February 18, 2014).

On the other hand, connections have been made between Development and "Pursuit of the Quality of Life," for the expanding middle classes (Offer, Ayner, 1996; Calvert-Henderson, 2006); and the eradication of Poverty from among the poor, with special focus on the poorest of the poor (United Nations, 1997, 2008).

Education: Education, like the other two Instrumental Processes of *Democracy* and *Development* is not amenable to one standard universal definition. Education as organised instruction for the transfer of knowledge and experience of one generation to the next had been first assigned to religious institutions. Western colonisation brought to the colonised nations the supposedly secular "Schooling" model with its several levels – Primary (or Elementary), Middle, and High (now Higher Secondary) schools and in some countries Universities in the Western Model as in India, and South Africa (Bhola, 2006).

While old categories of Education by *Sectors* and *Levels* persist, new categories and descriptors have appeared on the educational scene as for example — *Formal, Non-Formal, and Informal Education* (Coombs 1974, 1985). Formal Schooling which was first focused on the 3-R's branched into Vocational Education at one level, and Technical and Specialised Universities on the other. Non-formal Education offered by non-school agents in non-school setting itself came to be in many forms – joining education with childcare and health, education including content on agriculture science, and teaching new modes of income generation to the slum dwellers and the urban poor.

In a world where half the population cannot read and write, *literacy* promotion has remained an essential for Development and Democracy. Literacy used to be defined as "Teaching of Reading and Writing in the Mother Tongue." That definition does not make sense any more. It is not any more even teaching Literacy the National Language. Bi-Literacy and even Tri-Literacy – most often English being one of the languages of Literacy – has become a necessary qualification for the upward bound and entrepreneurial classes all around the world (United Nations, 2002; Bhola 2009).

The difference between "Independent, Self Learning" versus "Being Taught" and its extension into the ideal of *Lifelong Learning* are other intriguing constructions in what used to simply Education. Educational Visionaries today are talking of not only Independent Individual Learning, but also of Lifelong Learning, Learning Communities, and Learning Cities and Regions (Longworth, 2006).

Categories of Objectives

Inclusion: Inclusion, literally meaning "including much or all," today has acquired various highly politicised connotations: e.g., who will be the prior candidates for Inclusion — Gender, Caste, Class, Ethnicity, *Race or What?*

At the global level, Inclusion has been focussed sharply on Women, who as the Chinese have said, "Hold up Half the Sky." United Nations interest in Gender Equality and Women Empowerment goes back several decades, marked by such landmark agreements as the Beijing Declaration and Platform for Action and Convention on the Elimination of All Forms of Discrimination against Women, adopted by 189 world governments at the Fourth World Conference on Women (1995), with 30,000 individuals from civil societies in attendance. The latest Milestone on the road to Gender Equality and Women's Empowerment is the creation during July 2010 of "UN-Women." This is an independent institutional arrangement but will merge with and then consolidate the already existent parts of the UN system that had focused exclusively on Gender Equality and Women's Empowerment – for example, the Division for the Advancement of Women; International Research and Training Institute for the Advancement of Women (INSRAW); Office of the Special Adviser on Gender Issues and Advancement of Women (OSAGI); as also the United Nations Development Fund for Women (UNIFEM) (www.unwomen.org).

Inclusion in India

In an earlier section we have made some comments on Inclusion in India in our discussion of Constitutional Democracy. Suffice it to say that attention to the inclusion of Women in institutions of the state and civil society has continued as evidenced by the International Conference on Women's Literacy for Inclusion and Sustainable Development hosted by the Ministry of Education, Government of India during September 8-10, 2011, on behalf of E-9 Member nations. Shrimati (Madam) Pratibha Patil, the first woman President of India from July 25, 2007 to July 25, 2012 showed deep commitment to promoting gender equality in all sectors of life and work (Bhola, 2014).

Inclusions in South Africa

Inclusions aside, history of South Africa first offered the challenge of Accordance between the Afrikaners and Anglos before the country would come to face any problems of Inclusions as understood today. The Dutch emigrants (also called Afrikaners, or Boers) had settled in South Africa since 1652. The British took control in 1795, to lose it again to Afrikaners. By 1948, the Afrikaner National Party had gained control of the Government. The *Accordance* between the Afrikaners and Anglos remained uncomfortable. While the Anglos were present in the nation's Parliament and Courts and Universities, they were unwelcome guests in the halls of the powerful.

Overall, the 1948 Government was an exclusive regime with near-complete control of Politics, Economy, and Culture. Even the Church had been bent into an instrument of Apartheid and the Devil was quoting scripture to suit his corrupt purposes. The Black majority, the original inhabitants of the land now called South Africa, did not have the right to vote. The Coloured – (those born of the unions of Afrikaners and imported Indonesian mates); and Asian Indians did have a minimal level of rights.

With the dawn of Independence, with Nelson Mandela at the helm, South Africa was indeed re-born. The new South Africa now belonged to all – without exceptions. The spine of the Constitution as adopted was wrapped with Compassion (Mandela, 1994). There was Forgiving without Forgetting of the deeds of Oppressors. The Truth and Reconciliation Commission developed in association with Bishop Desmond Tutu was an act both of genius and generosity. F.W. De Klerk, the last Afrikaner President who handed over power to the new President of Independent South Africa, Nelson Mandela in 1994 is known to have been impressed.

In due course of time, hard realities did appear. The new Constitution promising equal rights did not just conjure up an "egalitarian" community out of Tribes and Clans, each with their own hierarchies of privileges of class and gender. Indeed, the University Educated Black Africans soon became a New Aristocracy assuming huge political power and hoards of stolen Money. New problems of Inclusion arose with movements of Africans from other countries of Southern Africa – Zambia, Zimbabwe, and Nigeria. It wasn't the Rainbow Nation as once dreamt of.

Equity: Inseparable from Inclusion

Inclusion, as was pointed our in the beginning of the preceding section literally means "including much or all," and in today's political culture means Inclusion of Other or Outside for *Gender, Caste, Class, Ethnicity, Race.* Equity, which in common parlance means Fairness, now is often joined with Justice. Thus defined, Equity is inseparable from Inclusion. Indeed, in our elaboration of Inclusion above one can hear loud echoes of Equity.

Sustainability

Sustainable Development as re-defining development that does not hurt the environment was elaborated in an earlier section. Sustainability as a movement to engage in Stemming Global Warming as a national mission needs separate attention.

In India: The central government has had an Environment Ministry since 2006 which has done important work in developing National Environment Policies. It now has a full-fledged National Action Plan on Climate Change (NAPCC), with focus on Energy and Land. The Government has recently approved an allocation of 46,000 crore of Indian rupees on a *Green India* Mission to be pursued over the next 10 years. According to a ministerial announcement: "The National Environment Policy is intended to be a guide to action: in regulatory reform, programme and projects for environmental conservation; and review and enactment of legislation, by agencies of the central, state and local governments..... The policy also seeks to stimulate partnerships with different stakeholders, i.e. public agencies, local communities, academic and scientific institutions, the investment community, and international development partners, in harnessing their respective resources and strengths for environmental management. The dominant theme of this policy is that while conservation of environmental resources is necessary to secure livelihoods and well-being of all, the most secure basis for conservation is to ensure that people dependent on particular resources obtain better livelihoods from the fact of conservation, than from degradation of the resource."

Against this background, some highly interesting projects are in process as for example the multiple initiatives taken up by the world-known philanthropist Bill Gates and India's own local stalwarts — too many to be mentioned here.

In South Africa: The Durban Climate Summit, November-December 2011 was blessed by Pope Benedict XVI – he has now come to be called the Green Pope. Bishop Desmond Tutu compared the Summit with his country's struggle against apartheid, and prayed for its success. But this movement was not blessed with its own "Mandela;" and nothing dramatic has been done in regard to Climate Change initiatives. There are rays of hope as several initiatives are being taken by the South Africa's Department of Environmental Affairs to integrate climate change responses into local Development as for example one with cooperation with Germany's GIZ.

Designing Social and Behavioural Interventions for Delivering Innovation and Change on the Ground

Social Configurations of Actualising Innovation and Change

The concept of Context introduced earlier can be further expanded in Social Configurations of Change defined by Innovators and Adopters as proposed in Bhola's Configurations-Linkages-Environment-Resources (CLER) Model. Both the Providers and Beneficiaries involved in transactions of planned change are part of a complex system of social Configurations (C) formed by Individuals, Groups, Institutions and sub-Cultures of their own; and using Linkages (L) both formal and non-formal. Both providers and recipients will need Resources (R) including the Conceptual, Informational, and Material of Personnel, and Institutional Capital as well as Time (CIMPIT). The Participants and the Beneficiaries indeed may not be responding to the same Environments (E). Managing the complex drama of their interactions requires imagination and commitment, and a comprehensive model such as the CLER Model (Bhola, 1988, 2013b).

The following Graphic explains how the model accommodates Planning, Implementation and Evaluation of the Processes of Planned Change and Innovation Diffusion. [*See* Graphic Below]

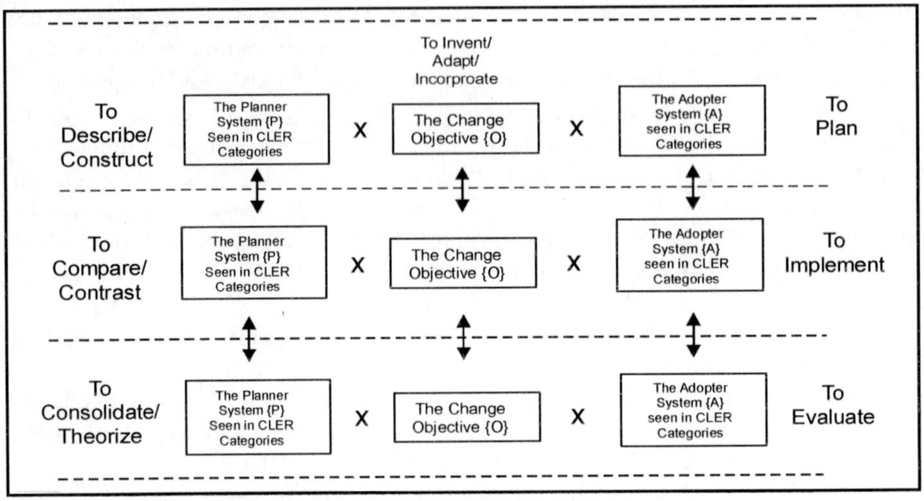

Fig. 4.3: Innovation for Reform: The CLER Model as a Systemic Strategy

Modelling for Praxis: From Policy into Practice

In this final section, we present a "Model for Planned Action: From Policy into Practice." Once again, we will have to let the Graphic below to carry the maximum burden, and with the minimum of commentary.

← — — — Historical Framework of Political Economy of a Nation — — — →
V V V V V V V V V V V V V V V V V V V V V V V
Policy Processes of:
Formulation – Planning -- Mobilisation – Implementation -- Evaluation
Λ Λ Λ Λ Λ Λ Λ Λ Λ Λ Λ Λ Λ Λ Λ
V V V V V V V V V V V V V V V

The CLER Model Showing
Configurations, Linkages, Environment and Resources of Agents and Adopters:

Planner System X Objectives of Change X Adopter System
\|/
The Logic of Action:
Dialectics between the Institutional and the Instructional

Fig. 4.4: Model for Planned Action: From Policy into Practice
Source: Adaptation from: (Bhola, 2013a).

As shown in the Graphic 3 above, Policy making is a process rooted in the History, and Political Economy of a country. In going from Policy to Practice, we need to deal with the processes of Formulation, Planning, Mobilisation, Implementation and Evaluation. The relationship between and among these processes is not Sequential, but

Dialectical. Estimation of Resources available for Implementation and Anticipation of difficulties may influence the very Formulation of Policy; and obligations and anxieties about Evaluation to show results may also determine what policy declarations are made in the first place; and how Plans are worded, and so on (Bhola 1998 (a), 1998(b), 2000, 2003, 2004).

The CLER (Configurations-Linkages-Environments-Resources) Model Showing the Dialectic between "Planner System", "Objectives of Change" and the "Adopter System" has been presented in some detail in a separate section above. The last but not the least important conceptual part of the Graphic is "The Logic of Action: Dialectics between the Institutional and the Instructional."

By Way of Conclusion

Policy elite and peoples — Borrowing from and lending to each other

We had begun this paper by describing the Embedded Objective of The International Seminar on organised by the National University of Educational Planning and Administration (NUEPA) in collaboration with UK-India Education and Research Initiative (UKIERI as promoting Educational Policy Borrowing and Lending among policy makers, planners, implementers and evaluators participating in this event.

We like to end the paper by suggesting that the process of Policy Borrowing and Lending that began and had for a century or more remained to be the Playground of the Power Elite is no more exclusive to the Policy Elite. There are new players on the playing field.

In the new Age of the Internet with its Social Media, Policy Borrowing and Lending has exploded into People's Business. At the larger level, the communication technologies of TV and Videos on the Internet have expanded knowledge about how the others live creating visions of new possibilities in commoners' lives. New conceptions of the role of women and new appetites of middle classes have changed the world. Most importantly, the Social Media, in the form of widely available and low priced cellphones have brought the world peoples into a new power house of politics. Policy makers and the Peoples are borrowing and lending from and to each other.

Notes

1. The purposes and goals of the UK-India Education and Research Initiative (UKIERI) cover a wide area of interests and are not limited to Formal and Non-formal Education. UKIERI Annual Report (2012-2013) lists it programmatic interests along Four Strands. Strand 1: Leadership Development; Strand 2: Innovation Partnerships; Strand 3: Skills Development; and Strand 4: Enhancing Mobility. Additional Sections of the UKIERI Report discuss: Corporate partnerships in UKIERI; Key Event and Activities (2012-13); Awards (2012-13); Awards Analysis (2012-13); and Memoranda of Understanding and Agreements. In addition, Education is sought to be integrated with Health Maintenance, improved Agricultural and Industrial Skills for Income Generating and promoting Environmental sensibilities.

References

Andre, G.F. (1972): Lumpen Bourgeoisie and Lumpen Development: Dependency, Class and Politics in Latin America. New York and London: Monthly Press Review.

Berger, P.L. & Luckman, T. (1966): *The Social Construction of Reality*, Garden City, NY: Doubleday.

Bertalanffy, Ludwig von (1968): *General Systems Theory: Foundations, Development, Applications*. New York: George Braziller.

Bhola, H.S. (1988): The CLER Model of Innovation Diffusion, Planned Change and Development: A Conceptual Update and Applications. *Knowledge and Society: An International Journal of Knowledge Transfer*, 1(4): 56-66.

Bhola, H.S. (1996): Between Limits of Rationality and Possibilities of Praxis: Purposive Action from the Heart of an Epistemic Triangle, *Entrepreneurship, Innovation and Change*, 5: 33-47.

Bhola, H.S. (1998a): Constructivist Capacity Building and Systemic Programme Evaluation: One Discourse, Two Scripts, Evaluation: *International Journal of Evaluation Theory and Practice*. London, U.K.: Tavistock Institute, 4 (1998): 1-22.

Bhola, H.S., (1998b): They are Learning and Discerning: Evaluation of an Adult Education Project of the National Literacy Cooperation of South Africa. *Studies in Educational Evaluation*, A Pergamon Press Journal, 24 (1998): 153-77.

Bhola, H.S., (2000): Practical Policy Analysis for Educational Policy Making under Globalisation, *Journal of Educational Planning and Administration*, XIV (3) (July 2000): 233-48.

Bhola, H.S., (2002): A Discourse on Educational Leadership: Global Themes, Postmodern Perspectives. *Studies in Philosophy and Education: An International Journal*, Kluwer Academic Publishers, 21(2): 181-202.

Bhola, H.S. (2003): Policy: A Holistic Perspective, *Journal of Educational Planning and Administration*, XVII(1): 85-104.

Bhola, H.S. (2004): Policy Implementation: Planning and Actualisation, *Journal of Educational Planning and Administration*, XVIII(3), (July 2004):.295-312.

Bhola, H.S. (2006): Access to Education: A Global Perspective. In: Oduaran, Akpovire and Bhola, H.S. (Ed.), *Widening Access to Education as Social Justice: Essays in Honour of Michael Omolewa*, Berlin, Heidelberg, New York: Springer/UNESCO/UIE, pp. 44-68..

Bhola, H.S. and Gomez, Sofia Valdivielso (2008): *Signposts to Literacy for Sustainable Development* [Two complementary studies by the joint winners of the 2004-2005 International Award for Literacy Research.] Hamburg: UNESCO Institute for Lifelong Learning (UIL).

Bhola, H.S. (2009): Literacy. In Bates, Marcia J. and Maack, Mary Niles (Ed.): *Encyclopaedia of Library and Information Sciences*, in four volumes, Third Edition. New York/London: Taylor and Francis.

Bhola, H.S. (2011): Systems Theory Perspective on Education for Rural Transformation: In the Dialectic between Global Contexts and Local Conditions, *Journal of Educational Planning and Administration*, XXV(1) (January-March): 5-19.

Bhola, H.S. (2013): Education for Rural Transformation (ERT) in India – Dialectics between Theory and Ideology; and the National and the Global, *Journal of Educational Planning and Administration*, XXVII(3) (July): 257-80.

Bhola, H.S., (2013a): Google search of December 22, 2013, using the Title "The Epistemic Triangle – Framework for Building Theory, Doing Research, and Implementing Change."

Bhola, H.S., (2013b): Google accessed on December 24, 2013 showed 4,700 Results in 0.25 seconds; More than 100 citations including CLER Model authors papers published in 1965, 1988, 1994.

Bhola, H.S., (2014): Essentiality of a Policy Framework for Promoting Literacy, Adult Education and Lifelong Education (pages 74-96)." In Gupta, Shaibal (ed.): *Compendium on Literacy and Inclusive Development*, New Delhi: National Literacy Mission Authority, Ministry of Human Resource Development, Department of School Education and Literacy, Government of India.

Calvert-Henderson. (2006): Quality of Life Indicators, Accessed on www.Google.com, 8 January 2006.

Checkland, Peter (1999): Systems Thinking, Systems Practice: Includes a 30-Years Retrospective. Wiley Publication.

Coombs, Philip H. (1974): Attacking Rural Poverty: How Non-Formal Education Can Help, World Bank Series.

Coombs, Philip H. (1985): *The World Crisis in Education: The View from the Eighties*, Oxford University Press.

Ekanga, Basile (2005): Social Justice and Democracy: The Relevance of Rawls's Conception of Justice in Africa. European University Studies, Series XX, Philosophy, Vol. 682. Frankfurt am Main: Peter Lang.

Harding, Sandra (Ed.) (2004): *The Feminist Standpoint Theory Reader*, New York and London: Routledge.

Inkeles, Alex, and Smith, David H. (1974): *Becoming Modern: Individual Change in Six Developing Countries*. Cambridge, Massachusetts: Harvard University Press.

Jameson, Fredric (2010): *Valences of the Dialectic*, Verso Publication, Available through Amazon.

Kovel, Joel (2008): *Dialectic as Praxis*. Electronic Resource, Basingstoke: Palgrave Macmillan.

Library Thinktank, (2013): http://library.thinktank.org/26466/history_of_democracy.html [Accessed December 31, 2013]

Longworth, Norman (2006): *Learning Cities, Learning Regions, Learning Communities: Lifelong Learning and Local Government*. London and New York: Routledge / Taylor & Francis Group.

Mandela, Nelson (1994): *Long Walk to Freedom*, London: Little Brown and Co.

Meadows, Donella H. et al (1972): The Limits to Growth: A Report for the Club of Rome's Project on the Predicament of Mankind. New York: Universe Books.

Meadows, Donella H. (2008): *Thinking in Systems: A Primer*. Earthscan.

Midgley, G., (Ed.) (2002): Systems Thinking. In four volumes, London: Sage Publications.

Offer, Ayner (Ed.) (1996): *In Pursuit of the Quality of Life*. Oxford, U.K.: Oxford University Press.

Phillips, D. and Ochs, K. (Ed.), (2004): *Educational Policy Borrowing: Historical Perspectives*, Oxford Studies in Comparative Education. Oxford: Symposium Books.

Sen, Amartya, (2009): *Idea of Justice*. Boston: Belknap Press of Harvard University Press.

Steiner-Khamsi, Gita and Waldow, Florian (Ed.), (2012): *World Yearbook of Education 2012: Policy Borrowing and Lending in Education*. Routledge, Taylor and Francis Group, New York: USA.

The Economist (2014): Essay: Democracy, What's Gone Wrong with Democracy, March 1, pp. 47-52.

United Nations, (1997): First United Nations Decade or the Eradication of Poverty, 1997-2006. www.un.org/esa/socdev/poverty/poverty.htm

United Nations, (2002): United Nations Literacy Decade: Education for All (UNLD) 2003-2012). www.unesco.org/education/litdecade

United Nations, (2002): The Johannesburg Declaration on Sustainable Development. World Summit on Sustainable Development, Johannesburg, South Africa, 2-4 September 2002. <www.johannesburgsummit.org/html/documents/summit_docs/1009wssd_pol_declaration.doc>.

United Nations, (2008): Second *United Nations Decade* for the *Eradication* of *Poverty* (2008-2017). www.un.org/esa/socdev/social/poverty/2nddecade.html

Wetherell, Margaret; Taylor, Stephanie and Yates, Simeon J. (2001): Discourse Theory and Practice – A Reader. London, U.K. / Thousand Oaks, CA. USA/ New Delhi, India: Sage Publications. Reprinted 2002, 2003. This book has also been published as an e-book by The Open University.

Wikipedia, (2013): http://en.wikipedia.org/wiki/History_of_democracy [Accessed December 31, 2013]

Wikipedia, (2014): The Fourth World Conference on Women: Action for Equality, Development and Peace, September 4-15, 1995, Beijing, China; Beijing Declaration and a Platform for Action. New York; and for additional background: United Nations, 1993, World Conference on Human Rights. The Vienna Declaration and Programme of Action, June 1993. New York. (Accessed in www.unwomen.org).

5
Education, Global Citizenship and Democracy in Post-2015 Landscapes[1]

Kenneth King

Education has been long claimed to have a direct relationship with economic and social development, including increased productivity, health, reduced mortality, population control, etc. These claims go back to the very early 1960s and 1980s (Schultz 1961, UNESCO 2002, Colclough, 1980), in association with the World Bank's studies of the influence of education, and especially primary education on other sectors, and they go right upto the *EFA Global Monitoring Report, 2013/14*. Arguably, some of these most claimed connections of education with many other dimensions of development helped in the processes of lobbying for a place of education in the post-2015 global development agenda. In these debates, the case for education is made both as a stand-alone goal, and as a goal that is inseparable from the successful delivery of all the other goals.

In this chapter, we shall look particularly at the "democratic dividend" from education, both through the lens of global citizenship as well as more generally through education's influence on political participation. Perhaps surprisingly, these two discussions seem to take place in the literature on parallel lines, though it might seem that they should be interrelated. They do, however, come together a little in relation to the MDG and post-MDG agendas.

Case for Education in Relation to Political Participation in 2002 and 2009

With the publication of the first, full length report in 2002, there was a detailed discussion on the relationship between education and development as the very first chapter of the report. This was entitled "Education for All is Development" (UNESCO, 2002). It looked at three different arguments for supporting education goals: "The first derives from ideas of human rights. The second is a framework informed by notions of individual capacity and capability. The third perspective concerns the ways in which education helps people and societies to achieve other desired development goals" (*ibid*, 30). From two of these perspectives, there is an argument about the relationship between education and political participation. From a right angle, education is seen to provide some of the essential "scaffolding" for securing the right to participation in social and political activity. Second, from Sen's capabilities approach "these substantive freedoms (that is, the liberty of political participation.....) are among the *constituent components* of development" (*ibid*, 32). Interestingly, the chapter does not refer to greater political participation as one of the non-market effects or externalities of investing in basic education. We shall see that this will prove to be one of the largest contrasts between the 2002 and 2013/14 GMRs.

In terms of our later discussion of global citizenship, it should be noted that the actual term does not appear at all in the GMR of 2002. Citizenship is certainly mentioned, particularly as an element in lifeskills education, along with education for peace, and human rights in settings of serious conflict or post-conflict. "Good citizenship" is also seen as one of the outcomes of education alongside generic skills, and positive attitudes towards learning (*ibid*, 80). But beyond this, there is little discussion of the concept in its relation to social and political development.

Before turning to the GMR of 2013/4, we should acknowledge that the GMR of 2009 with its focus on "Why Governance Matters" also paid attention to how education acted as a "catalyst for development" through "unlocking the wider benefits of education" in other development objectives (UNESCO, 2009: 29-37). Within this key section, there was a crucial analysis of "Democracy and Citizenship: From Local to Global" – which brings together the twin concerns of this present chapter. But it is valuable to note that its examination of the powerful effects of education on democratic participation starts with the caveat that this relationship is far from universal or straightforward. There are well-educated societies that are not model democracies, and societies with relatively lower levels of education which have rather well-developed democratic traditions (*ibid,* 36).

One of the most influential pieces of research in this area of education and democracy (Evans and Rose, 2007a; revised 2012) is drawn upon by the GMR of 2009. From cross-country research on education and democratic attitudes in 18 countries of Sub-Saharan Africa, it concludes that schooling is by far the strongest factor explaining support for democratic approaches. This research also provides the evidence that higher levels of schooling strengthen these positive attitudes towards democracy. A "killer finding" derives from this work: "People of voting age with a primary education are 1.5 times more likely to support democracy than people with no education, rising to three times more likely for someone with secondary education" (UNESCO, 2009: 36). We shall note that this finding will be picked up in later years, but the GMR of 2009 treated it with two cautions. First, the finding could not be simply extrapolated to other regions, and equally there was no single model of democratic governance. But, second, it was not the case that any old education could have this apparently powerful effect; it would have to be "investment in education of good quality" that might act as among the most influential forces for democracy (*ibid*).

Education in Relation to Democracy and Good Governance in the GMR 2013/14

Where the GMR of 2002 dedicates just seven crucially important pages to the chapter "Education for All" is Development" (*ibid,* 29-35), and the GMR of 2009 has nine pages on the same topic of education as a catalyst of development, the GMR of 2013/14 has a whole chapter of no less than 45 pages allocated to the argument that "Education transforms lives" (*ibid*, 140-85). Doubtless, this attention to arguing the case for education in relation to other possible development goals was also affected by the imminence of the next global agenda being decided by the United Nations. Indeed, the introduction to the chapter admits this: "This chapter provides comprehensive evidence that progress in education is vital to achieve all new development goals after 2015" (UNESCO, 2014: 140).

The chapter marshals detailed evidence about the powerful influence of education on a large number of development challenges. These include: a route out of poverty, improvement of employment prospects, protection against unemployment in rich countries, closing gender-wage gaps, improved chances of a healthier life, reduced infant and maternal mortality, as well as fertility, containment of disease, protection against non-communicable diseases, elimination of hunger, a contribution to the solution of environmental problems, and finally women"s empowerment (*ibid*, 140-69; 177-85).

Education, Democracy and Good Governance

But it is also in relation to education's "key role in promoting democratic values" that the Report sees a particularly crucial contribution to the post-2015 development framework (*ibid*, 170). We shall look in turn at several of the different ways in which, it is claimed, education contributes to "expanding democratic engagement." Under the general banner that "Education builds the foundations of democracy and good governance" (*ibid*), the report looks at seven different dimensions of education's relationship with democracy.

One of the most fundamental of these is "the vital role of education in promoting human rights and the rule of law" (*ibid*). The contribution of "teaching and of education" in "promoting rights and freedoms" is enshrined in the preamble to the Universal Declaration of Human Rights (UDHR) (UN, 1948). It is worth noting that the key articles 19, 20 and 21 which specify the right to freedom of expression, and to peaceful assembly, and the right to take part in the government of the country and in elections by universal and equal suffrage, do not actually use the word "democracy." This is understandable as most of the world in 1948 was very far from having the right to free elections. Nor does the UDHR say anything about the quality of education in its famous article 26 about the right to education.

The GMR claims, however, that it is "good quality education" that helps people to make more informed judgements about key issues and helps their engagement in political discussion. It is admitted, however, that there are in many parts of the world, very weak, even corrupt, forms of justice and of democracy. We should note also that while some of the discussion is held at the level of education contributing to "political participation"; a great deal more is concerned quite explicitly with education's role in building democracy and good governance.

In this connection, the GMR acknowledges that the argument has been made by the UNDP (2012) that a "democratic governance goal" should have been in the MDGs, and should be considered for the post-2015 development agenda. This role of education in relation to democratic values is claimed to be substantiated by some 40 years of analysis showing that a 10 per cent increase in secondary enrolment is linked to a 1.8-point increase in the Polity IV index, which measures the extent of democracy on a ten point scale. It is conceded that 40 years is too short a time to measure the role of education in the emergence of democracy. Nevertheless, the GMR does then proceed to claim that studies over more than 100 years "show that universal primary education and literacy have been vital for countries to move from authoritarianism to democracy" (UNESCO, 2014: 170). Such claims about the democratic transition need to bear in mind that some of the largest concentrations of the present illiterate 774 million in the world are to be found in democratic countries such as India, and equally that a full nine years of compulsory education had been implemented effectively in China even before the MDGs were agreed. However, the GMR then turns to what it considers even stronger evidence of the key role of education in promoting the "social and cultural foundations of democracy" (*ibid*).

Education and Political Knowledge

We are then offered some quantitative analysis about how "Education improves political knowledge." In Europe, apparently, people who have "four more years of schooling" spend 50 per cent more time, on average, in getting insights from reading newspaper articles on politics and current affairs (UNESCO, 2014: 170). However, it is not mentioned with whom the four more years of schooling are being compared. Further quantitative analysis then claims that in 12 Sub-Saharan African countries, 63 per cent of those without formal schooling had any understanding of democracy as compared with 71 per cent of those with primary education and 86 per cent of those with secondary (*ibid*). Although we are not told in the GMR what an understanding of democracy consisted of, it could be claimed by contrast that if as many as 63 per cent of those with no schooling at all understood the meaning of democracy, seven years of primary schooling do not appear to have made much difference (just a 7 per cent increase). A similar point could be made about the evidence from Malawi, where almost 80 per cent of those with no schooling could provide a definition of democracy. This is as it should be, even if the addition of primary education meant that all but 3 per cent could produce a definition (*ibid*, 170-71).

It is important to ensure that these claims about primary' educated respondents' understanding of democracy (which date from 2005 and 2007) bear in mind the appalling quality of primary education in Malawi which we are told about in other sections of the GMR 2013/14. Apparently even for better-off children, "the quality of education is so low that 72 per cent are in school but not achieving the minimum learning standards" (*ibid*, 195). So even if it may seem impressive that all but 3 per cent of Malawians of voting age with primary school education can define democracy, we need to recall that only "3 per cent of the poor and 8 per cent of the rich (are) completing primary education and achieving the basics" (*ibid*). Where this leaves their understanding of democracy will need to be further examined.

Despite this contrast between one of the main messages of the GMR 2013/14 which is about the teaching and learning crisis in basic education on the one hand, and understanding of democracy on the other, there is still said to be powerful evidence that primary education and, even more, secondary education do increase support for democracy. Apparently, across 18 countries of SSA those of voting age with primary and secondary education are 1.5 and 3 times more likely, respectively, "to express support for democracy" than those with no education (*ibid*). What is not completely clear, at least from the GMR, is whether these relationships hold up, regardless of the quality of the schools, which we were earlier told was critical in these relations.

Support for Democracy

Similar claims are made in the GMR for the impact of education in strengthening support for democracy in the Arab states of Egypt and Tunisia, in other pre-dominantly Muslim countries such as Jordan, Lebanon, and Pakistan. In respect of urban Pakistan in particular, where it was found that only 35 per cent of respondents supported democracy, those with secondary education were only 15 percentage points more likely to support democracy than "those with less than primary education" (*ibid*). Leaving aside the uncertainty about the meaning of "less than primary," the finding is used to argue for the "urgency of increased investment in education" given that education levels remain extremely low and "fully fledged democracy has yet to take hold" (*ibid*, 171). This particular argument seems to come dangerously close to making the case for education as a form of securitisation.

Other claims about the impact of more education on positive attitudes towards democracy are made for Latin America. But in a GMR volume where one of the principal concerns is with quality education and quality teaching, it is perhaps surprising that the many studies quoted on attitudes towards democracy pay so little attention to the different qualities of primary and secondary schools but seem mainly to focus on mere years of education, whether in primary or in secondary. For example, one study claims that "an additional year of schooling raised voter participation by seven percentage points" (*ibid*, 172), but there seems to be no interest, in this section, in exploring whether one year of very poor schooling has the same impact as a year of high quality schooling.

Education and Political Participation

Beyond strengthening support for democracy, the GMR argues strongly that a higher level of education "raises political participation" (*ibid*, 172). Different dimensions of this participation cover readiness to vote, engagement in "democratic activity" such as campaigning, attending rallies, signing petitions etc. But although the claim is that citizens with secondary education were twice as likely to take part in peaceful demonstrations or sign petitions as those with primary, the overall figures for either were extremely small (e.g. in China and in Turkey (*ibid*, 172)). These two countries are of course interesting cases, as they contain very high levels of young people with full secondary education. It could be argued that the more obvious conclusion from the surveys is that despite very high levels of both primary and secondary education, there is actually very little expressed interest in political participation. Furthermore, given that nine years of compulsory education has been in place in China by law from the late 1990s, it is becoming increasingly difficult to contrast those citizens with only primary education versus those with secondary education. Indeed, the contrast between those with primary and those with secondary may actually in some countries be a reflection of age, as the great bulk of all young people have had both primary and secondary education. In other words, the education contrast may be hiding a difference in age.

Education, Tolerance and Social Cohesion

A next illustration of education's role in building the foundations of democracy in the GMR 2013/14 is taken from studies about the role of education in encouraging tolerance and social cohesion, whether in attitudes towards race, religion, immigration, or towards people with HIV. Again, it is argued that there is "a difference between a primary and a secondary education" when it comes to such issues. But again there is no discussion of whether it may be as much age as education that is responsible for any marked differences in attitudes. Also, the failure to get behind the simple labels of primary and secondary education may be masking significant other differences. For instance, very high dropout rates characterise secondary education in many parts of Latin America, but does this produce a difference in attitudes between the large numbers of secondary non-completers and those who finish? The same might be asked of primary school completers and dropouts.

Intriguingly, there are one or two issues where more education does not seem to make a difference, at least in some regions. For instance, in the Arab states, as many as 9 out of 10 people express intolerance towards homosexuality, regardless of education (*ibid*, 173). The response of the EFA GMR to this is interesting: "This suggests that education can take time to have an impact on ingrained attitudes" (*ibid*, 173). In other words, the basic assumption is that education is potentially part of the solution, whereas it is just possible that education might itself be part of the problem. In addition, in countries where there are very distinct kinds of primary or secondary school with frequently different levels of achievement (e.g. private, aided, and public), it is conceivable that the label primary or secondary may actually be concealing important distinctions in attitudes. But the Report continues to use mere years of education rather than quality of education as a key marker. Thus, in respect of trust and tolerance, the attraction of a quantitative generalisation, as noted earlier, is more powerful than disaggregation of schooling by quality, type or level of completion: "A review of estimates from various studies suggested that one year of schooling increases the probability of trusting people by 2.4 percentage points and the probability of civic participation by 2.8 percentage points" (*ibid*, 175).

Significantly, however, the GMR 2013/14 does accept that schooling can be as much part of the problem as part of the solution in some situations. When it comes to countries with increasing levels of income inequality reflected in increased segregation in education through private schooling, levels of social cohesion have declined. In the same manner, social cohesion was lower in 15 high income countries in settings where there were more unequal education outcomes (*ibid*).

Education Helps Prevent Conflict

Some of the more controversial quantitative generalisations in this GMR come from the claims about education and the prevention of conflict. While it is admitted that low levels of education do not automatically lead to conflict, they are nevertheless seen as an important risk factor (*ibid*). Again, the attraction of killer headlines such as: "doubling the percentage of youth with secondary education, from 30 per cent to 60 per cent, would halve the risk of conflict" or "if the male secondary school enrolment ratio were

10 percentage points higher than average, the risk of war would decline by a quarter" obscures the possibility that the different qualities of different types of secondary education may be more important than mere secondary education. Some of these killer generalisations are even applied to the past — which seems completely counter-intuitive: "Globally, an increase in primary enrolment from 67 per cent to 100 per cent would have resulted in a 35 per cent decrease in the probability of civil war over 1980-1999" (*ibid*, 176). It is worth continuing to stress that in a volume that is concerned primarily with quality education for all, it seems odd to produce quantitative generalisations that have no connection with educational quality.

Education and Corruption

One of the last dimensions of education and democracy dealt with in the GMR is the claim that "Education helps reduce corruption" (*ibid*). Again, there are studies proclaiming that across almost 80 countries "the level of educational attainment is the most powerful factor predicting lower levels of corruption" (*ibid*). But the growing concerns about corruption, especially in South Asia, suggest that the cultures of petty and grand corruption cannot be captured in any such simple way as level of education.

Education as Essential for Justice

The final section of the discussion on education and political participation claims that "Education is essential for the justice system to function" (*ibid*, 177). It is certainly the case that lack of education, especially in English or French in Sub-Saharan Africa, can be a major setback in situations where the courts do not operate in the local languages, but the way the courts operate is much less to do with levels of education or languages of instruction than with other political and cultural constraints.

Reflections on Education, Political Participation and Democracy

The chapter, of which the section on education for democracy is a part, seeks to elaborate "education's unique power" in relation to many other sectors (*ibid,* 185). The purpose is to secure for education a central position in the post-2015 development framework (*ibid,* 184). Its ambition is to demonstrate that not only is education a human right, and a key goal on its own, but that it is "an investment that pays off in every sphere of people's lives and aspirations" (*ibid,* 185).

But as far as the GMR making the case for a "democratic governance goal," it is interesting to note that the UN Secretary General's High Level Panel (HLP) of Eminent Persons on the Post-2015 Development Agenda covered much of the same ground in their report of May 2013 as the GMR 2013/14 would do some eight months later. The HLP proposed as one of eleven illustrative goals, "Goal # 10: Ensure good governance and accountable institutions." Their list of targets within this goal covered the following, several of which are very close to those issues we have just discussed:

a) Provide free and universal legal identity, such as birth registrations
b) Ensure that people enjoy freedom of speech, association, peaceful protest and access to independent media and information

c) Increase public participation in political processes and civic engagement at all levels
d) Guarantee the public's right to information and access to government data
e) Reduce bribery and corruption and ensure officials can be held accountable (HLP, 2013: 50).

While the HLP talked a good deal about good governance as well as participatory governance, they did not actually use the words "democracy" or "democratic" at all in their main text or the key Annex II about the eleven illustrative goals.[3] The contrast with the EFA GMR 2013/4 is rather sharp. As we have just seen, democracy and democratic are used a good deal (51 and 30 times respectively) in the GMR; while "good governance" is used only twice. The reason for this clear distinction is presumably that the HLP was very hesitant about appearing to assume that good governance meant democracy or western democracy. On the other hand we have seen that the GMR 2013/14 has reviewed a great deal of the relevant literature about explicit support for democracy and expanding democratic engagement. It has had no hesitations in analysing education's claim to promote democratic values. Equally, it has quite openly sought to show that "education helps people understand how democracy functions and what its benefits are" (UNESCO, 2013/14: 170).

A second issue for reflection we have raised about the GMR discussion on education's role in getting people to understand democracy is whether the principally quantitative approach adopted in much of the literature reviewed by the GMR is suitable for deciding about such a topic, and especially in a report which has been concerned with a very dramatic crisis of learning quality in basic education. Equally, we have been aware that the simple contrasts between primary and secondary education mask the massive differences within these categories, and not least when "one year of schooling" is claimed to make a significant difference (*ibid,* 175). The importance of quality education is mentioned firmly at the outset of the discussion, but the emphasis overall is strongly placed on education's instrumental effects. We end the section "with little insight into the complex chemistry of how various elements react, under what conditions and with which resultant by-products" (McGrath, 2014: 35).

A third reflection in this set of arguments about education-and-democracy in the GMR is that there is almost no discussion of citizenship education in this section we have reviewed, and no mention at all of global citizenship education, to which we turn next. It is almost as if these terms are from two different domains.

Rise of Education for Global Citizenship

Given the attention paid to good governance and democratic engagement in the GMR 2013/14, it might be anticipated that there would also be a discussion about global citizenship. This term has been rendered more salient by its being identified as one of three key pillars in the UN Secretary General's Global Education First Initiative (GEFI) of 2012, even if it has been also recognised as a possibly controversial or faddish term (Tawil, 2014). We have already noted that there was neither discussion of the concept in the first full GMR Report of 2002; nor was it discussed in the GMRs of 2009 or 2012; nor did it merit discussion in the HLP of 2013. However, it does secure attention in the GMR 2013/14 as a separate section in the key chapter 7 on "Curriculum and assessment strategies that improve learning" (*ibid*, 275-297). Perhaps surprisingly, as we have just noted, it is treated quite separately from the GMR's discussion of education for democracy and good governance.

Before turning to examine its role in the GMR, we should acknowledge that the term global citizenship has an ancestry long before it was selected as a core element within Education First.[4] Indeed, cosmopolitanism and the notion of being a "citizen of the world" have been ideals for many people, young and old, for generations, but especially in the late 1960s and 1970s, as international travel, greater leisure, global movements and student mobility began to make the world smaller. In parallel, traditional moral and civic education in schools began to reflect more of a one-world approach through the rise of new nations and nation building, development education, and global issues. Schools were increasingly claimed to be about much more than tests and diplomas, and many made global links.

It is some of these global concerns that the GMR 2013/14 pointed to in its call for "transferable skills for global citizenship." These skills were said to be beyond the foundation skills which had been carefully analysed in the previous GMR of 2012 (UNESCO, 2012; King, 2014). It was claimed that they illustrated a whole series of attributes, "such as critical thinking, communication, cooperation, problem-solving, conflict resolution, leadership and advocacy" (*ibid,* 309). It would appear from this listing that global citizenship itself is not a transferable skill, but rather that transferable skills are needed to ensure the acquisition of global citizenship. On the other hand, global citizenship education is said to include issues such as "environmental sustainability and peace-building" as well "core values such as tolerance, appreciation of diversity and civic responsibility." So it rather looks as if "conflict resolution" is a core or transferable skill, while "peace-building" is an aspect of global citizenship. Being clear whether global citizenship is itself a skill, an attitude or an outcome and a result of an educational process is surely important to its promotion. But a closer analysis of this key section on global citizenship should help clarify this.

However, in the multi-country review of which transferable skills are highlighted in national curricula (*ibid*; Amadio, 2013), there is no mention of whether conflict resolution is so regarded. In fact there are only two major items highlighted in the section on global citizenship in the GMR 2013/4: one covers "responsible attitudes and behaviour towards the environment" and the other is "education for peace-building" (*ibid,* 295-97). It will be recalled that these were just two of a whole range of development issues where it was claimed that education had a substantial impact (above, p. 2). It is perhaps surprising that education for greater political engagement and awareness as discussed earlier is not explicitly picked out under global citizenship. Greater political interest was nevertheless claimed as one of the outcomes of Northern Ireland's Local and Global Citizenship programme, in the discussion of "Education for peace-building": "As a result of this approach, students became more interested in local and international politics and had greater expectations of democratic environments in schools" (*ibid,* 297).

Global citizenship is thus treated through just two lenses, environment and peace-building, and unlike education-for-democracy there is no discussion of whether exposure to different levels of education makes a significant impact on its achievement. Nor is there any discussion of the relationship between global citizenship and globalisation; indeed the latter term does not appear in the GMR 2013/14 at all. Global citizenship is mentioned in the discussion of the ten most important teacher reforms that policy makers should adopt to promote more equitable learning for all. In particular, it is said to be one of the outcomes of fostering transferable skills through interdisciplinary and participatory learning.

The wider debates about how citizenship and civics education may be located and contrasted in a whole continuum of conservative and progressive approaches to both content and pedagogy have been tackled by Tawil (2013; 2014). He has not only critically reviewed the "political dimension of citizenship education" but also examined how global "civic megatrends" are being integrated into citizenship education. Such trends include awareness of international migration, the global economy and changing patterns of work, the impact of the ICT revolution, the increasing global population and the changing role of women etc. (Tawil, 2013: 4). From this perspective, these trends can enrich existing forms of national or local curriculum. They encourage, according to Tawil, a sense of shared destiny with humanity and the global community, an understanding of humanity's interdependence, and a commitment to act and engage in civic and social action. On reflection, Tawil thinks it is more intelligible to refer to "citizenship education in a global world" than to use the potentially contested notion of "global citizenship education" (Tawil, 2013: 6).

A Pillar of the Global Education First Initiative (GEFI)

It would be interesting to know more about the origins for the inclusion of Global Citizenship as one of the three pillars in the Global Education First Initiative. In September 2012 when the Initiative was first announced there were still three years left before 2015; so it was natural and even tempting to suggest one more "big push" before the deadline. This was especially the case for the remaining millions of out-of-school primary age children which was the first GEFI pillar: "Put every child in school." Equally, the second pillar of "Improving the quality of learning" had become a very high priority by 2012, and was on everyone's lips. The mystery is surely why global citizenship is included along with Access and Quality. Is there any clue to this in Ban Ki-moon's own explanation of the Initiative?

The first sentence of his one-page rationale from September 2012 is the strongest possible endorsement of the impact of education on many other sectors:

Education is a major driving force for human development. It opens doors to the job market, combats inequality, improves maternal health, reduces child mortality, fosters solidarity, and promotes environmental stewardship. Education empowers people with the knowledge, skills and values they need to build a better world. (Ban, 2012)

While the first part of this rationale speaks directly to the well-known evidence about education and other outcomes, the last sentence is more of a global vision or global ambition. Hence when the Secretary General (SG) turns to a statement specifically on global citizenship, he reiterates education's potential to "build a better world." In other words, he goes beyond the value of education to the individual and the family, and affirms its contribution to peace, good relations and to care for the environment.

Like many other South Koreans, he turns to his country's own history of transition from poverty to prosperity to explain the centrality of education. There is nothing further said by the SG about Korea's increasingly global role, as a long term aid donor, as a member of the OECD and of DAC, as host to the Busan aid effectiveness forum in 2012, and as future host of the World Education Forum in May 2015; but conceivably these could be seen as illustrations of Korea itself becoming a global player or global citizen.

In the more detailed website blurb on the third pillar or priority – Global Citizenship – there is a good deal said about global challenges and global solutions. These "interconnected global challenges" go far beyond education's role in helping to secure an entry to the job market, or the other claimed impacts of education on health, wealth and productivity. The global citizenship agenda needs to be "transformative" in many different ways. This term "transformative" is highly suggestive. Just 3-4 months earlier in Shanghai at the 3rd World Congress on Technical and Vocational Education and Training in 2012, the main background document for the meeting was entitled *Transforming technical and vocational education and training,* and it used the term transformative 19 times in just 20 pages of text. More importantly it used the word dramatically to re-conceptualise traditional TVET and address the multiple challenges of a globalising world (UNESCO, 2012b).

Be that as it may, Education First's conception of global citizenship is intimately connected to education answering the big questions of the day. Sustainable development will not be achieved by technological solutions, political regulations or by financial instruments. Rather, it "requires transforming the way people think and act."

Having suggested that education will require a transformative lens if global citizenship is to become a reality, a number of barriers to such citizenship are noted. The first and most obvious is the education system itself! With its powerful focus on exams, graduation and jobs, it stands directly in the way or raising global citizens.

The second barrier is that existing curricula are said to be part of the problem. Allegedly they reinforce stereotypes, exacerbate divisions, and engender fear and resentment of other groups and nationalities (http://www.globaleducationfirst.org/220.htm). This seems a pretty large generalisation, even if it may have been true historically of apartheid South Africa. In addition, the notion that change is feasible with the adoption by teachers of "a vision of ethical global citizenship" is rather a tall order (*ibid*).

A third barrier is lack of teacher capacity. Here the challenge is precisely that teachers are claimed to be part of the problem. But if the transformation of teaching and learning is the objective, there is a massive teacher reform process needed. The focus of the change seems to be rather narrowly focused on "non-discrimination and positive support to the disadvantaged" as if the problems are as much within the school as outside (*ibid*).

A last barrier is the inadequate focus on values. Again there is the claim that schools actually reinforce "social pathologies" and "gender-based violence," whereas they ought to be promoting an ethos that promotes the wider values of peace, human rights, respect, cultural diversity and justice.

In conclusion, the website blurb on global citizenship presents an ideal world against a reality of traditional examination-oriented learning. The reforms required talk of the need for innovative and participatory teaching and learning. In other words, the teaching reforms talk of a complete transformation of approaches to learning.

There is a brochure on the Education First Initiative. It mostly reproduces the material about the three pillars from the website, but it does surprisingly include Foster Global Citizenship as one of the key actions to help the world achieve the three goals of Education First. Three items are mentioned for Global Citizenship: Cultivate a sense of community and giving back to society; ensure schools are free of all forms of discrimination; invest at least 5 per cent to 6 per cent of GDPs in education (Ban, 2012: 27).

What is however very far from clear is the current status of activity around the fostering of global citizenship. There is a listing of barriers to global citizenship, but there is almost no indication of what may have happened to this objective in the one and a half years since the initiative was launched in September 2012. The only two indications of specific lessons from teaching good citizenship are said to be in India and Ghana, but it is not clarified whether these are as a result of Education First's funding. Nor is there any way of following up on the reference to these two countries. Of the different commitments to support Education First listed on the site, many of them from the private sector, none is explicitly targeted at global citizenship. At least from the evidence available on the official site, therefore, this third pillar of Education First remains very much an ambitious aspiration, and a hoped-for transformation. By contrast the pillar of improving the quality of learning is getting very high-level visibility.[5]

Relationship with the Post-2015 Processes

We have examined in this brief review some of the ways in which it is hoped that "education's unique power" may influence other development issues, including democratic engagement and political participation. In parallel, we have reviewed where education for global citizenship fits into the jigsaw, and considered how its transformative ambitions may contrast with the realities of the many barriers to citizenship education in a globalising world. Before concluding, it may be useful to revisit the ongoing post-2015 processes, and see where democratic engagement and global citizenship may fit into these. The following are a few of the most recent, relevant reference points.

It will be recalled that as far as the HLP was concerned, good governance was the preferred discourse rather than democracy, while citizenship, not to mention global citizenship, did not appear at all.

UNESCO may have ultimate responsibility for putting the flesh on the Education First Initiative's bones. Certainly, global citizenship was mentioned in the 2013 UNESCO General Conference's discussion of its fundamental principles, thematic priorities, and within one of its five objectives for *Education beyond 2015* (UNESCO, 2013).

In the February 2014 *Indicators for Sustainable Development Goals* of the Sustainable Development Solutions Network (SDSN) which reviewed indicators for ten goals, there were a series of indicators for education and skills, from early childhood through to TVET. It is worth noting that both in respect of primary and of secondary, the draft report mentioned the importance of citizenship. By the time of the SDSN producing in May 2014 *An action agenda for sustainable development* (SDSN, 2014b), the indicators were no longer specified, and like the HLP above, there was no mention of citizenship, global citizenship, or democracy.

However, in the Global Education for All meeting, held in Muscat in May 2014 by UNESCO, in the *Muscat Agreement,* education was claimed to be an essential condition for global citizenship, amongst other targets. Both global and local citizenship were seen to be central to the post-2015 education development agenda. Moreover, apart from the targets for all the different levels of education, global citizenship was itself picked out as a target with a link to sustainable development:

Target 5: By 2030, all learners acquire knowledge, skills, values and attitudes to establish sustainable and peaceful societies, including through global citizenship education and education for sustainable development. (UNESCO, 2014b: 3)

The same is true of a place for citizenship in our final document for this chapter. The intergovernmental Open Working Group (OWG) on Sustainable Development Goals (SDGs) has played a crucial role in determining the next development agenda, and in its *Outcome Document* of July 2014 it presented its 17 Goals, along with their respective Targets. Its Goal 4 on Education was very close to the Muscat Agreement. It too had a target that mentioned global citizenship, but there is a danger that this element may be lost in a target that includes so much else, including multiple references to sustainable development:

Target 4.7: By 2030 ensure all learners acquire knowledge and skills needed to promote sustainable development, including among others through education for sustainable development and sustainable lifestyles, human rights, gender equality, promotion of a culture of peace and non-violence, global citizenship, and appreciation of cultural diversity and of culture's contribution to sustainable development (OWG, 2014: 9).

Indeed, this is the only place in the 20 page document where citizenship is mentioned while sustainable and sustainable development are mentioned no less than 100 and 55 times respectively. Interestingly, neither democracy nor democratic are mentioned in their own right in the Outcome Document, except in a single reference to the Rio+20 outcome.

Conclusion

This chapter has taken seriously the claim in the *Concept Note* of the international NUEPA seminar of March 2014 notes that "Education holds the key to democracy and development"(NUEPA, 2014: 1). It has looked critically at the assertion that education "is instrumental in developing a democratic society while supporting the development process" (NUEPA, 2014: 1), and has used the latest documentation from the GMR 2013/14 and from the post-2015 process to examine some of the evidence behind the claim. It remains surprising after this initial review of the evidence that education-for-democracy and global citizenship education seem still to inhabit separate worlds. It will doubtless be valuable to track what happens to these two concepts including in their relationship with education for sustainable development, both in the September 2015 meeting of the United Nations General Assembly, and beyond.

Notes

1. An earlier and longer version of this paper was given at International Seminar on "Democracy, Education and Development: Issues Relating to Inclusion, Equity and Sustainability," March 06-08, 2014, NUEPA, New Delhi
3. Good governance or participatory governance were used 16 times in the HLP Report; by contrast 'democratic' was only used once in connection with financing, and 'democracy' not at all in the main text and goal annex. (http://www.globaleducationfirst.org/220.htm)
4. See Mason's valuable account of some of this history in 'The ethics of a cosmopolitan citizenship education in a globalised world' (2002). He traces the ancestry back to Kant.
5. See http://www.globaleducationfirst.org/4455.htm for high level event of 24th September 2014 on 'Quality Education for the World We Want'.

References

Adams, A. (2012): *The Education Link: Why Learning is Central to the Post-2015 Global Development Agenda.* Washington: Centre for Universal Education, Brookings.

Amadio, M. (2013): "A Rapid Assessment of Curricula for General Education Focussing on Cross-Curricular Themes and Generic Competences or Skills." Background paper for EFA Global Monitoring Report, 2013/14, UNESCO, Paris. Accessed at http://unesdoc.unesco.org/images/0022/002259/225939e.pdf

Ban, K. (2012): "Statement from the Secretary General. Launch of the Global Education First Initiative, United Nations, September 2012, New York. Accessed at http://www.global educationfirst.org/289.htm

Ban. K. (2012): *Global Education First Initiative.* United Nations, New York. http://www.globaleducationfirst.org/files/GEFI_Brochure_ENG.pdf

Colclough, C. (1980): *Primary Schooling and Economic Development: A Review of the Evidence.* Staff Working Paper, Washington: World Bank.

Evans, G. and Rose, P. (2007a): Education and Support for Democracy in Sub-Saharan Africa: Testing Mechanisms of Influence. Paper presented at 'The Micro-Foundations of Mass Politics in Africa,' East Lansing, Mich: Michigan State University, 12–13 May.

Evans, G. and Rose, P. (2007b): "Support for Democracy in Malawi: Does Schooling Matter?" *World Development.* 35 (5): 904-19.

Evans, G. and Rose, P. (2012): Understanding Education's Influence on Support for Democracy in Sub-Saharan Africa. *Journal of Development Studies,* 48 (4): 498-515

High Level Panel (HLP) of Eminent Persons on the Post-2015 Development Agenda (2013): *A New Global Partnership: Eradicate Poverty and Transform Economies through Sustainable Development.* 30 May 2013, United Nations, New York.

King, K. (2014): Youth, Skills Development, and Work in the Education for All Global Monitoring Report 2012: Learning from Asia or for Asia? *Prospects* 44: 141-58.

King, K. and Palmer, R. (2013): "Post-2015 Agendas: Northern Tsunami, Southern Ripple? The Case of Education and Skills," *International Journal of Educational Development*, 33. 409-25.

McGrath, S. (2014): Education, Teaching and Developmental Outcomes – Any New Chemistry? *NORRAG News* 50, 35. Accessed at www.norrag.org

Mason, M. (2002): "The Ethics of a Cosmopolitan Citizenship Education in a Globalised World" Thirty-Sixth Annual Conference of the Philosophy of Education Society of Great Britain, 5 – 7 April 2002, New College, Oxford.

NUEPA (2014): *Concept Note.* International Seminar on Democracy, Education, and Development, 6-8 March 2014, NUEPA, New Delhi

Open Working Group (OWG) (2014): *Outcome Document of the Open Working Group on Sustainable Development Goals*, 19 July 2014, New York. Accessed at http://sustainable development.un.org/focussdgs.html

Schultz, T. (1963): *The Economic Value of Education.* Columbia University Press, New York.

Sustainable Development Solutions Network (SDSN) (2014a): *Indicators for Sustainable Development Goals. A Report by the Leadership Council of the SDSN*. February 14, 2014, SDSN, New York.

Sustainable Development Solutions Network (SDSN) (2014b): *An Action Agenda for Sustainable Development: A Report for the UN Secretary General*, May 5, 2014, SDSN, New York.

Tawil, S. (2013): *Education for "Global Citizenship": A Framework for Discussion.* Working Paper 7, Education Research and Foresight, UNESCO, Paris.

Tawil, S. (2014): Education for "Global Citizenship": Beyond the "Fuzzword." NORRAG Newsbite, 3 February 2014. Accessible at http://norrag.wordpress.com/2014/02/03/education-for-global-citizenship-beyond-the-fuzzword/

United Nations (1948): *The Universal Declaration of Human Rights*, 10 December 1948, United Nations, New York.

United Nations (2012): United Nations Secretary-General's Global Education First Initiative. United Nations, New York. Accessed at: http://www.globaleducationfirst.org/220.htm

UNDP (2012): *Measuring Democracy and Democratic Governance in a Post-2015 Development Framework.* Discussion Paper, New York: United Nations Development Programme.

UNESCO (2002): *Education for All: Is the World on Track? EFA Global Monitoring Report 2002.* Paris: UNESCO.

UNESCO (2009): *Overcoming Inequality: Why Governance Matters. EFA Global Monitoring Report 2009.* Paris: UNESCO.

UNESCO (2012a): *Youth and Skills: Putting Education to Work. EFA Global Monitoring Report 2012.* Paris: UNESCO.

UNESCO (2012b): *Transforming Technical and Vocational Education and Training: Building Skills for Work and Life. Main Working Document.* Paris: UNESCO

UNESCO (2013): *Education beyond 2015.* 37C/56, Paris: General Conference of UNESCO.

UNESCO (2014a): *Teaching and learning: Achieving quality for all. EFA Global Monitoring Report*, 2013'/14. Paris: UNESCO.

UNESCO (2014b): 2014 *GEM Final Statement: The Muscat Agreement*, Global Education for All Meeting, UNESCO, Muscat, Oman 12-14 May 2014

UNESCO & UNICEF (2013): Envisioning Education in the Post-2015 Development Agenda, Global Thematic Consultation. Executive Summary. Draft

6

Democracy, Deprivation and Dispossession

Multiple Narratives of Democracy in North India*

Badri Narayan

All over the world, various forms of democracies are suffering through multiple forms of democratic deficit. In many cases, election, as central method to take democracy forward, fails in many ways. The existing power-holders and dominant sections often dictate governments that emerge out of democratic elections. They create hurdles in ensuring equality and participation as key values of democracy.

This chapter documents the multiple experience of democracy in North Indian society through the narratives of small Dalit groups in eastern Uttar Pradesh (UP). This chapter traces the sense of relative deprivation of small Dalit groups in eastern UP as revealed through their narratives of democratic experiences.

State-Led Democracy and the Marginalised

India is the world's largest democracy. One of the achievements, highlighted as an important outcome of democracy in the country is the growing sense of empowerment the weaker sections of society. The Indian experience shows that empowerment and marginalisation sometimes go together at times supplementing each other or countering each other. So marginalisation appears in our everyday life in both ways – it is real and constructed.

In its constructed form, marginalisation evolves and develops in the context of state-led democracy, where state appears as a resource-distributing and opportunity-providing agency. It is interesting to observe that these narratives of marginalisation mostly emerge as critical and complaint based against democracy, since these are based on aspiration and desire for a better life of the marginalised communities. In the Indian context, state is perceived as the primary instrument of delivering democracy.

During our fieldwork in northern Indian villages, especially in UP, we observed that in popular parlance state and democracy are being perceived as synonymous to each other. Both state and democracy are understood by the rural people in their everyday life as *"sarkar."* The idea of *sarkar* in vernacular life means bit different from European meaning of government that is perceived as rational governing agency. It means government and powerful people (*huzoor*, modern masters or political leaders — *neta*, powerful people, who may or may not directly be part of the government but attain power in the corridors of the state), who all run the government directly and indirectly or the *sarkar banane ke liye chunav* (electoral politics for entering in government.)[1] This *sarkar* in its combined meaning of state and democracy invokes lot of undirected and uncontrollable social aspiration despite the "global dominance of ideas of liberalisation" (Kaviraj 2005: 2). Sudipto Kaviraj rightly observed that "there is no end in sight of the Indian society's strange enchantment with the modern state" (*ibid*). This very enchantment may be the one of the causes of enormous rise of dissatisfaction against the state and state-led democracy.

While observing the working of state-led democracy in villages, it appears that no one seems to be satisfied with democracy. All the people we talked to had a large number of complaints against the state-led democracy. The major complaint was that the government was not doing anything for them. There may be two reasons for this response. First, identify that the person asking questions might be a government official and hence they deliberately enhance the intensity of their problems in the hope of getting some benefits. Secondly, the state-led democracy, in its present form, has given rise to a great deal of expectations among the people, which they express in the form of deprivations.

However, further probing and longer interviews revealed that each person is benefitted from the state-led development and democracy although not upto the level of expectations. The state-led democracy in India relied on various strategies to fulfil the urges and desires of communities and deepen democracy at the grassroots. Forming categories as a technique of managing democracy appeared as one of the modes of delivering protective discrimination to provide support and benefit of democracy to the weaker sections of population. To deepen democracy and attack the caste system, the Indian constitution, along with other measures like the abolition of caste system, formed a system of reservation based on these categories in three sectors — electoral representation, government employment and educational institutions (Kaviraj 2005: 13).

These categories linked with census and numbering play an important role in governance. While exploring the politics of making of category Ian Hacking (1975) and Arjun Appadurai (1993) said that numbers were elegant, discrete, comparable, and meaningful within and across categories and units. Dirks also reconstructed the meaning of numbers and said numbers could be used to generate information concerning the caste composition of discrete areas of imperial control in relation to military recruitment, police control, land settlement operation, market intervention, and legal policy (Dirks 2003: 199-200). These categories were formed by the colonial governance for population counting but later on they were used for protective discrimination and electoral mobilisation.

This reinvention of categories later evolved as a powerful tool of electoral mobilisation of marginal communities in India like the Scheduled Castes (SCs), Scheduled Tribes (STs) and Other Backward Castes (OBCs), during democratic elections. The demands for shifting categories by upper, middle and lower castes are the outcome of their growing sense of marginalisation in the allotted state location and the hope to come out from it by changing state created categories.[2] In governance, these categories are considered as homogeneous entities but in reality they contain multiple forms of heterogeneities and various layers of social locations for these castes.[3]

It is interesting to observe that sometimes during electoral mobilisations, political parties and media believe that these categories work well as they help to mobilise larger percentage of voters in favour of certain political parties. It is only when the distribution of democratic resources take place that these heterogeneities, stories of marginalisation and narratives of dispossession, become visible. Hope for a better future binds them all together. All groups, big and small, come together for a common cause. A case in point is the Mandal Commission agitation, when even smaller groups of OBCs and SCs rallied together for common gains such as government jobs, housing and other development policies aimed to strengthen the weaker sections and provide equitable social justice within the target group. This was the dream that was shown to these marginalised communities by the ruling political party.

The desire of the dominant and vocal sections of these categories to take more share of the resources resulted in an inequitable distribution of resources based on caste. This situation created competition among the different marginalised castes at various levels with the smaller and less powerful being left out of the share of the resources. These communities now want to shift to other categories as they believe that they will get more benefits in this way. The trend among them is to try to shift to lower state-created categories as they feel that these categories are being given more benefits by the government. The ruling political party and other parties use these desires that emerge from the deprivation of these communities for strengthening their base among the respective communities.

Political Parties and Marginalised Committees

Even political parties support the demand of communities to move to lower categories as can be seen by the fact that the Samajawadi Party (SP) government, in UP, is in the process of sending its recommendations to the Centre for including 17 OBCs in the SC category. These castes are Kahar, Kashyap, Kewat, Machuwa, Mallah, Nishad, Kumhar, Prajapati, Dheevar, Bind, Bhar, Rajbhar, Biyar, Batham, Gond and Tairaha. The SP had included these castes in the SC category by managing to intrude in the Centre's rights to change quotas and categories. The SP sources accused previous chief minister and Bahujan Samaj Party (BSP) chief, Mayawati, of depriving these castes of their rights to protect her political interests. Under Mulayam Singh Yadav's government, in October 2005, a Government Order (GO) was passed, providing equal facilities as SC to these 17 most backward OBCs. This move of Yadav was stayed by the Allahabad High Court following a writ filed by the BSP. After Mayawati became the CM, she withdrew the recommendations of the previous SP government and quashed it on June 6, 2007.[4] But, before quashing the previous government order, Mayawati wished the Centre to increase the SC reservation quota by another eight per cent before these 17 castes were to be included.

However, all these recommendations have a vested political interest as SP sources opined that these 17 castes that constitute 15 per cent of the total population of UP were capable of changing the forthcoming Lok Sabha election results in favour of the SP. Mayawati feared her defeat and thus withdrew the proposal sent by the SP government earlier.[5]

Indifferent to the vested interests of the political parties a strong tussle emerged among many middle and most backward castes to be included in the government and state created low categories. This is because of the benefits of reservations and quotas that the low categories enjoy now that translates into assured government jobs. While some OBCs wish to acquire SC status, a section of SCs like Musahar, Nat, Kanjar, Bansphor, etc. are demanding to be included in the ST category, as they feel that the STs are given more benefits by the government. This wish of theirs was vocal in a recent conference held at Barahi Navada, near Varanasi, on November 26, 2012. Another protest meeting was held at Ganga Prasad Memorial Hall, Lucknow, on March 7, 2013, where caste leaders of nine SC groups, from Bhadohi, Jaunpur, Varanasi, Allahabad, Kaushambi, Fatehpur, Unnao, Barabanki, Lucknow and Lalitpur met and handed over a memorandum to the state government to press their demands of being included in the ST category instead. These leaders felt that the change in category would help them get jobs in Aanganwadi, accrue facilities of various health schemes and get the benefits of reservation, something that eluded them so far. Earlier, this group had congregated at Fatehpur, on February 12, 2013, to press these demands.

Numbers, Capacities and Usurping Benefits

These small Dalit groups reasoned that some big and influential castes within the SC category had usurped all the benefits meant for the entire section for their own good. Being small, insignificant and not vocal, by the time their turn came, every benefit was taken away by the bigger, powerful, and dominant Dalit castes and they were left empty handed. With the shrinking of facilities within the SCs, these small castes now desire to crossover to the ST category. Their justification for this crossover is that they had originally been forest dwellers who had later moved to plain land and became a part of the SCs but in the process they had been outcompeted by the bigger, powerful and more dominant SC castes. This problem is not that of the castes that wish to move into the ST category now but is a challenge faced by 62 of the 66 castes among Dalits in UP.

Musahars: Democratic Experience and Desires

The Musahar is a community that is believed to be an offshoot of the Bhuiya tribe of Chhota Nagpur. To the community the word "*musahar*" derives meaning that signifies flesh-seeker or hunter (*masu* meaning flesh, *hera* meaning seeker). Some interpret it to signify rat-taker or rat-eater (*musa* meaning rat) (Joshi and Kumar 2002: 20). Musahars belong to the Scheduled Castes and according to the 1981 census, their total population in UP is 126,018. The Musahar (SC) of UP also called Vanmanus, Banjara or Gonrare mainly distributed in the districts of central and eastern UP. Musahars are the most efficient soil cutters (*ibid*: 13). According to Asharfi Sadai, "The Musahar and earth are like a two in one" (*ibid*, xvi). Their language is Awadhi.

The Musahars of Mirzapur are of an altogether different stock. In the local language, they are called "*vanamanus,*" which means forest dwellers. They collect honey and make *pattals* (plates made of leaves). They are a tribal group, once hunters and gatherers, collecting fruits and flowers from forests (*ibid*, 139). They are mainly landless community that works as palanquin-bearers, agricultural labourers or labourers in brick kilns, while some are involved in piggery. Modern developmental programmes have made only little impact on them. While earlier, till 1995, the focus of the Indira Awas

Yojana was directed on the Musahars only but now this facility has been extended to all SC castes and so the Mushars did not get proper housing facilities as they do not have the voice to claim their rights (*ibid*, 96). Recent surveys indicate that the spread of education among the Musahars is extremely limited - just three per cent (*ibid,* 1) According to the 1981 census, only 6.95 per cent of them are literate. In India, the average literacy rate of the Musahars was 52 per cent. Out of this aggregate, 64.13 per cent were men and 39.29 per cent were women (*ibid*, 90).

The homes of the Musahars are usually small thatched huts consisting of 10 × 10 × 6 space (*ibid*: 7). Goats, cows, oxen, buffaloes are among the major livestock of these people (*ibid,* 49). Musahars are Hindu by name. Other Hindus neither dine with them, nor accept them into their social fold (*ibid,* 70). They worship deities like Dudh Beer, Tulsi Beer, Deena Bhadari, Shabari (*ibid,* 144). They don't have pictures of these gods in their homes. Instead, they make objects of clay and worship these as symbols of their deities. They offer *kasar* or plantain to gods (*ibid,* 148).

The Musahars like singing, dancing, acting, etc. (*ibid,* 79). They have their own identity. Some people consider them to be a dissipated lot just for the reason that they drink liquor and take pork (*ibid,* 136). After almost 60 years of post-colonial Indian democracy and governance, the Musahars, in spite of being a part of state generated development narratives, articulate their own experience of democracy that are quite different from the narratives of other dominant castes. Here we narrate Musahars narratives of Indian democracy as documented from three villages of eastern Uttar Pradesh, near Varanasi. Their tone, tenor and diction of telling democratic experiences are quite different from urban educated people. The core of their accounts revolve around how state-led democracy reached them, how they experience it, feel it and benefit from it. Our focus is to understand their relationship with democracy around the tangible presence of developmental initiatives of the state in the form of housing, loan, education, employment and livelihood initiated under state-made category based schemes of development and social justice that affect their everyday life.

Experiencing Democracy: Myths and Realities

Our field research among the Musahars, in three villages, reveals the process of their low political visibility among Dalit groups because of their small population, lack of capacity to aspire and acquire for a better share in democracy, and their inability to produce their community leaders, etc. they feel as though they are still standing outside the circle of democratic benefits even among SCs. One may observe their confusion in some cases towards state generated modernity that reflects through state led frame of education, livelihood and lifestyle. We know that in Indian context the state plays an important role in spreading modernity in everyday life of the people especially in the rural areas (Kaviraj 2005: 1)

The first village that we studied was Dallipur. It is 12 km from Varanasi, on the way to Jaunpur. The village profiles mixed caste population with Kurmi (800/900 households), Musahar (250 households), Chamar (400 households), Gupta (100 households), Patel (200 households) and Brahmin (10 households). The village has a primary school, two wells and four hand pumps. Inside the Musahar hamlet there is a pond, Kajahariya Pokhar. The Pradhan of this village is of the Chamar caste (a dominant Dalit caste). The Musahars live in their own hamlet called "*mushhar patti.*"

The second village that we visited was Anai. The village has a population of around 3000. The land of this village is good for farming and nearly 320 households are involved in this sector. A canal flows through this village and alongside there are also 50 tubewells with electricity connection. All households have electricity connection. There is a primary school in the village where children of all castes, including Musahars, study. This village is a part of Mangalpur. The Pradhan of this village belongs to the Patel caste. The village has a mixed caste composition with 2800 Brahmin households, 60 Musahar households, 200 Chamar households, 60 Khatik households, 25 Muslim households and 200 Patel households. This village is totally illiterate but children of the present generation have started going to school.

The third village was Jungalpur Kathiranv. The population of this village is nearly 22,000 with voter strength of nearly 15,000. This is a big village with a mixed caste composition. There are 1500 Chauhan households, 300 Musahar households, 100 Gupta households, 1000 Patel households, 100 Muslim households and 20 Yadav households. The Pradhan of the village, Arun Kumar Gupta, belongs to the Vaishya caste, which comes under the OBC category. The village has 52 ponds and eight schools. The village has schools, health centres and is connected to the main road. It has electricity, water supply and has adequate irrigation facilities. All these infrastructural facilities make it appear as an ideal village. My team members and I were involved in constantly documenting the experiences of democracy of the Musahar community in all three villages through long term qualitative interviews.[6]

During our fieldwork, we observed that the presence of state-led democracy in the everyday life of people works simultaneously in different communities in two ways. Firstly, it makes them economically dependent on the state, and secondly, it makes them feel more deprived than other communities. Alongside, among the SC and ST communities, which have been provided special protective discrimination under the notion of social justice through various welfare measures, the communities which have the capacity to acquire and capacity to aspire, (Appadurai 2004: 59) have attained a minimum level of development by appropriating a larger share of the welfare measures. In such a situation, many Dalit communities receive only a small share of the benefits through the trickledown effect. However, even among these communities no common pattern is visible. Only the communities, which have assertive organic leaders, are able to claim some share of the benefits. The form in which the claim is made is, however, like that of a subject (*praja*) placing his request (*fariyad*) before the king (*raja*). In fact, the communities often use the word "*fariyad*" when describing their demands from the bureaucrats, who are the representatives of the state-led democracy. In such a situation, it often appears that even today the democracy has taken the form of kings and subjects, where the subjects place their requests (*fariyad*) for share in resources and welfare measures before the king. The Dalits communities that are able to increase their capacity to make "*fariyad*" are able to get a larger share of the democratic resources.[7]

Claiming to be Poorest in Democracy

Musahar respondents began their narratives to prove that they are the most marginal of all SC communities.[8] For example, the Kanjars, who live in the Kanjar *basti*. They tell very emphatically that they did not get anything from the *sarkar* (government). Some nominal state benefit reached to them through the trickle-down effect. When they accepted that they were getting some benefits from the state they described themselves as being in a disadvantageous position in the comparison with other OBCs and Dalit castes that are more visible in democratic politics and are dominant communities benefitting from the government's social justice schemes.[9]

The experience of democracy, which emerges from their narratives, seemed to be true even at the ground level when we analyse the structure of political parties working in this region. They have no Member of Legislative Assembly (MLA) or Member of Parliament (MP), even after 70 years of Indian Independence. They have around 65 Pradhans, who won in the recent local body elections, in this part of UP. So if democracy means political participation they still hold one of the most disadvantageous positions even among Dalit castes. While showing their dissatisfaction about their political participation, Surmati, a 55-year old woman of Musaharpatti, of Dallipur village, says, "*Humro jati me abe tak kauno lal batti na mila ba bhaia*" (Our caste has never got any red beacon car). Here *lal batti* (red beacon light) is sign of ministerial berth that is given to the ministers and chairmen of state bodies by the government.[10]

If democracy means equal distribution of resources by the democratic state, they assert that they have no access to any of the welfare schemes launched by the government for the uplift of the downtrodden sections. The benefits of reservation make no sense for them. In Dallipur village, most of the Musahars are illiterate, except a lone 20-year youth Rajkumar, who has passed intermediate examination. Some of their children go to school but most of them don't pass High School. Many children drop out of school to become child labourers and supplement the family income. For earning their livelihood, they work as labourers in agricultural fields, brick kilns, etc. About 15 to 20 youths of this caste have migrated to Gujarat in search of work. In any case, the school near their hamlet provides education to the children only till class 5.[11]

The people of this community still live in small, thatched huts. Their *patti* is like village slum. This is a harsh reminder of the tangible and intangible artefacts of the Indian democracy that have survived in the last 60 years in these villages. In the name of development, there are some *pucca* (brick and concrete) houses. These *pucca* houses were allotted in the decade of the eighties under the Indira Awas Yojana. These dwellings are instead used for rearing pigs, while they themselves live in mud huts. The reason for this is that they were told that these houses were too weak and fragile to stay in and could collapse anytime. These houses had large windows through which ghosts and spirits could enter. Their mud houses either have no windows or have very small ones. These superstitions made them stay away from these dwellings. Ramrati, a woman of the Musahar community of Dallitpur told us, "When Indira Gandhi was alive we were given small houses. The houses have now broken down. We have never lived in those houses because ghosts and spirits can enter into them.[12]

Dominant and Powerful Dalit Groups Usurp Their Benefits

All the Musahars in the three villages complain that no one bothers about them, while the welfare schemes including National Rural Employment Guarantee Act (NREGA) are grabbed by other powerful castes. According to Surmati a 55-year old woman, of Dallipur, the entire benefit of NREGA is taken away by the Thakurs, Brahmins and Kurmis. "Our men only drink and remain at home and there is no unity among them. This is the reason why, in spite of being an SC seat, when Raj Kumar, the only educated youth of this caste, contested the election of Pradhan, the Musahars were divided in two groups and he lost. Instead, Sunnar Chamar, of the Chamar caste, won the polls.[13]

The Musahars of this village had several complaints against Sunnar Chamar. According to them, "Before the elections he used to almost live in this hamlet but after winning the election he doesn't bother about us." Ramkali, a 65-year old woman says, "We do not get any benefit of the government's welfare schemes. No one listens to us." When we asked her why they do not meet political leaders and government officials Ramkali opined, "The upper castes listen to the people of their own castes. No one heeds to lower castes like us."[14]

Though poor none of the Musahars of these villages have BPL (Below Poverty Line) or *Antyodaya* cards meant for the poorest of the poor but instead they all have APL (Above Poverty Line) cards. By no criteria can these poor Musahars be counted among above poverty line. They say the village Pradhan had assured them that they will be given the appropriate card later as their dream is to get the "*lalka karad*" (red Antyodaya card) and *"ujarka karad"* (white BPL card), while they have *"piyarka karad"* (yellow APL card).[15] The Musahars, of Dallipur village, dwell around a pond called *Kajrahia Pokhar*. Despite of their constant demand for the lease *(patta)* of this pond, which is the main source of their sustenance and livelihood, they did not get it. But ironically the state and local dominant communities consider their use of the pond as illegal because they don't have right to use it. The narrative of Ramsurat Baba (65 years), of Dallipur Village, about Kajarahia Pokhar (pond) reveals the story of their marginalisation by the post colonial democratic state, through which the story of this marginalised community emerged. "We have been living here for five generations. Cantonment Sahib brought our ancestors here and settled them in order to perform free labour on the landlord's land. Till now no land has been leased to the Musahars. The pond belonged to our ancestors but it has been forcibly taken away from us by the Kurmis. We have appealed to the higher officials for getting back our pond but there is no hearing.[16] Raj Kumar informed us that in order to get back their pond the Musahars staged demonstration in front of the District Magistrate (DM)'s office but no action was taken. A little wasteland, along the side of the pond, is used by the Musahars. When the water of the pond rises and fishes are spawned, there are regular skirmishes between the Kurmis and the Musahars."[17]

Narratives of Comparative Disadvantage

The narratives above deal with the feelings of the Musahars regarding their constant ongoing comparative dispossession from their livelihood sources and the poor quality of life in the modern democratic state. Battling against hunger they have forgotten their traditional cultural resources. When asked them if they remembered their traditional folk songs, Phoolmati (55 years), of Dallipur village, said, "Those who sit under fans and coolers can remember their songs. Our need is to fill our stomachs. We have no time to remember or sing any song.[18] Sometimes their discourses reflect that their past was better. Due to unequal distribution of democratic resources and malfunctioning of state-led schemes they felt insecure. According to the women of the community, "Everyone is busy earning and eating. Who is concerned about the poor? All the leaders and officers come here, listen to our problems, give us false assurances and then leave."[19]

In India, there are provisions for bank loans on cheaper interest rates for disadvantageous and poor communities. In addition there are many micro credit groups with the help of NABARD (National Bank of Agricultural and Rural Development) working in this area.[20] However, even government loans meant for them are beyond their reach. Due to their illiteracy and ignorance they fear taking loans. Lallan (47 years), of Dallipur village, says, "God knows on which paper they will make us put our thumb impression. In 1980, I took a loan of Rs. 5000, out of which Rs. 800 was taken away by the agent. With the remaining money, I bought a pig but it died. I made no profit. All Thakurs and Brahmins take loans on our names. Their loans are written off.[21]

Although they have social interaction with the other Dalit castes but when it comes to getting benefits they are made to stand at the end of the queue. They are totally deprived. The BSP movement started in this region around the mid-80's to correct the vices and bias of the upper castes and dominant middle caste-led state democracy. Even during the BSP regime, under the leadership of Mayawati, the Dalit woman Chief Minister of UP, when there was hope to develop a new Indian democracy, they found no space. In the last 10 years, they never existed in the polity or concerns of our democracy. They did not even get the benefits of the ambitious projects for Dalit villages, like Ambedkar Gram Yojana, during Mayawati's reign. Though the village fulfilled all the criteria for an Ambedkar village, they never got it. Instead, the neighbouring village, which has a Chamar majority, wangled the said status.

When we asked the Musahars of Anai village whether they had taken any loan from the bank they replied in negative. The reason was that the Pradhan had told them that if they took loan it would need five generations to repay it, as the interest rates were high. Lalai, a resident Anai added that even if they took loan, the block office staff and the middlemen took away a large percentage of the money. If a loan of Rs. 10,000 was taken, nearly Rs. 3000 was lost as commissions. Although they received only Rs. 7000 they had to pay interest on Rs. 10,000. Thus no Musahars applied for bank loans.[22] All from this Musaharpatti accepted their poverty as their destiny. Unlike the people of Dallipur village, they are silent about their rights. They somehow manage to exist in the village by performing various menial works. They have neither any agricultural land nor the traditional occupation of making leaf plates.

The residents here feel that they have got nothing substantial from Indian democracy. This caste, despite being SC, has not been able to develop the capacity to enjoy the caste status that they rightfully deserve. They have no visibility or voice that could draw attention of the state or democracy towards them. This caste has neither heroes nor the educated lot that is must for visibility. They cannot come together for democratic politics. Their struggle for two square meals a day is huge. They have no place in democracy. The development projects are far away from them.

While narrating the experience of their everyday life in the village, Lalai, of Anai Village, tells us that the Musahars lead very miserable and poverty-stricken lives. He said that his ancestors lived and died here. Earlier, they used to earn their living by making leaf plates from Mahua trees. The plates were supplied to various castes during weddings and other occasions. However, now plastic plates are available. There is almost no demand for leaf plates. He added that the Musahars used to live in the jungles and were dependent on forest products but now with large scale deforestation, their livelihood has been taken away. Today, they earned their livelihoods by working as labourers in the nearby fields. This is a story of their dispossession in a democratic state.[23] Lalai told us that the Patels have a stronghold. They control the ponds. Sukhrani, a Musahar resident of this village stated, "Earlier, we lived in the west of the village but when the population of Brahmins and Thakurs increased, we were pushed to the south of the village." No Musahar here received any benefits from the government's welfare schemes. He added, "We do not get any government money or benefits. Whenever some scheme is launched the upper castes grab all the money.[24]

The women of the village say that they sometimes get some medicines and sometimes a little ration from the fair price shop but they are neither aware of the benefits to which they are entitled. In spite of various government welfare schemes for the uplift of the downtrodden sections they suffer from poverty, hunger and misery, as they are outside the ambit of these schemes. Although they are all below the poverty line they have not been given BPL cards. After a lot of running round, they were allotted the white APL cards. They only get a little wheat and rice with this card but do not get sugar, kerosene oil, palm oil, etc. When the SP came to power, the Musahars were promised houses but although more than a year has passed they have still not been given houses. When they go to the government officials with their requests (*fariyad*), they are turned away.[25]

The reason why their requests are not heard by the administration is that they don't have any leaders among them who can submit their *fariyad* to the *sarkar* (administration) in an effective way. No one in the village is literate. There is no one to fight for them and place their demands before the political leaders or the government. They have not yet developed their community leaders who can understand the state language and its *niyam-kanun* (rules-regulations) and are able to translate the state language in the community language. They have not yet fitted into the state-led pedagogic democracy.

Fariyadi Matters

The story of Musahars in Jangalpur village is a little different. Here, there is a youth Srinath, who has emerged as a community leader. He is illiterate but articulate and he has proved to be an effective *fariyadi* in a couple of cases, which brought a few state benefits. Like in Dallipur village, the Musahars of Jangalpur, also did not have any right over the pond in the village since the Muslims had a 15-year lease on it. They ran from pillar to post to get the lease on the pond but to no avail. However, recently, after a long fight, Srinath, succeeded. He told us, "I had sent repeated requests and applications to the DM but there was no effect. One day I went straight to the DM's office and told him, '*Huzoor*, if you are the king of the government (*sarkar*), we are the king of the jungle.' *Huzoor*, please give us one chance and see the result. Our wives and daughters do not have place to even throw the ashes of the stoves." The DM was impressed by Srinath's attitude and ordered tea for him. He gave him Rs. 100 and promised to try to give him the lease on the pond. On the other hand, Hyder Ali, of the Muslim community of the village, who had the 15-year lease on the pond and used to rule over it, was also trying to get the lease extended. However, the DM supported Srinath and the Musahars were given lease on the pond for 10 years.[26]

Since independence, several Five Year Plans have been carried out and a large number of welfare schemes have been passed but this is the first time that the Musahars, of Jangalpur, managed to get a lease of the pond. Before this, in 1982, the Musahars were allotted 11 houses under the Indira Awas Yojana. During Mayawati's reign, 18 quarters were constructed and 28 households were given land on lease to construct houses. However, they could not construct their huts on them since the land allotted to them by the Pradhan was surrounded by Muslims. They did not allow the Musahars to settle there since the Musahars rear pigs, which the Muslims perceive as not only dirty and unclean, but unholy as well. The Musahars were unable to fight for land in some other part of the village since by that time Mayawati had been removed from power.

Another *fariyad* of Srinath about distribution of scholarship for their children was also heard by local officials. He informed, "Since the Musahars are categorised as SC, when scholarships were distributed to OBC children in the school, the Musahar children were denied the scholarships. My son had told his mother that this time when the scholarships are given please buy me a pair of shoes. However, we were told that the scholarships were meant only for OBC children and the SC would be given scholarships later. After waiting for two months, the scholarships did not come. We felt bad since we had promised to buy shoes for our son. I was angry. I headed for Banaras to meet the DM with my *fariyad*. I said, "Sahib, I have brought a *fariyad*. We are Musahars, poor and illiterate. We are dying of hunger. My son goes to school. It is very cold but he goes bare-footed. The scholarships were distributed to OBC children again yesterday after being distributed to them two months ago. The SC children were not given scholarships. If we had been given, we would have bought shoes for our children. It is very cold."[27] The DM said, "Go, you will get the scholarship within two days."

However, after two days we did not get the promised scholarship. After two months, when I went to the DM's office for the lease of the pond the DM recognised me. He asked me if I got the scholarship. I replied in negative. He was angry. He called for his car. After he reached, all of us again placed our *fariyad*. Several other officers also came. We were given the scholarships.[28]

Similar to the two other villages, the Musahars of Jangalpur have also not obtained the benefits of any government-loan schemes for the welfare of the poor and downtrodden sections. On asking the Pradhan, about the facility of obtaining loan he replied that once someone took loan from the government the person's sons and grandsons will also not be able to repay it. It was because of this fear that most people did not avail the loans. However, some people did take loans. One of the experiences of taking government loan was narrated by Lalai of village Dallipur. He said, "I applied for a loan for Rs. 5000 but got only Rs. 4000. The middlemen and agents pocketed the rest. I bought three pigs. Two died. I suffered a big loss as the interest increased and the bank officials kept asking me to deposit the interest. I am unable to pay the interest, leave alone the principle. The bank officials and village Panchayats in collusion do not give us the entire amount we had applied for but we have to pay interest on the full amount. It is because of this fear that very few people take loans.[29]

While maintaining pride in their identity as "king of the jungle" they claim their dispossession in modern state but alongside they also continue to disapprove in some sense the modern state defined lifestyle. According to them, the reason why the Musahars do not want to stay in the Indira AwasYojana houses allotted to them is that they see "ghosts" in those houses and prefer to live in the jungle where they are happier.

Conclusion

This study shows that the Musahars, who belong to the SCs and are one of the most marginalised Dalit castes, have several complaints from the state-led Indian democracy. While narrating these complaints and their experiences of democracy they continuously try to prove themselves as "most poor," and expression(s) like "not getting anything from sarkar" appears again and again in their narratives. They feel that other castes, which are dominant and powerful, either upper or middle or even other Dalit castes usurp their democratic rights and benefits. They don't have educated and assertive leaders who can present their *fariyad* to the local administration. They also don't have their own MPs or MLAs, who can represent them in the government. There is no *lalbatti* given by the *sarkar* for any leaders of their community. They hesitate in taking loans from government loaning schemes for the SCs and poor. They refuse to live in houses allotted to them under state given housing schemes because of the traditional notion of community habitat. These are the discourses that emerged from the narratives of our respondents of the *Musaharpattis*, of all three villages, under our study, namely Dallipur, Anai and Jungalpur.

Thus, in their experience, democracy raises desire but also gives rise to dissatisfactions, which are reflected in their complaints to the state. The state sponsored schemes empower various communities but also make them more and more dependent on the state gradually. As diagnosed by Sudipta Kaviraj, "state in the Indian context, as distinct from the European, has been the primary source of modernity. Even in the age of liberal economy the enchantment of state is still undiminished" (Kaviraj 2005: 2). Democracy in contemporary form in India has turned into state-led democracy or *"sarkari cheez."* The political agencies expected to be involved in deepening democracy turned their politics into "gift politics" like distributing blankets, cheap rice, free tablets and *wajifa* (scholarship) for students, pension schemes and so on. For these, political parties are not linked with the dissemination of the values of democracy but distributing gifts to allure their subjects (*praja*) to mobilise them for the coming elections. In this process, all the marginalised castes expect gifts from political parties, which is the only meaning for democracy for them.

It is a notable fact that the caste and communities among middle and Dalit castes, which are numerically dominant, get more attention of the state and political parties due to electoral considerations, as they comprise a larger vote bank. Those who have incorporated well in the state democratic logic of development and modernity through modern state framed education, or have developed their caste leaders, who can represent their demand to the state, get larger share of the welfare projects of democracy. The castes that have not fully prepared themselves to be accommodated in democracy and in the modernity and development frame, suffer from democratic deficit.

Despite low numbers, these castes should develop education and collective leadership within themselves that might strengthen the "politics of presence" among them and give them a voice. However, the renowned post-modern thinker Derrida states, "Voice alone does not guarantee any presence." Several other elements must be added to it. This would ensure that others don't drown their voices and present them in a wrong light. It is necessary that within the community, other than the aspiration for development, they should develop such elements that make them "political." An eminent political scientist, Rajni Kothari, also suggests the value of political consciousness among caste. He suggests politicisation of caste played an important role in the facilitation of democracy and the growth of social awareness (Dirks 2003: 286).

These castes have failed to develop their identity and honour (read caste-based glory). They have still not reached the ground to stand on to strongly express their political and developmental aspirations. They have not been able to use identity and aspirations into their "politics" and thus use these as resources of growth. They are miles away from the door of democracy. It is must that these castes should be able to express their political achievement within the democratic framework.

Notes

* The excerpt of this chapter has been published in chapter 3 of the Book 'Fractured Tales: Invisible in Indian Democracy', 2016, OUP, New Delhi, pp. 82-98.

1. The meaning of terms and concepts like state and democracy is likely to vary between intellectuals and common people, and also between literates and illiterates, underprivileged population of various kinds (Kaviraj 2005: 2).
2. Similar observation was done by Dirks who says that During the Mandal crisis caste leaked simultaneously out of the traditional worlds of the subaltern and the village and into the middle-class enclaves of new India. Through the design of the new constitution, the Nehruvian state undertook an immense project of social reform, using the state as the primary instrument to tear down the thousand years' indignities of the caste system (Kaviraj 2005: 13).
3. The state linked various categories in Indian constitution to distribute social welfare to the downtrodden communities. These categories are the Scheduled Castes (SCs), Scheduled Tribes (STs) and the Other Backward Classes (OBCs). Presently in Uttar Pradesh the SCs are 64 in number, the STs are 15 in number and the number of Backward classes are 234. The SCs and the OBCs are scattered in various districts of UP. The STs can be found in eastern UP (http://scholarship.up.nic.in/index.asp).
4. SP takes on Maya, proposes Dalit status for 17 OBCs, Milleniumpost, April 2, 2013, Lucknow, Team MP.

5. *Ibid.*
6. Most of the respondents like Ramsurat Baba, Phulmati, Srinath look towards the state for their own benefit and are dependent on the state. The methodology employed to elicit oral histories was the *baat se baat* methodology, which involved extracting information from semi-structured conversation. The purpose was to identify persons of different ages with interesting narratives and an encyclopedic memory of the past of the village, local history, culture, traditional knowledge, and so on. We chose three sets of individuals from each *patti*, including both men and women, to collect their subjective oral narratives about the village past, in order to see the variation in memory between the various castes, generations, and genders. The three age groups were people above 70 years of age, those in their fifties or thereabouts, and those in the age group of approximately 20 years.
7. Interview with Srinath, village Jungalpur, district Varanasi by Brijendra Gautam on 25.4.13
8. *Ibid.*
9. *Ibid.*
10. Interview with Surmati aged 55 years of Musaharpatti of Dallipur village, district Varanasi on 25.4.2103 by Archana Singh.
11. *Ibid.*
12. Interview with Ramrati aged 45 years of village Dallipur, district Varanasi dated 25.4.2013 by Archana Singh.
13. Interview with Surmati aged 55 years of village Dallipur, district Varanasi dated 25.4.2013 by Archana Singh.
14. Interview with Ramkali aged 55 years of village Dallipur, district Varanasi dated 25.4.2013 by Brijendra Gautam.
15. *Ibid.*
16. Interview with Ramsurat Baba, village Dallipur, district Varanasi, dated 25.4.2013 by Archana Singh.
17. Interview with Rajkumar, village Dallipur, district Varanasi, dated 25.4.2013 by Archana Singh.
18. Interview with Phoolmati, village Dallipur, district Varanasi, dated 25.4.2013 by Archana Singh.
19. Interview with the women of village Dallipur, district Varanasi dated 25.4.2013 by the field staff of Dalit Resource Centre.
20. *Ibid.*
21. Interview with Lallan, village Dallipur, district Varanasi, dated 25.4.2013 by Brijendra Gautam.
22. Interview with Lalai, Anai village, district Varanasi, dated 25.4.2013 by Archana Singh.
23. *Ibid.*
24. Interview with Sukhrani, village Anai, district Varanasi dated 25.4.2013 by Brijendra Gautam
25. Field diary, Dalit Resource Centre dated 25.4.2013.
26. Interview with Srinath, village Jangalpur, district Varanasi, dated 25.4.2013 by Brijendra Gautam.
27. *Ibid.*
28. *Ibid.*
29. Interview with Lalai, village Dallipur, district Varanasi, dated 25.4.13.

References

Appadurai, A. (1993): "Number in the Colonial Imagination.' In Breckenridge, Carol A. and Veer, Peter Van der (Ed.), *Orientalism and the Post-Colonial Predicament*. Philadelphia: University of Pennsylvania Press, pp. 314-39.

Appadurai, A. (2004): "The Capacity to Aspire: Culture and the Terms of Recognition." In Rao Vijayendram and Walton, Michael, *Culture and Public Action*. Delhi: Permanent Black. pp. 59-84.

Beetham, D., Bracking, S., Kearton, I., Weir, S.(Ed.) (2003): *International IDEA Handbook on Democracy Assessment.* BRILL.

Chakravarty, D. (2003): *Provincialising Europe, Post-Colonial Thought and Historical Difference*. New Delhi: Oxford University Press.

Dirks, N.B. (2001): *Castes of Mind: Colonialism and the Making of Modern India*, Princeton: Princeton University Press.

Hacking, I. (1984): *The Emergence of Probability: A Philosophical Study of Early Ideas about Probability, Introduction and Statistical Inference*. Cambridge University Press.

Kaviraj, S. (2005): On the Enchantment of the State: Indian Thought on the Role of the State in the Narrative of Modernity. London: SOAS.

Prasad, M. (1995): *Uttar Pradesh ki Dalit Jaatiyon ka Dastavej*. New Delhi: Kitabghar.

Srinivas, M.N. (2000): *Social Change in Modern India*. New Delhi: Orient Longman.

Steele, J. Michael. (2002): "Formal Probability." *International Encyclopaedia of Social and Behavioural Sciences*, 18: 12099-13004.

7

Higher Education and Development in Africa

Teboho Moja

Most of the higher education in Africa remains elite, with gross enrolment rates (GER) lower than 10 per cent, although some of the systems are now massified and have increased their GER slightly to over 15 per cent. In none of the African countries, higher education systems are close to the threshold for a universalised system at GER of 50 per cent. India, on the other hand, compares well with the other systems in Africa that have crossed the GER line of 15 per cent to be a massified system. Another feature of higher education in Africa is the fast expansion that has taken place in the last couple of decades and that the expansion has mainly occurred due to the opening up of systems to allow private providers to offer higher education programmes. This is the situation in India as well. The countries in Africa and India are characterised by the existence of a youthful population that means there is a large number of youth in need of access to higher education that the systems are not able to cater for.

India and countries in Africa face a development challenge of supporting and supplying their economies with high skilled labour expected to be produced by their higher education systems. This creates a double-pronged challenge of having masses of people not accessing education, and in particular, higher education as well as the shortage of skilled human power to support and grow the economy. With increased access, though not sufficient, the tendency has been to focus on undergraduate programmes with low research capacity to produce knowledge, a key driver for the global knowledge economy. These countries therefore face development challenges that have led to their lower rankings on the development index.

Equity and Higher Education Development

The access, equity and development debate poses challenges. In debates linking access to development one cannot ignore issues of equity. For example, in the early days of transforming the system in South Africa debates centred on which of the three issues to focus on to address the needs of a new democratic society. One perspective was that promoting access would translate into equity opportunities for all and with masses of people in the system of higher education there was a strong likelihood of them contributing to the development of the country. The other perspective was that development should be prioritised and arguments were made for maintaining an elite system that focussed on access to critical disciplines that are likely to contribute directly to economic development. The first perspectives could be translated as arguing for a mass low quality education system that would address equity issues with limited contribution to development. This perspective argued for an elite high quality system that does not address equity issues but attempts to address development needs of a country. Both perspectives tackle one aspect of the problem but what is really needed is a perspective that addresses all three aspects. A middle ground is needed and options had to be found that would address all three factors because the role of higher education for development does not depend on one or the other but both. In this paper the South African strategy to address access, equity, and development issues is presented.

The debate on the role of higher education in development in Africa has metamorphosed over a number of decades but comes back full circle to the agreement that higher education plays a role in development. Africa has suffered the assault of the limited perception of what role higher education was to play in development and continual shifts that de-emphasised the importance and role that higher education could play in development. African governments post the colonial era have shifted back and forth on their policies in supporting higher education. The shifts occurred partly due to internal pressure and external pressure. Internal pressure was exerted post independence due to governments' expectations of the direct role that higher education was to play to advance their development agendas. External pressure was exerted by international development agencies defining Africa's priorities and mode of development. In response to internal pressure there were attempts made to control higher education systems for political gains. For decades the relationship between governments and universities in particular oscillated between attempts to take complete control of it through the control of budgets and institutional governance systems to underfunding and interference in its governance systems.

The external pressure was exerted when the World Bank de-emphasised the role of higher education in development for Africa and pressurised countries to adopt policies that cut budgets to higher education and redirect those funds to the school sector. The World Bank arguments were based on the rate of return studies that indicated that there were higher rates of returns for investment in the school sector than in the higher education sector, for example, 10.8 per cent for higher education compared with 19 per cent for primary education (Psacharopoulos 1986). African governments convinced by those compelling figures and their general disenchantment with the role that universities were playing in advancing their development agendas implemented the World Bank policies. It was at the turn of this century that a policy shift was made to recognise the role that higher education played in development and in reducing poverty in developing countries influenced by reports such as the WB/UNESCO Task Force Report 2000. Another influential and significant report by the World Bank was released in 2002 on the role of higher education in constructing knowledge societies.

Reconceptualising the Role of Higher Education in Development

The debate on the role of higher education in development is settled and shifted to the role it plays in economic as well as social development. Often the role is expressed mainly in economic development terms and less in terms of social development. There are fora where social development is addressed, for example, the Third "Higher Education in the World Report" commissioned by UNESCO and produced by the

Global University Network for Innovation (GUNI) in 2009 addressed the issue and tried to put social development back on the agenda focussing on the social responsibility of higher education. How does higher education contribute to development?

There are two areas in which higher education plays a direct role in development. The first is that higher education produces graduates/labour with skills needed to support the knowledge intensive economy. The second is that it produces knowledge through research and publications. There are studies that indicate that in Sub-Saharan Africa, for example, with the addition of 1 year of tertiary education the GDP increased by 0.25 per cent points and 0.40 per cent in terms of productivity (Bloom, 2006).

High-level skills and knowledge are key factors to sustainable development and that is what places higher education in the centre of strategies for advancing and supporting development efforts. This realisation accounts for the global surge in the demand for higher education places, unprecedented growth and expansion of higher education systems in Africa too. Since there is no doubt in the notion that higher education plays a role in development the questions we need to address is how higher education plays that role, what are the obstacles for playing that role, and how can their graduates and research they produce contribute to development? To address these questions I would like to first look at the four perspectives of universities and development that explains the strategies that have been used with limited success in the past in the context of Africa. It is those roles and perspectives that need to be re-thought as we explore the role that higher education plays in development. The perspectives locate the role of universities in blocs formed by two crossing axis of knowledge and development. I have chosen to use knowledge in this case since universities still play a major role in knowledge production.

The vertical axis (in Figure 1) represents development and range from the point that universities have no role or part to play in development strategies to universities having a role/part in development strategies. The horizontal axis moves from universities having no role or perhaps marginal role for producing new knowledge (research) in development strategies to playing a role in producing knowledge for development. (Maassen and Olsen, 2007). What we have are four blocs that represent the roles of

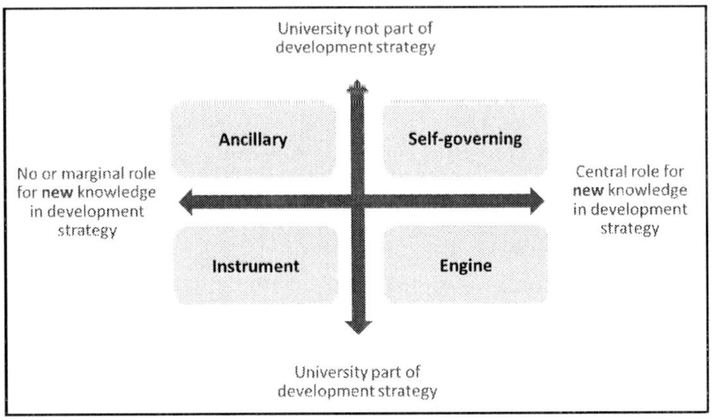

Fig. 7.1: Higher Education in an Ancillary Role

universities in development – the ancillary, self-governing, instrument and engine – that I explained further.

The first perspective assumes that the key role that higher education plays, especially in Africa, is to produce professionals and civil servants, and that there is no need for them to play an active or direct role in national development. Universities set up in the colonial period were set up for that purpose and unfortunately continued to play that role post-independence. As a result numerous institutions were set up mainly as teaching institutions and professional schools with less emphasis on research and knowledge production. The outcome has been the production of an elite class that were provided with upward mobility opportunities who then account for the high private returns that have been used in arguments against the development and support of higher education. The ancillary perspective of higher education was understood and translated into "luxury auxiliary" hence the lack of support by the World Bank policies and this led to the underfunding of this "fee free" luxury. Governments then convinced that higher education was a luxury activity responded in most cases by becoming more hostile especially towards universities and often resorted to direct interference with "luxury activities" that cost governments a lot of money.

Higher Education as Self-Governing Institutions

The second perspective is that higher education is important to development, but there in no need for a direct role in national development. The claims for autonomy are informed partly by this notion, with academics demanding their right to decide who is trained, how they are trained, and what knowledge to produce on their own or in cooperation with other international academics. As tax dependent institutions governments never bowed to self-governance and instead tightened the grip especially when they became even more tight-fisted with funding and the funding levels dropped. Recently, in Africa as elsewhere, there has been an increase in governments demanding broader accountability from higher education institutions.

Higher Education as Instrument for Development Agendas

The third perspective is that of higher education as an instrument for development agendas. Institutions were perceived as providers of expertise to address national agendas such as poverty alleviation, improving agricultural development or addressing other major issues such as health, business etc. An international example of this notion is to be found in actions such as the recent launching of a "New Sustainable Development Solution Network" by the Secretary-General of the United Nations Ban Ki Moon. The network is made up of a global network of research centres, universities and technical institutions to help achieve sustainable development post the 2015 Millennium Development Goals (August 09, 2012 – UN Press Release). Development aid in the past has been more attracted and directed to this instrumentalist notion and support has been directed to national agendas such as poverty alleviation, community upliftment, etc., through the use of researchers as consultants and in most cases independent consultants. This has been good but need to be rethought and redirected to reduce dependency on aid. Knowledge used in these instances has sometimes been recycled "old knowledge" or "imported knowledge." This notion has stifled knowledge production and/or sometimes limited production to applied knowledge for immediate and direct use only. As a result, there has been less knowledge production in Africa that is more visible despite pockets of progress that is unconnected and not sustainable.

Higher Education as the Engine for Development

The last perspective is that of higher education as an engine of development. In the knowledge economy there are other knowledge producing institutions but the university has remained the main knowledge institution. Universities continue to play a role in knowledge production, transmission and archiving it. Another role that the higher education institutions have continued to play is that of producing the human resources to support the knowledge driven economy. This is the notion that needs more attention. Currently there is recognition of the centrality of knowledge to development and as a result there has been massive expansion and a diversification of systems to meet the growing demand and skills variety. Some governments in Africa are looking at ways to increase post-graduate enrolments, encourage knowledge production and increase research output/ISI publications. The African Union is paying attention to ensuring that higher education is central to development hence their attention to the need to increase doctoral studies and a focus on setting up the Pan African University on the continent with a focus on science training.

How can We Address Access, Equity and Development in Higher Education Reforms?

Access and participation rates are used as indicators of development in by the World Economic Forum literature. Many countries in reforming their higher education systems tend to focus on increasing participation rates. The reasons range from the need to increase skilled labour figures, a response to the growing demand for higher education following a success of universal access programmes and the Millennium Development Goals (MDG) that promoted access to schooling, and the concern about growing figures of out of school youth that are perceived as great threat and political time-bomb if they are not placed in any formal system of education.

South Africa as an example in this paper has put forward its strategy to address issues of equity access and development in various policy documents. There is a focus on establishing a single coherent, differentiated and articulated post-school system to promote access and equity issues. The post-school system is to comprise of a range of types of institutions such as universities, further education and training colleges, community education and training centres. The goal is to have 1.5 million (GER of 23 per cent) students in universities and about 4 million (GER 60 per cent) students in other forms of formal education. (DHET, White Paper 2013)

The development strategy worked out together by the National Planning Commission, the Department of Science and Technology and the Department of Higher Education and Training aims at increasing knowledge production through research and expanded graduate training programmes. The goal is to triple the current number of doctoral graduates from 1,420 to 5,000 per annum, increase the numbers of academics with doctorates from 34 per cent to 75 per cent, and to develop world class research centres while boosting the current science research councils. (NDC 2011)

Rethinking Policies that Link Higher Education and Development

The role of higher education in development is no longer contested and there is evidence that knowledge and higher education are important for sustainable development. As we move forward with ways of rethinking policies and strategies to support higher education, we need to keep in mind some key premises.

First, we need to keep in mind that access, equity and development issues are linked and need to be tackled together. African countries and countries like India need to find ways of addressing equity issues which impact their democratic societies as well as forge ahead with their development agendas. The inequities in accessing higher education have their root in the broader societal issues that include poverty levels, geographic locations of education facilities, access to low quality basic education that leaves students unprepared for higher education etc. It is clear that access issues need to be tackled in the entire education pipeline and not only at one level. As access opportunities open up, the next issue to tackle is access to what kind of programmes. Most of the industrialised countries are shifting focus to access into Mathematics; Science, Engineering, and technology (MSET), developing countries have a double challenge of access to all programmes to address equity issues as well as access to MSET for development. The other challenge is that of increasing participation rates at the post-graduate level to improve qualifications of the academic staff as well as to provide countries with high-level skills for knowledge production and use.

Second, in addressing the development issue, we need to address the persistent attempts to depict the relationship between knowledge and development as a direct one. These attempts are usually made with the best of intentions, which are to demonstrate "relevance," utility, applicability and belies the deep desire to "do something" in what is frequently a parlous situation. There is a role for higher education in producing applied knowledge but that should not be pushed to the core of what universities are about. Such attempts all misunderstand the relationship between knowledge and development. Hence their attempts to convert the university into an applied knowledge producing institution, eroding its longer-term and far more critical mission, which is to produce the next generation capable of producing knowledge and innovation on a renewable basis.

Besides, the university is much better at indirect, long term knowledge capacity building than at direct short term knowledge application, at which many of the new knowledge institutions of the knowledge economy (parastatals, NGOs etc.) are far more efficient. These adjunct institutions of the knowledge economy are dependent upon a vibrant university sector from which they draw their self-renewable knowledge generative capacity (new PhDs) without which they could not run, and on which they depend. This is why a vibrant secondary knowledge production landscape only occurs successfully in countries which have a stable PhD producing university sector – mostly the developed North.

Third, the African universities are characterised by high numbers of undergraduate admissions and very low numbers of post-graduate students. The absence of strong post-graduate students in universities weaken the self-generative capacity of higher education in Africa and their ability to make a substantial contribution to new knowledge production. Neither governments nor universities see it as a priority to cultivate the university's capacity to produce knowledge and to develop its generative capacity. Governments have mainly bought into the erroneous picture of the relationship between knowledge and development as being direct. Governments in Africa are still seized by the traditional image of national universities as being there to educate the next generation of state or civil service functionaries, hence their focus and support of the teaching model of a university rather than the research model of a university. There notion of a university's relevance to society is narrowly defined with an expectation of short term "relevance" to society to address issues such as poverty alleviation, empowerment, or another short term fashionable concept, which all point to a direct, unmediated, instrumental conception of the relation between knowledge and development. The need for universities in developing countries to strengthen their research capacities and play a role in contributing to development is captured in the quote by Mr. Musa Sirma the Chairperson of the East African Consortium Council of Ministers at the opening of the East African Higher Education Forum when he said:

> "The difference between the world's upcoming economies and the stable economies lies in how much research goes into economic development and how much of the new knowledge is utilised." (Sirma, 2012)

There is a continuing challenge in defining the role that universities in developing countries need to play to balance the needs of society as well as to play the traditional role that universities play especially in countries of the north. The Association of Commonwealth Universities in their campaign "The World Beyond 2015" to raise awareness on why and how universities should respond to global challenges recently raised this issue once more. (MacGregor, 2014)

References

Bloom, D; Canning, D and Chan, K (2006): *Higher Education and Economic Development in Africa.* Washington DC: The World Bank.

Department of Higher Education and Training (203): White Paper for Post School Education and Training – Building an Expanded, Integrated Post-School System. November 20.

GUNI (2009): *Higher Education at a Time of Transformation — New Dynamics for Social Responsibility.* Global University Network for Innovation, 3rd "Higher Education in the World Report" commissioned by UNESCO and produced by the Global University Network for Innovation (GUNI).

Maassen, P. and Olsen, J. (2007): University Dynamics and European Integration. *Higher Education Dynamics*, 19.

MacGregor, Karen (2014): Universities and Development – A Core Mission Dilemma, *University World News*, Global Edition Issue 311. March 09.

Moon, Ban Ki (2012): *New Sustainable Development Solution Network*, August 09, 2012 – UN Press Release.

National Development Commission (2011): *National Development Plan – Vision for 2030.* South African Government. http://www.npconline.co.za/medialib/downloads/home/

Psacharopoulos G, Tan J.P. and Jimenez E (1986) "The Financing of Higher Education in Developing Countries: Exploration of Policy Options" Washington, DC: The World Bank.

Sirma, Musa (2012: East African Higher Education Forum Opens in Arusha. October 24 – 26 2012. Arusha, Tanzania.

World Bank/UNESCO (2000): *Higher Education in Developing Countries – Peril or Promise.* The Task Force convened by the World Bank and UNESCO.

World Bank (2002): Constructing Knowledge Societies: New Challenges for Tertiary Education. Washington DC: The World Bank.

8

The Sustainable Learning Paradigm

Global Case Studies to Inform and New Models to Guide 21st Century Development and Democracy

Judith Parker

The vocabulary around continuous or lifelong learning is not new. In fact many would argue that the idea and necessity of lifelong learning is an accepted norm. But that idea is punctuated by the reality of events that suggest closure. However, moving to a new school for the next grade level or graduation ceremonies can no longer be viewed as the end or accomplishment of a packet of learning. They are a milestone of accomplishment but only one milestone in a series that will commemorate and comprise learning.

This paper is driven by two main issues: Learning must be ongoing; but even more so, learning must be sustainable. This idea of sustainable learning might take some investigation. The term sustainable has become part of a catch phrase when applied to such topics as development, energy and agriculture. So why hasn't it become part of the language of learning? This paper will investigate this applicability and how and why it should be added to the lexicon of terms like adult learning, transformative learning, action learning, etc.

Sustainability as a Framework

In 1987, the United Nations released the *Brundtland Report*, which included what is now one of the most widely recognised definitions: "Sustainable development is development that meets the needs of the present without compromising the ability of future generations to meet their own needs" (WCED, 1987, UN 2005 a). This definition contains two key concepts. First, the importance of meeting present needs. Second, the most critical is the idea of maintaining an eye to the future needs. This implies the "idea of limitations imposed by the state of technology and social organisation on the environment's ability to meet present and future needs" (US, 2005b). Meeting current needs requires identifying those current needs by utilising critical thinking skills. This requires preparing future generations to identify and meet the needs and facilitating their task by handing off the responsibility and ensuring that resources are available. All of these are hallmarks of sustainability.

This United Nations 2005 World Summit Outcome Document refers to the "interdependent and mutually reinforcing pillars" of sustainable development as economic development, social development, and environmental protection" (US, 2005b). "A sustainable agriculture is one that, over the long term, enhances environmental quality and the resource base on which agriculture depends; provides for basic human food and fibre needs; is economically viable; and enhances the quality of life for farmers and society as a whole" (UN, 2005 c).

While sustainable has its roots in these concepts of development in economics, agriculture and environmental practices, it has been applied to numerous other fields including innovation. Allen, Gojer, Gavrilova-Aguilar and Philpot (2012) note that sustainable innovation is process-based, not project-based and that it includes providing ways of improving the quality of human life while not exceeding the supporting capacity of existing ecosystems. They add that when sustainable is used in the context of innovation, it refers to the "degree to which a programme of change is continued after the initial resources provided by the change agency are ended" (*ibid*, 256). This concept might be most appropriately applied to learning. One would hope that the change in knowledge or skills is continued after the focussed educational event and serves as the foundation for further learning.

The concept of sustainability is also consistent and complementary to several ideas that are central to today's learning theories. Brookfield, Illeris and Knowles offer just a few examples. Brookfield (1986) defined critical thinking or critical reflection as "reflecting on the assumptions underlying our and others" ideas and actions, and contemplating alternative ways of thinking and living" (p. x). Brookfield (1986) described nine concepts of the critical thinking process but then synthesises them into two key activities: "identifying and challenging assumptions" and "exploring and imagining alternatives" (p. 15). Brookfield's (2005) focus on critical reflection as an essential component of learning suggests the sustainability of that learning.

Illeris (2004) offers a model of an inverted triangle which places two psychological poles, Piaget's cognition and Freud's emotion at the top two corners and society at the lower vertex. He stresses that these 3 dimensions of learning, cognitive, emotional and social, "are always integrated parts of the learning process and in practice do not exist as separate functions" (p. 20). This integrated holistic model of learning is consistent with the concept of sustainability.

Malcolm Knowles professed his theory of andragogy for adult learners and established assumptions that suggested a continuum of learning and a hope of sustainability. Knowles, Holton, & Swanson (2005) report that he formulated these assumptions into his six core andragogical principles: "the learner's need to know, self-directed learning, prior experience of the learner, readiness to learn, orientation to learning and problem solving, and motivation to learn" (p. 183). Of these, two seem especially significant for this paper; the facts that adults learn best when the learning is about something they need to know and is connected to previous knowledge. Both of these indicate sustainable learning.

However, searching every variation of sustainable learning in databases, resulted in a plethora of references on learning about sustainable environmental practices. It seems to have been applied to almost every process and product imaginable. Yet, isn't the adjective, sustainable, applicable to the most important process and product, learning in the twenty first century to guide development and democracy? Within the realm of learning vocabulary, lifelong learning is the most closely connected term to sustainable learning. In practice, educators test for short term knowledge acquisition that will likely not be remembered in the near future. Educators teach about the transitory nature (not the death) of theories. Whether it is new technology or new theories, they tend to be a part of a long tradition of evolution and development. While there seems to be a natural propensity to categorise and clump, sustainable lifelong learning must be viewed as a continuum from cradle to grave.

Continuum Model for Sustainable Learning

This continuum model requires transitions not terminations. A parallel can be seen in our analysis of visible light and its place in the larger electromagnetic spectrum. Whether one is studying radio waves, microwaves, infrared waves, visible light, ultraviolet, x-rays or gamma radiation, one is studying waves that all travel at the same speed and have the same general properties but vary only in their wavelength (or frequency). The labels for segments of the continuum arose from the pragmatic reality that different detection devices developed at different times in history detected different segments of the spectrum. Similarly, labels have been used to indicate periods in ones educational development. While adjectives such as elementary, middle, high, higher, adult, etc. might be useful for credentialing purposes of teachers, they created a false sense of division along what should be a continuum of education from birth to death. The first educational experience of a newborn should be the beginning of sustainable learning throughout life.

Jarvis (1985) explains the necessity of lifelong learning for everyone because society itself is fluid and always changing as well as learning itself is changing and needs to become lifelong rather than recurrent at times of status change. This fluidity has demonstrated itself in the evolution of the terms that describe society. While Peter Drucker is credited with advancing the term knowledge society in the 1960's, Bennett and Bell (2010) provide some insights into the development of the term. They explain how over a twenty year span, the term information economy gave rise to information society which became the knowledge economy and finally the knowledge society. They indicate that this shift from "describing economy to society reflects the social and cultural transformation that occurs as a community adjusts to new technologies, industries, and ways of life" (p. 412). "Knowledge society is qualitatively different from the former terms because it is more holistic and views people as possessing rich and diverse forms of knowledge important for a progressive society" (pp. 412-13). This should provide an insight into the current thinking on a more holistic paradigm.

In light of these societal needs, the learning continuum for sustainability must develop in two directions. It must certainly consider the entire timeline of one's life but must also connect links across the breadth of topics that one is learning at any given time throughout that timeline. Both of these dimensions are essential to this new paradigm and will be considered below.

Length: The Timeline of Life

Ideas of lifelong learning provide a framework for discussing the learning continuum. Farmer (2012) suggests that this timeline begins very early in one's existence. She explains that "humans are constantly bombarded by stimuli, even before they are born. They become aware of stimuli through their senses and make decisions as to whether to ignore the stimuli or deal with them" (p. 29). She explains the influence of developmental issues on reacting to these stimuli and learning as young children become adolescents and then adults.

Bennett and Bell (2010) accept Jarvis's broad definition of lifelong learning which includes "preconscious as well as conscious learning resulting from the transformation of experience in all contexts and stages in life and integration into the individual's personal biography. This definition underscores the social context of learning and the continual changes in self-identity and life world that are both the outcome and the genesis of new learning. In the knowledge society, individual's ability to learn from experience in ways that enable them to cope with continual change becomes the curriculum for lifelong learning" (p. 415). This explains the need to explore and integrate more examples of formal, non-formal, and informal learning.

While formal education is consistent with a K-12 model of education, Kasworm, Rose & Ross (2010) report that "currently, research indicates that most adults engage in some form of learning in their daily lives" (p. 1). However they indicate a difference in the use of the term adult and continuing education over time. Today, adult and continuing education refers to activities that are specifically designed to bring about learning in those individuals designated by society as being adults while historically adult and continuing education was used interchangeably with "home education" or "popular education" (p. 1).

Wolf and Brady (2010) indicate that "for older adults, this (lifelong learning) is both a process of understanding and influencing the world and an important life course goal, a way of living in community and understanding the contradictions of a lifetime of experience; (p. 369). They also explain this process in terms of Paulo Freire's description of praxis as "naming, reflecting, acting, and re-evaluating one's own world" (p. 369). This longitudinal view of learning must be supplemented with an investigation into the broad, holistic nature of learning.

Breadth: Holistic

Holistic suggests an integrated approach to learning as opposed to segmented elements. Wheatley (1999) provides some insights into this idea in her explanation of the new science. She attributes the machine imagery of the seventeenth century to Isaac Newton and Rene Descartes. This imagery contained the belief that studying the parts of a machine was the key to understanding the whole. She notes that the main difference between the new science or quantum mechanical view is the focus on holism rather than parts. "Systems are understood as whole systems, and attention is given to relationships within those networks. In this admittedly bizarre view, relationship is the key determiner of everything. Subatomic particles come into form and are observed only as they are in relationship to something else. They do not exist as independent things. There are no basic building blocks" (pp. 10-11).

The application to the real world and education begins to become evident. Wheatley (1999) in her explanation that "we are beginning to recognise organisations as whole systems, construing them as "learning organisations" or as "organic" and noticing that people exhibit self-organising capacity" (p. 15). This might provide a useful model for sustainable learning.

In addition, models for education already exist. Hoffman (2012) supplies real life data and demonstrations of systems that are successful in other selected studies from Australia, Austria, Germany, the Netherlands, Norway, and Switzerland. She describes "countries that are doing much better by their young people – supporting them to achieve academically at higher levels, keeping them in school, and most importantly, structuring the transition from school to work so that almost everyone has training for an initial career and enters the workforce smoothly" (p. 4). She admits that her "motivating idea for her book was to put before American educators and policy makers some examples of systems of education that get better results than the United States does for the large group of young people who do not opt for a university education" (p. 167). Her book is about eliminating the boundaries between school and work and the borders between countries and admitting that everyone needs to work together and learn from each other. While it is easy to get caught up in the familiar educational model that has been the norm, Hoffman encourages American educators and policy makers not to remain in the silos of K-12, higher education, and the private sector. She demonstrates the necessity of collaboration between the systems that should prepare people for careers and the demands of the careers that they will enter. She goes a step further in calling for an end to the artificial distinction between academic and vocational when describing education. Her descriptions sound like the elements of sustainable learning. Mazarr (1999) echoes this picture by explaining that "knowledge-era learning" must become more "holistic" and "hi-tech"; it must "emphasise creativity and participation" and be "characterised by more choice and competition" (p. 285).

Bennett and Bell's (2010) explanation of the required knowledge and skills for society, confirms the need for learning that crosses the traditional subject matter lines. They note that "the curriculum for lifelong learning in the knowledge society must include "cognitive skills that enable individuals to cope with and optimally thrive on the complexities, uncertainties, multiple choices, and multiple realities" of that society. These include "perceptual skills and the ability to appreciate alternative perspectives". These skills allow individuals to acquire meaningful knowledge and to make viable choices amid constantly changing options. Additional skills needed in the knowledge society include multitasking, non linear and systems reasoning, information navigation, reflective practice, pattern recognition, and the ability to distinguish between the significant and the banal" (p. 416). "Perpetual skills" could certainly be another term for sustainable. Whether it is the formal learning in educational institutions, the non-formal learning in community groups, museums, or libraries or the informal learning from experiences of daily living, boundaries must be crossed.

Sustainable Learning Paradigm: The Applicability of Sustainable to Learning

The literature noted above provides a picture of the importance of sustainability when applied to a variety of educational venues. The term itself implies a transcendence of time and place. It includes practices, habits and a lifestyle. Sustainable practices are those that are repeated, foundational and informed whether applied to sustainable agriculture or healthy eating. Surely learning practices and habits in the twenty first century must include all of these characteristics. Sustainable learning is consistent with several established theories and practices of adult learning.

Wilson (2006) suggests that staff development must be "strategic" and consistent with the culture, mission, and vision of the organisation. Likewise, if learning is to be sustainable, it must be strategic to one's personal mission, goal and role in society. Sustainable implies doing good things today that will make things better tomorrow. It is positive in the short term but with positive long term consequences. Learning must be lifelong and lifewide.

Length: The Timeline of Life

Farmer's (2012) suggestion that any stimulus provides an opportunity for learning even at very early stages of life is the foundation for a cradle to grave or a conception to grave theory for sustainable learning. Unfortunately, the reality of today's education structure inhibits this sustainability. Consider that only a few generations ago, education was considered to begin in first grade. Some children attended kindergarten but not everyone. Then the climb up the segmented education ladder began with well defined beginnings and endings. The children who excelled or at least minimally met the requirements of grade one were moved to a different classroom with a different teacher for grade two. That closing the door on the first grade classroom at the end of the school year also was symbolic of trapping the first grade learning in that room. Opening the door to the second grade classroom the next fall was a symbol of new beginnings with a new teacher in new surroundings with new knowledge (often disconnected to the previous knowledge). This ceremony was repeated annually until the student reached the last grade in the building and was now ready to advance to middle school or junior high school depending on how that school district segmented their first through twelfth grade responsibilities. Now the door closed on an entire building of knowledge and a very new beginning occurred the following fall. Now the teachers were specialists and the movement between subjects was further demonstrated by the students physically moving from room to room. Each room contained the teacher as subject matter expert and the specialised equipment to facilitate learning in only that subject.

The story repeats between this intermediate phase of the first through twelfth grade educational experience and the final stage of high school. Building doors again closed. But most significantly, for most students, this transition to high school was considered to be the beginning of the end of their education. When the door slammed shut at the end of grade twelve, there was open space ahead. But often students were ill-prepared to navigate this vast landscape. College or technical school was an option but just as kindergarten was considered a pre-education option, any formal education after grade twelve was post education and outside the scope of mainstream America.

Over the past decades, kindergarten became the beginning of the now standard K-12 education expanding the previously grade one to twelve norm. Soon this pre-grade one year expanded to preschools often beginning to provide educational environments and experiences to toddlers and infants. But often these were another series of open and closing doors between rooms of pre-schools. While segments were added to the educational years, the segmentation still remained limiting the sustainability of any learning.

At the other end of grade twelve, the expansion continued. Employers were demanding more specialised training and documented learning in the form of certificates or degrees for their new hires. Community colleges bridged the gap between K-12 education for everyone and college for the elite. Accessibility had improved but continuity had not.

While societal requirements have added segments before and after grade one through twelve, little attempt has been made to provide continuity throughout the curriculum. A review of curricula at the national, state, and district levels reveals silos of subject matter clusters. In addition, while STEM (science, technology, engineering and mathematics) education is key, it is segmented from literacy. Often these clusters attempt to build on previous grades but this connection is often on paper in a carefully filed document. The author has taught science workshops to elementary and middle school teachers. These teachers often are frustrated if they are in groups with teachers of other grades arguing that they want grade specific content and activities to take back to their classrooms. But they are also surprised to learn what is being taught in grades below and above their own. Comments demonstrate not only their surprise at the content but also at the alarming revelation that the content is not remembered from year to year. It is the acceptable culture of learn and retain for the test or possibly until the door closes on that classroom at the end of the year. Sadly they realise that the students are not likely to remember what they are teaching once their classroom door is closed at the end of the school year.

An example of successful boundary crossing can be seen in a programme initiated by a large multinational corporation, 3M. Its research and development department hired employees that were technically trained at a wide range of levels from the technician to the senior researcher with an earned doctorate. Technicians with a two year vocational degree were often hired to do the hands on work in the lab. But with this degree, their career growth was limited. However they acquired important tacit knowledge about the company culture and business unit dynamics. Recognising this asset and realising the expense and often impossibility of hiring scientists and engineers at higher levels, the company recognised the value of providing technicians the opportunity to earn a bachelor's degree or beyond.

The corporation developed two partnerships with academic institutions. One partnership was with a local liberal arts college, Augsburg College, with a quality physics and chemistry department. The other was with a medium size university, University of North Dakota, in a neighbouring state that offered quality engineering degrees. Courses from the local college were offered on the corporation's site during the workday by college faculty or company employees with credentials that allowed them to become adjunct faculty of the college. Access to courses was facilitated by this arrangement but the rigor of the course work was consistent with that offered to traditional undergraduates on the college campus. Sometimes employees needed to travel to campus for special upper level courses and shared the classroom with the traditional age students bringing their knowledge of real world work applications to the academic campus and bridging the gap between academia and the workplace.

The second partnership involved videotaping on campus engineering classes and making them available to employees enrolled in the courses. Tests were proctored by company management or staff. While it might see that the employees/students would be at a disadvantage, it was actually the on campus students who complained that the off campus employees had access to video tapes of lectures that they could replay to review or study for an exam. In response to the complaints, the university made videotapes of the lectures available to on campus students through their campus library. Employees were required to attend on campus labs during the summer in a compressed format so they often took vacation time or worked out special arrangements with their supervisors to live on campus for several weeks during the summer. In each instance, that traditional school/work gap was being bridged.

Breadth: Holistic Integration

There is a clear link between length, breadth, and sustainability. In elementary school, teaching across subject matter lines in order to develop the breadth of a subject is easier. However, while the elementary school teachers are generalists who could more easily connect subject matter areas, they are often constrained by a curriculum mandating a number of minutes each day for each subject. In middle school, in an effort to provide content from a teacher with more specific and in-depth subject matter content knowledge, the siloing of content begins and continues through high school and afterward through college.

Many liberal arts colleges see their mission as providing links across academic disciplines but the majority of these attempts are demonstrated in extra-curricular activities. Only a few courses provide these connections in a serious vigorous course format. One example exists at Muhlenberg College in Pennsylvania which offers a Physics or Music course for music and physics majors. The course was developed and is co-taught by one of the physics professors who is also a musician in collaboration with a music professor at the college. It is amazing to watch music majors who would not likely have selected a physics course now enthusiastically carrying their instruments into the science building for a class involving physics equipment. They might not have been excited about a lecture on the general principles of waves and sound but they were excited to see the visual display of sound produced by their own instrument. Both disciplines were broadened by the experience. The sustainability of the learning will likely be substantial since the new knowledge in an unknown discipline was linked to an area in which they had an interest and expertise.

But once past undergraduate subjects, the funnel of educational content quickly narrows to an area of specialisation which tends to continue through life. Even the student who enters the workforce directly or enrols in a technical school for further skill based training will learn a focussed set of skills for a particular job and other learning will be relegated to a second tier category of hobby or interest.

Some insights into a useful approach to promoting sustainability might be gleaned from Hoffman (2012) whose ideas are grounded in strong philosophical issues surrounding the concept of preparing for and progressing in a "calling" or "vocation." This places the learning of specific skills within the context of a broader educational framework. She states that liberal education is a clear strength of higher education in the US. However, rather than the dichotomy of academic liberal education versus vocational training that prevails on the US educational landscape, Hoffman advocates for country models of education that integrate successfully liberal education into learning for work and result in economic development. These would appear to serve those involved in traditional liberal arts education, those pursuing a profession, and those preparing for research intense careers in academia or national laboratories. Hoffman is careful to distinguish between traditional continuing technical education (CTE) and her term, vocational education and training (VET). Strong employer involvement is a hallmark of VET. She describes VET as "an education system that in partnership with employers holds itself accountable not only for career preparation but for moving young people into productive roles in the labour force has a different orientation than one in which completion of a degree or credential is the end point of the education system's responsibility" (p. 6). But a strong VET system includes "a qualifications system, engaged employers, and workplace learning" (p. 169). It clearly involves the breadth of numerous stakeholders and the longevity of lifelong learning. But even then, one size does not fit all and she describes three models of VET education distinguishable by their differing priorities of economy, politics, or society. But she provides the foundation for thoughtful discourse among potentially every segment of society, in the US and around the world. Her ideas are applicable to every person who intends to become or remain gainfully employed, with or without a university education. In a knowledge society and a global economy, it is important to share best practices and consider their application in a variety of settings.

Breadth and inclusiveness can also be achieved by crossing national and cultural boundaries. The same multinational corporation referred to earlier offers a few examples. The corporate headquarters and the large corporate research and development facility were located in the Mid-west of the United States. Smaller but often technology focussed laboratories and technical centres were located globally. Traditionally, courses are developed at the corporate headquarters and distributed globally with little attention to diversity or cultural differences. However, when the traditional human resource development function at 3M was reorganised, the technical education function reported to the vice-president of research and development and new opportunities arose for more inclusive, sustainable learning to occur. Several examples are described below.

When this corporation was organising a video conference course on imaging technology, the design was intentionally inclusive of locations in Italy, England, and New York as well as the headquarters laboratory. These locations housed the laboratories that were specifically focussed on imaging and therefore the internal company experts on imaging technology. Times were organised to include the workday in all locations and sessions were recorded in case a connection was lost and/or for archival purposes. Technical employees in the locations remote from the headquarters had an opportunity to showcase their knowledge and expertise before colleagues around the globe.

Two additional examples exist in courses developed to meet the specific needs of the growing Asian region of the corporation. One involved the need for leadership development of technical centre managers and the other focussed on capacity building of training expertise within each national technical centre. Each technical centre manager was a country national who had an academic degree in a science or engineering discipline and rose to his leadership position based on his longevity with the organisation but had little if any training in leadership. This leadership need was addressed by the development of an action learning programme which included 12 technical centre managers in the Asia region. It was a hybrid model integrating a face-to-face session attached to an annual regional technical managers meeting with online learning. Each manager was asked to submit a proposal of a real issue in his technical centre that would benefit from the learning project. Management at headquarters selected the three projects whose results might be replicable in other locations and have the most influence in the overall business results of the region. The twelve technical centre mangers were divided into three teams to learn and make recommendations on the assigned issue over a fourteen months' period. The Global Technical Education Manager at the corporate headquarters and a consultant who was born and raised in Taiwan served as co-instructors for the course. The goal had several facets. Obviously the results would be valuable. But more so, the leadership capacity of the individuals was being developed and would result in capacity building in the region as a whole. While members of the team took on required roles to accomplish the task and the learning, it was essentially an inclusive peer relationship.

The second example involved capacity building of training expertise within each national technical centre. Like the manager, the employees in each technical centre were country nationals who were academically trained scientists and engineers. They embodied the technical expertise within that country and were responsible for training sales people, customers, and anyone needing technical knowledge about a product. But they had little training experience or skills. To address the problem, one option was to designate an itinerant expert trainer from headquarters to visit all the locations, teaching the technical employees how to be trainers. But this did not build the training capacity in each country. The option that was chosen was for the technical manager in each country to designate an outstanding employee to become the expert trainer for that location. These employees were brought together in Singapore where there was a larger regional technical centre. The Global Technical Education Manager from headquarters again partnered with a consultant who had been training technical employees throughout Europe to be technical trainers. They developed a train-the-trainer model. The selected employees from the Asia region spent one and a half weeks in Singapore for the training. The initial half week was spent training them on the role of being a trainer and successful techniques to implement. The next half week, they were taught how to teach the course in which they had just participated. For two and a half days of the following week, they co-taught a section of the course to employees in Singapore. Each evening, they all met with the two instructors to debrief the experience and have a question and answer session about issues that arose. After this event, they were instructed to teach the course to their peers in their home country technical centre. They were encouraged to make any changes necessary that would make content and examples more country and culturally specific. After training in their home country, they were required to have a phone conference with one of the two co-instructors to debrief the session and ask questions. Only then did they receive their completion certificate for the course. This was to emphasise that the learning did not just occur in Singapore but that it was not complete until they had utilised those learned skills in their home environment. This also built a learning community among the now expert trainers in each country that crossed national boundaries and built a training capacity within the region as a whole as well as in each specific country technical centre.

Implementing the Sustainable Learning Paradigm

Sustainability suggests several elements: intensity and rigor; longevity – a long term commitment aimed at long term results. Lifelong learning is not just a casual endeavour but requires planning and attention; intensity and longevity. Anyone planning and preparing for a physical workout might initially assess their current strengths, weaknesses, opportunities and threats. One might consider a preference for individual or group activities, competitive sports or just performing to one's personal best. Learning styles inventories help in assessing the learning style preferences. But clearly, learning throughout one's life should be a well planned succession of integrated learning experiences resulting in sustainable learning.

Brain science research suggests that "exercising" the brain is as essential as exercising the body to maintain optimal mental and physical health. On the first day of class a few semesters ago, students in the author's class were taking turns introducing themselves and indicating why they were enrolled in this author's class. One student, probably in his early fifties stated that his doctor told him to get an advanced degree. The statement caught students' attention and he continued to explain that his doctor recommended him to enrol in a degree programme to keep his mind sharp as he is aged. The doctor felt that the rigor of taking courses for credit toward a degree was more beneficial to mental health than just taking a non-credit course in a subject of interest. Just as a few trips to the gym won't ensure continued physical health, a few short courses will not ensure mental acuity. For example, elder hostels and community based learning programmes have long attracted adults more as a hobby than a serious learning endeavour. But this man had taken his doctor's advice and was enrolled in a graduate programme in adult learning and leadership.

Learning Culture

The way forward is not simple but is certainly clear and is required. A culture change to establish a new paradigm of sustainable learning must be developed. The shift to this new paradigm would require a change in culture to a learning culture that is pervasive throughout society not just in the educational system itself. A portrait and the dynamics of such a culture are not unlike what Schein (2010) describes for a learning culture in an organisation. A learning culture must:

- assume that the appropriate way for humans to behave in relationship to their environment is to be proactive problem solvers and learners.

- have members that must hold the shared assumption that learning is a good thing worth investing in and that learning to learn is itself a skill to be mastered.
- contain the shared assumption that solutions to problems derive from a deep belief in inquiry and a pragmatic search for "truth."
- be built on the assumption that communication and information are central to organisational well-being and must therefore create a multichannel communication system that allows everyone to connect to everyone else.
- have leaders and members who believe that analysing and reflecting on their culture is a necessary part of the learning process.

He refers to a learning culture as one that has a "learning gene" in its DNA. Developing this learning culture could initially appear to be a daunting task. But establishing strategic goals for a sustainable educational paradigm would focus and integrate the educational activities across society.

This learning culture will demand a new type of leader that Schein (2010) labels a learning leader. He describes this new learning leader as one that

- must be able to perceive the problem, to have insight into the culture.
- requires not only insight into the dynamics of the culture but also the motivation and skill to intervene in their own cultural process.
- must have faith in people and must believe that ultimately human nature is basically good and, in any case, malleable.

This description is consistent with Wheatley's (1999) description of a quantum mechanical view in which "Leadership, an amorphous phenomenon that has intrigued us since people began organising, is being examined now for its relational aspects" (p. 13).

Hoffman (2012) admits that the U.S. has "pockets of excellence" (p. 170) which may present a good starting point for success but lacks an overall system. Some changes have happened but mostly in methodologies. Observing today's elementary and middle school classes reveals discussions and connections. Many of the methods that surfaced in the adult learning classroom have become rooted in the K-12 classroom as well. But once the climate of testing and fact regurgitation surfaces, the focus is diverted from learning, critical thinking, analysis, etc., all the skills that educators and employers agree are essential for today's and tomorrow's society and workforce.

Kasworm, Rose & Ross (2010a) note that "the world of adult and continuing education focuses both on individual learning and on the varied organisations that support and enhance the process of learning. The aim of this learning endeavour is to broadly equip adults to effectively engage in the world through individual and collective actions within the spheres of family, work, and community" (p. 4). Schein (2010) expresses a similar sentiment by noting that "culture is our learned solution to making sense of the world, to stabilising it, and to avoiding the anxiety that comes with social chaos, then we have taken the first important step toward deeper cultural understanding" (p. 400). The learning leader can find support in today's technology in the task of achieving this goal and establishing a learning society.

Technology as a Facilitator

The challenge that the learning leader faces in establishing a learning culture can be supported by technology. Technology's ability to establish continued connections will foster idea growth to establish a sustainable paradigm of learning across subjects. Cerf (2010) comments that "one thing we know for sure is that the Web is a collaborative medium unlike any we've ever had before. We see people working together, playing together, interacting in social settings using these media. We hope that will emerge as the new tool for education" (p. 120).

Roles and responsibilities of the educator are altered with technology. Internet access makes content available to everyone, everywhere. The teacher can focus on being the facilitator at every grade. Farmer (2012) describes the developmental issues that influence learning throughout a lifespan and also notes the different skills that digital natives possess and how that will influence their learning. She notes that "In face-to-face education, the teacher is likely to activate curriculum-based stimulus, and call attention to it. In e-learning situations, the teacher sets up the structure that provide stimuli for the information-interaction process, but the student might have to pro-actively seek the stimulus" (p. 30). Students can sit in one location and access literature and science with the touch of a screen or keyboard. Content is no longer person or place specific. Doors are not slamming between grades or subjects. But how this will be integrated into this new paradigm is still emerging with some issues and problems becoming obvious. But consider that learning has evolved before as information became more readily accessible.

Kelly (2010) notes that "in fifteenth century Europe only one in 20 adult males could write. After Gutenberg's printing press came along around 1440, mass-produced books changed the way people read and wrote. The technology of printing expanded the number of words available (from about 50,000 words in Old English to a million today). More word choices enlarged what could be communicated. More media choices broadened what was written about..... Painting, music, architecture, dance were all important, but the heartbeat of Western culture was the turning pages of a book. By 1910 three-quarters of the towns in America with more than 2,500 residents had a public library. We became a people of the book" (pp. 122-123).

Kelly's data continues to illustrate the dramatic changes that have occurred as our mechanism for obtaining information has changed. "Today some 4.5 billion digital screens illuminate our lives. Words have migrated from wood pulp to pixels on computers, phones, laptops, game consoles, televisions, billboards and tablets.... We are not people of the screen. And of course, these newly ubiquitous screens have changed how we read and write" (p. 123). And they have changed how we perceive the right to access information. That information is available 24/7.

Anderson & Wolff (2010) indicate that "the Internet is the real revolution, as important as electricity; what we do with it is still evolving. As it moved from your desktop to your pocket, the nature of the Net changed. The delirious chaos of the open Web was an adolescent phase subsidised by industrial giants groping their way in a new world. Now they're doing what industrialists do best-finding choke points. And by the looks of it, we're loving it" (p. 164). Whether it is from the perspective of the industrialist or the consumer, the maturing on line world is providing opportunities for the growth of the learning culture. Whether they are labelled digital natives or the net generation, the students in today's academic institutions have indeed grown up with the internet and technology at their fingertips but they still need to develop the skills needed to learn.

Cerf (2010) claims that "the problem is – and this is true of books and every other medium – we don't know whether the information we find (on the Web) is accurate or not. We don't necessarily know what its provenance is. So we have to teach people how to assess what they've found. That's a skill, a critical-thinking capacity, which is important no matter what the medium. It's just more dramatic in the World Wide Web where there's so much juxtaposition of the good stuff and not-so-good stuff and flat-out-wrong stuff or deliberate misinformation or plain ignorance" (p. 120).

Anderson & Wolff (2010) offer a sobering thought about the Web which is not 22 year old. "It has reached adulthood. An entire generation has grown up in front of a browser. The exploration of a new world has turned into business as usual. We get the Web. It's part of our life. And we just want to use the services that make our life better. Our appetite for discovery slows as our familiarity with the status quo grows" (p. 127). In a rapidly changing and fast paced world, it is difficult to imagine that the appetite for discovery will slow. But it is imperative that the momentum behind applying technology to learning in new and different ways does not slow.

Clearly the learning leader has a great deal of work to do. Schein (2010) outlines some of the issues and challenges that leader will face in stimulating sustainable learning in a global twenty first century society. The leader will need to "unfreeze the organisation." This requires the "creation of psychological safety" meaning that the leader must have the emotional strength to absorb much of the anxiety surrounding change and remain supportive through the transition phase. Schein (2010) notes that "a paradox of learning leadership is that the leader must be able not only to lead but also to listen, to involve the group in achieving its own insights into its cultural dilemmas, and to be genuinely participative in his or her approach to learning and change" (p. 382). If a culture of sustainable learning is to be achieved, listening to various opinions, involving stakeholders at all levels, and active participation in the process will be required.

Learning opportunities and a vast range of resources will surface because of the openness of the web. Bennett and Bell (2010) explain that "the thirst for openness of knowledge in democratic society began during the Enlightenment and is revolutionised through new public knowledge forums found on the Internet" (p. 412). Bennett and Bell (2010) add that "a central and largely implicit premise behind the knowledge society is that open access to information will improve society and quality of life. This premise incorporates both individual adult learning as well as collective learning for the betterment of civil institutions and social structure, and it is consistent with the long held emphasis of social justice in adult and continuing education"(p. 411). Anderson & Wolff (2010) note that "the great virtue of today's Web is that so much of it is non-commercial. The wide-open Web of peer production, the so-called generative Web where everyone is free to create what they want, continues to thrive, driven by the non-monetary incentives of expression, attention, reputation, and the like" (p. 164). Kelly (2010) provides an example in the statistic that "right now ordinary citizens compose 1.5 million blog posts per day" (p. 123). Kelly (2010) continues that "the amount of time people spend reading has almost tripled since 1980. By 2008 more than a trillion pages were added to the World Wide Web, and that total grows by several billion a day" (p. 123). Cerf (2010) adds that "at Google we see 23 hours of video being uploaded to YouTube per minute and I'm sure that will increase over time. So trying to project what tools will be available over the next 40 years is really daunting" (p. 120). Daunting or not, this openness and the tasks ahead will be influenced by future societal trends taking shape.

Future Trends

The sustainable learning paradigm must be an essential component of the coming decades with its corresponding challenges and opportunities at every level. On an individual level, Schein (2010) advises that "As the world becomes more complex and interdependent, the ability to think systemically, to analyze fields of forces and understand their joint causal effects on each other, and to abandon simple linear causal logic in favour of complex mental models will become more critical to learning" (p. 371). Jarvis (1985) echoes the sentiment that as society moves toward this new information technology society, it is essential that the designs of "learning be such that they encourage critical awareness about all forms of information they receive, whether their teacher is in the classroom, the purveyor of information through the media, or the billions of pages of circulars, or even the programmer of a computer learning package" (p. 14).

On an organisational level, Argyris (1999) warns that "twenty-first corporations will find it hard to survive, let alone flourish, unless they get better work from their employees. This does not necessarily mean harder work or more work. What it does necessarily mean is employees who've learned to take active responsibility for their own behaviour, develop and share first-rate information about their jobs, and make good use of genuine empowerment to shape lasting solutions to fundamental problems" (p. 229).

Kelly (2010) sees a opportunity for technology to meet these challenges. Kelly (2010) notes that "book reading strengthened our analytical skills, encouraging us to pursue an observation all the way down to the footnote. Screen reading encourages rapid pattern making, associating this idea with another, equipping us to deal with the thousands of new thoughts expressed every day. The screen rewards and nurtures thinking in real time. In books we find a revealed truth; on the screen we assemble our truth from pieces" (p. 125).

Bennett and Bell (2010) add their analysis of the pros and cons of the generation for whom screen reading is the norm. They note that "The net generation born between 1981 and 1984 is entering adulthood and members bring with them a set of traits that includes familiarity with technology, optimism, ability to multitask, diversity, and acceptance of authority. Other traits, however, may pose challenges for supporting their learning.... Members of the Net generation are also characterised by shallowness in reading, lack of critical thinking, and naiveté about intellectual property and information authenticity of internet resources" (p. 417). The need to address these issues at every level support the argument for a sustainable learning paradigm.

Conclusions

Sustainability seems to be everywhere! This could be just another example of the "red car" phenomena; only after one has purchased one does one notice how many others are on the road. Or it could be an over-reaction to the "use it up" and discard the unusable. The focus of sustainability is on connectedness of used and discarded; a focus on today as a result of yesterday and tomorrow as a result of today. Sustainable is not only an appropriate adjective for learning but it describes the only realistic approach to learning in the twenty first century. This new inclusive paradigm expands the length of learning and its breadth, no matter what one's role in society. Bennett and Bell note that "the ongoing challenge for members of the knowledge society will be to live successfully in the tension between the public and the private, the individual and the collective, the open and the closed. Negotiating these tensions will be what balances the paradoxes of the knowledge society" (p. 418).

While Wheatley (1999) notes that "the quantum mechanical view of reality startles us out of common notions of what is real" (p. 11), the startling acknowledgement of the need for sustainable learning must be recognised. Sustainable is in everyone's vocabulary at every level of learning with regard to environmental issues, recycling, and resources. The challenge now is to begin at the earliest possible occasion to provide the stimuli for expanding the concept of sustainability to learning. This is essential to the economic, educational, social and political climate of the planet.

References

Allen, J., Gojer, A., Gavrilova-Aguilar, M., & Philpot, D. (2012): "Sustaining Organisational Innovation." In Wang, C.V. (Ed.), *Technology and Its Impact on Educational Leadership* (pp. 254-71). Hershey, PA: IGI Global.

Anderson, C & Wolff, M. (2010): The Web is Dead. Long Live the Internet. *Wired,* 18 (9): 118-127, 164, 166.

Argyris, C. (1999): *On Organisational Learning,* second edition, Malden, MA: Blackwell Publishers.

Bennett, E.E. & Bell, A.A. (2010): Paradox and Promise in the Knowledge Society. In Kasworm, C.E.; Rose, A.D., & Ross-Gordon, J.M. (Ed.), *Handbook of Adult and Continuing Education* (411-20). Thousand Oaks, CA: Sage Publications.

Brookfield, S. (1986): *Understanding and Facilitating Adult Learning*. San Francisco: Jossey-Bass.

Brookfield, S. (1987): *Developing Critical Thinkers.* San Francisco: Jossey-Bass.

Brookfield, S. (2005): The Power of Critical Theory: Liberating Adult Learning and Teaching. San Francisco: Jossey-Bass.

Cerf, Vinton, Google's View. *Smithsonian*, July-August, 2010, 41 (4): 120.

Farmer, L. (2012): "E-Learning for K-12 Learners and Adult Learners." In Wang, V.C.X.

Farmer, L., Parker, J, & Golubski, P. Pedagogical and Andragogical Teaching and Learning with Information Communication Technologies, pp. 28-43. Hershey, PA: IGI Global.

Hoffman, N. (2011): *Schooling in the Workplace.* Boston: Harvard Education Press.

Jarvis, P. (1985): "Thinking Critically in an Information Society: A Sociological Analysis." *Lifelong Learning*, August 6, 1985, pp. 11-14.

Kasworm, C.E., Rose, A.D., & Ross-Gordon, J.M. (2010): "Adult and Continuing Education as an Intellectual Commons." In Kasworm, C.E., Rose, A.D., & Ross-Gordon, J.M. (Ed.), *Handbook of Adult and Continuing Education*, Thousand Oaks, CA: Sage Publications, pp 1-12.

Kelly, K. (2010): "From Print to Pixel," *Smithsonian* July-August 2010. 41 (4): 122-28.

Knowles, M., Holton, E., & Swanson, R. (2005): *The Adult Learner*. Burlington, MA: Elsevier.

Mazarr, M. (1999): Global Trends 2005: An Owner's Manual for the Next Decade. New York, NY: St. Martin's Press.

Schein, E. (2010): *Organisational Culture and Leadership,* fourth edition. San Francisco: Jossey-Bass.

United Nations General Assembly: *Verbatim Report* meeting 8 session, 60 Integrated and coordinated implementation of and follow-up to the outcomes of the major United Nations conferences and summits in the economic, social and related fields, page 44, on 16 September 2005 (a). Retrieved July 12, 2012.

United Nations General Assembly: *Verbatim Report* meeting 8 session, 60 page 46, Mr. Bolton, *United States* on 16 September 2005(b): Retrieved July 12, 2012.

United Nations Association of Great Britain and Northern Ireland (UNA-UK) (2005 c): World Summit Outcome Document: A Glass Half Full? Retrieved July 12, 2012.

Wheatley, M. (1999): Leadership and the New Science: Discovering Order in a Chaotic World. San Francisco: Berrett-Koehler Publishers.

Wilson, J. (2005): Human Resource Development: Learning and Training for Individuals and Organisations. Philadelphia: Kogan Page.

Wolf, M.A. & Brady, E.M. (2010): Adult and Continuing Education for an Aging Society. In Kasworm, C.E., Rose, A.D., & Ross-Gordon, J.M. (Ed.), *Handbook of Adult and Continuing Education*, pp. 369-78. Thousand Oaks, CA: Sage Publications.

World Commission on Environment and Development (1987): *Our Common Future*. Oxford: Oxford University Press.

9

Vocational Education and the Challenge of Development in South Africa[1]

Volker Wedekind

The post-World War II international development agenda has been informed by various seemingly contradictory understandings of the relationship between education and development. On the one hand education is viewed as a form of capital that individuals and societies are able to invest in, and that deliver returns on that investment. On the other hand, there are arguments that suggest that investment in education either reproduces the existing inequalities or saturates the labour market and causes qualification inflation with little impact on development. Within these various debates there are further divisions related to the relative value of primary, secondary or tertiary education and also the value of general versus vocational education. In the current juncture the role of technical and vocational education and training (TVET) in the development of societies is receiving new attention internationally and in South Africa.

This paper will first outline the broad development approaches to education, and then trace the key education reform moves in South Africa over the past twenty years in the light of these wider approaches. The chapter focusses specifically on the TVET sector as this is the part of the education system that is most explicitly linked to the labour market. It will be argued that the need for the system to respond to urgent societal pressures and the demands of the labour market have remained in an uneasy tension. Thus TVET institutions are constantly under pressure to be responsive in multiple and complex ways and struggle to achieve these objectives.

Debates about Education and Development

The period after World War II saw unprecedented growth in the global economy. Through a well-coordinated system of international financial and developmental institutions, the destroyed economies of Europe and Asia were reconstructed. This led to much optimism about the potential of the global economy to continue on a path of growth that would progressively incorporate the developing world into the developed world.

While the initial approach to development was one of modernisation and investment in infrastructure, by 1960 the focus of development theory shifted to the role that education, health and mobility played in making sense of patterns of development. Theodore Schultz's presidential address to the American Economic Association distilled the core ideas of the Human Capital Theory (HCT), which argued that much of what had previously been understood as consumption should rather be viewed as investment in human capital (Schultz 1961). Schultz argued that differences in wages, the gap between investment in infrastructure and the rise in productivity can all be better explained if expenditure on education and health are factored in as investment.

HCT has had a profound effect on the views policy makers have of the function of education. Rather than being a social good or focused on the development of an individual, education and skills development is tied up with economic growth. Investment in education enhances the human capital of a society and therefore improves the development of that society. International agencies such as UNESCO and the World Bank dispersed these ideas throughout the world and significant investment in education was realised.

By the mid-1970s there were already a number of strident critiques of HCT. Spence (1973) and Stiglitz (1975) showed that education credentials were more important as a screening and signalling device rather than demonstrating any greater productivity. Dore showed how this qualification inflation process was like a disease, particularly in developing countries (Dore, 1976, 1980). Bowles and Gintis (1975) argued more fundamentally that HCT completely removed any class analysis from economic understanding. Despite these critiques the notion that education could remove inequality and lead to greater economic growth held sway. Michael Young's 1958 satirical piece coined a term, "meritocracy," which ironically became widely used to refer to the way education enables individuals to achieve based purely on merit rather than class.

The predominance of HCT in guiding education policy makers also brought about an increased focus on vocational education and training. In order to meet the demands of the labour market, greater emphasis was placed on stand-alone vocational programmes as well as integrating vocational education into the general education programme. Already in 1965 Phillip Foster raised concerns about the focus of education becoming too narrowly aligned to specific job-related skills, arguing that the distinction between general and vocational education was a fallacy (Foster, 1965). Foster's landmark study of education in Ghana over more than a century showed that educational reforms that had tried to align the schooling system more directly to the world of work and the immediate needs of society had failed consistently to achieve the desired outcomes. A significant part of Foster's argument centred on the "realism and rationality" of the Ghanaian children and their parents in working out what was in their best interests despite the intentions of the policy makers to steer them toward specific occupations (King & Martin, 2000).

Perhaps less rationally there is also extensive literature that shows that TVET continues to suffer from negative perceptions that impact on the learning pathways that are possible and result in poor choices made by learners (Gale 2011). In South Africa, as with many countries around the world, TVET is perceived to be the last resort for those that have not been able to cope with an academic career. Despite attempts to market TVET pathways, young people vote with their feet and strive to enter university programmes, with the belief that this will lead to better types of jobs. Why this perception exists even in contexts where being skilled in a trade is a more likely to lead to employment than a general university education requires further interrogation.

The above debates have circulated in the academic and policy domains throughout the second half of the twentieth century. In the early 1990s vocational and technical education emerged again as a key development strategy. Technical and vocational education has resurfaced within the discourse of the World Bank and other international agencies such as UNESCO (including the establishment of UNEVOC in 2000), and has been a feature of all the developing economies that have experienced growth. For example, the recent BRICS[2] summit held in Durban in 2013 included for the first time a study group on vocational education skills development. Investment in TVET is seen as a key part of the success of emerging economies.

Education and Development in South Africa

Since the transition to democracy in South Africa, education has been seen as central to the "fight" against poverty, unemployment and as a vehicle for dismantling the system of racial privilege. Much of the initial focus was on getting young people back into school. Enrolments increased and generated new challenges related to quality of the educational experience. However, despite sustained – albeit slower than desired – economic growth, the employment patterns remained bleak. Increasingly the focus of debate and policy intervention has shifted from the failures of the schooling system to the needs of the TVET and skills system. If this can be strengthened, so the mantra goes, economic growth will follow and unemployment will decrease. A speech at the University of Witwatersrand the South African Deputy President at the time, Kgalema Motlanthe, made the following statement which is illustrative of this focus:

> "Economic productivity is the fruit of long-term investment in the national education system. Short of an education system geared to the particular developmental needs of the country, we will be hard put breaking into high-level economic productivity that can extricate us from the inter-generational cycle of poverty."

This faith in the investment in human capital as a means for addressing South Africa's economic and social challenges is widespread, not only in government but also in wider society.

A recent survey once again highlighted the acute crisis South Africa faces with respect to unemployment. Twenty eight per cent of South Africans are unemployed and looking for work with only thirty eight per cent employed either full-time or part time (IPSOS, 2013). Various estimates suggest that there are as many as 3,5 million people who are not in employment, education or training – the so-called NEETs (Cloete, 2011). It is little wonder then that over the past two decades education and training as strategies for addressing job creation and unemployment have been central to government's priorities. Particularly the vocational education system, centred on the colleges, and the Sector Education and Training Authorities (SETAs) have been the focus of the strategy. In March 2013 the President of the Republic of South Africa signed the Further Education and Training Colleges Amendment Act into law. This was followed in November 2013 by the approval of a White Paper on the Post-School Education and Training system, which has in turn introduced a range of new amendments to existing policies. These marked the latest stage in a series of reforms to the South

African technical, vocational and occupational education and training system. These reforms have introduced major changes to the institutional landscape, the qualifications, the curriculum, and the demographics of the system. While the reforms have been premised on a notion of making the college system more responsive to the needs of the labour market, and to a lesser extent the wider developmental agenda of the state, the outcomes remain uncertain. The degree to which the various critiques of HCT help to explain this tension around the TVET system will be discussed in the context of the reforms.

A Brief Historical Review

Like almost all aspects of South Africa's society, TVET and the development of the vocational colleges (branded Further Education and Training (FET) Colleges until they were renamed TVET Colleges in 2014) are inextricably bound up with the history of colonialism, apartheid, and the particular form of racial capitalism that developed on the southern tip of Africa. The college system inherited by the first democratic government had evolved primarily out of a technical training system that had, in turn, emerged in the first quarter of the twentieth century as a response to the mineral revolution and the development of the Apartheid state (Badroodien, 2004; Motala, Vally & Spreen, 2010). The system was designed as a vehicle for artisan training linked to apprenticeships, where the colleges provided the theoretical components and the practical training was largely done on the job or in training centres attached to large companies. Though small, this dual system (parallel learning on the job and in formal educational institutions) was effective at providing the skills needed in the economy and in the public sector, with the bulk of training happening in state owned enterprises, large corporates and municipalities. With the economy moving into recession in the mid-1970s, and political and economic pressure to broaden the skills base and create a black middle class, the system was slowly opened up to young people of other races but became increasingly disconnected from the work-based apprenticeship system (Chisholm, 1983). By the time the first democratic election was held in 1994, the technical college system consisted of more than 150 institutions of very uneven quality, delivering a dated curriculum, and producing fewer and fewer qualified artisans.

Education Reform

One of the striking features of the early post apartheid educational policy is that it was shaped primarily outside the education community. Arising from worker struggles in the 1970s and 1980s, a proposal was developed by the unions, employers, and the state departments for an integrated education and training system that would ensure formal recognition of skilled workers and associated pay increments. The South African Qualifications Authority (SAQA) Act of 1995 established the qualifications authority that was to oversee the National Qualifications Framework (NQF). Not only did the NQF seek to map out all existing and new qualifications on one framework, but it also described the entire education system on eight levels, divided into three bands (General, Further and Higher).

The vision of the NQF designers was a radical one. Driven by a desire to enable the recognition of skills and to encourage training for workers in order to improve their productivity and employability, the NQF resulted in far reaching changes to both the schooling and college systems, and also to a lesser degree the university system. The intention was to enable the seamless articulation of qualifications across the system that would allow progression from the lowest to the highest levels. Furthermore, by framing the entire education system in terms of outcomes that needed to be achieved at each level and for each unit of knowledge, it was possible to imagine formally recognising knowledge and skills that had been achieved on the job or through life experience. This recognition of prior learning was a key mechanism for ensuring that people were not held back by their lack of formal qualifications. At the heart of the NQF lies an implicit belief that recognition of and investment in human capital will benefit the individuals concerned and necessarily grow the economy to the benefit of society as a whole (Young and Allais, 2013).

Perhaps the most widely critiqued aspect of the NQF was the fact that qualifications and part qualifications had to be specified in terms of their exit level outcomes rather than in terms of duration of time or content to be covered. The vocational education and training system had to be dramatically overhauled as a consequence of the new logic of the NQF. All forms of training were to be encoded on the NQF as part or whole qualifications. Knowledge had to be described in discrete units (known as Unit Standards) that could be separately assessed. This had the consequence that the entire education system had to adopt an outcome oriented pedagogy, which generated significant confusion for teachers at all levels of the system (Harley and Wedekind 2004).

The Green Paper on FET was released in 1998 and linked the FET Band to a "range of government policies... (including) macro-economic, industrial, labour market and human resource development policies."[3] The Green Paper was explicitly aligned with notions of life-long learning, increased productivity and employability and foregrounded the human capital orientation over broader educational or social objectives. The vision put forward was a dramatic reorganisation and reorientation of the FET Band, that is the three levels (numbered 2, 3 and 4) between basic education (Grades 0-9) and higher education. The Green Paper presented a critique of the inherited system that highlighted the lack of coherence, the lack of articulation, poorly coordinated funding mechanisms, poor linkages to industry, a distorted labour market and a system that was marked by low morale, poor work ethic and low professional self-esteem amongst educators (Department of Education, 1998). What was proposed was an expanded and revitalised college system that was responsive to the local economic conditions.

The 1998 Green Paper was followed by a series of other policies and legislation developing, not only the institutional form, the qualification structure, but also the levy mechanisms to fund the system. By the year 2000 the policy was in place to develop a sophisticated system of skills development based on the notion of stakeholder participation coupled with incentives and new qualifications was in place. The intention was that those in employment would become more productive and also better rewarded for their skills, while employers would employ more people because the increased productivity would result in economic growth.

The actual implementation changes to the system prioritised the institutional dimension, with significant energy and resources focussed on the merging of colleges. The 152 public technical colleges and training centres were merged into 50 multi-campus FET Colleges under the authority of the provinces and governed by Councils (Wedekind, 2010). The second major intervention in the system was close to R2 billion worth of investment in the re-capitalisation of colleges between 2006 and 2009. This was a response to the critique that the colleges did not have the infrastructure or equipment to play the role that was envisaged for them in the various policy documents.

During this period the FET Band functioned only in name. The notion of an integrated band straddling school, colleges and the workplace was not seriously developed at institutional, conceptual or curriculum level. The school system retained its basic distinction between primary and secondary schools, and very few students exited the school system at the end of Grade 9, or NQF Level 1. The envisaged growth of the vocational part of the FET Band had not materialised despite the above-mentioned recapitalisation of colleges, and colleges remained outside of the public and official spotlight. In 2006 Parliament passed the FET Colleges Act which provided for a clear separation of the FET schooling component from the FET colleges, and introduced a new governance structure that vested significant powers in the College Councils.

The FET Colleges Act also set in place a new curriculum framework. The National Certificate (Vocational) (NCV) was envisaged as a full-time qualification on three levels of the NQF that essentially provided for an alternative pathway to the schooling system. This qualification was a completely new type of offering, incorporating both subject specialisation in a vocational field as well as generic skills in communication, mathematics and life-skills. The intention was that learners would exit the college system with a good general vocational education, with some specialisation, but would have had significant practical experience as part of the programme through work in college based workshops and exposure to workplaces. The focus on communication and language, life-skills and mathematics as a core component was in response to critiques from employers that students were able to do the technical aspects of a job but would often fail when it came to broader and basic level skills of communicating with colleagues and customers, doing basic mathematical tasks and not managing their lives.

The aims of the NCV as articulated by the Department of Education ten years after the publication of the Green Paper align once again to the overall focus of the vocational education sector: The NCV is a qualification which "aims to solve the problem of poor quality programmes, lack of relevance to the needs of the economy, as well as low technical and cognitive skills of the FET college graduates" (Department of Education, 2008, p. 11). Linking to definitions used by UNESCO and the ILO, the 2008 plan for colleges defined vocational education as being a general education that prepares people for occupational fields so that they have a basis for effective participation in the world of work, that it produces environmentally aware responsible citizens, and that it increases employment opportunities and alleviates poverty (Department of Education, 2008). Thus, clearly the intention of the system remained framed by a strong HCT approach, but the overall definition of vocational education recognised the wider social and general education dimensions that Foster's fallacy paper had highlighted in 1965.

Like much vocational education worldwide, the general public did not understand its purpose, and so it was viewed as a programme for those not able to cope with academic school curriculum demands. Principals of high schools actively advised their academically less able pupils to transfer to colleges, reinforcing a stigma about the colleges, but also creating a huge problem with pass and retention rates in the colleges. While the curriculum was vocationally oriented, it was not academically less demanding than the school curriculum. Indeed, Umalusi, the quality assurance agency responsible for both colleges and schools undertook comparisons between similar subjects at schools and colleges and found that the vocational requirements were similar and in some instances more demanding than the school subject (Houston, Booyse & Burroughs, 2010). Other criticisms came from industry who argued that the new curriculum was too academic, ironically that the core components were not necessary, and that the full-time nature of the programme over three years meant that existing employees could not access the qualification.

When the new government was installed in June 2009 after an internal revolt within the ruling party, the administration was significantly reformed. Tensions that had existed between the Departments of Labour and Education with respect to the oversight of the skills system, and the failure at provincial level to focus resources on the colleges in the context of more high profile attention on schools, resulted in the decision to split the Department of Education in two by creating the Department of Basic Education and the Department of Higher Education and Training (DHET). The DHET was given responsibility for all post-school education as well as Adult Education, including the FET colleges. It also was given those skills development responsibilities previously attached to the Department of Labour and became the ministry responsible for the National Skills Development Strategy (NSDS), the National Skills Agency, the Sector Education and Training Authority (SETAs) and the National Skills Fund (NSF). For the first time all the components of the skills development system were housed under one ministry.

The third NSDS lists the following as pressing challenges that it is responding to (DHET, 2011: 6):

- Inadequate skill levels and poor work readiness of young people entering the labour market, compounded by inadequate linkages between institutional and workplace learning "thus reducing the employability and work readiness of the successful graduates from FET and HET institutions."
- The plight of the longer term unemployed who lack basic numeracy and literacy, entry-level skills, work experience and work-based training
- Specific skills shortages in artisanal, professional and technical fields
- An over emphasis on learnerships without progression. "Substantial programmes that improve qualifications, support career pathing, enable greater flexibility and mobility and increase productivity" are needed.
- The failure of business to equip their workforce
- stemic blockages within the skills system

The strategy attempts to address these "pressing challenges" through focussing the resources more coherently via better planning and coordination. As far as the colleges were concerned, the strategy places them as central to the skilling and re-skilling of youth and adults. As far as curriculum goes, the much criticised NCV is to be reviewed, while the older "N-courses" (linked explicitly to apprenticeships), which previously had been scheduled for phase-out, are to remain a part of the programme mix, and be updated, where necessary. Once again one can clearly see that the underpinning discourse informing these interventions retains a strong HCT dimension.

The National Planning Commission (NPC), tasked with drawing up a development plan for the country, released the *National Development Plan* in 2011 which laments the quality, size and output of the college system, and once again argues that urgent attention needs to be focussed on the quality of the system in order to improve the employability of the graduates. Indeed, in the view of the NPC, improving educational outcomes is the first of five factors that are necessary in order to raise employment. With respect to the college system, the NPC proposes to increase the size of the system to about 1,25 million learners by 2030, but makes the point that not "focussing on quality is likely to be expensive and demoralising for young people, further stigmatising the system" (National Planning Commission, 2011: 18). While the Planning Commission claims to adopt a capabilities approach to development, the education section retains a HCT orientation by prioritising the investment in skills and linking education directly to employment and employability.

The most recent policy intervention has been the White Paper for Post-School Education and Training (Department of Higher Education and Training, 2014). The White Paper's purpose is to provide a vision for the integrated post-school system. Colleges are once again a central feature of the White Paper. The assessment of the colleges is frank:

FET colleges are varied and diverse but, with some notable exceptions, they are mainly weak institutions. With their present capacity, colleges can neither absorb significantly larger numbers of students nor achieve acceptable levels of throughput (Department of Higher Education and Training, 2012: 10).

There is acknowledgement that many of the prior reforms such as the decentralisation of governance, the re-capitalisation programme, and curriculum reforms were not successful either because they were premature or because they were inadequately conceptualised. This is a recognition that many reforms were not successful, though there is no real reflection on the original intentions. This is noteworthy primarily because many of the proposed reforms are very similar to previous iterations.

Colleges will be the primary sites for vocational and occupational qualifications focussed on fields such as engineering, construction, tourism and hospitality, business administration and educare (early childhood development). The colleges will offer both general vocational qualifications such as the NCV and focussed programmes for specific occupations. A range of options are discussed in the White Paper related to the nature of the NCV and the introduction of new NCV programmes at Level 5 of the NQF,[5] changes to the NATED 191 courses, offering skills courses and short courses, a possible role in the delivery of a new National Senior Certificate for Adults, and the need to ensure progression into and articulation with higher education programmes both in terms of existing programmes and new bridging programmes.

The picture that emerges from the White Paper suggests that not much has been achieved since the first policies were being drafted almost two decades ago. The colleges appear not to have delivered what was envisaged and remain a weak link in the overall development plan of the country. The solutions and interventions remain largely the same – improve the lecturers, improve the qualifications on offer, and build partnerships and linkages in order to be responsive and enhance the employability of students.

When placed next to each other, the Green Paper of 1998, the various skills and economic development strategies that have followed, and the White Paper of 2014 all have similar intentions. The FET system has consistently been viewed as a vehicle for solving critical social problems and specifically for addressing a crisis in employment. Across the fifteen years under discussion in this paper, policy texts and commentators have focussed on the need for colleges to be responsive to the needs of the employer, and for colleges to produce learners who are employable. As new policies have been developed, they lament the same problems in the colleges: poor quality, lack of articulation, poor alignment with economic priorities and poor linkages with industry. The responses over the years have attempted, albeit in different ways, to address these concerns. Yet, if the analysis presented in the 2014 White Paper and the National Development Plan is correct, it would suggest that there has been little or no progress at all in the college sector, and possibly that the system has deteriorated.

Discussion

Why then have colleges and the wider TVET system apparently failed? The focus of the critique centres on the failures of policy and the weaknesses of the institutions and their staff. There has apparently been no loss of faith in the potential of the education system to solve the economic problems. However, the failure of the college sector to improve the employability of their graduates and to significantly reduce unemployment may have less to do with the poor quality of the colleges and their weak linkages to industry and is more likely to be a feature of the structure of the economy, and how economic policies have been implemented that privilege a particular model of growth. A comprehensive discussion is not possible here, but there is significant evidence to suggest that there has been little attempt to fundamentally restructure the economy and that transformation has focussed on the formation of a small black elite (Maharaj, Desai & Bond, 2010). Economic growth has been largely jobless.

That is not to suggest that colleges cannot improve, but colleges cannot be held responsible for the limited creation of new jobs in the economy. This raises questions about the simplistic assumptions made by human capital theory and the nature of the relationship between education and economic growth where there is a persistent belief that skills shortages are a major constraint on economic growth (Allais, 2012; Wheelahan, 2010). Whether this belief is based on naivety or on a symbolic necessity that has little to do with fundamental change is debatable (Young, 2008).

Being "responsive" education institutions cannot be understood as focussed solely on meeting the needs of industry. Employers tend to focus on their immediate needs and few have long-term orientations. Given the rapidity of change, being responsive requires anticipation of developments and planning and risk. Colleges cannot depend on this coming from industry. Furthermore, maximising returns on investment also does not always result in support for training that formalises qualifications. This can be result in increases in labour costs that employers may wish to avoid. Responsiveness then needs to also take account of wider societal issues that may at times be at odds with the perceived needs of employers. Educating citizens that are aware of their rights in society and the workplace may not be a priority for employers but is a crucial contribution to society. And focussing on the needs of students while they are at the college during a formative period of their lives is also a dimension of responsiveness.

The tension between skills training and education, which has been a feature of much of the debate around education and training, relates directly to Foster's fallacy critique (1965). The Human Capital approach, with its associated discourses of responsiveness and employability, places great store on skills, understood as a "practice" or "task," rather than a wider understanding of education that encompasses knowledge, skills, values and dispositions. Skills tend to be understood in discrete units (whether soft or hard) and can be separately assessed in no particular sequence. This has been the basis for much of the logic of the NQF and the system of unit standards and skills courses (Allais, 2007). While this approach makes sense from the perspective of accreditation of certain skills, it fails to grasp the complexity of the interface between knowledge, skills, occupational commitment and identity (what Felix Rauner and colleagues refer to as "competence" (Jude, Hartig & Klieme, 2008; Rauner, 2005)). This notion of competence is premised on an understanding that in order to develop real expertise in an aspect of the work process, a worker needs to understand the context, the underpinning knowledge and the socio-cultural and environmental impact of the work. This defines "skilled workers" as being able to function in a complex setting and to be able to understand the work they do holistically, rather than as a fragmented set of practices (Gamble, 2009).

There have been attempts at various points in the period under discussion to strengthen the educational dimensions of the vocational system. The introduction of the NCV was a case in point, where the qualification included general education components alongside occupation specific modules. The critique of the NCV has often focussed on the time it takes and that it includes too much general education (numeracy, literacy and life-skills) and not enough hands-on practical aspects. Yet, if done well, this is precisely what learners should be getting. What is absent from the discourse on skills is an indepth engagement with what vocational *education* is: its inner structure and demands. The vocational education systems that are most highly regarded internationally all have a strong formal education dimension that complement the work-based and practical components. This recognises that preparation for work does not have to be only about work. Formal educational spaces open up possibilities that cannot be realised in the workplace. In order to develop an education system that goes beyond training requires an educational theory of vocational education, which is largely absent in South Africa.

What is apparent when tracking education reforms across the first two decades of post-apartheid South Africa is that there is little evidence that policy makers have taken on board any of the critiques of HCT. There remains a consistent belief that if the institutions are modernised and reformed, they can deliver the desired economic growth and address issues such as inequality, unemployment and poverty. Revisiting the critiques of HCT in the current context is critical to ensuring that education does not carry central responsibility for the failures to resolve these challenges. It is well worth repeating Phillip Foster's warning that education institutions "are remarkably clumsy instruments for inducing prompt large-scale changes in underdeveloped areas" (1965, p. 144) is well worth repeating. It is not that education systems are unimportant, but rather that they do not predictably do what policy makers expect of them.

Notes

1. This chapter is based on an earlier paper on employability and education reform in South Africa's TVET system that was published as a chapter (*See* Wedekind 2014). Parts of this chapter draw on earlier versions of that paper.
2. A club of 'developing' countries comprising Brazil, Russia, India, China and South Africa
3. Minister SME Bengu, Foreword, page 3.
4. Level 5 is a post-school level that has higher certificates and the first years of diplomas and degrees in it.

References

Allais, S.M. (2007): The Rise and Fall of the NQF: A Critical Analysis of the South African National Qualifications Framework. Ph.D. Thesis, University of Witwatersrand, Johannesburg.

Allais, S.M. (2012): "Will Skills Save Us? Rethinking the Relationships between Vocational Education, Skills Development Policies, and Social Policy in South Africa.' *International Journal of Educational Development,* 32: 632-42.

Badroodien, A. (2004): "Technical and Vocational Education Provision in South Africa from 1920 to 1970." In McGrath, S., Badroodien, A., Kraak, A. & Unwin, L. (Ed.), *Shifting Understanding of Skills in South Africa – Overcoming the Historical Imprint of a Low Skills Regime*. Cape Town: HSRC Press, pp. 20-45.

Bowles, S. and Gintis, H. (1975): "The Problem with Human Capital Theory — A Marxian Critique." *American Economic* Review, 65 (2): 74-82.

Chisholm, L. (1983): "Redefining Skills: Black Education in South Africa in the 1980s." *Comparative Education,* 19 (3): 357-71.

Cloete, N. (2011): The Waste of Talent in South Africa. *IIEP Newsletter,* XXIX (2),:9.

Department of Education. (1998): Green Paper on Further Education and Training: Preparing for the Twenty-First Century through Education, Training and Work. Pretoria: Government Printer.

Department of Education (2008): *National Plan for Further Education and Training Colleges*. Pretoria: Government Gazette 31712.

Department of Higher Education and Training (2011): *National Skills Development Strategy III*. Pretoria: Government Printer.

Department of Higher Education and Training (2012): *Green Paper for Post-School Education and Training*. Pretoria: Government Printer.

Department of Higher Education and Training (2014): *White Paper for Post-School Education and Training*. Pretoria, Government Printer.

Dore, R. (1976): The Diploma Disease: Education, Qualification and Development. London: George Allen & Unwin.

Dore, R. (1980): "The Diploma Disease Revisited." *IDS Bulletin*, 11 (2): 1-12.

Foster, P.J. (1965): "The Vocational School Fallacy in Development Planning." In Anderson, C.A. and Bowman, M.J. (Ed.): *Education and National Development*. Chicago: Aldine.

Gale, C., (2011): "From Prejudice to Prestige: Vocational Education and Training in Ghana." *Norrag News*, 46 (September):112-115

Gamble, J. (2009): "The Relationship between Knowledge and Practice in Curriculum and Assessment," *Umalusi Occasional Papers*. Pretoria: Umalusi.

Harley, K and Wedekind, V (2004): "Political Change, Curriculum Change, and Social Formation, 1990 – 2002. In Chisholm, L. (Ed.) *Changing Class: Education and Social Change in Post-Apartheid South Africa*. Pretoria and London: HSRC and Zed Books, 195-220.

Houston, J., Booyse, C. & Burroughs, E. (2010): *The 'F' in NC(V): Benchmarking Common Subjects in the NSC and the NC(V)*. Pretoria: Umalusi.

IPSOS (2013): "19 Years after Democracy South Africans still have to Deal with Slow Progress in Terms of Job Creation, Unemployment and Inequality, *IPSOS Survey*, IPSOS.

Jude, N., Hartig, J. & Klieme, E. (Ed.). (2008): *Kompetenzerfassung in pädagogischen Handlungsfeldern: Theorien, Konzepte und Methoden* (Vol. Bildungsforschung Band 26). Berlin: BMBF.

King, K. & Martin, C. (2000): "The Vocational School Fallacy revisited: Education, Aspiration and Work in Ghana 1959-2000." *Centre for African Studies Occasional Papers*, No. 85. Edinburgh University.

Maharaj, B., Desai, A. & Bond, P. (Ed.) (2010): *Zuma's Own Goal: Losing South Africa's War on Poverty*. Trenton, NJ: Africa World Press & The Red Sea Press.

Motala, E., Vally, S. & Spreen, C.A. (2010): "Reconstituting Power and Privilege or Transforming Education and Training?" In Maharaj, B., Desai A. & Bond, P. (Ed.), *Zuma's Own Goal: Losing South Africa's 'War on Poverty.'* Trenton, NJ: Africa World Press & The Red Sea Press, pp. 241-60..

National Planning Commission (2011): *National Development Plan: Vision for 2030*. Pretoria: Government Printer.

Rauner, F. (2005): "Work Process Knowledge and the Development of Vocational Competence." Muscat: Oman Conference.

Schultz, T.W. (1961): "Investment in Human Capital,". *American Economic Review*, 51: 1-17.

Spence, A.M. (1973): "Job Market Signalling." *Quarterly Journal of Economics*, 87: 355-74

Stiglitz, J. (1975): The Theory of Screenings, Education and the Distribution of Income. *American Economic Review*, 65: 283-300.

Wedekind, V. (2010): "Chaos or Coherence? Further Education and Training College Governance in Post-Apartheid South Africa." *Research in Comparative and International Education*, 5(3): 302 15.

Wedekind, V. (2014): "Going Around in Circles: Employability, Responsiveness and the Reform of the College Sector." In Vally, S. and Motala, E. (Ed) *Education, Economy and Society*. Pretoria: UNISA Press, pp. 57-80.

Wheelahan, L. (2010): Why Knowledge Matters in Curriculum: A Social Realist Argument. London: Routledge.

Young, M. (1958): *The Rise of the Meritocracy, 1870-2033*. London: Thames & Hudson.

Young, M. (2008): Bringing Knowledge Back. In: From Social Constructivism to Social Realism in the Sociology of Education. London: Routledge.

Young, M. & Allais, S. (Ed.) (2013): Implementing National Qualifications Frameworks across Five Continents. Abingdon: Routledge.

10

The Employability of Tertiary-Level Graduates in India

Santosh Mehrotra

With gross enrolment ratio (GER) in higher education hitting 18 per cent, well past the 15 per cent mark that is seen as the point of transition from an elite to a 'mass' higher education system (2011-12), the problem of quality and employability of graduates has come even more sharply into focus than before.

Education of the Workforce

In India 146 million (or 30 per cent) of the workforce out of 485 million in 2012 were illiterate. Over half (52 per cent or 253 million) of the labour force are those only with education upto secondary level. (But 40 per cent of this 52 per cent have less than middle-level of education, and the majority of this 40 per cent consists of those with primary or less education.) An additional 15 million have tertiary level technical education, about half of whom have diploma or certificate level and the other half of this group has graduate level technical education (*See* Table 10.1). In other words, barely 3 per cent of the workforce has technical education at tertiary level, and another 7.2 per cent has general academic education at tertiary level.

NSS data allow an analysis of the workforce by three types of employment: self-employed, casual labour, or regular salaried work. It is not surprising that hardly any illiterates have regular salaried jobs. Most illiterate are either casual workers or in self-employment, usually engaged in low productivity work.

Just over half the workforce has education up to secondary level. Well over half of those who have education up to secondary level are self employed. However what is more worrying is that as many as 75 million of those with secondary education actually are in casual work. Given that nearly half of all those in the workforce have secondary education the fact that nearly a third of all those with secondary education are in casual work (without any social insurance) should be worrying to policy makers.

The total number of those with higher secondary education (34.4 million) and those who have graduate level education and above (35.6 million) is roughly similar in the workforce. What is notable, however, is that half of those with only higher secondary education are self employed. Under a third of those with higher secondary education are in regular salaried employment (while only 15 per cent of those with secondary education have regular salaried jobs). However, half of those with graduate level education or above are in regular salaried employment. What is worrying is that nearly four million of those with higher secondary level of education are engaged in casual work.

What is notable from Table 10.1 is that technical education below graduate level as well as at the graduate level and above significantly raises the probability of one getting a regular salary job than if one were a graduate with only general academic education.[2] The good news is that the share in the workforce of those with any tertiary level education has risen from 7.3 per cent in 2004-05 to 10.3 per cent in 2011-12.

Both the labour market as well as tertiary education outcomes for men and women are rather different. It is well known that the labour force participation rate of women in India is well below that for men and in fact is one of the lowest in the world. Even more worrying is the fact that it has been declining. While there were 351 million males in the total workforce of 485 million in 2012, there were only 134 million women in the workforce. Nearly half of the women in the workforce are illiterate but less than one-third of men in the workforce are illiterate.

If women acquire education up to graduate level, whether it is general or academic or technical education, there is a high likelihood they will get regular employment. In fact the probability of their getting regular employment is slightly greater with graduate education if they are women rather than if they were men (*See* Table 10.1).

In Table 10.2 we present the sectoral distribution of the workforce by level of education both with general as well as technical education. As in the case of Table 10.1, the information for the entire workforce is presented by category: (a) illiterate, (b) general education up to secondary level, (c) with general education up to higher secondary level, and finally (d) those with graduate and above general education. The remaining two of the six categories presented are for technical education, below graduate and then graduate and above level. As one would expect, two-thirds of all illiterate workers are in agriculture. It is also notable that construction employees are a significant share of all illiterate workers.

Two-thirds of those who have graduate level of education enter services employment. This is more than seven times as many as those who enter manufacturing sector employment. It is well known that services account for 25 per cent of total employment in the Indian economy, while manufacturing accounts for only 11 per cent of it. In fact services account for the majority of those who have technical education as well. Half of those with below graduate technical education are employed in the services sector. That share rises to 80 per cent for those with technical education of graduate level. In other words, the services sector accounts for the majority of those with some tertiary level education, including those with technical education. On the ground one example of this is reflected in the following fact: that IIT graduate engineers more often than not end up in finance and other services. Manufacturing and non-manufacturing employment accounts for less than a third of all technical education graduates who have employment.

If India remains a services driven economy, rather than one in which manufacturing and non-manufacturing industry (construction, mining, electricity) predominates (as in China), the educational system is a reflection of this situation. Moreover, if India's agriculture is not as productive as in China, one reason is that the majority of the workforce in agriculture remains illiterate or with very low levels of education.

Table 10.1: Distribution of Labour Force (Million) by Sex, Level of Education and Types of Employment, 2004-05 and 2011-12

Level of Education		*2004-05*					*2011-12*				
		SE	**RE**	**CL**	**UE**	**LF**	**SE**	**RE**	**CL**	**UE**	**LF**
						Mal e+ Female					
General education	Illiterate	102.0	7.9	71.9	0.67	182.5	76.4	7.7	61.5	0.67	146.2
	Upto Secondary	132.2	32.5	58.2	5.47	228.4	135.5	38.1	75.3	4.48	253.4
	Higher Secondary	12.5	6.8	1.5	1.41	22.2	18.4	10.8	3.7	1.60	34.4
	Graduate & above	9.6	10.9	0.4	1.94	22.9	13.8	18.4	0.9	2.52	35.6
Technical education	Below Graduate	2.6	4.2	0.4	0.85	8.0	2.1	5.2	0.5	0.81	8.6
	Graduate & above	1.7	3.0	0.1	0.48	5.2	1.4	4.4	0.1	0.53	6.5
Total		**260.6**	**65.3**	**132.5**	**10.8**	**469.2**	**247.6**	**84.6**	**142.0**	**10.6**	**484.7**
Male											
General education	Illiterate	45.1	4.9	37.4	0.43	87.9	38.4	4.8	35.8	0.46	79.5
	Upto Secondary	98.9	27.9	46.6	3.69	177.1	104.6	32.3	60.6	3.40	201.0
	Higher Secondary	10.8	5.6	1.3	0.83	18.5	15.7	9.0	3.3	1.13	29.1
	Graduate & above	8.7	8.6	0.3	1.08	18.7	12.4	14.2	0.7	1.58	28.9
Technical education	Below Graduate	2.1	3.3	0.3	0.51	6.2	1.8	4.3	0.5	0.52	7.1
	Graduate & above	1.4	2.4	0.1	0.28	4.1	1.2	3.4	0.1	0.33	5.0
Total		**167.0**	**52.7**	**86.0**	**6.8**	**312.5**	**174.1**	**68.0**	**101.0**	**7.4**	**350.6**
Female											
General education	Illiterate	56.9	3.0	34.5	0.24	94.7	38.0	2.8	25.7	0.21	66.8
	Upto Secondary	33.3	4.6	11.5	1.77	51.3	30.9	5.8	14.6	1.08	52.4
	Higher Secondary	1.7	1.2	0.2	0.58	3.6	2.6	1.9	0.3	0.47	5.3
	Graduate & above	0.9	2.4	0.0	0.86	4.2	1.4	4.2	0.1	0.93	6.7
Technical education	Below Graduate	0.5	0.9	0.1	0.35	1.8	0.3	0.8	0.1	0.29	1.5
	Graduate & above	0.2	0.6	0.0	0.21	1.1	0.2	1.1	0.0	0.20	1.5
Total		**93.5**	**12.7**	**46.3**	**4.01**	**156.7**	**73.4**	**16.6**	**40.8**	**3.2**	**134.2**

Source: Author's estimates based on NSS unit level data

Note: Higher Secondary education includes both regular and diploma/certificate courses. The abbreviations used are SE - Self-Employed, RE - Regular salaried Employed, CL - Casual Labour, UE - Unemployed (open), LF - Labour Force.

Table 10.2: Industry-Wise Distribution of Workforce (Million) by Sex, Level of Education, Types of Employment in India, 2011-12

Level of Education	*Male*				*Female*				*Male+ Female*			
	SE	*RE*	*CL*	*Total*	*SE*	*RE*	*CL*	*Total*	*SE*	*RE*	*CL*	*Total*
General Education (Illiterate)												
Agriculture & Allied	27.2	0.4	20.1	47.6	30.5	0.2	19.0	49.6	57.7	0.6	39.0	97.3
Manufacturing	3.1	1.7	2.1	7.0	4.9	0.4	0.9	6.1	8.0	2.1	3.0	13.1
Non- Manufacturing	1.1	0.4	11.9	13.5	0.1	0.2	5.2	5.5	1.2	0.6	17.1	19.0
Services	6.9	2.3	1.7	10.9	2.6	2.1	0.7	5.3	9.5	4.4	2.3	16.2
Total	**38.4**	**4.8**	**35.8**	**79.0**	**38.0**	**2.8**	**25.7**	**66.6**	**76.4**	**7.7**	**61.5**	**145.6**
General Education (Upto Secondary)												
Agriculture & Allied	58.9	0.8	27.9	87.6	20.3	0.3	9.8	30.4	79.1	1.1	37.8	118.0
Manufacturing	10.7	10.5	5.0	26.2	7.2	1.4	1.4	10.0	17.9	11.9	6.4	36.2
Non- Manufacturing	3.4	2.7	22.6	28.6	0.1	0.1	2.8	2.9	3.4	2.7	25.4	31.6
Services	31.7	18.4	5.1	55.2	3.3	4.0	0.7	8.0	35.0	22.4	5.8	63.1
Total	**104.6**	**32.3**	**60.6**	**197.5**	**30.9**	**5.8**	**14.6**	**51.3**	**135.5**	**38.1**	**75.3**	**248.9**
General Education (Higher Secondary)												
Agriculture & Allied	7.64	0.13	1.49	9.26	1.41	0.00	0.18	1.59	9.04	0.14	1.67	10.85
Manufacturing	1.31	1.93	0.30	3.53	0.57	0.22	0.05	0.84	1.89	2.15	0.34	4.37
Non- Manufacturing	0.44	0.48	1.17	2.09	0.00	0.02	0.07	0.09	0.44	0.50	1.23	2.18
Services	6.33	6.42	0.37	13.12	0.66	1.62	0.05	2.33	6.99	8.04	0.42	15.45
Total	**15.7**	**9.0**	**3.3**	**28.0**	**2.6**	**1.9**	**0.3**	**4.8**	**18.4**	**10.8**	**3.7**	**32.8**
General Education (Graduate & above)												
Agriculture & Allied	4.06	0.09	0.24	4.39	0.40	0.01	0.03	0.44	4.47	0.10	0.26	4.83
Manufacturing	1.01	1.75	0.06	2.81	0.23	0.18	0.01	0.42	1.24	1.92	0.07	3.23
Non- Manufacturing	0.35	0.56	0.32	1.23	0.02	0.06	0.03	0.10	0.37	0.61	0.35	1.34
Services	6.97	11.8	0.13	18.87	0.78	3.97	0.04	4.79	7.75	15.7	0.17	23.67
Total	**12.4**	**14.2**	**0.7**	**27.3**	**1.4**	**4.2**	**0.1**	**5.8**	**13.8**	**18.4**	**0.9**	**33.1**
Technical Education (Below Graduate)												
Agriculture & Allied	0.50	0.01	0.09	0.60	0.07	0.00	0.02	0.09	0.57	0.01	0.11	0.69
Manufacturing	0.14	1.61	0.11	1.86	0.05	0.06	0.01	0.12	0.19	1.67	0.12	1.98
Non- Manufacturing	0.16	0.49	0.13	0.78	0.00	0.03	0.01	0.04	0.16	0.52	0.14	0.82
Services	1.01	2.23	0.13	3.36	0.22	0.73	0.01	0.96	1.22	2.96	0.14	4.32
Total	**1.8**	**4.3**	**0.5**	**6.6**	**0.3**	**0.8**	**0.1**	**1.2**	**2.1**	**5.2**	**0.5**	**7.8**
Technical Education (Graduate & above)												
Agriculture & Allied	0.14	0.02	0.03	0.19	0.01	0.00	0.00	0.01	0.16	0.02	0.03	0.21
Manufacturing	0.10	0.75	0.02	0.86	0.01	0.03	0.00	0.04	0.11	0.78	0.02	0.90
Non- Manufacturing	0.08	0.24	0.02	0.34	0.00	0.03	0.00	0.03	0.08	0.27	0.02	0.37
Services	0.92	2.36	0.01	3.29	0.16	1.0	0.00	1.17	1.08	3.36	0.01	4.46
Total	**1.2**	**3.4**	**0.1**	**4.7**	**0.2**	**1.1**	**0.0**	**1.3**	**1.4**	**4.4**	**0.1**	**5.9**

Source: Author's estimates based on NSS unit level data

Note: Same as in Table 10.1.

The disconnect of the education system with agriculture is also evident from the two tables above. Of those with technical education – whether at diploma/certificate level or graduate level – very few work in the agriculture or allied sectors (forestry, fishery, horticulture, animal husbandry). This disconnect is especially manifest (and tragic) since the agricultural extension system in the country, which was responsible for the success of the green revolution in India in the 1970s and its spread in the 1980s, has all but collapsed in most states. Part of the problem may be that most of the higher education institutions are in urban areas, in fact concentrated in cities and towns. Settlement clusters with a population of more than 10 000 and less than 100 000 have very few institutions of higher education in their proximity (Planning Commission, 2013).

We turn now to examine the tertiary education system, and directly to issues of employability of its graduates.

Rapid Growth of Tertiary Education System

It has long been known that the rate of open unemployment of university graduates is greater than that of those with lower levels of education (*See* Table 10.3). This in itself is not surprising since those with lower levels of education cannot afford to be openly unemployed; they are often too poor to not work at all, and cannot rely upon the goodwill of the family/parents to keep body and soul together. Open unemployment rates are much lower for those with lower levels of education, even though they may be severely underemployed, working less than the full year. This rate of open unemployment of those with higher education does seem to be declining, according to the NSS (Employment-Unemployment Rounds of surveys), even though marginally.

Table 10.3: Incidence of Open Unemployment for 15 Years and Above Age Group, by Level of Education, 2004-05 and 2009-10 (UPSS)

Level of Education	*2004-05*	*2009-10*
Not Literate	0.3	0.3
Literate Without Formal Schooling	1.2	0.3
Below Primary	1.2	0.7
Primary	1.4	1.2
Middle	2.7	2.1
Secondary	4.8	2.7
Higher Secondary	6.4	5.2
Diploma / Certificate	10.4	9.6
Graduate	8.8	6.9
Post Graduate & Above	8.1	6.7
All Level of Education	2.3	2.0

Source: National Sample Survey 2004-05 and 2009-10.

Yet, GER in higher education has continued to rise. The number of government higher educational institutions grew from 6.4 million (2006-07) to 8.9 million (2011-12), an increase of 26 per cent. As much as 94 per cent of the government institutions in higher education are managed by the state governments (a serious challenge for the management capacity of State governments).

However, it is the private institutions which are growing faster than the government ones. Private ones accounted for 54 per cent of all institutions offering higher education in 2006-07, the remaining being government ones. The share of private ones had risen to 59 per cent by 2011-12 from 54 per cent in 2006-07, merely within five years. Their numbers grew from 7.5 to 12.8 million over the same period. But we also know that the capacity of both state and central governments to actually regulate private educational institutions is very limited, and there remain major issues with the quality of private higher education in the country (except in a miniscule minority of institutions). This is a foundational reason for employability being compromised.

Yet another reason for the concern over employability arises from the fields of study that students in higher education are enrolled in. Of the 13.8 million enrolled in 2006-07, 40 per cent were enrolled in Arts courses – raising a question about their employability in the first place. These are precisely the workers that we noted in Section 1 that are likely to end up in the unorganized segment employment in the services sector. An additional 18 per cent were studying the Sciences, 16 per cent were in Commerce and Management, and another 13 per cent were studying Engineering; these could be regarded as potentially more employable than at least the Arts graduates. The remainder (about 12 per cent or so) were spread, in descending order of their share between Education, Medicine/Nursing/Pharmacy, Law, with Agriculture/Veterinary bringing up the rear (with less than one per cent of enrolment) in a country where half of the workforce is still employed in agriculture. Even education and medicine/nursing/pharmacy are areas that are facing shortage of workers in the economy, but they account for a limited share of all students. It is difficult to assess whether this is more a problem of demand to studying such disciplines among students, or the seats available is well below demand. In any case, this is an aspect of the mismatch of skills that our employers are complaining about in respect of the education sector.

By 2011-12 the absolute numbers enrolled in Arts courses had increased by over a million, even though their share had dropped precipitously by 10 percentage points to 30 per cent of total enrolment. However, this lower share is still completely out of line with the requirements in the Arts. It is likely that these students are in higher education for no reason other than that they have few other choices. It is also likely that career counselling facilities for school leavers are very limited. It is also likely that in the absence of a formal Labour Market Information System (LMIS), the employers – both private as well as public – are still unable to send signals out to students graduating from higher secondary institutions as to which sectors need more workers. In the absence of a formal LMIS, student may register at Labour Exchanges (managed by the central government's Ministry of Labour), but such exchanges are mainly a place to direct those registered with them to government offices.

The drop in the share of Arts students (mentioned above) was almost entirely explained by the dramatic increase in the share of Engineering enrolment, which rose from 13 per cent to 25 per cent of total tertiary level enrolment in India. It is the absolute increase in Engineering students enrolled that is stunning: from 1.8 to 5.5 million between 2006-07 and 2011-12. For this reason the quality and employability of Engineering graduates will be a further subject of discussion we will pick up in this chapter. Since overall enrolment in higher education increased dramatically over the period, there were sharp increases in that five year period in other disciplines as well – science (from 25 to 30 million), education (from 6 to 13 million), commerce and management (from 23 to 34 million), medicine/nursing/pharmacy (6 to 12 million), but their relative shares in total enrolment did not change much. As noted earlier, most of the change in shares was on account of the decline in Arts and increase in Engineering.

A related fact that impacts the employability of higher education graduates is that the vast majority are studying in affiliated colleges, where the quality of education is a problem. The importance of such colleges is notable at all levels: while they enrol 87 per cent of all students in higher education, they enrol over 90 per cent of undergraduate students, over 70 per cent of the postgraduates, and even 17 per cent of doctoral students are enrolled in colleges. In other words, if there are issues around the employability of higher education graduates, it is because the quality of the majority of affiliated colleges is abysmal. This fact must be read along with the fact noted earlier that private institutions have seen a phenomenal growth in numbers between 2006-07 and 2011-12 from 7.5 to 12.8 million, increasing their share to nearly 60 per cent of all students enrolled in higher education. In other words, a very high share of the increase in enrolment in higher education in recent years is in *colleges* that are run by *private bodies.* This increase in enrolment is obviously an indication of the rising demand for higher education, driven in turn by the sharp growth in school education. However, the 'diploma disease' (a term coined by Ronald Dore, 1976) is also probably behind the rise in higher education enrolment, in the sense that there are not enough vocational courses for those nearing completion of school education so that they continue in general academic courses at tertiary level for want of an alternative. White collar jobs in any case are neither available to any student with less than a university education nor are government jobs available for less than a university education, and even though government jobs are not growing (Mehrotra *et al*, 2012), the diploma disease is partly driven by the desire to get a government job.

Underlying Causes of the Problem of Employability

We should begin by noting that the fast enrolment growth alone is not responsible for the problems of quality and employability of Indian graduates of higher education. There were pre-existing problems in the system that have only become bigger in magnitude with the sharp increase in enrolment since the middle of the last decade.

One pre-existing problem was the 'diploma disease' that already existed. Students continued into first secondary, then senior secondary, and then in turn to higher education for no reason other than that there were few alternatives. In a slowly growing economy until the 1980s, with two-thirds of employment still accounted for by agriculture, and with few institutions of higher education in rural areas, the 'urban bias' in terms of the locational concentration of higher education institutions in urban areas was quite prominent. With non-agricultural employment not growing very much outside of the public sector, the focus of those who acquired higher education in an earlier era was to obtain a government job. However, as we noted earlier, government jobs grew very slowly in the 1990s and then actually declined in absolute terms in the 2000s (Mehrotra *et al.*, 2012).

Why the Pressure of Numbers Grew upon the Higher Education System

Until the end of the 1980s the school education system was narrowly based, and so was the higher education system. The Central Government increased allocations significantly to school education from the early 1990s (the District Primary Education Programme began), supported with large bilateral and multilateral assistance. External assistance began for the first time in India's education sector's history only in the early 1990s (Mehrotra *et al*, 2005). With net primary enrolment rates increasing to 96 per cent by 2007, the pressure on higher levels of the school system, and hence on higher education only increased. As we will discuss below, the system was not prepared for such massive pressure on the higher education infrastructure and human resources, especially at a time when the focus of government spending had shifted to expand access to schooling to universalize elementary education (witness the Sarva Shiksha Abhiyaan, SSA, in the 10th Five Year Plan), and accordingly the secondary system (the Rashtriya Madhyamik Shiksha Abhiyan followed in the 11th Plan). It was only during the 11th Five Year Plan (2007-12) that there was an attempt to increase public allocations to higher education (from about Rs 18,000 crore during the 10th Plan period to Rs 90,000 crore during the 11th Plan period, not all of which could actually materialise due to the fiscal constraints imposed by the sudden onset of the global economic crisis and its aftermath on India from late 2008).

Thus the first reason for poor quality in higher education is the upward pressure from larger and larger numbers finishing school resulting from government efforts to universalise elementary education, especially after the Right to Education Act in 2009. The second reason for the upward pressure arose from the deliberate effort to increase female enrolment, though that effort was concentrated at increasing transition rates of girls from elementary to secondary education. Almost all states provided bicycles/cash transfers to enable households to purchase cycles to encourage girls to continue into secondary schooling, after completing 8 years of elementary school. Although in 2007-08 the Gross Attendance Ratio at higher secondary level for girls and boys was the same in urban areas (30.5 for females and 29.6 for males), this share may well increase significantly as the incentives for girls' continuation into secondary school (that started only in the late 2000s) affects the cohorts that would now be entering higher education.

A third source of increase in demand for higher education arose from the labour market. Economic growth between 2003-04 and 2011-12 averaged an unprecedented 8.4 per cent per annum, driven by manufacturing, infrastructure and services. Concomitantly, there has been a Lewisian shift in the labour market since 2004-05 onwards. There has always been a decline in the share of workers in agriculture, but the total workforce in absolute terms was always growing in agriculture until 2004-5. After that, for the first time in the history of the Indian economy, there has been an absolute decline in the number of workers in agriculture, with workers moving to construction, manufacturing and services. Even though the employment elasticity of manufacturing has not been high, non-agricultural employment has grown significantly with faster GDP growth (Mehrotra *et al*, 2014). The economy created on average 7.5 million non-agricultural jobs between 2004-05 and 2011-12, though much more in construction (which benefitted unskilled and mostly ill-educated workers leaving agriculture) and services, than in manufacturing. However, organised sector jobs, especially regular jobs, grew in absolute and relative terms.

Naturally, the demand for skilled workers has grown in all services and manufacturing, though the demand for unskilled and semi-skilled workers has grown faster, as the fastest growth in non-agricultural employment has been in construction.

Reasons for the Quality Problems that Led to Issues of Employability

(a) *Teacher and instructor shortages:* One of the most serious problems that arose with rapid expansion of the higher education system – in fact its 'massification' – is the shortage of teachers. The Planning Commission estimates (2013) that a doubling of faculty from the current 800,000 to 1.6 million is required during the period 2012-17. A study of higher education salaries across 28 countries shows that Indian university faculty salaries are among the highest in the world (on a purchasing power parity basis). Hence, the demand for teachers may not be a problem, but it is finding teachers for general academic education with the requisite skills that is going to remain a problem, especially at senior levels (above the Assistant Professor level).

The most serious problem is finding teachers/instructors for vocational education courses (polytechnics, Industrial Training Institutes and vocational education in secondary schools), and engineering colleges that have grown dramatically in number, and especially teachers who have some practical industry or work exposure.

(b) *Private sector growth with little regulation affected quality:* We have noted in the previous section that private sector enrolment in higher education already accounted in 2006-7 for 54 per cent of total enrolment, and it had grown to 59 per cent, even while the public sector enrolment also increased in absolute terms. Private universities may cost nearly 3-4 times of public university fees, but the rise in costs may not be to a proportional increase in quality and graduate outcomes. However, private expansion has happened without commensurate growth in capacity or even willingness of the state to monitor outcomes or put in regulatory frameworks.

Typical of this situation is the growth in engineering colleges acroreoss the country, but especially in south India. The political class as well as the builder-developer entrepreneurs have contributed to a growth in engineering enrolment by 25 per cent between 2006-07 and 2011-12, much higher than in any discipline. As noted earlier, in absolute terms it led to engineering enrolment growing from 1.8 million to 5.5 million, a tripling in five years, thus contributing a massive 60 per cent of the total growth in higher education enrolment in India.

The regulatory capacity and integrity of the staff of All-India Council for Technical Education (AICTE), the body charged with the responsibility to regulate higher technical education in India, was highly questionable. In fact, in 2008-09 as many as 20 senior staff of the one regulatory body in the field of technical education (the equivalent body to the University Grants Commission meant to regulate universities) had police first information reports against them, and seven of the senior most staff, including the erstwhile chairman of AICTE, were actually in jail – all charged with corruption in the approval to create new colleges, given the discretion that AICTE enjoyed in granting approval. The end result of this process was that faculty from engineering colleges, who were the ones who normally staffed senior positions in AICTE, began to shy away from coming on deputation to AICTE. Its staff capacity, limited as it was even earlier, was further eroded as a result. However, despite this situation prevailing for several years following 2008-09, the AICTE continued to approve new colleges. The political pressure to open new engineering colleges – coming as it does from politically connected business or politicians themselves standing to gain from converting their unaccounted for money into 'white' – has been unrelenting.

India's Supreme Court, slowly realised the growing menace of capitation fees and the failure of existing legislative and regulatory mechanisms to take strict action against erring institutions. Such institutions have over a period of time perfected the professional college admission system into process akin to the stock market. "Highest bidder is the ultimate buyer." In April 2013, the Supreme Court delivered a major judgement, making AICTE into a mere advisory body, removing from it its power of approval of technical colleges. However, the judgement also handed over the powers of regulation to UGC, which had even less capacity to regulate, burdened as it is to manage a growing number of central and state universities. As a result, the Supreme Court, in a revised judgement restored the powers of approval to AICTE in April 2014, but the ability and willingness of AICTE to regulate remains highly questionable.

Unfortunately, the UGC too faces problems normal to a bureaucracy in India, made difficult by a situation in which government institutions at tertiary level have grown from 6.33 to 8.9 million between 2006-07 and 2011-12. central government institutions (central universities, IITs, IIMs, IISERs, Schools of Planning and Architecture, National Institutes of Technology, and other technical institutions and other universities) have grown, but they still account for barely 5 per cent of all government institutions at tertiary level. The remainder are all managed by state governments, and their governance capabilities will have to be strengthened enormously before the state-level institutions of higher learning could be better regulated and monitored.

(c) *Accreditation system has a very narrow coverage:* Although institutional accreditation through the National Assessment and Accreditation Council (an autonomous body funded by UGC, created in 1994 in Bangalore) has been growing, at present in India, accreditation is voluntary for higher education institutions. Out of 612 universities in the country, only 172 of them have been accredited by the National Assessment and Accreditation Council (NAAC). Out of the universities accredited, 67 have been placed in Grade A, 99 universities in Grade B and only 6 in Grade C, based on scores awarded during the process of accreditation. Only about one-fifth (4529 out of 22, 500) eligible colleges, where the majority of tertiary education students are enrolled, have been accredited (Planning Commission 2013). A bill — National Accreditation Regulatory Authority for Higher Educational Institutions Bill, 2010 — was introduced in Parliament to make it mandatory for every higher educational institution in the country (other than institutions engaged in agricultural education) to be accredited by an independent accreditation agency; however, like so many bills of the Ministry of Higher Education, it has been hanging fire for the last several years.

(d) *Skewed funding of public institutions:* First, household spending and private investment have grown more rapidly than government spending on higher education in recent years. Second, "government spending, and particularly state government spending, has fallen far short of the funding requirement in the face of a dramatic expansion of the system and the rising expectations of the people in terms of quality, access and equity" (Planning Commission, 2013: 118). The central government's share is about 30 per cent, while the state governments spend the remainder 70 per cent, most of it under the non-plan category. The latter category is mostly absorbed by salaries of teaching and non-teaching staff, leaving very little for capital investment or development work. The third source of difficulty of public higher education institutions is that half of the central plan funds (Rs 20,630 crore) went to central institutions (which enrol, as we noted above, only 5 per cent of all students of higher education), with state universities, colleges and polytechnics receiving about Rs 10,450 crore. Moreover, central institutions received about Rs 25,000 crore as non-plan grants during 2007-12 (the 11th Plan), but state institutions received no non-plan grants. In sum, the state universities, colleges and polytechnics, enrolling 95 per cent of all tertiary education students in the country, remain severely underfunded. Quality is bound to be affected in publicly-funded higher education institutions as a result, and hence the employability of their graduates.

(e) *Quality of technical and vocational students and courses poor:* There are two sets of problems afflicting technical and vocational education (TVE) programmes at tertiary level. We will discuss the quality and employability of engineers, who are in the Degree programmes, that account for most (85 per cent) of total tertiary technical enrolment (or 18.4 million), separately later. The remaining 15 per cent of tertiary enrolment (or 3.3 million) in technical education is in Diploma programmes. The latter can offer employability almost immediately, provided they are in the trades/disciplines that are in demand, and are of requisite quality, based on industry requirements in respect of standards and competencies. However, their enrolment level, especially in Polytechnics is very low, partly because the number of polytechnics itself is very low relative to need.

Polytechnics in the country offer three year generalised diploma courses in conventional subjects such as civil, electrical and mechanical engineering. The courses are now diversified to include electronics, computer science, medical lab technology, and hospital engineering. Women's Polytechnics offer courses in garment technology, beauty culture, textile design, and library science. There are 1,292 polytechnics under the aegis of the Ministry of Human Resource Development with a capacity of over 2.95 lakh offering three-year diploma courses in various branches of engineering with an entry qualification of 10th pass. Besides, there are 415 institutions providing a diploma in pharmacy, and 63 for hotel management, and 25 for architecture.

The number of polytechnics increased slowly from 1,203 in 2001-02 to 1,266 in 2005-06 with corresponding rise in intake from 2.36 lakh to 2.65 lakh. The proportion of polytechnics is high in the southern states (46 per cent). Further, the proportion of public sector institutions at degree level in the country is only around 20 per cent, the remainder being in the private sector. On the other hand around 80 per cent of diploma level institutions are in public sector. At the beginning of the 11th Plan period (2007-12) 125 districts (of India's 641 districts) did not have even a single polytechnic. Over the years, the diploma courses have lost the skill components and are perceived as diluted version of degree education. The government faces many challenges in respect of polytechnics: static curricula, poor industry interface, lack of flexibility to respond to needs, obsolescence of equipment, lack of trainers, and inadequate funding.

In the old economy, skill development largely meant development of shop floor or manual skills. Even in this area, there are major deficiencies in our workforce which need to be rectified. In the new or knowledge economy, the skill sets include professional, conceptual, managerial, operational, and behavioural ones (interpersonal skills and inter-domain skills). In the twenty first century, with greater intra-industry trade and integration of economies across border, knowledge domains and skill domains also multiply and become more and more complex. Neither our engineering degree colleges nor our diploma-awarding polytechnics are equipped to offer skills for the new economy.

During the 11th Plan period, there was a sharp expansion in the AICTE approved institutions. In addition to the unprecedented expansion in the numbers of the premier centrally-funded technical institutions like IITs, IIM, NITs, IISERs etc. the number of AICTE approved institutions in the country during the period of the 11th Plan (2007-12) almost doubled. They rose from 4,491 in 2006-07 to 8,361 in 2011-12 and annual intake went up from 907,822 in 2007-08 to 2,046,611 in 2011-12. Similarly, number of polytechnics increased with corresponding rise in intake from 417,923 in 2007-08 and 1,083,365 in 2010-11. This is not surprising as of the 11th plan outlay of Rs. 84,943 crore for the Department of Higher Education, Rs. 27,334 crore was earmarked for Technical Education out of which the actual expenditure up to 2010-11 was 89 per cent (11th Working Group report, Planning Commission).

Community Polytechnics (CP) are wings of the existing polytechnics intended to provide a platform for transfer of appropriate technologies to rural masses and to provide technical support and services to the local community. At present, there are 669 CPs in the country. During the Tenth Plan period, about 13 lakh persons had been trained in them in various job-oriented non-formal skills/trades.

To summarise this discussion on technical tertiary education, the poor quality of technical education, a bulk of which falls under the states and mainly in the private sector, is due to the poor governance structure, unqualified faculty, absence of research and industry interface and low finances. There is great need to strengthen State level technical institutions which constitute nearly 90 per cent of the technical education sector. A total number of 3,241 engineering institutions exist in India out of which more than 90 per cent are private unaided institutions (PUIs). These have remained very poorly regulated.

Improving Employability of Graduates of Tertiary Education: What can be Done?

Drawing upon the preceding analysis, we present in this final section some policy implications. These relate to focussing explicitly on employability in future actions related to higher education, both in the general academic education sphere as well as the technical education sphere. We discuss each in turn in this final section.

a. Tightening Entry into General Academic Education at Tertiary Levels, and Utilising Colleges Differently

We have seen in the previous section that despite the fall in the share of Arts students in total enrolment in higher education from 40 per cent in 2006-07 to 30 per cent in 2011-12, their absolute numbers increased (from 5.5 to 6.6 million). These students are unlikely to be much in demand in the labour market in an economy that is diversifying its product and services mix rapidly. The vast majority of these students are enrolled in the affiliated colleges (which enrol 87 per cent of all students in higher education), mostly in the private sector. When they get jobs, they are likely to be in low-productivity service sectors, mostly in its unorganised segment, ill-equipped to obtain positions in any job-role other than sales/marketing. There is no case for any further growth in such courses or students.

The central government would need to take a firm position that these colleges should curtail admission of more students, and they could be incentivised by being partly financially compensated for admitting in the second shift vocational course students.[2] This can become a way of ensuring that the Community College (CC) idea that the 12th Plan is propagating is given an appropriate home. A framework for setting up CCs based on the North American model has been endorsed by the Central Advisory Board on Education. CCs already exist: 336 of them in 17 states, and receive technical support from a Jesuit organization (Indian Centre for Research and Development of Community Education, Chennai). The 12th Plan speaks of the need to take technical support of this organization to build on the current initiatives to create a robust framework for skill-based education in higher education (Planning Commission 2013).

b. Expanding Community Colleges

Community Colleges (CCs) can provide modular credit-based courses with entry and exit flexibility that conforms to the National Skills Qualification Framework (NSQF) that was notified by the central government in December 2013. They will offer programmes leading to certificates (after one year), diplomas or associate degrees (after two years) with options to transfer to regular degree programmes.

The 12th Plan notes (Planning Commission, 2013) that their curricula will include an appropriate mix of academic and vocational skills and will be in line with national occupation standards, determined by employer-led Sector Skill Councils. Assessment of vocational skills and training provided by community colleges will be done in accordance with assessment protocols developed by Sector Skill Councils. Their faculty will typically consist of a permanent core, who will teach fundamentals (language, mathematics, science) and a large pool of adjunct or part time faculty, enabling specialisation. Online courses would be integrated with face to face instruction to enhance quality. As regards location, they could be established in the premises of the existing colleges, polytechnics or even higher secondary schools, and use online training and industry sites, wherever possible.

Community colleges can "provide career oriented education and skills to students; contracted training programme for local employers; and remedial education for secondary school graduates not ready to enrol in traditional colleges, giving them a path to transfer to 3 or 4 year institution." Such colleges could be established as affiliated colleges of universities governed, guided and managed by the newly created Ministry of Skills and Entrepreneurship in the Central government or autonomous institutions connected to Sector Skills Council (Planning Commission, 2013).

c. *Improving Employability of General Academic Students in Tertiary Education*

To improve the employability of graduates of general academic higher education or technical education at least 5 kinds of actions are necessary: improving soft skills, offering internship to students, updating curriculum, better regulation of private providers, and getting industries to provide teachers and instructor.

First, *soft skills are missing* in graduates both of general academic as well as technical degrees. Aspiring Minds, a consultancy firm, conducted an employability study of 40,000 Indian technical graduates. It tested English communication, quantitative skills, problem solving skills, and programming skills. It was found that in high growth factors, such as business process outsourcing, employability of university graduates was only 38 per cent. There was also a difference in quality of graduates between the top tier and lower tier schools, making it 2 or 3 times harder in terms of cost and effort to identify an employable graduate from a normal campus compared to reputed colleges, for example, Indian Institute of Technology.

Second, students need to experience work environments, through *internships*. Indian university or technical education students lack exposure to work while studying. In mature labour markets practical experience in work through internships is common. This normally involves active collaboration between career offices in university on the one hand and public and private organisations on the other. This required proactive behaviour on the part of the university as well as industries. There are many good examples of this happening in private universities. The Hero group, for example, a motorcycle manufacturer, has made large investments to set up a new university in Gurgaon, focussed on practical oriented education to improve employability. Similarly one of India's largest software company, Infosys, have set up a large university university-like campus in Mysore and also one on its campus in Bangalore and elsewhere, where they conduct training on a very large scale

Outdated curriculum also needs to be updated and connected to labour market needs. But labour market surveys of the National Sample Survey Organisation happen only once in 5 years. In any case, they are not of the kind that can serve as any guidance to potential students, trainees or student work counselors. The Annual Survey of Industries, although conducted every year, is very narrow in scope, confined as it is to a section of organised industry. Similarly, graduate employability studies are rarely conducted and this makes any kind of evidence based curriculum revamp very difficult. Moreover with most employment being in the informal sector it becomes difficult to collect information, which makes taking data-driven decisions even more difficult.

Accreditation. If more and more university and technical education is being delivered by private providers it is very important to have a stronger accreditation framework. Regulation and monitoring of universities is governed by the UGC and technical education by the AICTE. These bodies lack the capacity to implement monitoring standards. Surprisingly a very small proportion of all universities and colleges have been accredited in India.

*Lack of teachers. I*ndustry associations and industry bodies must be willing and able to provide teachers and instructors. India's IT industry body, the National Association of Software and Services Companies (NASSCOM) set up the Sector Skills Council and launched the Foundation for Skills in Integrated Product Development Programme at 15 Indian colleges. The programme outlines curriculum for course ware and incorporates an internship programme that will help to make students more employable.

d. Rising Number of Girls Need More Vocational Courses at School and Tertiary Level

We have noted in the previous section that enrolment of girls has been growing at secondary level at an increasing pace. Vocational courses at secondary and tertiary level are not available which are expected by girls and their parents and which are consistent with cultural norms. Girls are less likely to work in construction activity, where jobs are growing the fastest. They are also less likely to be found in manufacturing. However, the services sector is different. Nevertheless, there is a possibility that girls acquiring secondary/higher secondary education may not be able to enter the formal labour market, if either service sector jobs are not growing commensurate with the supply of labour, and/or vocational education or training is not available in the vicinity of their homes for girls. In that situation, the labour force participation rate of women which are already low in India may not rise (Mehrotra and Sinha, forthcoming). Female labour force participation and employability will rise only if the courses that are available suit the girls' requirements, i.e., the requirements of first time secondary education graduates. They will prefer to enter modern services like organised retail, BPO, computing and personal beauty services. If appropriate courses are not available in the vicinity of where these first time graduates live, the possibility that their parents will allow them to undergo further education or to take up jobs in the formal labour market is undermined. We would, therefore, argue strongly for a rapid expansion of vocational education at both secondary as well as higher secondary levels, where service sector skills can be imparted with industry participation in the vocational courses. However, this also means that the number of polytechnics will need to increase sharply, and upward educational pathways in the form of admissions to polytechnics must be made facilitated (through a certain percentage of reserved seats) for higher secondary/ secondary graduates of vocational courses.

The GDP growth rate can be enhanced by 2 percentage points a year by raising the female labour force participation rate by pro-women and job-enhancing policies (OECD, 2014).

e. Technical Tertiary Education: Improving Employability

We have discussed above the issues with the employability of those graduating from technical education (whether at degree or diploma level) due to the quality of education imparted. In response, in 2002-03, the Government of India with financial assistance from the World Bank launched a Technical Education Quality Improvement Programme (TEQIP) as a long-term programme of 10-12 years implemented in three phases, for systemic transformation of the technical education system. The first phase of TEQIP (2003-09), covered 127 institutions (including 22 private unaided institutions (PUI)). The second Phase of TEQIP (TEQIP-II) covered around 200 institutions.

Based on the need to improve quality of engineering education in private unaided institutions, MHRD proposes a parallel project, TEQIP-III, solely for PUIs, aimed at improvement in the quality of faculty and strengthening institutions. The programme will also focus on pedagogical training of faculty for effective teaching; and enhancing institutional and system management effectiveness.

Finding the Faculty for Engineering Colleges and Polytechnics

Due to the shortage of faculty, many engineering colleges are forced to recruit fresh engineering graduates as teachers. These fresh recruits need training in pedagogy as well as knowledge upgradation. The existing institutions that can impart training are limited. Also, it is not feasible for the college to release these teachers for undergoing training. The plan is to set up a new part-time Masters' degree in Engineering Education to be conducted by the IITs. The degree, designed for faculty from engineering colleges will be conducted online, through live video lectures using the NKN, thus eliminating the need for participants to be relieved of normal teaching duties. It is estimated that 7000 young faculty can be trained each year. Approximately 1500 faculty from IITs and other institutions will teach the courses in the evening and weekends. IIT faculty will also be able to identify and motivate many of these young candidates to carry on a Ph.D. programme. It is aimed to train approximately 30,000 college-faculties in the 12th plan in this manner and another 30,000 to 40,000 in the 13th Plan.

Another proposal would be to introduce a new three year programme leading to a Dual Masters Degree, i.e. an M. Tech degree in the domain area and a Masters degree in Educational Skills and Pedagogy.

Addressing the Capitation Fees Extortion

It is necessary to provide adequate financial support to ensure quality. AICTE must compute and publish realistic costs of engineering education (both capital and operating expenditure) and arrive at benchmark figures for fees in private colleges. Mechanisms of incentivising State engineering institutions on the lines of upgrading Regional Engineering Colleges to NITs or the process adopted by TEQIP to fund institutions must be adopted for all technical institutions including private ones.

Need for More New Technical Education Institutions

During the 11h Plan, 20 IITs and 300 new polytechnics were proposed through the PPP mode and private sector participation. Both these schemes could not take off due to poor response from the private sector. The resource limitations of the Government necessitate funds and investments from the private industry in the Higher Education sector and more so in technical institutions where the viability is more certain. By making necessary changes in the above schemes, it is hoped that during the XII Plan, greater private sector investment will be created.

Teacher Training

National Council on Teacher Education should revise teacher education syllabi to include a separate paper on VE in B. Ed. & M. Ed. programmes for teacher preparation. Further, B. Ed. (Voc.) programmes may be expanded and strengthened. Students of B. Ed. and M. Ed. programme will be given hands-on practice through internship programme in work place/industry.

The teachers who will teach the expanded vocational education programme (*See* discussion below) also need training. A component of induction and in service training is inbuilt in the revised scheme of Vocationalisation of Secondary Education. An induction training of 30 days duration will be organised by the State Coordination Cell for VE or District Education Office for all vocational teachers. Regular in-service teacher training programmes of 7 to 10 days on pedagogy, subject content and other related aspects of VE should be organised for all teachers every year.

Vocational Education in Schools

In addition to the above MHRD has launched the National Skills Qualifications Framework (NSQF) which is the proposed overarching academic architecture for vocational education in the country (*See* Mehrotra, 2015, for an extended discussion). A unified mapping of Class 9 to 12 and up to level 7 (Bachelors in Vocational Education) has been done and a detailed scheme drawn up for strengthening skills and developing vocational education by involving CBSE/State Boards, Technical Education Boards, Universities and National Skill Development Corporation and industry. The idle infrastructure of existing institutions and buildings could be utilised for speedy implementation. These vocational courses would have a component of general education also which would facilitate mobility into and from mainstream education. Also, being modular in nature it would provide multiple entry and exit options to the students. The National Occupation Standards being created by NSDC are intended to drive the competency-based curriculum preparation for skill development in the country, with the involvement of industry.

NSQF levels 1-2 will prepare students for the work environment, generic competencies, understanding career options and pathways and develop positive attitude towards life, work and further education. National Certificate for Work Preparation 1 (NCWP 1) will be issued to those who have cleared NVEQ level 1, which would be equivalent to Class 9, opting for vocational course units along with general subjects. The National Certificate for Work Preparation 2 (NCWP 2) will be issued to those who have cleared NVEQ level 2, which will be equivalent to Class 10, again with a combination of general subjects and vocational course units.

During discussions on the NSQF strategy, it has been felt that the exit levels into the workplace would be trade specific. Some sectors like IT may not have a requirement of level 2 competency, but others, say retail, may employ youth after level 2 also. These would be guided by the NOS being developed for different sectors. These exit points would be useful not only for the students in the formal schooling, but also draw back school drop outs for achieving requisite levels of competency to enhance their employability. At the same time they could receive a school certificate also.

The experience gained from the pilots of NSQF in Class 9 in Haryana and West Bengal will enable firming up the curriculum and courses in vocational education. The pilots have a provision of offering vocational courses both as an additional subject and in substitution.

Learners will be able to acquire vocational qualifications in a particular occupation from level 3 onwards, i.e., Class XI and subsequently upgrade their qualifications through gradual acquisition of competencies.

Sector Skill Councils will determine the minimum levels of competencies prescribed for that NSQF level. For children seeking entry into level 1 of the NSQF, this process will be in compliance with the Right to Education Act, 2009. If there are "competency gaps" identified in a candidate, then the candidate will have to undertake the required units through a "bridge course" to acquire those competencies. Academic qualifications would be assessed and certified by educational bodies and NSQF would be assessed and certified by respective Sector Skill Councils.

Concluding Remarks

This paper began by mapping the educational level of different segments of the workforce, and identified a number of profoundly troubling trends. The massification of higher education, following the rapid growth of school education has caused a precipitous fall in the quality and employability of tertiary education graduates in India. The paper went on to analyse the reasons for this decline in quality and employability in general academic as well as vocational/technical education.

We identified the following priority actions that governments need to focus on. First, there is need for tightening entry into general academic education at tertiary levels, and utilising affiliated colleges differently. Secondly, there is a strong case for expanding community colleges, so that those entering post-secondary education are prepared for the world of work. Thirdly, we made a series of suggestions for improving the employability of students attending the general academic tertiary courses, who form the majority. Fourth, there is a great need to create the enabling environment in higher education for greater womens' participation, so that women who wish to join the labour force do not find their education or training wanting. India has one of the lowest female labour force participation rates, and a rising female labour force participation has intrinsic value in empowering women; it also has the potential of raising the growth rate of the economy. Finally, we make a series of suggestions to ensure that growth in a rapidly diversifying economy and the development of a knowledge economy is not held back by the poor quality and employability of technical education graduates.

Notes

1. The rate of unemployment of those with graduate general academic education is only slightly lower at 7.3 per cent than for those with technical education below or at graduate level (8.8 per cent).
2. The central government can incentivise this action in central universities, while the central government's fund allocation to state universities can be used for this purpose to ensure effective action at state level as well.

References

Dore, Ronald (1976): *The Diploma Disease: Education, Qualification and Development*, London: George Allen & Unwin.

Mehrotra, Santosh (Ed.) (2014): *India's Skills Challenge. Reforming Vocational Education and Training to Harness the Demographic Dividend*, New Delhi: Oxford University Press.

Mehrotra, Santosh (2015): *Seizing the Demographic Dividend. Policies to Achieve Inclusive Growth in India*, New Delhi: Cambridge University Press.

Mehrotra. Santosh; Parida, J.; Sinha, S. and Gandhi, A. (2014): Explaining Employment Trends in India, 1993-2012, *Economic and Political Weekly,*49 (32)

Mehrotra, Santosh; Sahoo, B.K.; Saha, Partha and Gandhi, A. (2012): Creating Employment in the 12th Five Year Plan, *Economic and Political Weekly,* 48 (19).

Mehrotra, Santosh and Sinha, S. (forthcoming): Why the Labour Force Participation of Women has been Falling?, *International Journal of Human Development and Capabilities.*

OECD (2014): *India: Economic Survey 2014,* Paris: Organisation for Economic Cooperation and Development.

Planning Commission (2008), The 11th Five Year Plan. Towards Faster and More Inclusive Growth, New Delhi: Sage Publication.

Planning Commission (2013): The 12th Five Year Plan. Faster, More Inclusive and Sustainable Growth, New Delhi: Oxford University Press.

11

Medical Education, Inclusiveness, Democracy and Development in Contemporary India

Roger Jeffery

Amongst the flurry of articles published in connection with the centenary of Abraham Flexner's 1910 report on medical education in the USA (Flexner, 1910) was an article that suggested that the situation in South Asia today is not so different from what Flexner described: medical colleges being established rapidly, by private entrepreneurs, neither always where there were adequate clinical facilities for student learning, nor universities to ensure academic oversight.

As in Flexner's United States, competition in South Asia for students' fees and an ineffectual accreditation process have resulted in questionable admission practices, stagnant curricula, antiquated learning methods, and dubious assessment practices. Accreditation systems, which were weak in nineteenth century America, are constrained in much of Asia by a combination of inadequate authority, insufficient resources, uneven enforcement, and occasional corruption (Amin *et al.* 2010: 333).

As all historians of American medicine have demonstrated, the reforms initiated after Flexner's Report radically reduced the numbers of places where medicine was taught, cut the numbers entering into medical education, provided monopoly powers to the nascent medical profession and helped create closer connections between medicine and science – as well as delivering much higher incomes to American doctors, and at best a second-class public health service.

There are, of course, many differences between the USA in 1910 and India in 2010. Insofar as services for the poor are concerned, for example, recent evidence affirms that the poor in many, if not most, parts of India do not find it difficult to reach a medical practitioner: in some surveys, they visit doctors more than do the rich (Das 2012: 454). The poor are, in practice, excluded from an achievable quality of medical care because the doctors available to them practice medicine so incompetently. The supposed democratic remedy to this situation – the provision of good quality, publicly-funded medical personnel – is working, if at all, only in a few of India's states. Furthermore, India's low level of investment in health care of all kinds – not just public health but also in medical care – is holding back its development at the same time as its economic growth is accelerating.

Medical education in India is, then, in dire need of reform. Two obvious challenges are, firstly, to raise the level of medical knowledge among medical graduates, and secondly, to increase the chances that this knowledge will be appropriately used. Outside a relatively small set of institutions, once these new doctors begin to practice they are likely to set aside much of what they know about 'good' medical practice, in the need to survive in a highly competitive market – whether this be the over-prescribing of antibiotics by doctors in small local clinics or the excessive prescribing of tests and interventions by those beholden to the large corporate hospital chains. A third issue, of how doctors already in practice – whether qualified or not – could have their competence checked regularly and raised by continuing professional education so that their everyday practice is made safer and more effective, is beyond the scope of this paper. What I argue here is the following:

The net effects of the outcomes of political processes surrounding these processes in India have rarely been conducive to increasing inclusivity, deepening democracy or accelerating development in India; and because history, global political economy and local politics matter, the chances for a major reorientation of medical education to achieve even some of these goals look to be highly unlikely.

Theoretical Context

Using education to enhance democracy, and ensuring democratic oversight of education, are usually understood as issues surrounding school education, which is expected to produce citizens for democracy; engagement with politics in positive, ethically acceptable ways, such as voting; involvement with civil society organisations to press social change; opposition to non-democratic ways of functioning, whether in formal politics or in other spheres of life. Good citizens are also expected to mobilise against threats to democracy, whether from the military or from within institutions, such as corrupt practices in elections or afterwards, on the part of those entrusted with the responsibility of ensuring due process and proper functioning of key social institutions such as colleges, professional associations or regulatory authorities. But medical education, like other forms of higher education, can also contribute to or hinder the creation of such citizens, and can be overseen through democratic or authoritarian processes. The principles of equality, liberty and justice – contested from different sides – seem to be directly related to development. How they play out in different historical transitions to local forms of modernity and development – and the role played by education in them – vary across nations.[1]

What kind of relationship might there be between higher education – in this case, specifically medical education – and democracy? Does it matter if institutions of higher education have not achieved a critical stage of knowledge generation? What happens if private capital plays an increasingly dominant role in an educational sphere apparently as important for the nation's health as medical colleges?

Because of doctors' symbolic significance in society – their roles at the critical times of birth, illness and death – expectations of how they should support social goals are much higher than for other skilled workers. Doctors sometimes object to these expectations: why, they ask, should they be expected to work in rural areas, at all hours or for restricted pay – unlike architects, engineers, IT specialists or economists, for example. But how they should be trained, employed, paid, and regulated, and what kinds of relationships they should be encouraged to develop with their peers, with other health workers, with patients and with the State, in a democratic society, remain highly contentious.

Clearly, very different arrangements for all these things are compatible with representative democracy, as it is found across the world, and as both have changed through time. In the UK, Reform Acts began to establish a real (though still far from universal adult) electorate from the middle of the nineteenth century, around the same time as the General Medical Council (GMC) was created and the British Medical Association was institutionalised as a superior form of Trades Union. At that point, doctors were mostly individual practitioners, like members of other liberal professions. The deepening of democracy – the move from civil, political, and to social citizenship, as T.H. Marshall described the process – went hand in hand with the rise of state-backed medical insurance, hospital medicine, and finally a National Health Service with most of the incomes of doctors provided by the State (Marshall 1963). Similar processes elsewhere in northern Europe were not matched in the USA, however. In Nazi Germany and Fascist Italy, professional associations of all kinds – of lawyers as well as doctors, for example – were subordinated to serve the interests of the ruling party, especially, in Germany, with respect to the hounding out of Jewish doctors. In the USSR, and in Communist China, independent medical professional associations were prevented from developing, as part of more general restraints on the right to organise or associate except as part of state-sponsored activities.

In colonial India, when the basic framework of regulating doctors was established, the Indian Medical Council (IMC) was established with strong official leadership. Its main purpose was less to ensure a strong medical profession in India than to appease and support the interests of the GMC in London and of British doctors more generally, by controlling the numbers of doctors entitled to work in the UK and in the Indian Medical Service (IMS) (Jeffery, 1979). Doctors in government employment were effectively forbidden from joining the Indian Medical Association (IMA), as soon as it began to ally itself with nationalist struggles (Jeffery, 1988). Post-colonial regulation of doctors has continued along similar lines. The Medical Council of India (MCI, which replaced the IMC in 1956) is still a highly bureaucratic body, with intensely politicised contests over the elected positions, and the IMA is largely the preserve of general practitioners and the owners and managers of small nursing homes and hospitals.[2]

So, while bourgeois liberal democracy is compatible with a wide range of forms of health provision, and of 'professional' activities and protections on behalf of doctors, authoritarian regimes and dictatorships of various kinds find it hard to tolerate independent professional associations. There is, then, a generally positive relationship between the professional bodies of doctors as civil society organisations, and democratic processes and institutions.

The issue for medical educators wishing to help doctors play their part in democracy is how medical education should be organised to promote democratic values. Of course, even the best medical schools cannot ensure that medical practice itself functions in alignment with democratic values. The State should attempt to regulate medicine so that it supports the public interest, and encourages doctors to behave in ways that meet not only their own interests but also those of society more generally – and to practice medicine conscientiously and in the interests of their individual patients. These sets of interests are not always in alignment. A long tradition of works on the sociology of the professions saw professional standards and social interests being safeguarded by moral and ethical values inculcated during professional education, and policed internally (*See*, for example, Chapter X of Parsons, 1951). Increasingly, sociological studies of medical schools and of the working of professional associations and their internal controls have suggested that they were weak means of ensuring that professional standards were maintained, and that external regulation was necessary to limit their misuse of monopoly powers (*See*, for example, Freidson, 1972).

The key interactions between medical education, inclusiveness, democracy and development in India thus relate to:

- How medical colleges are established and managed
- Where they are established
- Who – in terms of social origin – is admitted
- How medical colleges are regulated
- The formal, informal and hidden curricula they follow

Key Arenas of Contestation

Management and Numbers Trained: Under British colonial rule, all medical colleges were either state funded or were established and run by non-commercial trusts. All the senior positions in Government medical colleges were held by IMS officers from the IMS, British (or at least, European) until the IMS itself began to Indianise after the First World War. Independent colleges, such as the missionary medical schools in Ludhiana and Vellore, were run on similar lines – again by European doctors to begin with. The exceptions – the medical colleges started by nationalist Indian doctors in Calcutta, Madras and Bombay – were notable mostly for involving visiting independent practitioners in the teaching, especially of the clinical subjects. But all were keen to ensure recognition by the IMC and thus by the GMC and other international registering bodies. This system came under great strain in the 1930s, particularly over who was to control the IMC and, in particular, with respect to whether and if so how to exclude German Jewish doctors who had acquired qualifications that would allow them to practice in India (Bhatti, 1999; Roland, 1998). The colonial system continued to run along the same lines after Independence; new medical colleges were usually upgraded from medical schools that had previously focussed on training staff with lower qualifications. As state control began to slip, in the early 1970s, the system came under much greater strain. New colleges were being established under private ownership and management, in Bihar and Karnataka in particular. Questions were raised about their standards. In 1975 the GMC withdrew automatic recognition for Indian medical colleges: thenceforth, Indian doctors would need to pass additional examinations in order to work in the UK, and other countries followed suit (Jeffery, 1979).

The MCI had lost control over the opening of new medical colleges. If once permission had been granted to start a college, the MCI found it very difficult not to recognise degrees that were awarded 5 or 6 years later, especially if the owners were politically well-connected (as they had to be, in order to acquire the original permission). The GMC 'derecognition' decision came at the beginning of India's political Emergency;

in combination, these two factors probably contributed to the reduction to six in the number of colleges approved from 1974-1983. After this brief pause, however, the founding of new medical colleges – now predominantly with the government sector – gathered speed. Table 11.1 shows that, whereas immediately after Independence, almost all medical colleges were in the public sector, that position has progressively changed, so that now more than half of all colleges – and more than half the associated admissions and bed strength – are outside the public sector. Most non-government colleges are managed by so-called 'Trusts'. By 2013, only 175 of the 381 medical colleges approved by the MCI were managed by government – state or central – with fewer than half of the authorised seats (24,063 out of a total of 50,068, though not all were necessarily filled).

Table 11.1: Medical Colleges by Year of Founding, Management and Current Seats, 1834-2013

Period of Founding	*No. of Colleges*	*Per centage Government*	*Current (2013) Seats*	*Average Seats*
Before 1944	14	92.8 per cent	2658	190
1944-53	17	88.2 per cent	3215	189
1954-63	48	89.6 per cent	7605	158
1964-73	28	92.9 per cent	3715	133
1974-83	6	50.0 per cent	750	125
1984-93	37	24.3 per cent	4825	130
1994-2003	77	20.8 per cent	9800	127
2004-2013	154	32.5 per cent	17500	114
All periods	381	45.9 per cent	50068	131

Source: http://www.mciindia.org/InformationDesk/ForStudents/ListofColleges Teaching MBBS.aspx, accessed 14 February 2014.

The argument that the numbers of health personnel in India are inadequate (Rao *et al*, 2012) is often put forward as a justification for opening new medical colleges, as with the suggestions for a medical college in every district (Chauhan, 2012; Express News Service, 2014). The noted neo-liberal economists, Jagdish Bhagwati and Arvind Panagariya, now key advisers to the Government of India, see a conspiracy by the MCI to prevent new medical colleges and argues for the loosening of its 'stranglehold,' along with rapid expansion in the numbers trained (Bhagwati & Panagariya, 2013: 137, 186-87). Along similar lines, plans have been announced to increase the seats in medical colleges where the bed strength is 1,000 or more, to 200 seats (Ananthakrishnan, 2010: 160). The Planning Commission's *High Level Expert Group on Universal Health Coverage for India* (hereafter the UHCI Report) followed this line in recommending approximately 187 new medical colleges to be established during the 2010s in larger districts currently without a college, in order to: correct the severe imbalance in the distribution of medical colleges in the country..... we see each medical college as an integral part of the health system, responsive to and partly responsible for the health needs of one or two districts..... We believe this purpose can be served by functionally linking medical colleges to district hospitals and mandating a substantial proportion of local student enrolment (Reddy *et al*, 2011: 33).

This places raising 'quality' below the need for more 'quantity,' since (as even the UHCI Report admits) in the short and medium term there will be severe shortages of qualified faculty, and inadequate state funds to finance such an expansion. But there is also a confounding factor – the impact of international and internal migration of doctors. Current levels of emigration are unknown, but are likely to fall as some common destination countries raise ever-increasing barriers to the recruitment of Indian doctors (for the case of the UK, see General Medical Council, 2012). There is also some immigration: for example, Manipal University has branch campuses in Sikkim, Dubai, Malaysia, Antigua and Nepal, and is said to be interested in Sri Lanka. It claims that 'Over 3000 practicing doctors in the US and every 4th doctor in Malaysia is an alumnus of Manipal'[4] but does not say how many graduates from its overseas campuses return to India to work. As far as internal migration is concerned, the UHCI report assumes this away: either local student recruitment will lead to enhancement of the number of local doctors; or rural medical practitioners will be deployed locally at the SHC level: (Reddy *et al*, 2011: 30). In other words, whereas full-fledged doctors would remain free to work where and how they like, supporting staff are expected to have to abide by government rules.

Putting that largely on one side, and taking the UHCI's goal of one doctor per 1,000 population, with a steady-state population around 1.6 billion by 2050 (Bloom, 2012), then 1.6 million doctors would be needed. Assuming that each doctor works for 35 years; that only 90 per cent of students admitted to medical colleges remain in India; and that only 95 per cent of these practice medicine, there is a need for an annual admission of some 55,000. Variations in these assumptions would generate slightly different figures, but the general trend is clear. Admissions to medical colleges have already reached 50,000; while there might be some case for a short-term expansion to deal with the backlog, a 50 per cent increase in the number of colleges, with a further 24,000 seats, looks to be unnecessarily ambitious. The UHCI report hedges its proposals with many worthy statements about maintaining appropriate balances between numbers of different health workers trained, about the need for a transformation in the ethos of medical colleges, and ensuring local student recruitment. But knowing past practice in this field and with no visible political mechanism to implement these proposals, the simple expansion in the number of medical colleges will be seen as the most important – and most achievable – goal.

As Table 11.2 shows, the growth in the number of medical colleges was very imbalanced. In the four large South Indian States of AP, Tamil Nadu, Kerala and Karnataka, plus Puducherry, there are now 168 medical colleges with a total of 23,195 seats, serving a population of 252 million, providing 92 seats per million people. In the seven large northern/eastern States of Bihar, UP, Assam, MP, Rajasthan, Odisha and West Bengal, plus Jharkhand, Chhattisgarh and the small north-eastern States, there are 106 medical colleges with a total of 13,353 seats, serving a population of 691 million, providing 19 seats per million people.

Table 11.2: Medical Colleges by State, Seats, and Per Capita Seats, 2013

State	*No. of colleges*	*No. of seats*	*Seats per million population*
Karnataka	46	6,755	110.6
Kerala	25	3,100	92.8
Tamil Nadu	45	6,015	83.4
Andhra Pradesh	43	6,200	73.3
Delhi	8	1,050	62.5
Maharashtra	44	5,945	52.9
Gujarat	22	2,930	48.5
Others	36	4,175	38.9
Punjab	10	945	34.1
Haryana	7	800	31.5
West Bengal	17	2,450	26.8
Odisha	8	1,050	25.0
Rajasthan	10	1,650	24.1
Madhya Pradesh	12	1,700	23.4
Assam	5	626	20.1
Uttar Pradesh	30	3,477	17.4
Bihar	13	1,200	11.5
All-India	381	50,068	41.4

Source: http://www.mciindia.org/InformationDesk/ForStudents/ListofColleges Teaching MBBS.aspx, accessed 14 February 2014.

For comparison, in the UK there are 32 medical colleges with approximately 8,000 seats for its population of 63 million, or 127 seats per million people. Thus South India is training doctors at a rate not far off that in the UK, while northern and eastern India has an output only one-fifth of that in the UK, in proportion to its population. Since doctors tend to stay and work in the state in which they were trained, this pattern of medical college approval both reflects and reinforces major geographical imbalances. An alternative comparison is with Sri Lanka, where the medical profession was engaged in a long-running battle to retain some control over numbers of students and medical standards, in the face of attempts by the government of President Rajapaksa and his colleagues to allow in foreign universities to train doctors without requiring approval by the Sri Lanka Medical Council (De Alwis, 2011; De Alwis, 2014).

Regional imbalance is one of the more powerful arguments in favour of new colleges being opened in the 'under-served' States and districts. It is hard to argue against the idea; but perhaps even more surprising that correcting such imbalances has not become a more significant rallying cry in elections.

Social Origins of Students

The issues here are often cast in terms of conflicts between democracy, individual rights, and expertise: as Deng Xiaoping summarised the debate, is being 'red' more important than being 'expert'? Democratic principles are often read to suggest that access to medical colleges should be opened up, through quotas or other policies, to make the social composition of the medical profession closer to that of the population at large. In India, as far as we know, medical students are largely drawn from tiny elite of upper caste Hindus. The Sachar Committee reported that about 4 per cent of all students in seven premier medical colleges were Muslims (compared to their share in the general population of 13 per cent in 2001) (Sachar, 2006: 70). More generally, the Committee estimated that in 2004-05 over 60 per cent of all undergraduate medical students were 'Hindu-General', about 10 per cent were SC/ST, about 15 per cent were OBCs, and about 5 per cent each were Muslims and other minorities (Sachar, 2006: 70). At the postgraduate level the disparities were clearer: nearly 80 per cent were 'Hindu-General' with the remaining 20 per cent split about equally amongst the remaining categories (Sachar, 2006: 71). Although estimates of the distribution of Hindu castes are unreliable, the 'Hindu-General' category probably constitutes about 25 per cent of the total population, about 35 per cent are OBCs, 21 per cent are SC/ST, 13 per cent Muslim and the rest – about 6 per cent – are Christians, Sikhs, etc. While this table contains many possible sources of error, it suggests the approximate scale of the imbalances.

Table 11.3: Distribution of Medical Students by Religion and Caste, 2004-05

Medical students	*General Hindu*	*OBC*	*SC/ST*	*Muslim*
Undergraduate	60%	15%	10%	5%
Postgraduate	80%	5%	5%	5%
Total population	24%	35%	21%	13%
Undergraduate odds ratio	6.6	1.1	1.2	1.0
Postgraduate odds ratio	8.8	0.4	0.5	1.0

Source: For medical students Sachar (2006); for estimates of Hindu population by caste, Sen (2010), using 61st Round NSSO data.

In the UK, pressures of this kind have led to careful monitoring of admissions procedures, through committees that have had cross-party support. "Medical schools have put in place a number of widening access initiatives to encourage applications from young people from less advantaged backgrounds, and further work is needed to understand the impact these have had" (General Medical Council, 2012: 39). Claiming to recognise the increasing diversity of the British population, "The British Medical Association made clear in 2009 that doctors should be as representative as possible of the society they serve in order to provide the best possible care to the UK population" (Milburn 2012: 43; see also Panel on Fair Access to the Professions, 2009).

There has, at least to my knowledge, been very little debate in India that recognises the diversity of the patient population as grounds for more concerted efforts to diversify the medical student population. Rather, the debate has been carried forward in terms of the general need to advance the economic conditions of previously disadvantaged groups.

How Colleges are Regulated

Medical education in India, followed closely by nurse education, is not regulated solely with respect to Indian conditions and concerns or according to any single global notion of what should be in the curriculum and how it should be taught. As was already clear in the early twentieth century, decisions about the content and form of medical education in India have been made with an eye to powerful overseas agencies, in particular, the GMC in the UK (Jeffery 1979). Bleakley and his colleagues suggest that in a postmodern age of de-territorialising the educational corners of the world that have already been homogenised – through historical waves of imperialism and colonialism – can encourage the withdrawal 'of the colonial impulse and to encourage local innovations to fill the space, thus creating difference and heterogeneity. Interdisciplinary approaches to education follow this heterogeneous impulse, to create diversity' (Bleakley *et al*, 2011: 175). In practice, this remains unlikely, until the lure of employment elsewhere is removed: neo-colonialism and neo-liberalising pressures to allow the migration of skilled (but not unskilled) workers remain key to decision-making about the curriculum.

Equally problematic has been the role of the MCI, especially since 1996. Table 11.1 shows that in the mid-1990s there was a quantum leap in the number of colleges approved, and that more than 75 per cent of these were in the private sector. In 2001 the then MCI President, Dr Ketan Desai, was removed from his position and found guilty by the Delhi High Court of corruptly receiving gifts from the management of two medical colleges. Although he was later cleared by the Supreme Court, and returned to his position, he was again arrested on corruption charges in April 2010, and the MCI was superseded by a Board of Governors. Throughout this period, according to press reports, there was a steady growth in a variety of practices that allow medical colleges to appear to meet the MCI's detailed requirements, while actually failing to achieve the purposes for which the targets have been set. Private medical colleges have met the requirements for a set number of teachers, for example, by hiring part-time faculty who also have clinical practices, or teach at a nearby Government college as well. The availability of sufficient patients for clinical practice is hard to achieve in the hospitals attached to these colleges, because of the high fees charged, and the unwillingness of private patients to accept observation or treatment by medical students (Amin *et al*, 2010: 335). In these circumstances there is little evidence that the MCI is really able to maintain control over the medical curriculum – over what shall be taught, in what sequence, through what methods, for how long, and so on. Anecdotal but persuasive evidence suggests that when an MCI inspection is announced – usually giving at least two or three days' warning – medical faculty and patients are rounded up to fill lecture theatres and teaching wards (Sood & Adkoli, 2000; Goudar & Kotur, 2003). One of India's leading medical journals, the *National Medical Journal of India*, printed claims that "The medical education system in India may be on the verge of collapse," with "an alarming shortage of teachers, with those who exist being untrained in modern teaching – learning technology" and a "gross shortage of patients in many institutions." In addition, 'the curriculum is outdated, insensitive to modern concepts of the process of teaching – learning, rigid and discourages innovation' (Ananthakrishnan, 2010: 156). Thus longer-term and more meaningful goals – such as ensuring that the average medical college will be a source of innovation in teaching or research, or will implement best practices from other colleges – seem a long way off.

The formal, informal and hidden curricula followed 1978-79 represented one position in a continual pendulum. On this end of the swing, efforts were redoubled to persuade or compel doctors to work in rural areas, either for a brief time after graduating, or for longer periods. In pursuit of this goal, a whole series of schemes were introduced: the one at the end of the 1970s was called ROME, the Re-orientation of Medical Education. Medical students were to be exposed to conditions in primary health centres attached to their medical college, and this was supposed to prepare them to work in a PHC on graduation, and to remove their fears and misconceptions about conditions they would find in rural areas. When I visited some PHCs attached to medical colleges in Orissa in 1984, it was clear that these goals were very far from being achieved. Students went reluctantly, on poorly organised visits; they rarely stayed overnight, or were given anything meaningful to do while there; their 'misconceptions' were actually pretty much correct; and they came away with a reinforced determination to avoid working in a rural area if they possibly could do so.

A whole host of other considerations encourage the opposition to working – even for a short time – in rural primary health activities. New medical graduates are under great pressure to move towards lucrative career options as soon as possible: their parents may have paid out large sums to get them admitted to medical college in the first place, and then to support them through 6 years of study; they are ready to be married, and a good job will command a higher dowry or (for a woman) encourage an offer from an even more successful man. Despite 'bonds' that will only be repaid after completing a few years of rural service, or making entry into MD courses dependent on such service, very few doctors actually followed the paths into which they were being pushed. Many rural doctors' positions – then as now – remain unfilled for budgetary reasons; those who were appointed to them would often take leave, attempt to be transferred to more urban positions, or attend as infrequently as they could do. Once doctors had children, their incentive to live in a town, preferably quite a large one, increased even further, so that they could enter their children in 'good' schools and establish or take part in an 'English-speaking' upbringing. Where – as in the MGIMS, Sevagram – conscious and strong efforts are made to provide alternative orientations, they are hamstrung by the surrounding context as well as by MCI rules:

There is a greater value put on technical training, particularly that which involves the use of hi-tech. Consequently, PSM or community medicine specialists are viewed as lesser doctors. MGIMS itself is not insulated from these pressures as many of the undergraduate students expressed their concerns about "falling back in the race"due to the additional perspective building activities that MGIMS expects them to undertake. In our interaction, we found that they showed preference for those activities that appeared to have technical content such as the ROME camp (where they are given information about national health programmes, etc.) and were least appreciative of activities that were purely reflective, such as the orientation camp. This is in keeping with the current obsession in medical education to dominate information, rather than build skills (Madhiwala *et al,* 2010: 40)

In trying to change orientations away from high technology medicine and towards primary health care, the UHCI Report looks to medical colleges to play a major role:

Medical education also requires greater orientation of providers to the social determinants of health as well as to gender and equity issues. Health professional education should be directed towards population-based primary and preventive health care instead of being driven by a curative-treatment paradigm. Medical and nursing graduates in the country should be well trained, prepared and motivated to practice in rural and urban environments. Systems of continued medical education and continued skill improvements — linked to promotions and renewal of license to practice — should be introduced. We recommend the use of Information Communication Technology (ICT) for standardised teaching across institutions and the development of institutional networks to facilitate and disseminate c-learning packages and resource materials (Reddy *et al*, 2011: 32).

Of course, schemes to encourage consideration of 'gender and equity issues' will not be entirely unsuccessful. But most of the more embedded, structural issues, which lead to an over-valuation of doctors in comparison to other health workers, are located in society at large, not just within the medical colleges. India still has one of the most adverse nurse-doctor ratios in the world. The training of other paramedical workers has been turned on and off in direct relationship to the number of funded positions for them to fill, meaning that the health service regularly experienced shortages, and training programmes were poorly managed and supported. Even the UHCI Report devotes inadequate attention to the conditions in which paramedical training should take place.

There are, of course, many efforts to change the implicit nature of medical education in specific ways. On efforts to modernise pathology teaching see Kar *et al*, (2012); on opportunities for deeper learning through modular approaches, see Srikanth *et al*, (2011). Some of these concerns might seem a long way away from everyday practice, with some medical educators more concerned about cheating (Gitanjali & Basant, 2004). In general, the Medical Council of India specifies in considerable detail the allocation of time to different subjects, lecture time and so on, even to the length of the lunch break (Supe & Burdick, 2006: 1077). Even though revisions in 1997 attempted to promote small-group, problem-based learning and a greater emphasis on community health, the wider constraints and unfamiliarity with these methods of many medical educators makes it hard to introduce them full-heartedly. Many reviews of India's medical education system bemoan the stress on lectures, on rote-learning, on too early specialisation, and on a hierarchical medical college culture which that stresses the pre-eminence of the individual, 'heroic' doctor Student perceptions of their learning environments confirm this picture (Kohli & Dhaliwal, 2013; Tripathy & Dudani, 2013). "Strict and sarcastic" teachers were a common features of student perceptions (Abraham *et al*, 2006). For example:

> "Considering these scores, in our medical school, we can presume that the teachers are knowledgeable but are authoritarian, often get angry in the class and ridicule the students; the teaching over-emphasises factual learning and is teacher-centred; support system for students who get stressed is not adequate" (Kiran & Gowdappa, 2013).

Some authors in the UK argue that the cultivation of such a culture in medical school contributes to hierarchical attitudes towards patients not only within the medical school environment but also in later life as doctors:

> "Given the explicit acceptance of democracy as a model for our civic life in the early twenty first century, why do doctors so blatantly avoid the same principles of democracy in working autocratically or in faux meritocracies in healthcare teams? It is a puzzle, and this puzzle extends to medical education in the workplace, where medical students continue to be socialised into traditional heroic medical culture. First, they learn quickly that patients are really not at the centre of medical education, and second, democracy is not the first principle informing medical education" (Bleakley, 2010: 879).

Many efforts have been made in the UK, USA and the Anglophone world more generally to transform medical practice – over and above the content of diagnosis, treatment, prognosis etc. – by changing the style of medical education. For content, basic medical sciences have been supplemented with aspects of medical humanities and medical social science: the role of society in the causation of disease patterns, how patients come into contact with healers, how the healing process can be encouraged through better doctor-patient communications, better awareness of the possible contributions of nurses and other para-professionals of a network of healers, and an understanding of human psychology have been added into the medical curriculum. Awareness of how easily medical students become alienated from possible empathy with patients – distinguishing between pre-cynical as well as pre-clinical aspects of personal change during medical education – has driven changes to the sequence of training, leading some medical colleges to bring patient contact forward to the beginning of the student experience, and stressing patient history-taking rather than reliance on tests and 'objective' measures.

The purpose of medical education – for these reformers – is to benefit patients by improving the work of doctors. There should be feedback loops between the training of medical students, the work settings in which they will find employment, and the social and political structures within which this work takes place. In the UK, changes in the conditions of practice have led some medical educators to propose changes in the style of medical education, to keep in step.

Over the past 25 years or so, however, top-down expert hierarchies, based on seniority and position, have been challenged by the rise of patient groups, external review procedure – of new forms of surveillance of the doctors as well as of patients, or what Bleakley and his colleagues call 'monitory democracy'. This has, or so it is suggested, emerged from "accounting for practices to a variety of people" – in the USA, professional colleagues, patients and their families (and patient advocacy groups) as well as ethics committees, internal and external validating agencies etc. This can be understood as part of Foucauldian bio-power:

In medicine, the traditional process of representative democracy is being supplemented – and sometimes supplanted – by patient groups, national and local audit groups and processes, legal investigations, management surveillance, appraisals, patient safety practices and so forth. This sounds oppressive, but, as Foucault suggests, power is not usually exercised in modern structures by authorities wielding sovereign power over other. Instead, power runs through systems and is productive, just as it may be oppressive (Bleakley *et al,* 2011: 98)

They suggest that the emergent role of medical education is to democratise medical practice fully. Although the evidence is not yet there, Bleakley suggests that current medical education practices in the UK are beginning to shift from those that encourage autonomy in medical practice, to recognise and value collaboration, team-work and social responsibility – something we might recognise as being democratic. Peer evaluation by medical students, he suggests, can play a part in encouraging and supporting such a shift (Bleakley, 2010).

This approach is similar to that of problem-based learning (PBL), introduced in many medical schools outside India and recently being promoted by some medical educators within the country. This is designed to encourage a problem-solving approach to issues of diagnosis and treatment, rather than a reliance on standardised responses. This approach also "underlines 'learning how to learn' and stimulates self-directed learning as a central, pervasive objective of the teaching-learning process" (Sood & Adkoli, 2000: 210). But some would argue that these pedagogies hide their Western essentialist thinking behind apparently technical language:

> "There is a danger..... that proponents of certain learning methods (particularly problem-based learning ot PBL) and certain educational frameworks (such as competence) [will cause] these key aspects of the Western curriculum [to] become, like the Big Mac, ubiquitously present – homogenised, commodified, marketed, reduced to 'essentials' and instrumentalised' (Bleakley *et al*, 2008: 268).

As an example, Bleakley and his colleagues quote a discussion of Japanese learning practices, which seem to fit the model of passive students who fail to give feedback to teachers, and teachers whose only teaching style is narrowly-focussed lectures. But, Bleakley *et al*, argue, the paper's author gives little weight to the evidence that the standards of medical care in Japan are, on a number of indicators, apparently excellent (Bleakley *et al*, 2008: 269). With reference to India, such an approach might lead to the following kind of argument: as in Japan, in India students enter medical colleges after intensive preparation, through rote learning and a single-minded focus on science subjects at school. Breaking these patterns in medical colleges is neither easy nor particularly important or worthwhile. Rather, educators should work with these prevailing orientations, and not assume that pedagogical innovations from abroad are necessarily relevant to the Indian situation.

Conclusion

With respect to medical education, pace Rao *et al*, (2012) it is not at all clear that there is an overall deficit of health workers. It is true that many of these are unqualified, with unknown training and dubious skills. In view of the massive expansion of doctors over the past 15 years while under surveillance by an MCI management that has been accused of major weaknesses in the criteria demanded for new colleges, there are legitimate grounds to worry about the quality of training of many of those *with* qualifications. The skill-mix of the doctors is very inefficient, with too many wanting to be specialists and not enough prepared to carry out basic frontline primary care; and very unbalanced locations, both between urban and rural areas, and by state and region. The levels and effects of physician migration are basically unknown.

Faced with a similar situation 100 years ago in the USA, Flexner argued for more control over numbers, closer links to universities, and thus for 'fewer, better' doctors. In India, efforts to impose control over training standards are continually undermined by the politics of public and private medical education. Increasing the number of medical colleges, distributing them more widely across the country, and expanding the intake of existing colleges, are the most likely patterns to be followed over the next 30 years. Reforming the content and styles of teaching will take a back foot, for the foreseeable future, compared with desperately recruiting more medical educators merely to maintain the existing patterns.

Why is this bad for democracy, inclusion and development?

Firstly, student admission largely on the basis of ability to pay continues the model of the medical profession as an elite, urban, overseas-oriented occupation. It leaves the social distance between patients and practitioners one of the largest in the world – larger even than that in other highly inegalitarian societies, such as the UK and the USA. Very few doctors trained in these contexts will ever perceive their social role in the way that they are exhorted to follow – of community service. These doctors need to repay massive loans – subordinating medical decision-making to the lure of the market. At the same time, there is a growing gap between the promise of quality control, as mandated for the MCI, and a reality of uncertainty, in which both doctors and public have lost faith in central institutions of the state tasked with meeting urgent public health needs. Perhaps the attention of reformers should be reoriented away from medical colleges and towards medical practice itself: continuing education might be more successful, focussing on the doctors who remain in India, and on their everyday tasks, rather than attempting to change undergraduate training.

Odds ratios are compared to Muslim chances as 1.0: The figures are all estimates and subject to contestation and rounding errors, but a 'general-Hindu' youth is about 6-7 times more likely to be an undergraduate medical student than a youth from any other social group. Differentials for postgraduate students are very much larger, especially for comparisons between 'General-Hindu' and OBC and SC/ST students.

Notes

1. I do not here discuss two very important issues: the implications of India's hybrid system – integrated medicine, AYUSH colleges and their graduates – nor the relationship of medical education to nurse and other paramedical training processes and structures.
2. http://ibnlive.in.com/news/indian-medical-association-calls-for-nationwide-strike-today/267729-3.html accessed 20 February 2014
3. http://www.manipal.edu/documents/mu-fact%20sheet.pdf, accessed on 16 February 2014

References

Abraham, Reem R; Kamath, Asha; Upadhyay, Subramanya and Ramnarayan, Komattil (2006): Learning Approaches to Physiology of Undergraduates in an Indian Medical School. *Medical Education* 40 (9):916-23.

Amin, Zubair; Burdick, William P., Supe, Avinash and Singh, Tejinder (2010): Relevance of the Flexner Report to Contemporary Medical Education in South Asia. *Academic Medicine* 85 (2):333-39.

Ananthakrishnan, N. (2010): Medical Education in India: Is It still Possible to Reverse the Downhill Trend? *The National Medical Journal of India*, 23 (3):156-60.

Bhagwati, Jagdish and Panagariya, Arvind (2013): Why Growth Matters: How Economic Growth in India Reduced Poverty and the Lessons for Other Developing Countries. New York: Public Affairs.

Bhatti, Anil and Voigt, Johannes H. (Ed.). (1999): *Jewish Exile in India 1933-1945*. New Delhi: Manohar.

Bleakley, Alan. (2010): Social Comparison, Peer Learning and Democracy in Medical Education. *Medical Teacher*, 32 (11): 878-79.

Bleakley, Alan; Bligh, John and Browne. Julie (2011): *Medical Education for the Future: Identity, Power and Location*. Dordrecht: Springer.

Bleakley, Alan; Brice, Julie and Bligh, John (2008): Thinking the Post-Colonial in Medical Education. *Medical Education* 42 (3): 266-70.

Bloom, David E. (2012): Population Dynamics in India and Implications for Economic Growth. In Ghate, Chetan (Ed.), *The Oxford Handbook of the Indian Economy*, New York: Oxford University Press, pp. 462-95.

Chauhan, Chetan (2012): A Medical College in Each District of the Country: Govt. *Hindustan Times*, New Delhi, 2 August

Das, Jishnu and Hammer, Jeffrey (2012): Health and Health Care Policy in India: The Case for Quality of Care. In Ghate, Chetan (Ed.), *The Oxford Handbook of the Indian Economy*, New York: Oxford University Press, pp. 420-45. Oxford & New York: Oxford University Press.

De Alwis, Dinesh (2011): Sri Lanka: Strike Threat over Private Medical School. *University World News Global Edition*, 8 September: No. 188.

De Alwis, Dinesh (2014): Sri Lanka: Private Universities may 'Bypass' Professional Bodies. *University World News Global Edition*, 13 February: No. 307.

Express News Service (2014): Medical Colleges in All Districts. *The New Indian Express*, Hyderabad, AP, 17 February.

Freidson, Eliot and Lorber, Judith (Ed.) (1972): *Medical Men and Their Work*. Chicago: Aldine Atherton.

General Medical Council (2012): *The State of Medical Education and Practice in the UK 2012*. London: General Medical Council.

Gitanjali, B. (2004): Academic Dishonesty in Indian Medical Colleges. *Journal of Postgraduate Medicine*, 50 (4): 281.

Goudar, Shivaprasad S. and Kotur, P.F. (2003): Trends in Medical Education. *Indian Journl of Anaestheia*, 47 (1): 25-29.

Jeffery, Roger (1979): Recognising India's Doctors: The Establishment of Medical Dependency, 1918-39. *Modern Asian Studies*, 13 (2): 301-26.

Jeffery, Roger (1988): Doctors and Congress: The Role of Medical Men and Medical Politics in Indian Nationalism. In Shepperdson, Mike and Simmonsm Colin (Ed.): *The Political Economy of Indian Independence and the Indian National Congress, 1885-1985*. London: Gower, pp. 160-73.

Kar, Asaranti; Kar, Tushar; Dash, Kanaklata, Rout, Niranjan; Bhuyan, Pallavi; Panda, Sasmita and Mohanty, Raghumani (2012): Undergraduate Pathology Education: Meeting the Challenge Ahead. *International Journal of Clinical Medicine*, 3 (2): 83-87. doi: 10.4236/ijcm.2012.32018.

Kiran, H.S. and Gowdappa, Basavana H. (2013): 'DREEM' Comes True: Students' Perceptions of Educational Environment in an Indian Medical School. *Journal of Postgraduate Medicine* 59 (4): 300-05.

Kohli, Varun and Dhaliwal, Upreet (2013): Medical Students' Perception of the Educational Environment in a Medical College in India: A Cross-Sectional Study Using the Dundee Ready Education Environment Questionnaire. *Journal of Educational Evaluation for Health Professions*, 10 (5): 1-7. doi.org/10.3352/jeehp.2013.10.5

Madhiwala, Neha and Others (2010): Integration of Medical Education with Primary and Secondary Healthcare: Mahatma Gandhi Institute of Medical Sciences, Sevagram, Maharashtra. Mumbai: Centre for Studies in Ethics and Rights.

Marshall, Thomas Humphrey (1963): *Sociology at the Crossroads: and Other Essays*, London: Heinemann.

Milburn, Alan (2012): Fair Access to Professional Careers: A Progress Report by the Independent Reviewer on Social Mobility and Child Poverty. London: Cabinet Office.

Panel on Fair Access to the Professions (2009): Unleashing Aspiration: The Final Report of the Panel on Fair Access to the Professions. London: Cabinet Office.

Parsons, Talcott (1951): *The Social System*. Glencoe, Illinois: Free Press.

Rao, Krishna D.;, Bhatnagar, Aarushi and Berman, Peter (2012): So Many, Yet Few: Human Resources for Health in India." *Human Resources for Health*, 10 (19): 1-9.

Reddy, K. Srinath, and Others (2011): *High Level Expert Group Report on Universal Health Coverage for India*. New Delhi: Planning Commission.

Roland, Joan G. (1998): *The Jewish Communities of India: Identity in a Colonial Era*. New Brunswick, N.J.: Transaction Publishers.

Sachar, Rajindar (2006): *Social, Economic and Educational Status of the Muslim Community in India*. Pp. 404. New Delhi: Cabinet Secretariat, Government of India, p. 404.

Sen, Gitanjali and Basant, Rakesh (2010): "Who Participates in Higher Education in India? Rethinking the Role of Affirmative Action. *Economic and Political Weekly*, 45(39): 62-70.

Sood, Rita and Adkoli, B.V. (2000): Medical Education in India – Problems and Prospects. *Journal of Indian Academy of Clinical Medicine*. 1 (3): 210-13.

Srikanth, S, B., Thirunaaukarasu, K. and Mahajan, P. (2011): Modular Teaching: An Alternative to Routine Teaching Method for Undergraduate Medical Students. *Indian Journal of Community Medicine*, 36 (3): 237.

Supe, Avinash and Burdick, William P. (2006): Challenges and Issues in Medical Education in India. *Academic Medicine* 81 (12): 1076-80.

Tripathy, Sukanta, and Sharmila Dudani (2013): Students' Perception of the Learning Environment in a New Medical College by Means of the DREEM Inventory. *International Journal of Research in Medical Sciences*, 1 (4): 385-91.

12

Realising Rights to Education

Is Privatising Educational Services Equitable, Democratic, Inclusive and Sustainable?

Keith Lewin

In the latter part of the twentieth century most modernising states saw education as a public good that should be publicly financed and universally available up to the age of 15 years. Over the last two decades there has been a growing interest in the role that for-profit private providers of educational services can play in universalising access to basic education in low income countries and a lively debate around the various propositions for and against greater roles for private providers (e.g. Colclough, 1996; Kingdon, 1996; Lewin and Sayed, 2005; Rose, 2007; Heyneman and Stern, 2011; Srivastava, 2013; Ashley *et al.*, 2014). The mechanisms suggested include promoting "low cost private schools for the poor" and supporting the public financing of privately managed schools using vouchers. Neither offers a panacea to complex problems and there is much special pleading (e.g. Tooley and Dixon, 2003) and a gulf between some images of the enthusiasm for privatisation and the reality of commitments by development partners (Mundy and Menashy, 2012). This paper makes the case for continued emphasis on public financing and provision of basic education to promote equitable development. In so doing it accepts that private interests can and do have roles to play in educational development in low-income countries. However, there are limits of capacity, motivation, and financing that mean that the provider of last resort will always be public in all but the most fragile states, and that the access to education of the poorest will be best served by public investments that prioritise equity and are directed at redressing imbalances and since social justice.

This paper[1] sets the scene for the debates about whether private schools for the poor make sense. The first section defines terms building on earlier definitions (Kitaev, 1999; Lewin, 2007) which seek to reduce the ambiguities common in discussion of what is private and what is public. The paper is concerned with low *price* schools rather than low *cost* schools since this is what determines if they are accessible to the poor. The second section asks which children are likely to be most attractive to low price private schools and links this to an analytic framework of Zones of inclusion and exclusion developed by the Consortium for Research on Educational Access, Transitions and Equity (CREATE)[2] (Lewin 2011). The third part develops a simple taxonomy of types of demand for private schools and links this to discussion of patterns of enrolment as a taster for deeper analysis of supply and demand as discussed in the concluding remarks.

Terms of Engagement

Any discussion of the virtues and vices of public and private provision of education must define terms carefully. Schools can be wholly privately owned, unsubsidised, and unregulated on the one hand and wholly publicly owned, fully publicly financed and regulated by the state on the other. But even these apparently unambiguous categories can have blurred boundaries. Private ownership may involve those with close ties to public authorities, qualified teachers in private schools may have been trained at public expense, public schools may collect fees and contributions, and regulation may be more apparent than real and subject to conflicts of interest and rent seeking behaviour.

Confusingly, beyond any simple dichotomy of private and public schools there is a wide spectrum of arrangements for ownership, finance and regulation. Beneficial owners can be large commercial organisations, charitable foundations, small family owned business and individuals, religious and other faith based organisations, and employers (e.g. farms, mines, plantations). Some owners have legal identities and others do not. Some are registered not-for-profit organisations and others are registered for-profit businesses. In some tuition and other fees are charged while in others they are subsidised or not charged to all or some households. Some are audited and some are not. Some are required to pay tax, others are not, and some evade taxes. Some fall under public inspection systems and follow national curricula, others do not. Some fall under self-regulation systems of registration and inspection organised by associations of private schools, others are only regulated by markets operating with imperfect information.

Alongside these ambiguities, overlaps and occasional obfuscations there are other definitional problems in the debates around privatisation and services to the poor. This can be illustrated with reference to five issues.

First, discussions of *low cost* private schools often fail to distinguish between low *prices* for those who attend such schools, and low *costs* for those who provide the services. Low prices are necessary if there is to be participation from the poorest households for the obvious reason that those below the poverty line can only afford the lowest prices. Low prices must come with low costs if such schools are financed from fees charged to poor households if they are to remain solvent. Low prices and low costs must come with very low teacher salaries since these are the main recurrent cost. Low prices may coexist with average of high costs if the low prices are subsidised by voucher schemes or something similar. So it turns out that what some mean by low-cost private schools — schools serving low income households with low running costs per student and low cost facilities — are schools which are charged with the difficult if not impossible task of providing good quality learning experiences with teachers paid low salaries under poor physical conditions.

From an economic private profit. providers have an interest in the ratio between prices and costs since that is where their margins and profit are generated. Any market logic would suggest they should maximise the difference between prices and costs and successful schools will do this by raising prices to the highest levels their market will bear leaving the less successful to survive with lower margins. The logic of the market and a competition between providers is not consistent with maximising profit by delivering high quality educational services to the poorest at low prices.

Another interpretation of low-cost private schools assumes that voucher schemes or some related arrangement (e.g. conditional cash transfers) provide capitation or fee payments related to the number of children. If these payments generate income per child similar to those in publicly financed schools they cannot be described as low cost. The schools are operating at the same average cost per child as public schools. The poor may be able to attend if the direct costs to households are minimised because of the public subsidy. Without such subsidy such schools could not operate with low prices within reach of those below the poverty line. Payments to schools at average public levels of cost per child coupled with very low or no fees are therefore low price but not low cost.

Truly low price private schools must actually be free to households if they are to enrol the poorest who are well below the poverty line in low income countries. They cannot therefore operate without subsidy. If that subsidy is much less than the average cost per student in a public school there is a challenge to social justice and equity — why should the poorest receive lower cost schooling if they are in private rather than public schools? But if the subsidies are raised to the level of an average publically funded school place then the school would no longer be low cost relative to the majority of schools which are publicly financed.

Without labouring the point further it is clear that we have to use terminology carefully and that, more often than not, debates around low price private schools are really about whether or not public authorities should subcontract private providers to provide educational services, and if they do so whether this will be efficient and will reach the poorest. Thus low-cost private schools should be described as low price schools with low paid teachers, or simply as cheap schools.

Second, private schooling has no clear identity. Many different things can be more or less private or public. Where a school is wholly financed from fees paid by students and parents it can be described as a privately financed school. However it may benefit from publically financed teacher training, subsidies for textbooks, exemptions from value added tax and other forms of taxation, and it may receive pupils who pay fees reimbursed by public scholarships or conditional cash transfers. There are many other possibilities.

Similarly public schools which subcontract services, e.g. for cleaning, maintenance, security, and transport, may still be classified as public. If they employ additional teachers from funds raised from parents they may still be considered public up to the point where most of the recurrent finance is private. And if they are owned and run by non-state entities including faith-based organisations and philanthropic trusts but staffed by teachers on the public payroll they are both public and private.

Though private schooling is often contrasted with public schooling this seems to suppose that there is something intrinsically different about schooling financed in different ways. It is not clear this is true. There is no obvious sense in which the pedagogy and curricula of schools can be privatised unless it is copyrighted and patented and thus unavailable in the public domain without paying license fees. Privately financed schooling does not have these qualities, especially in low income countries. It should be a matter of public concern if it did. What happens in and around classrooms is recognisably similar in successful and failing public and private schools.

A key question remains what is private about private schooling? If it is not curricula and pedagogy, is it aspects of school management, the contracting of teachers, the deployment of the resources available, the chains of accountability, the relationships with parents, the selection by price inevitable with fee paying, the social exclusion favoured by some groups? And if so which if any of these attributes are inextricably linked to public or private ownership, finance, or governance?

Third, the private sector is often referred to as if it stands in a simple counterpoint to the public sector. But whilst states have unitary characteristics with officeholders with known responsibilities and accountabilities within bureaucratic systems of public administration, the private sector has no such coherence or public accountability. It is largely defined negatively as "not being public" rather than being positively located by defined attributes e.g. fee paying, for-profit, unaccountable to public authorities. Increasingly, some commentators have begun to include not-for-profit community based NGOs who own and run schools as private providers as if they were similar to commercial for profit providers. This is clearly not the case..

What is known as the private "sector" is in reality a collection of actors who have very different legal identities, motivations, governance and accountabilities. Large-scale domestic or international corporations have very different characteristics to domestic small and medium size enterprises. Informally organised household businesses are very different from community organised cooperative enterprises. We can note also that the organised private "sector" of employment and commercial enterprises in many low income countries is extremely small with very limited capacity. It may account for less than 10 per cent of total employment. It may also have very few businesses that employ more than 20 employees. Informal sector activity may be much larger and involve a majority of the population. But schools are neither informal organisations and nor does any country depend on non-formal education in the "private sector" as the core mechanism to deliver basic education.

Fourth, educational achievement in many low income countries has the characteristics of a positional good as much as those of an investment in individual or collective human capital. In emerging dual labour markets which offer vastly differential rewards to those employed in small but rapidly growing modern sectors where value-added can be high, educational qualifications mediate access to jobs. They determine who gets what in terms of income earning opportunities. Demand for private schooling is much more likely to be a function of differentiated demand for an education that offers a greater chance of gaining qualifications for access to modern sector jobs, than it is to be a signal of unsatisfied demand from those who are out of school and who may have never attended school. Competition between schools to drive up standards may in reality be better understood as a competition between households for comparative advantage within a largely zero-sum game of life chances than it is an expression of public commitment to national development goals. If so, then the public goods aspect of investments in education, that seeks to mitigate inequalities, promote equal opportunities and deliver rights to minorities, will be overshadowed by rationing access to education by price.

Fifth, states have a unique responsibility for national development. It is not clear that those in different sectors of private activity share a commitment to the same goals as states. Externally owned private sector commercial providers have no necessary connection with national development. Profit maximising national enterprises will tend to seek income over social equity, and higher net wealth students than lower net wealth students to maximise margins. Not for profit providers, set up with goals and philosophies that may not mesh with national priorities, may also be uncommitted to national development. And it can be problematic for faith based organisations.

Two strategies have been advanced to enhance educational development involving private providers. The first arrangement concerns the development of "low cost private schools for the poor" where private for-profit unsubsidised schools are used to provide schooling to those at or below the national poverty line. The second set of arrangements concerns the public financing and sub-contracting of service delivery to for-profit private providers through voucher schemes and other similar arrangements. Both these strategies have been advanced as ways to accelerate progress towards universal access to education within the frameworks of "Education for All" which have targeted 2015 as the date by which time all children should have access to basic education. In India and in East and West Africa there is continuing debate about the virtues and vices of the different approaches (Chimombo 2009, Lewin 2011, Bangay and Latham 2013, Dixon *et al* 2013, French and Kingdon 2010, Harma 2011)

For Whom are Low Price Private Schools Intended

There are many different ways of conceptualising access to education depending on the dimensions that are valued. CREATE has developed a model of zones of exclusion from education which it has used to shape its research in communities and schools and as a tool for policy dialogue (Lewin 2011). In each of the zones the patterns and causes of exclusion from education are likely to be different. They may also be different from community to community. The model charts participation by grade and identifies different groups of children of school age that fail to sustain access to basic education. Figure 12.1 presents the chart.

The generic model displays the nominal grade level along the x-axis and an indicator of participation on the y-axis. It shows a system in which about 20 per cent of children fail to enter Grade 1, 45 per cent reach Grade 6, and about 20 per cent complete lower secondary. The characteristics of each zone of exclusion are indicated in Figures 12.1 and 12.2.

The model can be used to highlight the different zones where private providers may be attracted to operate in different education systems. This is important since privatisation may differ greatly between educational cycles, the characteristics of supply and demand vary by zone, and prices and costs are likely to be quite different for different levels.

Zones of Exclusion and Inclusion

Zone 0 captures those excluded from pre-school.

Zone 1 contains those who never attend school. It includes those who could attend existing schools but do not, and those who are excluded by livelihoods, location, civil status, disability, social stigma or other vulnerabilities.

Zone 2 includes the majority of children who are excluded *after* initial entry, who drop out of school and fail to complete a full cycle. In an increasing number of countries these are the largest numbers of out of school children.

Zone 3 includes those in school but at risk of drop out, most obviously as a result of low achievement and poor attendance. These children can be described as "silently excluded" since they are enrolled but may learn little, attend irregularly, and/or are overage.

Zone 4 contains those who fail to transit to secondary education as a result of failing to be selected, being unable to afford costs, or located far from a secondary school, or otherwise excluded.

Zone 5 includes those dropping out of secondary grades.

Zone 6 contains those at risk of dropout from secondary school.

Zone of Inclusion. This contains children who are the appropriate age for grade, attend regularly, and achieve in-line with national norms.

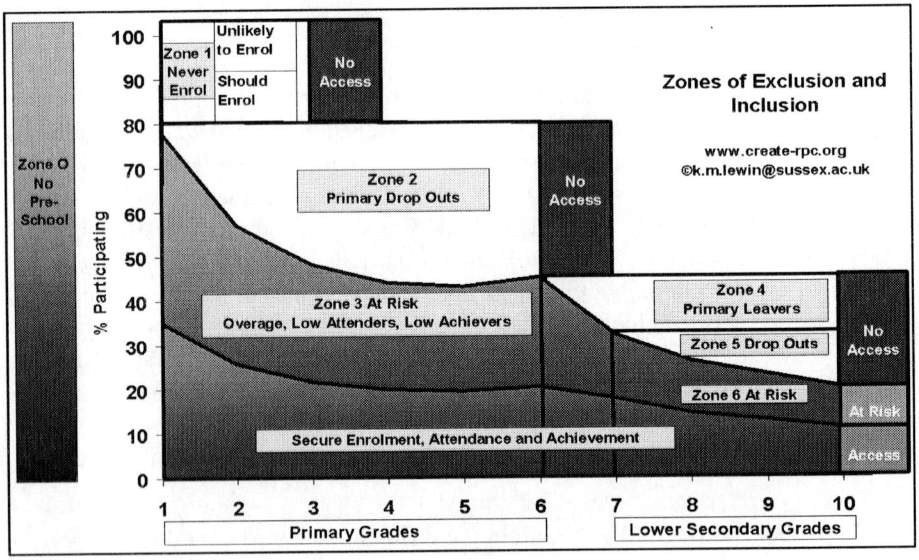

Fig. 12.1: Create Zones of Exclusion and Inclusion

To illustrate this with reference to Figure 12.1, some generic observations are as follows:

Zone zero — pre-school — is widely provided privately in low income countries with little or no state subsidised provision. Access is therefore rationed by price. Costs may be low or high depending on how provision is organised. In the worst cases children may be "warehoused" in large groups while their parents work in circumstances which provide some childcare but little of educational benefit. In contrast high quality and higher price preschools often exist for the children of the relatively wealthy. In some countries fee-paying participation in pr-eschools associated with high demand public schools is used as a method to ration access.

Zone 1 contains children who never attended school and are not likely to in future. These are disproportionately the poorest, those from excluded social groups, children with disability, illegal migrants, and those with nomadic lifestyles. They may include both urban and rural residents. The cost of reaching these children is likely to be higher than the cost for children from groups that are not disadvantaged. The prices that such households can afford are low. The reasons for non-enrolment vary but when they are structural they may be difficult to overcome. This zone is likely to include illegal migrants, those with disability, nomads, ethnic minorities, and children from other socially excluded groups. Children inside Zone 1 are unlikely to be attractive to low price for-profit private providers.

Zone 2 (and **Zone 5**) includes children who enrol in school and drop out at primary or secondary level. The most common reasons for dropout in low income countries are the costs of participation, including opportunity costs, and the lack of perceived relevance of schooling for future livelihoods and wellbeing. Many other factors may be significant in different community contexts. This group is unlikely to be attractive to private for profit providers unless the reasons why they have dropped out are understood and addressed. If the reasons are cost to household then fee paying will continue to exclude. If the reasons are to do with lack of perceived relevance and low achievement leading to low motivation these will continue to be a barrier. And the opportunity costs of returning to a fee paying school are higher than they are to a fee free school. Dropouts may re-enrol but the cheapest option for them will always be to return to a fee free public system. Some may enrol in private fee paying "second chance" schools in order to acquire qualifications with a labour market value that they have failed to acquire.

Zone 3 and **Zone 6** are those in school who are characterised as being "silently excluded" in primary or secondary school. Simply put this will include those who are attending irregularly, are substantially overage for their grade, and are in the lowest quintiles of achievement. These students find learning challenging. Those who are silently excluded are likely to be disproportionately drawn from poor households, though not all will be. Those with aspiring parents and resources may well be willing to pay for private schools that offer special programmes that offer in return the promise of more individual attention, remedial programmes and support to improve achievement. If this is so then this reflects a differentiated demand for schools which are perceived to be of higher quality. Those who transfer leave behind empty places in public school systems.

Zone 4 embraces those children who fail to make the transition to secondary school. Who goes to which secondary school is a critical issue in almost all low income countries. It is a strong determinate of life futures. Secondary schooling is a prized positional good for which those who can afford it are prepared to pay high prices. Private school operators may be attracted to secondary school provision for those unable to access fee free public schools where there are capacity limitations. In low enrolment Africa and South Asia there may be less than half the number of places available than there are primary school leavers creating opportunities for not state providers.

The zone of secure enrolment, attendance and achievement is the one likely to be of most interest to for profit private providers. These children are least problematic in motivation, enrolment status, attendance and achievement. They are disproportionately wealthy and urban, and more likely to have educated parents who value school achievement. It is in this zone are the children who will have the resources to attend higher cost fee paying schools and where demand for higher quality may drive school choice.

Patterns of Demand for Low Price Private Schools

Several different types of demand for private schooling coexist in low income countries. It is important to understand what these are since they affect school choice and whether propositions about the importance of choice to education system development are valid (Kremer and Muralidharan 2011, Cameron 2011, Siddhu 2011, Ohba 2012, Sommers 2012, Woodhead *et al* 2013, Akaguri 2014).

It is useful to spell out their characteristics. First, in some low enrolment countries there is demand arising from an absolute shortage of school places. This is not uncommon at secondary level in countries where Education for All programmes have rapidly increased the numbers of primary school leavers at rates well in excess of the growth in secondary school places (e.g. in Malawi, Tanzania, Uganda, Zambia). This demand can be called *excess demand.*

Second, excess demand can coexist with what can be called *differentiated demand.* This occurs when parents and students are dissatisfied with public schools and seek something different or better. In South Africa high price independent schools founded during apartheid remain alongside ex-white public schools that supplement their income with fees and remain in high demand. There are very few low price private schools largely because state schooling is widely available and fee free to those in the poorest quintiles of income. Where there are low price private schools these are small in scale, focussed in pockets, and often serving displaced and migrant communities. In Sri Lanka the highest demand is for national public secondary schools with some well-established high price private schools catering for those with particular preferences and the financial resources necessary to pay fees. Private tuition is common, some of which is low price. Almost all is supplementary rather than the first choice provider. In China high price private schools have been growing as a result of differentiated demand. Where migrants are disqualified from local school attendance in their destination community there is some lower price private schooling but this is less driven by differentiated demand than simple lack of available supply.

Differentiated demand also appears in relation to faith and cultural identity based schooling. Faith based schools offer an alternative to secular public schools. Fee paying high price private schools serve families who value academic standards, social exclusion, and broad curricula and who judge that many public schools fail to meet their needs. Madrasas and some Christian mission schools can be described as low price private schools which may or may not be fee paying or its equivalent.

Third, is demand that is predominantly driven by labour market employment practices, credentialism, and competition for social mobility. In this case educational achievement can be regarded as a positional good that provides access to well paid jobs and social status. More education and higher qualification may signal real differences in capability. If there is qualification escalation as a result of surplus demand the screening functions of educational attainment and qualifications may become more important. As a positional good in economic terms, education locates individuals relative to others in a zero sum game which benefits those who have more over those who have less. *Positional demand* is of growing importance. This interacts with the first two types of demand and is best understood as a competition between households and individuals, rather than schools, for scarce benefits that has global as well as national characteristics. It is reflected in the growing availability of league tables, candidate performance lists, and school choice driven by narrow considerations of examination performance and employability.

Fourth and lastly, economic liberalisation has resulted in more permissive attitudes towards private schools. This has stimulated demand through deregulation and light regulation and purposeful facilitation. As private schools have developed they have invested in generating demand through advertising, responding to differentiated demand, and creating opportunities to attend schools that were previously unavailable. To the extent that most of these providers are for-profit and commercially motivated they seek to expand through advertising and marketing what they regard as their unique selling points e.g. examination results, safety (especially for girls), social exclusivity, boarding facilities etc. The purpose of this *induced demand* is to increase market share and profitability. Induced demand includes within it the manipulation of differentiated demand and positional demand. As with much advertising and public relations promotion campaigns narrative can trump veracity and hyperbole eclipse reality.

Patterns of Enrolment and Possible Implications

A selection of charts of enrolment data from different school systems can be used to begin to see where there may be different types of demand and opportunities for the private sector may exist. The dotted line indicates the numbers of school age children at respective nominal grade levels. The other lines chart enrolments by grade in each of the years since 2000. The charts provide reminders that private service providers are operating at different levels of school systems where enrolment rates may be very different. The opportunities and risks of privatisation have to be seen in the light of the characteristics of different zones of inclusion and exclusion, different patterns of participation, and for a fuller analysis, patterns of income distribution. The latter generate financial limits to growth that constrain the proportion of children that can be enrolled in self financing private schools. In general such schooling is unlikely to be available to those outside the top two quintiles of household income unless unqualified teachers are used with rates of pay a fifth or a tenth of those for qualified teachers in government schools (Lewin 2007).

In Bangladesh, the enrolments by grade shows that there is a tipping point which is currently around Grade 4 where there are more children in the age group and there are enrolled in school. Not many more than 60 per cent of students make it through to the lower grades to secondary school which starts from Grade 6. Private schooling is largely driven by the kind of differentiated demand which seeks high quality than is available from free public schools, and which is available to those who can pay. There are many Registered Non-Government Primary Schools which are privately managed but publically financed. There are also a growing number of private madrasas. Above grade 5 there are not enough school places for all children and thus there may be excess demand for private schooling from those who are excluded. However, since the excluded are disproportionately in households below the poverty line, it is unlikely that most will be able to afford private unsubsidised schooling. Though there is a wide gap in enrolments between those in school and those in the appropriate age group at higher grades it is clear that private sector providers have not been able or interested in filling this gap otherwise the gap would have closed.

Nepal has had high levels of over enrolment and under enrolment relevant to the age-group in Grade 1 for over 30 years. This is because both over age and underage children are often retained in Grade 1 for more than a year before being allowed to proceed to high grades. Above Grade 4 there are more children in the age group than there are enrolled in school. As in Bangladesh at higher Grade levels there is substantial dropout and no indication that private providers have been filling gaps in provision. Private schools in urban areas do meet needs of rural parents at secondary level where local provision is insufficient, and fee paying schools in towns provide places for children who can pay. Those below the poverty line are unlikely to afford the costs.

In Burma all grades below Grade 5 have more children enrolled in the population. Above Grade 5 there is a steep drop in enrolments as a result of selection into secondary school. Access to secondary schooling is partly constrained by the cost to households of attending school. Though there may be opportunities for fee paying private schools to attract students who are currently enrolled at secondary level, it seems that many would be unable to afford the direct costs or private for profit schools given that more than 30 per cent of the population is likely to fall below the poverty line.

In Pakistan there is clear evidence of under supply of schooling at every Grade above Grade 2. By Grade 6 enrolments are less than half those in Grade 1 and the situation has only been changing slowly. In particular though enrolments appear to have increased in lower grades, drop out rates have not decreased. As in the other countries if private schooling was having a major impact on educational exclusion this would be evident in increased participation in higher grades. More likely, where the number of private schools has increased, they will have been enrolling children who were previously in public schools as may be the case with voucher like schemes like the Punjab Education Foundation.

Sri Lanka has full enrolment through to senior secondary. There are very few private schools operating and most of those that do exist cater to the children of the wealthy. Aside from a small cluster of historic and high cost elite private schools there has been no substantial growth of low price private schools. Rather there is intense competition, especially at secondary level, to gain access to the best public schools. This has led some national schools to become mega schools with enrolments over 5000. As in many other Asian countries private tuition is very common across most social groups and is a form of private schooling over and above normal day schooling. This is invisible in simple enrolment charts.

Cambodia has an evolving enrolment patterns common to the early stages of progress towards universal access. Enrolments in Grade 1-5 include many overage children and some underage. It is unlikely to many of these are in private fee paying schools since a large proportion of the population is at or below the poverty line. At secondary level enrolments are low and excess demand may support some private secondary schools but these will be limited in number as a result of income distribution. In contrast Vietnam has high enrolment through to Grade 10 and very few truly private schools that are fee paying. Above this level enrolments are much less than the numbers in the age group and, as in China, it is possible that some private community schools will develop. This may partly be the result of general satisfaction with public schools which generate region leading levels of achievement which are widely distributed across the school system rather than concentrated amongst a few schools.

In India at national level the tipping point where enrolments are less than the number of children in the age group has now reached Grade 4. Above this level of attrition remains high with less than half of all children succeeding in progressing through secondary school to Grade 9 and above. Enrolments by Grade aggregated across India are misleading since there are very large differences between and within states. In general the northern states have much poorer indicators of participation than those in the south. Under the Indian national programme to universalise access to primary school (Sarva Shiksha Abhiyan) more and more states are providing enough public school places to enrol all children but there remains a considerable journey left to travel. Differentiated demand is common whereby those with sufficient resources seek positional advantage through attendance at fee paying institutions where access is rationed by price. The availability of different types of private schooling varies greatly between states. It is common in some states for a substantial amount of provision to be in schools that are privately managed but publicly financed. In others the great majority schools are publicly managed but publicly financed. And in some states wholly private for profit schools account for a significant proportion of enrolment.

The enrolment pattern in four states is shown in the charts below. Uttar Pradesh, Rajasthan and Bihar are all northern states with lower enrolment rates and high dropout. In all these states enrolments in Grade 8 are a half or less of those in Grade 1. Andhra Pradesh is different and has high enrolments through to Grade 8 and relatively little dropout. Opportunities and constraints on the development of private education in each of the states are different for a complex set of reasons which have to do with current patterns of enrolments, demography, historic patterns of provision, the political economy of educational reform, household income distribution, and a variety of other factors beyond the scope of the short paper. What is clear from these data is that the possibilities are likely be very different at different Grade levels, and that variation between states is likely to be substantial.

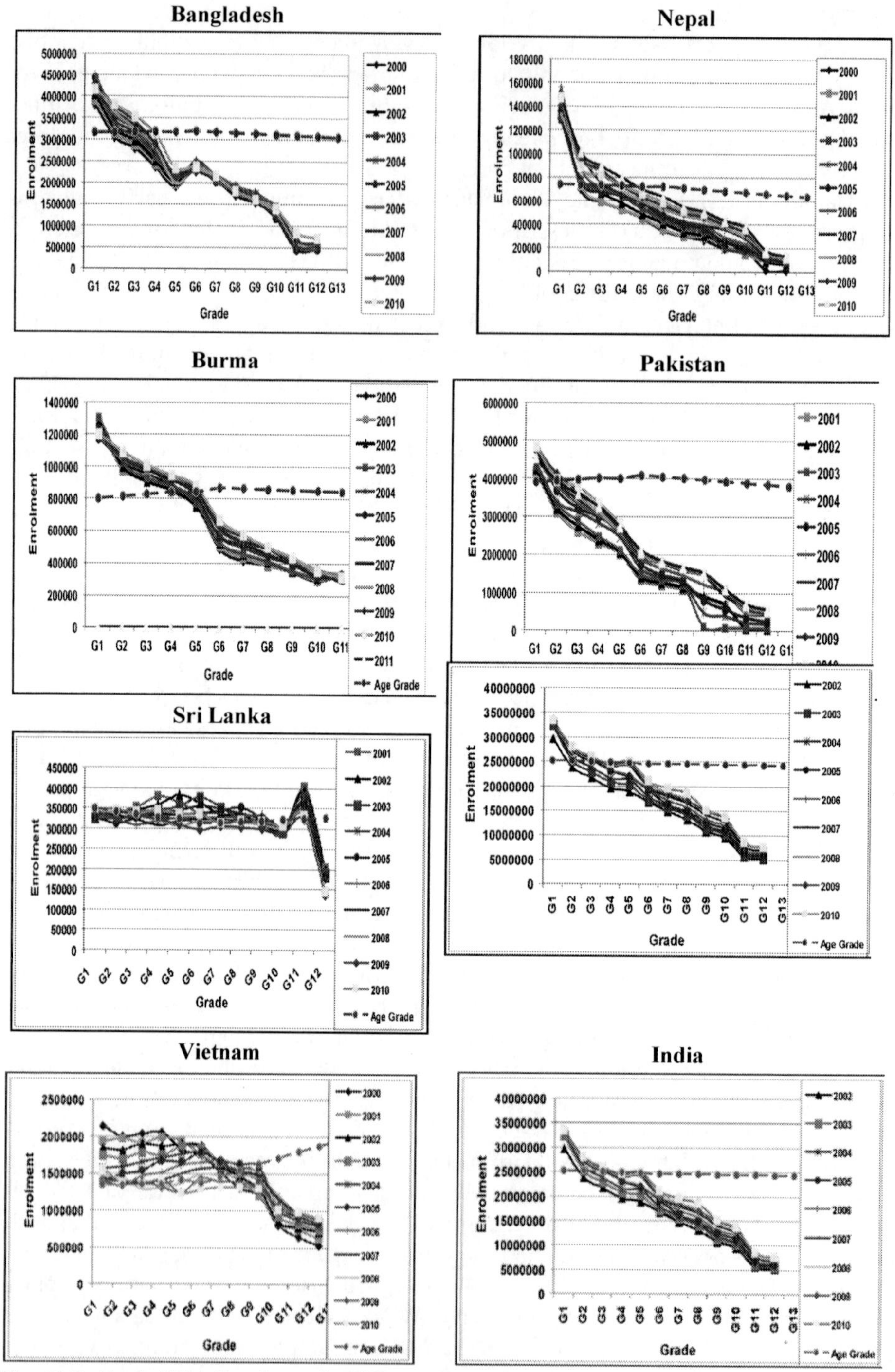

Fig. 12.2: Grade-Wise Enrolment in Different Countries

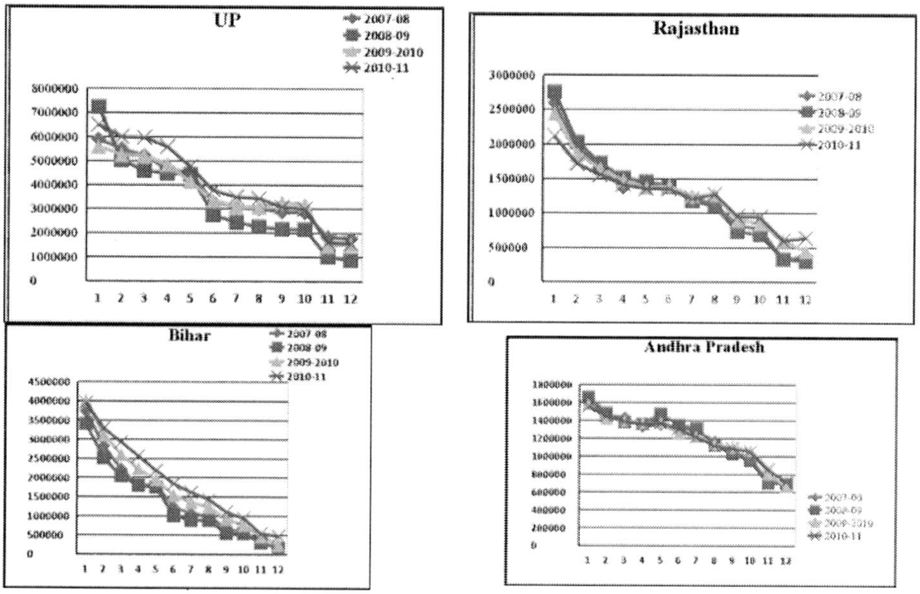

Fig. 12.3: Grade-Wise Enrolment in Different Indian States

Concluding Remarks

This short paper explores some aspects of the issues for educational development in the South and South East Asian region that relate to inclusion, equity and sustainability. It is part of work in progress that argues that continued investment in publicly financed and run basic education school systems remains at the core of development for a number of reasons.

- First, public systems are guarantors of the right to basic education. No other entity has either the responsibility or the means to deliver universal rights.
- Second, public systems have delivered much additional access at affordable costs and include many schools of quality as well as those that underperform. There is no systematic evidence of "private school effects" when appropriate controls are introduced for home background and selection effects and this is clear in the PISA data across 72 countries. In all countries some public schools out perform some private schools and *vice versa,* demonstrating that performance differences do not depend only on school type.
- Third, public systems reach children in communities of little or no interest to commercial providers. The reasons are obvious. Households below the poverty line have little discretionary income. Charging fees or other levies to households below the poverty line makes such households poorer. Only States can promote Rawlesian equity where investment of public resources is pro-poor. Free public schools can sponsor inter-generational mobility on a scale unsustainable in private institutions.
- Fourth, resource gaps in financing universal access to education cannot be

filled by private sector initiatives in sustainable ways. Reducing these gaps requires appropriate fiscal policy, the translation of political will into public financing, and the pro-poor redistribution of educational opportunity.

- Fifth, the opportunity costs of diverting public finance to largely unregulated private-for-profit providers are substantial. Every public dollar directed towards a for profit private school is a dollar less spent on improving a public school. Every dollar of profit represents a transfer from public funds to private national and international beneficial owners and shareholders.
- Sixth, systemic risks are real where dependence on private sector delivery of public services increases. When more than a small proportion of educational services is privately controlled, where public regulation is fragile, and self-regulation lacks transparency, there are risks of miss selling, cheating, tax fraud, and other malpractices. Where there are no requirements for public liability insurance and bonds to cover the costs of the failure of chains of schools the liability remains with the state and so do the costs.

These arguments make a case for continued large scale public investment in school systems. This case has to be accompanied with obligations for sector reform and the relentless pursuit of improved levels of efficiency and effectiveness. Constant attempts to enhance equity and ensure whole population benefits from improved quality are needed. The challenges are extensive and persistent. They mirror those for the reform of other systems that deliver public goods for which it is counterproductive to ration by price, e.g. basic healthcare, public security, clean water. These will be hindered not helped by diversion of resources to private providers of services, unless these serve public purposes efficiently. In low income countries with weak states and largely unregulated private providers of services, the need is to build modern states that can provide public goods of quality on a large scale. And which can manage private providers of services in the public interest if they are both efficient and equitable. Overall responsibilities for social development and educational provision cannot be divested to a mixed bag of market driven providers with many different motives. To do so introduces considerable systemic risk that cannot be easily offset. It jeopardises social justice and social equity.

Decisions as to how best to make use of the strengths of the private sector will always be politically shaped. There is merit in relationships that make use of opportunities to encourage constructive interactions between the public sector and private service providers. Demand from wealthy and middle-income households for private educational services is likely to grow and can release resources for use in public systems serving a broader constituency and those who cannot afford to pay. Aspects of infrastructure, learning material production, and training may benefit from engaging for profit and not for profit providers within appropriate procurement and regulatory structures. And where there is doubt about efficacy of public or private contracting small scale experiments outside the public sector and independent evaluations of effects can be very informative.

However, the role of the state in development is at the core of the debates around privatisation. The obligation of states to translate rights to education into realities is clear. Most investment in public capacity to develop education systems is needed where capability and performance is weakest in poor countries with low levels of attainment and achievement. This can help build good governance, reinforce collective national identities, generate confidence in States, promote reciprocity in the social contracts that modern states have with their citizens to collect taxes and provide public services. It can help reconcile the tensions that come from balancing national development priorities, individual aspirations and the development of education as both a positional good that allocates private life chances and a public good under pinning collective wellbeing. It can reduce the dependence that is so much part of the political economy of post-colonial states seeking national identities, especially in multi ethnic States, and can enhance national ownership of educational development strategies in a globalising world.

Public school systems have served OECD countries well, and been a core asset for those developing countries developing rapidly in East and South East Asia. They have contributed to more equitable development than would otherwise be the case, and the realisation of stable social contracts between governments and those they govern. Public systems must remain at the core of making rights realities. Investment in the next generation of children's knowledge, skill and capabilities is too important to be left to the vagaries of imperfect and largely unregulated markets and the ambitions of supply chain entrepreneurs.

Social democracy depends on fiscal policy that raises revenue to provide public goods that are valued. By 2030 all countries in the region will commit to providing equitable access and equal opportunities for education and training up to the age of 18 years. If governments fall short on their promises to provide educational public goods they risk diminishing social cohesion and social conflict. Today's children deserve governments, and external aid programmes, that deliver on promises to promote universal access and equal opportunities thorough to the end of secondary schooling. This has to result in the kind of accessible learning that is a public good that comes without a price to children and that is guaranteed by states not markets.

Notes

1. The author asserts his rights over the contents of this draft paper which shall not be circulated or distributed without reference to the author and which shall not be published in any form without prior agreement with the author.
2. The Consortium for Research on Educational Access, Transitions and Equity (CREATE was funded by the UK Department for International Development (DFID) to undertake research in Bangladesh, India, Ghana and South Africa. NUEPA was the CREATE Partner Organisation in India.

References

Akaguri, L. (2014): Fee-Free Public or Low-Fee Private Basic Education in Rural Ghana: How does the Cost Influence the Choice of the Poor? *Compare: A Journal of Comparative and International Education*, 44 (2): 140-61.

Bangay, C. & Latham, M. (2013): Are We Asking the Right Questions? Moving beyond the State vs Non-State Providers Debate: Reflections and a Case Study from India. *International Journal of Educational Development,* 33 (3): 244-52.

Cameron, S. (2011): Whether and Where to Enrol? Choosing a Primary School in the Slums of Urban Dhaka, Bangladesh. *International Journal of Educational Development,* 31 (4): 357-66.

Chimombo, J. (2009): Expanding Post-Primary Education in Malawi: Are Private Schools the Answer? *Compare: A Journal of Comparative and International Education,* 39 (2): 167-84.

Colclough, C. (1996): Education and the Market: Which Parts of the Neo-Liberal Solution are Correct?, *World Development*, 24 (4): 589–610

Ashley, L. (2009): Private Schooling in Less Economically Developed Countries: Asian and African Perspectives. *Compare: A Journal of Comparative and International Education,* 39 (2): 297-99.

Ashley, L.; Mcloughlin, C.; Aslam, M.; Engel, J.; Wales, J. and Rawal. S. (2014): The Role and Impact of Private Schools in Developing Countries: A Rigorous Review of the Evidence. DFID, UK.

Dixon, P.; Tooley, J. & Schagen, I. (2013): The Relative Quality of Private and Public Schools for Low-Income Families Living in Slums of Nairobi, Kenya. In Srivastava, P. (Ed.), *Low-Fee Private Schooling: Aggravating Equity or Mitigating Disadvantage*. Oxford: Oxford Studies in Comparative Education.

French, R. & Kingdon, G. (2010): The Relative Effectiveness of Private and Government Cchools in Rural India: Evidence from ASER Data. London: Institute of Education.

Härmä, J. (2011): Low Cost Private Schooling in India: Is It Pro-Poor and Equitable? *International Journal of Educational Development,* 31 (4): 350-56.

Heyneman, S.P. & Stern, J.M.B. (2013): Low Cost Private Schools for the Poor: What Public Policy is Appropriate? *International Journal of Educational Development.*

Kingdon, G.G. (1996): Private Schooling in India: Size, Nature and Equity Effects, *Economic and Political Weekly*, 31 (5): 3306 – 3314.

Kitaev, I. (1999): Private Education in Sub-Saharan Africa: A Re-Examination of Theories and Concepts Related to Its Development and Finance. Paris: UNESCO-IIEP.

Kremer, M. & Muralidharan, K. (2008): Public and Private Schools in Rural India. In Peterson, P. & Chakrabarti, R. (Ed.), *School Choice International*. Cambridge, MA: MIT Press.

Lewin, K.M. and Sayed, Y (2005): Non-Government Secondary Schooling in Sub-Saharan Africa? Exploring the Evidence in South Africa and Malawi. London: DFID.

Lewin, K.M. (2011): *Making Rights Realities: Researching Educational Access, Transitions and Equity*. Research Report of the Consortium for Research on Educational Access, Transitions and Equity. Brighton: University of Sussex.

Lewin, K.M. (2011): Expanding Access to Secondary Education: Can India Catch Up? in Lewin, K.M.; Little, A.W. and Hunt, F. (Ed), Access, Equity, and Transitions in Education in Low Income Countries; *CREATE Special Issue of the International Journal of Education and Development*, 31: 4, 382-94.

Lewin, K.M. (2007): The Limits to Growth of Non-Government Schooling in Sub-Saharan Africa. In Walford, G. and Srivastava, P.: *Private Schools in Developing Countries*, Symposium Books.

Mundy, K. and Menashy, F. (2012): Investing in Private Education for Poverty Alleviation: The Case of the World Bank's International Finance Corporation. *International Journal of Educational Development.*

Muralidharan, K.; Kremer, M. & Sundararaman, V. (2011): The Aggregate Effect of School Choice — Evidence from a Two-Stage Experiment in India. Paper presented at the IGC-ISI Development Policy Conference.

Ohba, A. (2012): Do Low-Cost Private School Leavers in the Informal Settlement have a Good Chance of Admission to a Government Secondary School? A Study from Kibera in Kenya. *Compare: A Journal of Comparative and International Education*, 1-20.

Rose, Pauline (2007): *Supporting Non-State Providers in Basic Education Service Delivery.* CREATE Pathways to Access Research Monograph No 4, University of Sussex.

Siddhu, G. (2011): Can Families in Rural India Bear the Additional Burden of Secondary Education? Investigating the Determinants of Transition. Sussex: Centre for International Education.

Sommers, C. (2012): Primary Education in Rural Bangladesh: Degrees of Access, Choice, and Participation of the Poorest. London: Privatisation in Education Research Initiative (PERI).

Srivastava, P. (2013): Low-Fee Private Schooling: Issues and Evidence. In P. Srivastava (Ed.) *Low-Fee Private Schooling: Aggravating Equity or Mitigating Disadvantage?* Oxford: Symposium Books

Tooley, J. & Dixon, P. (2003): Private Schools for the Poor: A Case Study from India, London: CFBT

Woodhead, M.; Frost, M. & James, Z. (2013): Does Growth in Private Schooling Contribute to Education for All? Evidence from a Longitudinal, Two Cohort Study in Andhra Pradesh, India. *International Journal of Educational Development,* 33 (1), 65-73.

13

Challenges of Inclusion

How are India's Schools Faring?

Praveen Jha, Satadru Sikdar* and *Pooja Parvati

Linkages between education, democracy and development is a complex terrain with no simple or unilinear answers; The well-known economist, John Kenneth Galbraith, once remarked that there is, in our time, no well-educated/literate population that is poor; and there is no illiterate population that is other than poor. Although Galbraith overstated his case but it would be difficult to disagree with the view that there is a strong instrumental linkage between education and overall well-being in any economy or society. Much of the recent work on human development has tended to explore such linkages in persuasive ways. Furthermore, as generally acknowledged across cultures and ages, education must not be reduced only to its 'instrumental role' as it is extremely important in an 'intrinsic' sense as well.[1]

In a developing country like India, the state has to shoulder the primary responsibility for provisioning of education. Thus, it is a matter of great concern that, given the diktats of the neoliberal policy frame, we are witnessing weakening of public policy commitments, which in any case had been indifferent at best even in the pre-reform era, towards *good quality universal basic education* in critical ways. The central tenets of a neoliberal policy regime are to facilitate ascendency of markets not only in what may be considered its 'traditional' domains but also in almost every walk of economy; in other words, it is not only the arena of material production and consumption but also the so-called social sectors and services such as education and health, which are subjected to the logic of the market. The period since the early 1990s, characterised by a strong push to a neo-liberal reforms programme, has fundamentally altered the role of government intervention in the economy and society in India, with far-reaching and pervasive implications. Like other arenas, the social sectors have also undergone significant changes, often organically linked with the neoliberal policies.

This paper seeks to investigate some of the core issues relating to the state of school education in contemporary India. In particular, we focus on core aspects relating to educational infrastructure and important outcomes and try to highlight some of the critical concerns relating to equity and exclusion. The paper draws on a variety of data sources including reports of the National Sample Survey Organisation (NSSO), reports of various government committees, budget documents of the Union government, District Information System for Education (DISE) data [published annually as Elementary Education in India: Analytical Report (Mehta, various years) by the National University of Education Planning and Administration (NUEPA)], reports of the All India School Education Survey (AISES), conducted by the National Council of Educational Research and Training (NCERT) and Ministry of Human Resource and Development, Government of India, and other relevant secondary literature.

After the introductory section, we have provided a snapshot of the context and major markers in this regard at the current juncture in Section I. Section II sketches the current status and gaps in outcomes of education at elementary and secondary levels across different social groups, religions, household occupation groups with a particular focus on economically and financially vulnerable sections. Section III examines the issues of quality and Section IV closes the paper with a couple of concluding remarks.

A Snapshot of School Infrastructure and Outcomes

School Infrastructure: As per the Constitution of India, public provisioning of education has primarily been a responsibility of the states, and thus state-specific factors have obviously been important in throwing up a diversity of outcomes. India currently houses the largest number of illiterates compared to any other country, accounting for almost one-third of the total number of illiterate persons in the world. Close to 8 per cent of the total population of children in the elementary school-going age (5 to 14 years) segment is reported to be out of school (for 2011-12) by the NSS 68th round data. Although, the official data reveal significant improvement in the count of literates during the last couple of decades, as the literacy rate for the country as a whole increased from 52.2 to 64.8 per cent in 2001, and 74 per cent in 2011, quality concerns continue to be serious. Further, as per the Census of India, there has been a narrowing of the rural-urban gap is literacy, from 28.41 in 1991 to 16.1 per cent in 2011. Nevertheless, deprivation levels among the vulnerable social and occupational groups are relatively high and significant.

The poor state of the country's public education system, create space for ill-equipped private schools, mainly targeted at low-income groups, desperate to see their children in 'decent' institutions. To many of them, schooling in English-medium private schools is seen as the first necessary step to escape from drudgery and poverty. As a result the number of private unaided primary schools in the country has increased almost six-fold and private recognised schools three-fold between 1970 and 2011 (1973 figure taken from Third All India Education Survey; And 2011-12 figures taken from Elementary Education in India Progress towards UEE Analytical Tables 2011-12).

Table 13.1: Growth of Private Schools Providing Elementary Education[2]

Year	Government	Private	Total	Private Schools as per cent of Total
1903	107196	38678	145874	26.5
1960-61	293936	88034	381970	23.0
1973	495756	53392	549150	9.7
1979	534260	45780	580040	7.9
1986	705560	113404	818964	13.8
2002	755792	140594	896386	15.7
2003	794265	125842	920107	13.7
2005	880545	157268	1037813	15.2
2011-12	1078407	299357	1377764	21.7

Source: Various statistical documents[3]

Over the same period, the number of government and local body schools went down by more than 10 percentage points. There are reasons to believe that the number of private unaided and unrecognised (by the government) schools may be substantially more than what we know from available official data as there has been a virtual mushrooming of teaching shops, particularly in the recent years, that are hardly visible. Many of these are operating in the lowest age category of 2-4 years, generally in urban areas, which are supposed to be feeders to English-medium teaching shops.

Coming specifically to some of the infrastructure indicators pertaining to the elementary level, as per the DISE data, student-classroom ratio (SCR) were 41:1 at the primary and 33:1 at the upper primary level in 2005-06, and they improved to 31:1 for primary and 29:1 respectively in 2010-11. In 2011-12, almost 34.6 per cent of primary schools and 26.87 per cent of upper primary schools did not have any toilet. 51.13 per cent of primary and 50.88 per cent of upper primary schools did not have any boundary wall. Drinking water facilities were not available in 6.64 per cent of primary and 6.11 per cent of upper primary schools.

Pupil-teacher ratios (PTR) for primary and upper primary schools declined from 24:1 and 20:1 in early 1950s to 31.37:1 and 30.2:1 in 2011-12 respectively (DISE, 2011-12). Clearly, the increase in teacher supply has not kept pace with increases in child population and attendance at schools leading to overcrowded classrooms with PTR at the primary level being as high as 58 in Bihar and 44 in Uttar Pradesh in 2011-12. In recent years, there has been an emphasis on increasing the number of upper primary schools at the all-India level with some improvement; now, on an average, one upper primary school is catering to 2.06 primary school in 2011-12, (which is close to SSA national norm 1:2), compared to 2.8 in 2004-05.[4] However, it is also worth noting that, the distance norm for schools, set by SSA, is yet to be met fully. According to the 8th AISES (2009) report, almost 10 per cent of habitations did not have primary schools within 1 kilometre and 14.6 per cent of habitations did not have upper primary schools within 3 kilometres.

Enrolment

As per the 68th round of NSS (2011-12), out of 211 million children in the age group 6-14 years, 196 million were enrolled; the percentage of out-of-school children works out to be 4.49. For the age group 11-13 years, the percentage of out-of-school children was relatively higher among girls (4.67 per cent) than boys (3.15 per cent). Between 1987-88 and 2011-12 enrolment status has improved for all age groups, both in rural and urban areas, as may be seen from Figure 13.1 below. In rural India, it was 54.4 per cent for children in the 6-14 year age group in 1987-88, which increased to 92.28 per cent in 2011-12; in urban India, the relevant figures, for the same age group, were 76.47 and 94.77 per cent respectively. For the 15-18 year age group, enrollment in rural areas increased from 27.26 per cent in 1987-88 to 64.15 per cent in 2011-12, and in urban India, the relevant figures were 48.79 and 74.44 per cent.

Gender disparity in enrollment has reduced considerably within both the age groups in rural as well as in urban regions. In urban India for the 6-14 age group, the gender disparity in enrollment came down from 7 per cent in 1987-88, to 0.2 per cent in

2011-12; for 15-18 age group, the gap came down from 14 to 3 per cent over the same period.[5] In the case of rural India, the gender disparity is higher than that in urban

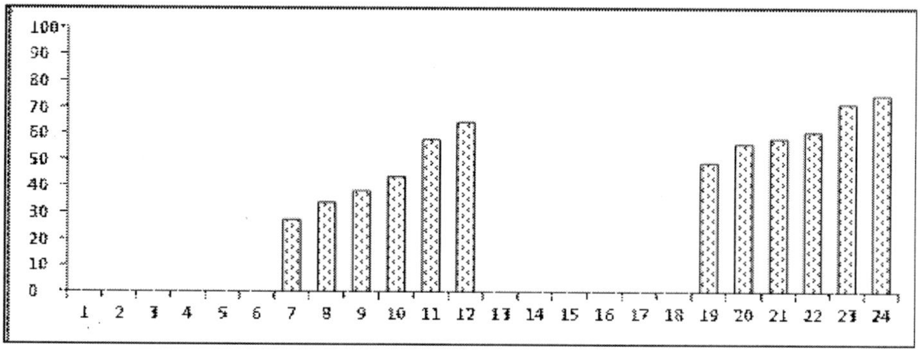

Fig. 13.1: All India Enrolment Status (1987-88 – 2011-12)

Source: Calculated from NSSO unit level data of employment-unemployment rounds (NSS 43rd, 50th, 55th, 61th, 66th and 68th rounds).

India: between 1987-88 and 2011-12, the gender gap in enrolment between 6-14 age group came down from 19 to 2 per cent, whereas in the 15-18 age group, it came down from 24 to 8 over the same period.[7]

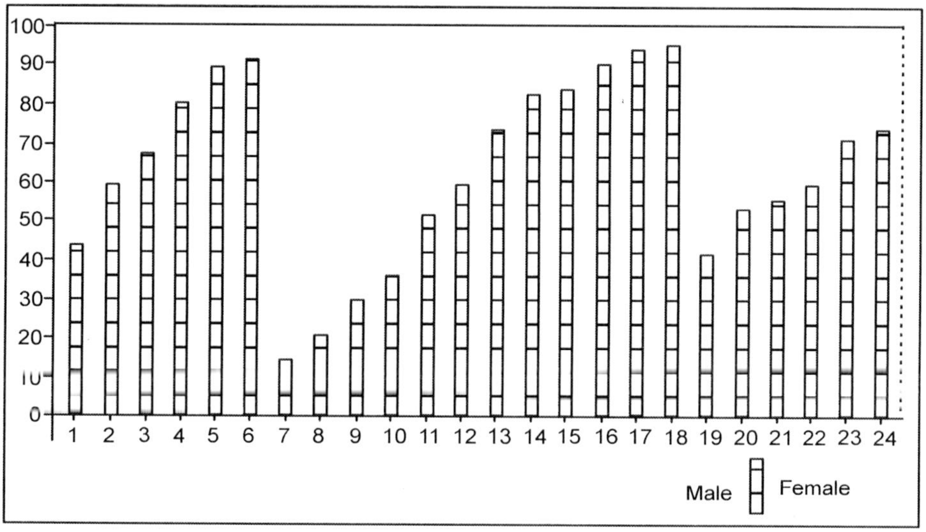

Fig. 13.2: All India Enrolment Status (Sex-Wise)

Source: Calculated from NSSO unit level data of employment-unemployment rounds (NSS 43rd, 50th, 55th, 61th, 66th and 68th rounds).

Although a reasonable progress has been achieved, significant disparities still exist along the lines of caste, religion and region. For instance, in 2011-12, among the 6-14 year age group, almost 9 per cent children from Muslim community were out of school, compared to 3.7 and 3 per cent from Hindu and Christian communities respectively. Similarly, in the same age band in 2011-12, proportion of out of school children from SC (5.3 per cent) and ST (5.3 per cent) households were almost double compared to the children from general category (2.8 per cent). Among, all social groups, estimated percentage of out of school children was higher in rural (5 per cent) than in urban (3 per cent) areas. Of those attending school in the 6-14 age group, more than 77 per cent attended government or aided school and 23 per cent were in private unaided schools in 2011-12. Dependency on government school is higher in rural areas (83 per cent) compared to urban areas (62 per cent). However, a shift of participation towards private aided schools has been taking place in the recent years for the country as a whole.

Disparities across Different Socio-Religious Groups

Disparities across Social Groups: The enrolment has increased at a rapid rate both in rural and urban areas, although there are noticeable disparities across social categories (Table 13.2). Between 1987-88 to 2011-12, there was a dramatic improvement in enrolment in the 6-14 year age group in rural areas from 39.22 per cent to 90.98 per cent among the STs, and from 44.39 to 91.55 for the SCs. A similar improving trend can be observed for the same age group as the urban areas. In 2011-12, enrolment rates in the 6-14 year age group were 95.2 per cent for General category, 94.95 per cent for OBCs, 93.52 per cent for SCs and 93.36 per cent for STs. The disparities across social groups are significant in case of the 15-18 year age group, both in rural and urban areas. In 2011-12, enrolment rates in this age group across different social categories were: 71 in rural and 79 per cent in urban for General category; 56 in rural and 73 per cent in urban for STs; 57 in rural and 67 per cent in urban for SCs. Enrolment rates for OBCs were better than that from SCs and STs.

Table 13.2: Disparity Enrolment across Social Groups

			1987-88	*1993-94*	*1999-2000*	*2004-05*	*2009-10*	*2011-12*
Between 6-14 Years	Rural	General over ST	19.97	18.56	19.00	13.06	6.21	3.52
		General over SC	14.80	12.68	12.63	8.02	4.04	2.95
		General over OBC	–	–	8.41	5.43	2.22	2.56
	Urban	General over ST	9.28	9.79	8.45	5.17	5.62	1.84
		General over SC	14.27	10.37	8.76	8.06	3.67	1.68
		General over OBC	–	–	5.72	2.88	2.46	0.25
Between 15-18 Years	Rural	General over ST	9.95	13.18	18.18	17.37	17.75	14.38
		General over SC	8.22	10.52	14.81	14.05	12.69	13.07
		General over OBC	–	–	11.72	8.41	5.70	4.88
	Urban	General over ST	2.17	9.11	10.80	9.67	5.37	5.75
		General over SC	18.83	16.61	20.72	22.04	13.88	11.68
		General over OBC	–	–	17.66	15.48	11.08	6.39

Source: Calculated from NSSO unit level data of employment-unemployment rounds (NSS 43rd, 50th, 55th, 61th, 66th and 68th rounds).

Despite improvement in enrollment rates during the last couple of decades, the problem of children dropping out remains a critical issue. In rural areas, chances of dropping-out are higher for STs than SCs among both of these age groups, whereas in urban areas, higher dropout rates are observed for SCs. In 2011-12, dropout rates in the 6-14 year age group for STs were: 3.76 per cent in rural and 1.13 per cent in urban areas; for SCs, comparative figures were 2.88 and 2.45 per cent in rural and urban areas respectively. Among all social categories, dropout in fact was significantly higher in the 15-18 year age cohort. In 2011-12, in rural areas, in the 15-18 year age group, dropout rates were 17.71, 15.06, 14.89 and 12.31 per cent for SCs, OBCs, STs and general categories respectively. In urban areas, in the same age group for 2011-12, dropout rates were 15.39, 11.42, 10.72 and 10.69 for SCs, OBCs, STs and general categories respectively.

We may also note here that the incidences of dropping-out were significantly higher for girls than the boys in both the age groups. In the 15-18 year age group, in rural areas, incidence of dropout for girls and boys respectively were: 15.9 and 14 per cent among STs, 20 and 15.8 per cent among SCs, 17.33 and 13.25 for OBCs and 14.46 and 10.55 per cent for general categories in 2011-12. In urban India, for the same year, within the same age band, incidence of dropout for girls and boys respectively were: 14 and 8.26 per cent among STs, 17.3 and 13.8 per cent among SCs, 11.72 and 11.18 for OBCs and 12.3 and 9.4 per cent for general categories.

As noted earlier, there is a growing desertion from the government schools for relatively better off both in rural and urban areas. As per the 2011-12 data, in the 6-14 year age group, 89 and 81 per cent of ST and SC children in rural areas depend on government schools compared to 66 per cent enrolled children of general categories. The dependency on government schools has increased among 6-14 years age cohort among STs in urban areas from 49 to 55 per cent between 2004-05 and 2011-12. Another point worth noting here is that dependency of girls on government schools is relatively higher than boys. The difference of boys and girls participation rate in government schools in rural areas were 6.6 for STs compared to 2.7 of general categories and in urban areas 8.2 for SCs compared to 1.9 for general categories. Further, we may also note that there is an overall shift from private aided to private unaided schools in 15-18 year age group, between 2004-05 and 2011-12, and this holds even for the SCs/STs children both in rural and urban areas.

Disparities across Religious Groups: Going by the trends between 1987-88 to 2011-12, gaps in enrolment rates across religious groups, in the 6-14 year age band, have become negligible.[6] In 2011-12, Jains were performing better than others although gender disparity exists even within this community. Buddhists fare better than Sikhs, Christians, Hindus and Muslims. Muslims continue to fare poorly in both rural and urban areas followed by Hindus during all the years under consideration. Generally there has been an improvement in enrolment in all age bands and across all religious groups, although at varying rates, with least progress among the Muslims. For instance, in 2011-12 the gap between Jains and Muslims in enrolment was almost 30 per cent in rural areas and 34 per cent in urban areas in the 15-18 year age group. Failure to complete education is a relatively serious problem among Muslim children. In rural

India, proportion of Muslim children dropping-out among the 6-14 year age group was 5 per cent in 2011-12, compared to 1.2 and 2.5 per cent for Sikhs and Hindus. The likelihood of female students dropping-out is higher across all religious groups.

As per the NSSO data for 2011-12, the participation rate in government schools in the 6-14 year age group among Hindus was 74 per cent in rural and 38 per cent in urban areas; for Muslims the respective figures were 74 and 42 per cent. We may also note that these rates remained almost same between 2004-05 and 2011-12, although there was a small shift from schools run by local bodies to private unaided schools. In the 15-18 year age groups, there is an increase in participation in government schools in rural areas (64.4 to 66.3 per cent); whereas, there is a small decline in urban areas (46.2 to 43.5 per cent) over the same period. Among major religious groups, as per the NSSO data for 2011-12, more than 76 and 65 per cent of Muslim and Hindu children respectively in the 15-18 year age cohort attend government schools in rural areas and comparable figures in urban areas are 47 and 43 per cent respectively.

Disparities across Occupational Groups: Occupational Groups represent different household types, as defined by NSSO on the basis of the household's sources of income during 365 days preceding the date of survey. In general, disparities in enrolment across all occupational groups have become negligible for the 6-14 year age group. However, for the 15-18 year age group, enrolment of children from the households in casual and agricultural labour are significantly lower compared to other occupational categories. As regards dropout rates in 2011-12 for children from casual agricultural labour households in rural areas: it was 3.79 and 17.07 per cent for 6-14 year and 15-18 year age groups respectively. In the same year these figures were 2.31 and 14.42 respectively for these two age groups for children from households working as self-employed labour in agriculture in rural areas. In urban areas, dropout rates were 3.75 and 18.9 per cent for 6-14 year and 15-18 year age groups respectively for children from casual labour households in 2011-12. For children from regular wage earning households in urban areas the dropout rates were relatively lower at 1.53 and 10.5 per cent for 6-14 year and 15-18 year age groups respectively.

Children from relatively weak economic background mostly attend government school. In 2011-12, 85 and 75 per cent of the total children enrolled from casual agricultural labour households in rural areas were in government school for the 6-14 year and 15-18 year age groups respectively. In the same year, for children from casual non-agricultural labour households in rural areas, these figures were 81.8 and 75.5 for these two age groups respectively. In urban areas, for the same year, from the casual labour households, 61.8 and 60 per cent for the 6-14 year and 15-18 year age groups respectively were enrolled in government schools, whereas children from regular-wage/salary earning households showed significantly lower dependency on government schools. For these households, in rural areas the participation rates in government school were 60.3 and 59.4 per cent for the 6-14 year and 15-18 year age groups respectively and in urban areas these rates were 31.1 and 38.8 per cent for the respective age groups.

It is worth noting that in urban areas, for 6-14 year age group, dependency on government schools has increased among children from casual workers' households (59.25 to 61.76 per cent) and reduced among children from regular wage/salary earning households (34.77 to 31.07 per cent) between 2004-05 and 2011-12. There is also a shifting trend from private-aided schools and schools managed by local bodies to the private unaided schools among children across all occupational groups. For instance, between 2004-05 and 2011-12, in rural areas, for 6-14 year age group, incidence of reduction in participation in private aided and local bodies managed schools were 6, 8 and 5 per cent for children from agricultural casual workers households, non-agricultural casual workers households, and self-employed households respectively. Over the same period data show an increase in participation in private unaided schools by 3, 8 and 3.6 per cent for the above noted household types respectively. In urban areas, over the same period, for the 6-14 year age group, incidence of reduction in participation in private aided and local bodies managed schools were 9.6, 2.4 and 3 per cent for children from households of casual workers, regular wage earners and self-employed; figures for increase in participation in private unaided schools were 7.4, 8 and 3.4 per cent for the respective occupational groups.

The enrolment, dropout and participation rates clearly show that weaker sections continue to depend in large measure on government schools, prospects for successful transition and completion of schooling are worrisome. In fact, careful examination of the relevant data clearly show that a significant section of Indian children continue to be deprived of several basic provisions under the Right to Education Act (RTE), 2009 even after 5 years. While there has been some advancement, as is evident from the growth in the number of classrooms and increase in access to schooling in remote areas, we still have a long way to go. The following section touches briefly on same issues relating to quality at the current juncture.

On Some Aspects of Quality

In the recent years, there have been several well-known studies and surveys across the globe, many of these of an ongoing nature to assess quality of education in schools.[8] In India, some of the recent initiatives in this respect include Annual Status of Education Report (ASER) by Pratham, National Achievement Survey (NAS) by National Council of Education Research and Training (NCERT) and Educational Development Index (EDI) by (NUEPA) using DISE data.[9] Apart from these, Indian Human Development Survey (IHDS-I in 2004-05 and IHDS-II in 2011-12) and EDWATCH survey by National Coalition for Education also provide important insights to the understanding of quality of education.

ASER mainly conducts surveys in rural areas every year and in 2013, it covered 568 districts in India. Quality of education is measured in ASER as "Reading and Calculation Proficiency of Students from Class I-VIII". While the indicators might be debatable, they provide an assessment of state-wise performances. The survey reports provide learning levels information with the help of their reading and arithmetic tools. Since 2005, it is providing information on learning levels among children in standard 3 to 5 and since 2012 also for children in standards 6 to 8. Sampling and assessment procedures of this survey had changed in 2007, and therefore information from 2007 to 2013 are comparable. The major finding emerging from ASER is that, on the whole there is no improvement over time and in fact with respect several indicators there are signs of deterioration in learning levels (Annual Status of Education Report (Rural), 2013, page 66).

NAS conducted by the NCERT also assesses learning capacity of students. However, there are differences both in design and the results between ASER (discussed above) and NAS. While the ASER surveys *households* in rural areas, the NAS conducts its surveys in *schools* both in rural and urban areas and both of them have different methodologies. NAS follows Trends in International Mathematics and Science Study (TIMSS) for preparing assessment method on Mathematics, and for assessment method on language it follows National Assessment of Educational Progress (NAEP). NAS has been done in three cycles, 2001 to 2004 (Baseline Achievement Survey), 2005 to 2008 (Mid-Term Achievement Survey) and 2009 to 2012 (Terminal Achievement Survey) to cover three key grades, Class III, Class V and Class VII/VIII. Students' abilities in language judged by listening, reading and recognition of words administered in 16 languages; abilities in mathematics is judged by numbers, basic operations — addition, subtraction, multiplication and division, money, measurement and data handling through a child-friendly test. For Class V children, apart from testing for Mathematics and language, questions were asked about environmental sciences, while for the children in Classes VII/VIII assessments included tests in Sciences and Social Sciences.

In general, results from NAS data show a better picture compare to other sources. For instance, recently released report for Class III (cycle 3, conducted in 2013) shows that about 65 per cent of the children were able to listen and respond correctly and about 86 per cent of the students were able to recognise a given picture. In Mathematics, 70 per cent of the kids were able to handle simple multiplication and 84 per cent students were able to handle data relevant to their context.[10] This survey also reported that "overall, Class III children in 34 states/UTs were able to answer 64 per cent of language items correctly and 66 per cent of Mathematics questions correctly". It may also be noted, that the differences in outcomes between boys and girls are negligible, as is the case with respect to outcomes for children across different social categories. (SCs, STs, OBCs and general). However, differences across states, with respect to outcomes, as per the social gender groups, tend to be quite significant.

National Council of Applied Economic Research (NCAER) in collaboration with the University of Maryland organised India Human Development Survey (IHDS-I) in 2004-05 which covered 41,554 households in 33 states and UTs. In 2011-12, the same households were re-interviewed as part of IHDS-II. These surveys have collected information on reading and writing skills among children. It emerges that among children between 8 to 11 years *reading capacity declined from 54 per cent to 52 per cent in between 2005 to 2012*; over the same period there is decline also in basic arithmetic skills from 48 to 45 per cent. In both these respects the children enrolled in government school trend to fare worse than their counterparts in other schools. These characteristics are higher for children enrolled in government schools.

The National Coalition for Education (NCE), New Delhi, conducted primary surveys in 10 states (Andhra Pradesh, Bihar, Gujarat, Jharkhand, Madhya Pradesh, Orissa, Punjab, Rajasthan, Uttar Pradesh and Uttarakhand) in 2008 and 2010, with the objective of analysing the functioning of elementary schools and budgetary allocations in the light of RTE for children between 6-14 years. This survey measured the quality of education with the help of survival and retention rates and transition rates. The cohort survival rates for Class 1-5 for the surveyed children was 89 per cent (for boys) and 84 per cent (for girls) in 2010; for Class VI-VIII the comparable rates was 92 and 88 per cent. Average transition rate from primary to upper primary level was 85 and 84 per cent. Using the data for 2010, the NCE report also generated Education Development Index (EDI) based on the correlation matrix which included 16 indicators for the Principal Component Index (PCI).[11] As in the case of other reports, results show considerable variation across states. With respect to access, states like Bihar, Uttarakhand, Odisha, Jharkhand and Rajasthan performed relatively poorer; with respect to infrastructure, Madhya Pradesh, Odisha, Andhra Pradesh, Bihar and Jharkhand are placed lower down the ladder. With respect to availability of teachers, performance of states such as Bihar, Rajasthan, Jharkhand, Uttar Pradesh and Madhya Pradesh did very poorly and the reported outcome were lowest for Bihar, Jharkhand, Uttar Pradesh, Rajasthan and Uttarakhand; in terms of equity indicators Bihar, Rajasthan, Jharkhand, Uttar Pradesh, Madhya Pradesh were among the poorest performers. Taking all the indicators together Bihar occupies the last place in terms the above noted EDI ranking.

One of the important reasons underlying differences of quality is the heterogeneity of schools under different management, although within the same management group there can be a remarkable variations. Per child expenditure, which is a relatively robust indicator of quality, varies widely even amongst the same broad category of schools. For instance, within non-residential government schools, (i.e., day schools), Kendriya Vidyalayas are considered to be relatively better than the rest. Kendriya Vidyalayas, especially made for children of government employees, had 11,48,340 students as on 31 March 2014; considering Rs. 2554.17 crore of expenditure on 2013-14 (RE), per child allocation was Rs. 22,242.28 per annum. Whereas, average per child expenditure on education in other government schools, taking into account expenditures by various departments of states and including central grants towards state (including mid-day meal), was Rs. 5,091 per annum.[12] It is quite likely that the differences with respect to per child expenditure are even more glaring and consequently there is larger heterogeneity in terms of infrastructure, quality etc. According to latest AISES (2009) report, number of unrecognised school was 39,015 with an enrolment of more than 3 million children (2,373,201 at primary stage and 790,683 at upper primary stage), whereas number of primary and upper primary school in rural India was 979,916 during the same period. As in the case of recognised private unaided school, fees structures for unrecognised have a large range.[13]

As stated earlier, 'quality' of education depends on a whole range of factors; however in our judgement, key to good quality universal education is adequate public provisioning of appropriate resources based on a realistic assessment of infrastructure for decent education. To name just one major gap: as per the recent assessments the shortfall with respect to teachers alone is 12 lakh (MHRD, 2010).[14] We may also note that the relevant data also show a positive relationship of reading and mathematical learning capability related with per child total expenditure (central and state).[15]

While introduction of para-teachers might have improved PTR, it has also critically impacted the quality of education. Despite the variability of para-teachers' definitions across various Indian states, there are approximately 500,000 para-teachers in the country. Correlating such appointments to decline in quality of teaching, many scholars have been questioning the wisdom of appointing para-teachers.

Concluding Remarks

India represents a combination of contradictory tendencies; while on one hand, the Right to Education (RTE) at the elementary level is a significant step (although the legislation and its working remain deeply flawed), on the other hand, an entire range of policies and processes have been unleashed which tend to make prospects of equity and inclusion even more difficult. Central to the above noted concerns are the powerful forces towards commodification of education. It is clear from the Indian experience that deficits of quantity and quality have adversely affected the deprived sections of society. Surely, 'commodification' of education has led to a situation where the number of private schools is increasing at a rapid rate even as deprived sections continue to rely on government schooling system where the educational standard may have gone from bad to worse.

It is quite possible that there is a crowding of children from relatively vulnerable socio-economic groups into schools that are at a lower or the lowest levels in terms of infrastructure, basic provisioning etc. Thus, even when there may have been a closing of the gap in terms of enrolment, distance among different social categories with regards to quality may have increased considerably.[16] It is more than evident that the well-heeled are increasingly 'voting with their feet' out of the government school system. In other words, it is quite likely that there has been a ghettoisation of children from less privileged background into institutions of relatively poorer quality. Furthermore, the mushrooming of private schools has a lot to do with the systemic neglect of government schools over the years. In the time of neoliberal reforms, such neglect has acquired added legitimacy and the choice between languishing government schools and ill-equipped shops in the name of private schools is hardly a choice. This is, to be sure, organically connected with the ascendency of the neo-liberal macro-economic policy regime.

One of the critical factors underlying failure of public policy in this context is inadequacy of resources. Even during the pre-reform period, public spending tended to be well below benchmarks suggested by various committees and experts. Further, inadequate spending over time has only meant that the state responsibility to finance quality education has moved to a continually shifting future date. It is worth recalling here that the Indian state through its several pronouncements over the years since independence, had promised highest priority to basic education.

However, given the worsening condition of state governments' finances and inadequate devolution of funds from Centre to States, expenditures on education incurred by the Centre become crucial to augment total allocations for this sector. However, the low increases in the Centre's expenditure on education, on a base that is already quite small, have not been able to compensate for the declining (per capita real) expenditure on education by States.

As is well known, the Indian Constitution, apart from laying the foundation of India's democratic institutions, also addressed the need to promote social and economic opportunities. In particular, it defined the 'fundamental rights' of all citizens and also identified 'directive principles of state policy' which supplement hard legislation and go beyond legal provisions. These directive principles urge the state 'to secure a social order for the promotion of welfare of the people' as well as to uphold a range of more specific entitlements, such as the right to 'free and compulsory education for all children' (Dreze and Sen, 2002). Any attempt to promoting democracy and development cannot be realised without ensuring this basic entitlement to all.

Notes

1. Professor Amartya Sen repeatedly emphasised the importance of its distinction of 'instrumental' and 'intrinsic' in several of his recent writings.
2. Government includes both government and local bodies. Private includes private aided, private unaided and private unaided unrecognised.
3. 1903 figure taken from 'Statistical Abstract Relating to British India 1903-1912, Digital South Asia Library; 1960-61 figure taken from Report of The Education Commission, 1964-66, Volume 2, page 461, by adding Pre-primary, Lower-primary and Higher Primary schools; figures for 1973, 1979, 1986, 2002 figure are taken from Third, Fourth, Fifth and Seventh All India Education Survey respectively; 2003 and 2005 figures taken from Elementary Education in India: An Analytical Report, 2011-12; and numbers for 2011-12 are from UEE Analytical Tables 2011-12.
4. Mehta, Arun C. (2004-05, 2011-12).
5. Even for the 19-25 year age band, there was a small decline in the gender discrepancy, from 10 to 7 per cent within the period in urban India.
6. It is also noted that in rural India, among 19 to 25 years age group, the gap had increased from 6 per cent to 11 per cent between 1987-88 and 2011-12; male enrollment had increased from 7.85 per cent to 21.54 per cent in between the same time period.
7. Data collected by NSSO that provides information on different religious groups, *viz.*, Hinduism, Islam, Christianity, Sikhism, Jainism, Buddhism, Zoroastrianism and other religions. Zoroastrians have not been considered in this analysis as they comprise only a small proportion in each age group.
8. Further, among these there are quite a few multi-country studies which include: (i) Early Grade Reading Assessment (EGRA) in 44 countries, (ii) Early Development Instrument (EDI) in 24 countries, (iii) Young Lives in 4 countries, (iv) Multiple Indicator Cluster Survey (MICS) in 55 countries, (v) UWEZO in 3 developing countries, (vi) Annual Status of Education Report (ASER) in 2 countries, (vii) Literacy Boost in 9 countries, (viii) Early Grade Math Assessment (EGMA) in 11 countries, (ix) Programme for International Student Assessment (PISA) in 32 OECD countries and some partner countries, (x) Analysis Programme of the CONFEMEN Education System (PASEC) in 13 countries, (xi) Progress in International Reading Literacy Study (PIRLS) in 49 countries, (xii) Pre-PIRLS in 3 countries, (xiii) Trends in International Mathematics and Science Study (TIMSS) in 63 countries, (xiv) The Southern and Eastern Africa Consortium for Monitoring Educational Quality (SACMEQ) in 14 countries, (xv) Latin American Laboratory for Assessment of the Quality of Education (LLECE) in 16 countries and (xvi) Literacy Assessment Monitoring Programme (LAMP) in 12 countries. Most of these studies collect information on reading

and simple arithmetic proficiencies. Some other studies like MICS and Early Development Instrument concentrated also in physical, social, emotional situation of children (Simons Kate Anderson 2012). Further, among these cross countries studies three studies has been conducted in India, e.g., ASER, Young Lives (in Andhra Pradesh), PISA (in Himachal Pradesh and Tamil Nadu only in the year 2009).

9. District Information System for Education (DISE) provides Education Development Index (EDI) measurement across all states with 24 variables covering four dimensions. The four dimensions are (i) access, (ii) infrastructure, (iii) teachers and (iv) outcomes. EDI calculates overall state wise performance ranking on the basis of these four dimensions, which cannot be consider as quality of education.
10. Press note of HRD Minister on releases of National Achievement Survey – Class III Report, PIB, 28-02-2014.
11. Zutshi, Bupinder; Rai, Ramakant; Padmakar, Paramshree; Gupta, Neema; Gupta, Umesh and Mishram Sandeep Chandra (2013).
12. Calculated by 2202-01/pop, and SSA per child exp.
13. A comparison among 20 private unaided schools in Delhi has been done by author, which is not any representative shows, annual charges vary from Rs. 10,000/- per annum to Rs. 1.5 lakh per annum. This is done by looking at by an examination of fees paid by the parents of who are working in one particular institution of Delhi.
14. Former Human Resource Development (HRD) Minister Kapil Sibal told the Rajya Sabha in 2010, about the estimates of 12 lakh shortage of teacher.
15. Jha P., Sikdar S. and Geetha P. (Forthcoming)
16. Department of School Education and Literacy, MHRD, GoI. Web link: http://mhrd.gov.in/nas1

References

DISE (2006, 2009): *Educational Development Index (EDI): A Suggestive Framework for Computation*, Department of Educational Management Information System, New Delhi: NUEPA (Version 1 & 2).

DISE (2005-06, 2006-07, 2007-08, 2008-09, 2009-10, 2010-11, 2011-12): *Flash Statistics Elementary Education in India: Progress towards UEE*, New Delhi: NUEPA.

Dreze, J. and Sen, A. (2002): *India: Development and Participation*, Oxford University Press, 2002.

Jha, P. (2005): Withering Commitments and Weakening Progress: State and Education in the Era of Neo-Liberal Reforms, *Economic and Political Weekly*, 40 (33) (August 13-19, 2005), pp. 3677-3684

Jha, P. (2007): Guaranteeing Elementary Education: A Note on Policy and Provisioning in Contemporary India, *Journal of South Asian Development*, 2:75.

Jha, P. and Parvati, P. (2008): India's Tryst with Elementary Education in the Time of Reforms: Policy Constraints and Institutional Gaps. New Delhi: Books for Change & Action-Aid.

Jha, P.; Sikdar, S. and Geetha, P. (forthcoming): Shifting Terrain of Public Policy Discourses for Financing of Education: An Overview, Routledge.

Mehta, Arun C. (2003, 2004, 2005, 2006, 2007, 2008, 2009, 2010, 2011): *Elementary Education in India: Analytical Report*, New Delhi: National University of Education Planning and Administration.

NCERT (2014): *National Achievement Survey (Cycle 3)-Class III: Achievement Highlights*, New Delhi: National Council of Educational Research and Training.

NCERT (2012): What Students of Class VIII Know and can Do: A summary of India's National

Achievement Survey, Class VIII, 2012, New Delhi: National Council of Educational Research and Training.

Pratham (2006, 2007, 2008, 2009, 2010, 2011, 2012, 2013, 2014): *Annual Status of Educational Report*, New Delhi: ASER Centre.

Simons, Kate Anderson (2012): *Multi-Country Assessments of Learning*. Discussion Document 1, Brookings Institution, Center for Universal Education.

Zutshi, Bupinder; Rai, Ramakant; Padmakar, Paramshree; Gupta, Neema; Gupta, Umesh; Mishra, Sandeep Chandra (2013): *Status of Elementary Education in India*, New Delhi: National Coalition for Education. Weblink: http://www.nceindia.org/wp-content/uploads/2012/01/Status-of-Elementary-Edu-in-India.pdf.

14

Equity and Education in India

The Definitive Decade of the 1950s

S. Irfan Habib

The decade of the 1950s is crucial in India's history of development, as it was during these ten years that most of the efforts for the building of a robust and independent India were initiated. Almost all those who took command of the newly independent India were inspired by the values of the freedom movement, they had struggled against the diverse deprivations during the colonial rule, spread across political, social, cultural, economic as well as educational domains. The decade began with a Nehruvian vision, which continued to impact our development model till the mid-seventies. However, there were other important players as well, who played a seminal role in putting the strife-torn nation together and devised policies in education and culture, which not only laid the solid foundations for future progress but also worked as a healing balm for the post-partition India. Maulana Abul Kalam Azad and Dr. B.R. Ambedkar had a key role as participants in the nation building process. Both were acutely conscious of the social and economic inequities of the newly independent country. The former battled with these deprivations as a minister while the latter helped formulate a constitution where equitable development was enshrined as the core pillar.

The freedom struggle can be seen as a social process involving the pursuit of several different ideals or values.[1] And, according to Krishna Kumar, one of the value orientations expressed in the context of education during the freedom struggle was equality. Both Azad and Ambedkar were committed to this ideal, besides others of course, in quite different ways.

Maulana Azad at the Helm of Education and Culture

Azad was born on 11 November 1888 in the holy city of Mecca. His family was one of those many elite Muslim families who decided to migrate to Hijaz in protest after the 1857 upsurge and the victory of the British. His father Khairuddin reached Mecca in 1858 and continued his higher studies. He soon became a great scholar, married an Arab woman of a distinguished family and finally decided to get back home in 1895 when Azad was seven year old. Azad studied at home all his life, probably one of the few scholars in recent times who did not hold any formal degree from a school or a university. He was educated at home by several competent teachers, all selected with strict norms by his father, who actually remained his most formidable teacher. His forays into education began early in life when he started writing serious columns in his paper *Al-Hilal*. By the time he took over as minister of education, science and culture,

Azad had thought and written immensely about education and its challenges in the newly independent India in the 1950s.

Thus Maulana Azad was not a run of the mill politicians but a scholar, who brought with him decades of experience as a writer and thinker on different aspects of Indian public life. Nehru visualised him as a "bridge" between the cultures of the East and the West, as the man who magnificently spanned in his person the gulf between the past and the future.... Without any English education, without speaking or writing in English, he was as easily and effortlessly at home in Western culture as in Indian or Eastern or Islamic culture. Nothing that was good was stranger to him.[2]

There is a sizeable opinion among scholars that Azad did not really have much to do with education personally, and the task was handed over to him by Nehru, who continued to play a key role in most of the policy formulations in educational and scientific matters. It is a fact that Azad accepted the responsibility on the insistence of both Nehru as well as Mahatma Gandhi. But this is also a fact that the choice fell on him because Azad was the best available person for the job. Both Nehru and Gandhi were aware of the fact that Azad was passionately committed to education, culture and scientific and technical progress. He surely had his limitations and Nehru always came forward positively to take care of them. On the death of Azad, Nehru called him 'a man of luminous intelligence and a mighty intellect with an amasing capacity to pierce through a problem to its core.' His erudition and high intellect led Nehru to compare him in European history, with 'the great men of the Renaissance, or, in a later period, of the Encyclopaedists who preceded the French Revolution, men of intellect, men of action'. Azad was neither a professional educationist, nor was so many others like Montessori, Tagore or Gandhi, yet their impact on education have been enormous. He was essentially a scholar, a man of thought, a litterateur, a divine, who found himself pitch-forked into a life of intense political activity and who, amazingly enough, was able to combine the exacting and almost mutually exclusive demands of the life of the mind and his life of intense political activity- a rare quality which he shared with his life-long friend and colleague, Nehru.[3] If we look retrospectively, Azad was the most eminently suited choice to bring India out of the morass it had gone into after partition. There was a need for a person of great vision and character who may be able to assess the situation correctly and adopt sound educational policies which would help, in the long run, to restore mental sanity and balance to national life and instil the right values in it.[4]

Dr. B.R. Ambedkar, the father of Indian Constitution and an indefatigable fighter for the upliftment and rights of the depressed classes wrote immensely on equity and education. Surprisingly he is not rated as one of the key educational thinkers of India though we know him well as a crusader against untouchability. There are elaborate accounts of his contributions to philosophy, sociology and religion among other fields but "there are very few attempts by scholars to project him as a great educationist. In fact more than half of his life was spent in educational institutions."[5] Ambedkar saw John Dewey, one of the greatest educationists of the twentieth century as his mentor, quoting his *Democracy and Education* extensively in his several works on social philosophy. His engagement with education for all began in the 1920s and continued for the next three decades. Once he got involved in framing the first Indian Constitution, his expertise and philosophy enriched the processes of equity at all levels being enshrined in our Constitution.

Education beyond Caste and Class

Soon after independence, one of the important issues for Azad was the democratisation of education, particularly when India had emerged out of 200 hundred years of colonialism, going through varied forms of discriminations and deprivations. His commitment to a change in British educational system can be seen in the 1920s during the non-cooperation movement. In his pamphlet *Talimi Taraqi-e-Mawalat*, published in the 1920s, he began with a statement that "Of all the bonds of association with the British government which needs to be broken forthwith, education is the most important one."[6] Maulana Azad emphasised on several Quranic principles and in the context of equity he stressed on *Adl* or justice, the supreme principle that brings the creative process to its completion.[7] Being at the back of the cosmic scheme of growth, Justice is all the more relevant to education as a process of harmonious nurture. Education for justice brings in a state of stable equilibrium between the antithetic entities, viz. individual freedom and social control, the spiritual and the scientific outlook, the religious and the secular system and national and international aspiration. Indeed, justice commands the pivotal place in Azad's general perspective, which has influenced his educational outlook quite profoundly.[8] He was conscious of the fact that class/caste ridden education system in vogue need to be replaced by a more inclusive and just educational order. In 1948, while addressing the educational conference, Maulana again reiterated that "Education, at any rate, must be pushed forward as rapidly as possible. We must not, for a moment, forget that it is the birthright of every individual to receive at least the basic education, without which he cannot discharge his duties as a citizen."[9] Maulana also realised that equity in education is not conceivable merely through the expansion of school education. He was aware of the huge adult population, which needed serious attention. For him adult literacy and education were crucial for any idea of inclusive and equity based education in India, particularly soon after the end of colonial rule.

Being primarily an Islamic scholar, he used Islam as a democratic and modernist movement, quite in contrast to what is being done in the name of Islam today all over the world. He observed Islam as "a perfect system of freedom and democracy whose function consists in bringing back to mankind the freedom snatched away from it."[10] At another place he defined Islam as "the message of democracy and human equality to the world suffering from chronic type of class discriminations."[11] Azad expanded Islamic values on a national scale, going beyond the narrow confines of the faith, to explain and understand the problems of the newly independent nation, particularly the access to education on a universal scale.

India's emergence on the 15 August 1947 as the largest democracy in the world was itself a great political achievement but it was a great challenge to education to train an unprecedented number of people in the art of democratic living. Azad being a great democrat himself took the challenge as an opportunity for making education a vanguard of the democratic life in the country. With a view to gearing education to the cause of democracy, he, in his very first official statement referred to Disraeli's verdict 'A democracy has no future unless it educates its masters'. In independent and democratic India, with universal franchise as the key principle, the voter was truly the master of democracy, whom Azad wanted to be educated and be aware. He was conscious of the sad inheritance, which had 85 per cent population of illiterates on the eve of independence. Several class and caste discriminations and disabilities were in place, which required to be urgently removed. He was convinced that the state needs to play a key role in combating such afflictions and provide the means of "the acquisition of knowledge and self-betterment."[12] However, the most disconcerting factor was the lack of necessary funds to carry forward the state's responsibilities. Azad conceded with a sense of guilt as minister of education that the Central Government has only one per cent allocation for education and he thus pleaded in the Constituent Assembly to raise the expenditure to 10 per cent.[13] He pursued the issue with passion and was able to raise the allocation from twenty million rupees to around 350 million during his tenure as minister of education.

On 30 September 1953 Azad addressed the nation through AIR, reiterating that "Every individual has a right to an education that will enable him to develop his faculties and live a full human life."[14] He strongly felt that our objective cannot be realised unless we get out of narrow-mindedness, which has been our greatest hindrance. In this new era of freedom, we should keep ourselves free from this disease as there is no other disease as dangerous for the healthy growth of national life. Elaborating further, he said: Like an actor it masquerades in disguise. In the domain of religion it appears in the form of blind faith and wants to deceive us in the name of orthodoxy. In politics it wants to overpower us in the guise of nationalism. In learning and culture it makes an appeal to us in the name of our nation and country. It behoves us not to be taken in by these fictitious names. We must remember that the root cause of all this is nothing but narrow-mindedness."[15] Azad was inspired by the values of our freedom struggle and he was convinced that those values should come in handy for nation building, where education should be seen as a right for all the citizens of this newly independent nation. In this context of age old discrimination and deprivation, Azad also emphasised on women's education, most of whom had been marginal. He felt that education of women is doubly purposeful: first that they need to be educated as citizens of free India, and second that their education facilitates the task of educating the younger generation.[17] He raised this issue in the Constituent Assembly as well in 1949 asking for multiplying the educational opportunities for the Indian women.[17]

In 1950 Azad spoke on the programme for national education at the third CABE meeting. He spoke extensively about equity and expansion of education in India, particularly to wipe out the deficiency in education created over a hundred years of colonial rule. He laid down four objectives for the next 10 years and two of the objectives were the provision of basic education on a universal, free and compulsory basis for all school going children and provision of adult education in order to wipe out the colossal illiteracy of our masses.[18] He further reiterated the two points in his 1952 address at another meeting of CABE.[19] While participating in the Constituent Assembly debates he emphasised on the overall significance of universal education as laid down in our constitution and the role of social education in the implementation of the plan of basic education for children between 6-14 year. Underlining the principle of equity he reiterated that educating the future citizens of India expeditiously and effectively is indispensible for shaping our future destiny.

His commitment to equity and the democratisation of education is also reflected in his strident position in the Constituent Assembly where he talked of equalising opportunities in the context of old caste, class and sex prejudices. He thus spoke in 1948, "If they have been left behind in the sphere of progress, it is not their fault. The society is to be blamed for this. It is all the more necessary, therefore, that the society, which has not until now placed them on an equal footing, should help in their advancement."[20] Towards this objective Azad was successful in framing the official policy of instituting special stipends and scholarships for students coming from the depressed classes.[21] This is all the more important today when we are in the midst of implementing the Right to Education Act; it's a tribute to Maulana Azad, as he took up this arduous task almost 60 years ago.

Ambedkar's Vision and Equity in Education

B.R. Ambedkar belonged to a well to do Mahar family of Ratnagiri district in Maharashtra. He was born on April 14 1891 in Mhow near Indore, in a family which was devoted to the Kabir school of thought. This Bhakti school was committed to the human attributes like compassion and benevolence. More than that the followers of this school had abolished the rigidity of the caste system, as its founder Kabir roundly condemned it. This background is important for the future evolution of Ambedkar as a thinker who steadfastly fought for equity and justice, and stood for inclusive development of society. After successfully finishing his school and college education in Bombay (now Mumbai), Ambedkar was given fellowship by the Maharaja of Baroda (now Vadodara) to study at Columbia University, New York. While at Columbia University, Ambedkar also came in touch with the great American educationist and pragmatic philosopher John Dewey (1859–1952). It was perhaps Dewey's philosophy of instrumentalism which might have led Ambedkar to undertake a critical analysis of concrete social problems and search for practical solutions for them. Ambedkar "fully endorsed Dewey's emphasis on education as a means to change the world and not merely to understand it."[22]

B.R. Ambedkar is amply recognised as a voice of the oppressed and deprived but his immense contributions to the cause of equity and justice in education are seldom talked about. Though his followers do chant "educate, organise and agitate" yet his educational philosophy has not been deservedly debated and discussed. In the 1950s, while a new India was being rebuilt Ambedkar played a crucial role in articulating and instituting concerns of equity, democratisation and universalisation of education. There is a perceptible influence of John Dewey, particularly his pragmatism and humanism as we find Ambedkar quoting Dewey's *Democracy and Education* in several of his writings. Like Maulana Azad, Ambedkar was also engaged in education at various levels much before independence. His experience as a thinker and as an activist was an asset in the 1950s when nation building began in earnest.

The progress of education in India as a universal right for all, beyond caste and class, is of a very recent origin. The colonial government claimed that they did initiate mass education, which I believe is questionable. As we know, it was after Wood's despatch that the British government began taking some interest in the education of the colonised Indians. It was Jyoti Rao Phule who, in his memorandum to the Hunter Commission in 1882, accused the British for their penchant in providing educational opportunities only to the upper castes, while collecting huge revenue from the illiterate Shudras and Atishudras.[23] Though it may be seen as the beginning of mass education in India no systematic effort was made by any leader to take this difficult task forward. It is in this context that B.R. Ambedkar should be seen as a sincere promoter of education based on equity and justice. Perhaps he is the only leader of the pre-independence period who had a vision for a people's education movement to realise universal education for all.[24]

Ambedkar submitted a memorandum to the Indian Statutory Commission in 1928 from the Bahishkrita Hitakarini Sabha where he emphasised that equality of opportunity need to be provided to the depressed classes. He supported the Board of Education in giving Muslims their due share in education but pleaded that similar benefits should be extended to other deprived classes as well. His insightful words need to be quoted which may be useful even in the present context where debates on affirmative action goes on. He said:

> "I am not making this statement in any carping spirit nor grudge the efforts that government have made in the matter of the education of Muhammadens. I must here emphasise that this country is composed of different communities. All these communities are unequal in their status and progress. If they are to be brought to the level of equality, then, the only remedy is to adopt the principle of inequality and to give favoured treatment to those who are below the level. There are some I know who object to this and adhere to the principle of equality treatment. But, I say government has done well in applying the principle to the Muhammadens. For I honestly believe that equality of treatment to people who are unequal is simply another name for indifferentism and neglect..... Economically speaking or socially speaking, backward classes are handicapped. I, therefore, think that the principle of favoured treatment must be adopted in their case."[25]

Here one can see how Ambedkar tried to rationalise and logically establish the need for a policy in favour of equality of opportunity. This is even insightful in the current debates on reservations, both for the government as well as for those who see such affirmative action merely as appeasement and political opportunism.

Ambedkar stressed on the increased state expenditure on education so that the benefits may reach to as many people, across castes and communities, as possible. Intervening in the debate in the Bombay Legislative Council on grants for education, he argued 'that unless we spend a sufficient amount of money, to see that every child that enters a school reaches the fourth standard, what we have already spent upon him is of no purpose whatsoever. According to Ambedkar, "It is only fair that our educational expenditure should be so adjusted that we should spend on the education of the people as much as we take from them in the form of excise."[27] As pointed out above, he wanted increased state expenditure in education to ensure that education is not the exclusive preserve and privilege of any caste, class, or community. He wanted to make it accessible for all. This is particularly important in view of the widespread inequalities in access to education in terms of caste and class. As long as inequality of educational opportunities was rooted in the unequal status and progress of different castes and communities, Ambedkar argued, equalising opportunities will not be of any avail. He believed "that equality of treatment of people who are unequal is simply another name for indifferentism and neglect."[28]

Ambedkar's commitment to equity and justice in education and other fields shall be clear if we briefly look at his political philosophy. For him democracy was a form of a society which unmistakably involves two things. The first is an attitude of mind, an attitude of respect and equality towards one's fellowmen. The second is a social organisation free from rigid social barriers. Democracy is incomplete and inconsistent with isolation and exclusiveness, resulting in the distinction between the privileged and the unprivileged — privileges for a few and disabilities for the vast majority.[29] Though much of Ambedkar's life-struggle remained inconclusive, his function as a source of inspiration for radical social action has proved longer lasting than that of any other leader of the freedom struggle, not excepting Gandhi. To this day, his name remains a live-wire that can charge political action for equality and related values.[29]

Conclusion

Both Azad and Ambedkar strived hard, of course in different ways, as I have tried to point out briefly, to build an equitable and just educational system. They left the battle incomplete, which should have been pursued with a similar passion. We surely took that forward but somehow got mired in the processes and compulsions of democratic governance. The process of modernisation, based on equitable development, has to engage with fundamental issues like the question of access, improvement in quality and the ensuring of social justice. The existing system — many features of which the country has inherited from colonial rule and maintained with marginal changes by the ruling classes — continues to be inimical to the interests of a large section of the people. Although changes have taken place in the field of education after independence, a major weakness of the system has been its limited character, as a result of which its impact on the marginalised has been very limited. The dalits, the adivasis and women are forced to remain at the periphery of the knowledge society that is being currently constructed. Free and compulsory education has been assured for the age group of 6 to 14 and facilities for higher education have been substantially upgraded. Yet, primary and secondary education has not become universal in the country, mainly because of economic and social compulsions.

Notes

1. Krishna Kumar, *Political Agenda of Education: A Study of Colonialist and Nationalist Ideas*, Sage Publications, New Delhi, 2005, p. 97.
2. Jawaharlal Nehru.
3. K.G. Saiyidain, *op.cit.*, p. 66.
4. *Ibid.*, p. 68.
5. K.S. Chalam, *Modernisation and Dalit Education: Ambedkar's Vision*, Jaipur, 2008, p. 33.
6. Cited in G. Rasool Abduhu, *The Educational Ideas of Maulana Abul Kalam Azad*, New Delhi, 1973, p. 83.
7. *Tarjumanul Quran*, Vol. 1, eleventh edition, p. 119 cited in *Ibid.*, p. 41.
8. *Ibid.*, p. 42.
9. *Speeches of Maulana Azad*, p. 29. In taking the argument of inclusive education forward Maulana also emphasised on the adult literacy issue. He said "It is obvious that with the extension of democracy, the problem of adult education has become even more important than it was in the past." (p. 32).
10. *Qawlii-faisal*, al-Balagh Press, Calcutta, 1921, p. 50, cited in Abduhu, *op.cit.*, p. 94.
11. *Presidential Address*, The Indian National Congress, March 1940, Ramgarh, p. 31.
12. *Speeches of Maulana Azad*, p. 260.
13. *The Constituent Assembly Debates*, 1949, p. 1556.
14. *Speeches of Maulana Azad*, p. 260
15. *Ibid.*, p. 20.
16. In his press conference on 31 May 1948 Azad remarked: "If women take to education, more than half of our problems will be solved. Educated mothers will mean children who can be easily made literate;" *Speeches of Maulana Azad*, p. 41. This was a progressive thinking on the gender issue than, which may not be acceptable to many in the contemporary context. Women need to be educated for societal and their individual good and not just to bring up educated well groomed children.
17. *The Constituent Assembly Debates*, 1949.p. 1552. cited in Abduhu, *op. cit.* p. 97.
18. *Speeches of Maulana Azad*, p. 126.
19. *Speeches of Maulana Azad*, p. 201
20. *The Constituent Assembly Debates*, 1948, p. 1952.
21. Abduhu, *op. cit.*, p. 96. In his survey of Azad's role in "what he called democratisation of educational opportunities" through the installation of scholarships for the students of backward classes, Saiyadain remarked that the provision on this head went up "about 75 fold, from 3 lakh in 1944 to 2.25 crore in 1960."
22. Lokhande, G.S. (1977), *Bhimrao Ramji Ambedkar: A Study in Social Democracy*. New Delhi: Sterling Publishers. p. 10,. cited in N. Jayaram, *Education and Emancipation*.
23. Chalam, *op. cit.*, p. 31.
24. *Ibid*, p. 32
25. *Bombay Legislative Assembly Debates*, p. 42, cited in Chalam, *op. cit.*, p. 26.
26. *Dr Baba Saheb Ambedkar Writings and Speeches*, Bombay, 1982, p. 40, cited in N Jayaram, *op. cit.*, p. 6.
27. *Ibid.*, p. 6
28. Ambedkar, B R, *Ranade, Gandhi and Jinnah*, pp. 36-37, cited in Dhananjay Keer, *Dr. Baba Saheb Ambedkar*, Bombay, 2009, p. 390.
29. Krishna Kumar, *Political Agenda of Education—A Study of Colonialist and Nationalist Ideas*, Sage Publications, New Delhi, 2005. p. 105.

References

Abduhu, G. Rasool Abduhu (1973), The Educational Ideas of Maulana Abul Kalam Azad, New Delhi, citing The Constituent Assembly Debates (1949).

Ambedkar, Baba Saheb, *Writings and Speeches* (1982), Bombay.

Azad, Abul Kalam (1921), *Qwalii-Faisal*, Cacutta: Al-Balagh Press.

Azad, Abul Kalam (1940), *Presidential Address*, The Indian National Congress, March, Ramgarh.

Chalam, K S (2008), Modernisation and Dalit Education: Ambedkar's Vision, Jaipur, citing Ambedkar, B.R., Bombay Legislative Assembly Debates.

Keer, Dhananjay (2009), *Dr Babashaheb Ambedkar,* Bombay, citing Ambedkar, B.R., *Ranade, Gandhi and Jinnah.*

Kumar, Krishna (2005), Political Agenda of Education: A Study of Colonialist and Nationalist Ideas, New Delhi: Sage Publications.

Lokhande, G.S. (1977): *Bhimrao Ramji Ambedkar: A Study in Social Democracy.* New Delhi: Sterling Publishers, cited in N Jayaram, *Education and Emancipation.*

15

Democratic Inequalities

The Dilemma of Elementary Education in India[1]

Vimala Ramachandran

Philosopher John Dewey argued that education was central requirement for a democratic and inclusive polity. (Dewey, 2001) But India's experience with electoral politics could lead one to argue that the classic doctrine does not apply to India. How does education or the lack of it and inherent inequality in quality and access to education impact on democratic practice?

At a formal level, democracy is about exercising choices. It is about franchise and it is about one-person one-vote and one-vote one-value. At a little deeper level, we also associate democracy with rule of law and institutions. We expect democratic societies to respect civil liberties and human rights, place value on an impartial judiciary. The existence of democratic institutions is a prerequisite for a vibrant democracy, although they do not ensure democratic practice. The Constituent Assembly understood that rights could be realised only if we create a level playing field.

An early twist in our tale of democracy and equality came in the failure to make Universal Elementary Education (UEE) a fundamental right of children, instead relegating it to the Directive Principles. Making universal elementary education a fundamental right would have had far reaching implications. Firstly (from the point of view of the government at that time) it would have involved enormous investment in schooling infrastructure. Secondly, making it a justiciable right would mean that citizens could take the government to court if access to school was not made available. As a result, even as UEE was accepted as the minimal non-negotiable requirement for ensuring a substantive practice of democracy, the founding fathers of democratic India did not make it a fundamental right. As a result, six decades after we declared ourselves a sovereign democratic republic, we have still to redeem the pledge made in 1950.

The relationship between education and democracy is like an invisible spiral that helps those in control remain there and those at the bottom alienated and voiceless. As it has manifested itself in Independent India, education impacts through its potential of enhancing the capability of people, the substantive practice of democracy more than the formal system of elections. Education has the potential of enhancing the capability of people. As Dreze and Sen convincingly argue: 'Capability' refers to the alternative combinations of functioning from which a person can choose. Thus the notion of capability is essentially one of freedom – a range of options a person has in deciding what kind of life to lead. Poverty, in this view, lies not merely in the impoverished state in which the person actually lives, but also in the lack of real opportunities – given by social constraints as well as personal circumstances – to choose other types of living' (Dreze and Sen, 2002 pp 35-36). Lack of access to education of acceptable quality actively inhibits the development of the capability of citizens to engage with democratic institutions thereby denuding the practice of democracy.

This paper explores how our education system has created new hierarchies and forms of social exclusion and inclusion – thereby challenging the very foundations of equality and equal opportunity and leaving an indelible mark on the practice of democracy. As noted in the prophetic words of Dr. B.R.. Ambedkar:

"On the 26th of January 1950, we are going to enter a life of contradictions. In politics we will have equality and in social and economic life we will have inequality. In politics we will be recognising the principle of one-man one-vote and one vote one value. In our social and economic life, we shall, by reason of our social and economic structure, continue to deny the principle of one-man one-value. How long shall we continue to deny equality in our social and economic life? If we continue to deny it for long, we will do so only by putting our political democracy in peril" (Dr. B.R..Ambedkar, 1949).[2]

Cumulative Burden of Exclusion

In 2003 I was engaged in a multi-sector qualitative research project. The object was to explore factors that facilitate or impede successful primary school completion among the lowest economic quartile of the population in Karnataka, Uttar Pradesh and Andhra Pradesh. This study explored different domains – the child, family, community and institutions (specifically the primary school, Integrated Child Development Services (ICDS) and other health related services) that impact on child health, nutrition and education and their inter-linkages, both positive and negative (Ramachandran *et al*, 2004). We spent considerable time in villages and urban slums, talking to women, interacting with children, observing schools and early child care centres and interviewing teachers and care givers.

The story was the same everywhere – poor and weak mothers giving birth to children growing up in an environment of extreme deprivation. Given the veritable absence of institutional support, an inter-generational cycle of poor health, nutrition and education is set in motion. Endemic malnutrition, partial or no immunisation, poor sanitation and hygiene and frequent bouts of illness sap children of energy and affect intellectual development. When children from the poorest communities reach pre-school age, their caste, location and economic situation becomes the defining variables framing their chances to access services such as supplementary nutrition and pre-school education. As they reach school-going age, all that they are assured of is that their name will be recorded in a school register as proof of formal enrolment. Their access to a school is determined by their economic status, place of residence, their caste, community or religion. However, what is not assured is whether they will be able to attend school uninterrupted – not merely because of ill-health but also because very little happens in the schools meant for the very poor. Teacher attitudes towards such children are, at best, indifferent and compounding the problem is the fact that most of the children, especially girls, work before and after school. There is no guarantee that they will learn to read and write – especially as they go to government schools or even low-cost private schools. If they live in a remote habitation or come from an impoverished community, the chances are that a local person with little qualification (popularly known as para-teacher or contract teacher) may teach them.

Nevertheless, parents were still eager to send their children to school and the children themselves were full of hope. Their aspirations, however, were tempered by opportunities as they exist or do not. The initial enthusiasm to participate gradually turns to resignation and apathy – children become irregular, hang around at home or on the streets and often start pitching into the work of their families – in most cases dropping out without learning anything. A few who can afford it may shift their children to a private school or send them to a tuition class. The inter-generational cycle is perpetuated, with the new generation being (at best) semi-literate, weak and apathetic or in many instances angry at a system that has treated them with such indifference.

Some of our more disturbing findings related to the abysmal state of government programmes designed to provide a social safety net for the poorest of the poor. Health, nutrition, and education have a decisive impact on a child's development. The health and nutrition status of both mother and child is clearly more significant in the early years since it affects later cognitive development. Persistent and cumulative neglect ensures a non-attainment of appropriate developmental milestones. Health and nutritional outcomes at each stage are carried on to the next, an inter-generational transfer of handicaps resulting in a downward spiral of poverty, ill health, malnutrition, and poor learning outcomes for children.

The point is not about the persistence of abject poverty, but that government schemes meant for the poor rarely reach those who need it the most. Children starting life with a handicap does not auger well for a democracy. It is the cumulative character of social, political and economic exclusion that frames the lives of poor children, influencing their ability to participate in schooling and social and political life in later years.

Has the Situation on the Ground Changed in 2014?

I was part of another large-scale qualitative study in 2012 (Ramachandran and Naorem, 2012). This time we were exploring the inclusion and exclusion of children in schools and in classrooms. The research team travelled across six states – Andhra Pradesh, Assam, Bihar, Odisha, Madhya Pradesh and Rajasthan – interacting with teachers, children and parents inside schools and in their homes. Blatant and subtle forms of discrimination were found in almost all dimensions of the school: (i) how children are seated in class, (ii) whom the teacher focusses her attention on, (iii) whom does she ignore, (iv) who gets to clean the toilets and do menial tasks, (v) who gets to drink water first and who has to wait in line, (vi) who is asked to lead the assembly, (vii) who can perform special duties during school function, (viii) who eats the mid-day meals etc. This list is endless. Issues such as gender, caste, poverty, appearance, skin colour, overt symptoms of illness or disease, cleanliness, language spoken at home emerged as important markers. A girl child from a poor Dalit or ST family, who is not "properly" dressed, is at the bottom of the pecking order in schools. Attitudes and practices of teachers in the classroom and in the school reflect prevalent social practices. Adolescent boys and girls that we interviewed and worked with said that the situation is much worse today than it was during the time when their parents went to school.

One of the overarching insights from this study is that we need to view inclusion and exclusion from different vantage points: from the outside (who goes to what kind of school); from the inside (what happens inside the school); and in society (who is visible and who is not visible, for example seasonal or new migrants are often invisible in data on out of school children). Equally significant is the influence of the larger society and social norms on what happens inside a school, the attitude and behaviour of teachers and the involvement or lack of involvement of parents and community leaders. Political and social assertion of the rights of Dalit and Adivasi also influence practices and attitudes. The differences between Andhra Pradesh, Bihar and Rajasthan are a case in point. While all three societies are highly stratified in terms of social and community identities, explicit caste-based discrimination is not so evident in schools in Andhra Pradesh or in Bihar while in Rajasthan discrimination was explicit. This may be due to the political environment in this state. Bihar and Andhra Pradesh have experienced social and political movements led by Dalit and other backward classes. In fact, Dalit and other backward communities have started playing a significant role in politics due to social mobilisation in the last two or three decades.

As the research teams travelled across the sample states one question kept cropping up: '*When and how will the situation change?*' There are no easy answers and given our track record of the last 65 years, some prejudices have only become more palpable. Issues such as caste, religion, economic status, place of residence and knowledge of English have become significant markers in our social and political life. Many older teachers admitted that the feeling of national unity and being one has been fading. Many of them attributed this to the way our electoral system has evolved whereby mobilisation of political support is done on the basis of social, religious, caste and cultural identities.

Several older teachers and parents said that taking the Constitution of India as the guiding spirit, teachers, administrators and community leaders need to be told that any violation of the right to equality and the right against discrimination will invite strict penal action. A non-negotiable code of behaviour needs to be communicated to all those who are involved in school education. This needs to be done in writing and prominently displayed in all schools and educational institutions. Simultaneously, children need to be involved in activities that enable them to understand and appreciate diversity, respect differences and formulate school level norms of behaviour. Involving children in creating an egalitarian atmosphere could bring moral pressure on teachers, administrators and local leaders not to differentiate or discriminate.

Enrolled in School without the Right to Education

Enrolment in primary schools recorded impressive growth in the 1990s and 2000s. Government and non-government surveys confirm that close to 97 per cent children between the age group of 6 to 11 years are enrolled in primary schools. More girls are in school as are many more children from socially and economically deprived communities. A large number of teachers have also been appointed in the last five years. The Right to Education Act was notified in 2010. In fact, if we are to go by the numbers published by the government, there is much to be upbeat about the primary education scenario in India.

Yet, despite the impressive data generated every year there is a sense of disquiet when we talk of education. A few months back some of my colleagues were conducting focus group discussions with parents of children who had dropped-out after Class 8. In almost all the villages, parents said that their children had learnt little. For example, a student of Class 8 of today cannot read what a child in class four could twenty-five years ago. Many of them enrol in secondary school but drop out soon because they are unable to cope. Parents also shared that children today can barely read and have rudimentary skills in mathematics and science. What is the use of such schooling, they asked.

Mere access to schooling, without commensurate focus on quality and learning outcomes is meaningless. For ten years now (since 2005) independent surveys and also government-sponsored surveys have called the bluff and declared loud and clear that all our children are not learning the way they should be. "In India, on a test of reading comprehension administered to Grade 5 students across the country, only 46 per cent of students were correctly able to identify the cause of an event" (NCERT, 2011). Only a third of students could compute the difference between two decimal numbers (NCERT, 2011). Another recent study found that about 43 per cent of Grade 8 students could not solve a simple division problem. Even recognition of two-digit numbers, supposed to be taught in Grade 2, tends to be achieved only by Grade 4 or 5 (ASER, 2011) (Dunder, Halil *et al*, forthcoming 2013). This is not all — careful scrutiny of the data reveals huge rural–urban, male-female, inter-state, and inter-community differences. We now know that one of the biggest markers is the kind of school a child attends — alongside poverty, social status and location that effectively determines the kind of school a child would attend.

For many decades now we have known that the social and economic status of a child's family is one of the strongest determinants of a child's educational attainment. The last 60 years of educational data as well as other socio-economic surveys (like NSS, NFHS) have demonstrated this link. In fact, this is valid not only for India but is a global phenomenon also. There is considerable evidence to show that the educational mortality of different social also classes is different and the cumulative burden of poor learning and exclusion becomes most visible in higher education (Deshpande, 2013). Bourdieu and Passeron, in their seminal work, also point out that the combination of the educational chance of the different classes and the chances of subsequent success attached to the different sections and types of schools constitutes a mechanism of deferred selection which transmutes a social inequality into a specifically educational inequality, i.e., an inequality of 'level' or success, concealing and academically consecrating an inequality of changes of access to higher levels of education (Bourdieu and Passeron, 1977: 158)."

The gap in achievement levels continues to grow as the child moves from primary to high school and university, with the cumulative burden of non-learning pushing children out at different stages. Reardon (2011) has argued that "The relationship between family socio-economic characteristics and student achievement is one of the most robust patterns in educational scholarship, yet the causes and mechanisms of this relationship have been the subject of considerable disagreement and debate." In India, the mix of family poverty, location (rural, tribal, urban slum etc.), caste/community identity, gender and parental occupation is known to be a significant predictor of education achievement among children (Vimala, 2009).

We all know that the fight for equity is ultimately a struggle for quality education. Equally, our socio-economic identity often determines the quality of education that is accessible to us.

Why and How did Equity and Quality Get Disjointed?

It is commonly believed that parents, who are well off, invest more resources and devote a larger proportion of their financial and social resources on their children's cognitive development. It is also argued that the rich have greater access to educational resources. The question, which then arises, is whether differentiation in the kind of schools that children attend, the quality of schooling and opportunities that are available reflects differences in income. Similarly, is it fair to assume that more educated parents (especially mothers) devoted more time and energy to the overall development of their children? (Rearden, 2011)

At another level, is there so much differentiation in the kind of schools children attend that it makes a significant difference to overall development and learning? Till the 1970s, we had heard about and met professionally successful people who had studied in a modest rural school or an urban municipal school. We also heard of numerous instances where a good school or a motivated teacher had been able to neutralise the odds that very poor children come with and enabled them to learn. Equally we have known of headmasters and teachers who made a big difference in the lives of very poor children, through encouragement and, most importantly, active academic support and guidance. Sadly, in the current scenario, such instances are becoming increasingly rare and in the last two to three decades, the difference in the ability of a child attending a rural primary school compared with children attending private school or a government school with a lot of resources is increasing.

The more worrying trend is that higher number of children who are poor and those from disadvantaged communities (SCs, STs, new migrants, Muslim) end up attending schools that are more likely to have very poor facilities, indifferent teachers (in government schools), poorly qualified teachers (in low cost private schools) or are multi-grade schools with two or more classes sitting together with one teacher. Such schools are now referred to as high-poverty schools and exist in both the government sector as well as the private sector. Further, income inequality has led to an increasing spatial segregation of high-income families from middle income and low-income families with the poorest often relegated to the outskirts of cities, inner city slums or specific habitations in rural areas. This spatial segregation of the rich from the middle class and from the very poor essentially implies that children are going to different kinds and differentially endowed schools.

Government data also reveal another side of the picture. According to NSS 66th round data (2009–2010), a startling 14.25 million children in the age group of 6 to 14 years were estimated to be "not attending." According to DISE data, 135.2 million students are enrolled in primary schools (an increase of 10 million children between 2005–06 and 2010–11). While more and more children move from primary to upper-primary, only 57.8 million children were enrolled at upper primary level in 2009–10. Further, these numbers drop sharply in high school and secondary schools and age specific attendance ratio decreases sharply.

The 64th round of the National Sample Survey Organisation also confirmed that close to 84 per cent children from the poorest economic quartile attend government and government-aided schools. As we go up the economic ladder the proportion of children attending government schools comes down and those attending private school goes up. If we look deeper, even among the poor who are able to attend private schools go to the 'low cost' private schools where the quality of instruction is; at best, marginally better than in government schools and infrastructure is far worse.

It is indeed noteworthy that more than 90 per cent of rural as well as urban households reported having a school with primary classes within one km. But availability of schools with middle or secondary level classes differed considerably between rural and urban sectors. Only 61.6 per cent of rural households, compared to 82.5 per cent of urban households, had a middle school within one km. For secondary level classes, the proportion was 30.7 per cent for rural as compared to 68.6 per cent for urban households. Further, about 33 per cent of rural households did not have any secondary school within a distance of 3 km (Report 532, NSSP 64th Round, 2009). Hence, it is fair to say that access is not equal and the ability of children to continue with their education is largely determined by location and availability of public transportation.

Crossing the secondary education barrier is a major hurdle before young people can hope to enrol in colleges and universities. Quality of secondary education exerts a huge influence on opportunities after school. Thomas Weisskopf points out that, "In India roughly 40 per cent of higher education students are enrolled in relatively low prestige arts programmes / bachelors programmes. This percentage is 60 for SC and 75 for ST..... The question is what kind of higher education do they have access to? (Their) academic performance and how many finish their degree in the stipulated time..... (there are) varying estimates, but in professional courses the percentages are far lower than the general category. Why do SC/ST students fall behind in during the course?"(Weisskopf, in Tilak, 2013).

In fact, this is not a new revelation. Way back in 1972 Suma Chitnis's work in Maharashtra revealed that overwhelming majority of SC students (in the sample she was tracking) were "studying in grade D colleges" and their performance in the course was poor and drop-out rates were also high. She also found that a higher percentage of SC students were enrolled in non-professional courses and in non-science courses (Chitnis, 1972). Reviewing the higher education terrain, Prof. Tilak (2013) feels that "In India the emphasis is laid either on quantity or quality or equity, not on all three at the same time and we end up with a scalene, a triangle of three unequal sides."

Going forward, having overcome the first barrier of access to primary schooling, there is no guarantee that attending school can guarantee learning. As discussed above, ASER 2011 revealed that nationally only 48.2 per cent of class 5 children could read simple class 2 level texts and only 29 per cent of class children could solve a two-digit subtraction problem. These findings reflect a mere tip of the iceberg and the reality on ground is quite sombre. While many more children may be enrolling in school, the big question before us is whether they are learning, and to what extent, does the kind of school they attend influences this learning? The recent PISA test results (2011) have also raised similar issues.

When most administrators, educationists (even those working in government institutions) and the larger education community agree that measuring inputs and enrolment is inadequate, the question that arises is why does government data focus so much on enrolment, retention, teacher appointments, teacher training, infrastructure and supplies and to a far lesser extent on learning? Why is it that we, as a nation, do not shrug at the thought that millions of our children attend school and emerge barely literate! What does it say about our education system? And how did we reach this situation?

Quality, the Heart of Equity

India attained Independence in 1947. Mahatma Gandhi had dreamed about a school system that was rooted in the social and cultural context while at the same time ensuring good quality secular education that is accessible to all children in the country. But as the first government assumed office "education for all" was quickly forgotten. We plugged along with the colonial system, partly because there were more pressing economic and political issues to tackle. Gandhiji's plea for 'Nai Taleem' (a fresh approach) in education was lost in the din of building a command economy, which meant focussing on heavy/basic industries, institutions of higher technical education etc.

It is not that education was neglected. In addition to regular schools, the government did set up a chain of 'Kendriya Vidyalayas' that were fairly well endowed and of good quality. But the real attention was reserved for higher education, as the ruling elite was committed to building quality institutions for professional and technical education. National institutes of technology, science, medicine and management produced graduates, who compared with the best in the world. It is no surprise that India had managed to ride the current global information technology wave in the 1990s with confidence.

In the early 1950s, education and quality were seen as coterminous, in part because education was a privilege of the few who could afford it. Most children, even from upper middle-class families, studied in government schools. With modernisation and escalated demand for education, pressure for rapid expansion in the public education system increased. By the mid-1960s, as increasing number of children started enrolling in school, the country also witnessed a gradual increase in the number of private aided and unaided schools. As the sixties rolled by, people with means moved out of public (government) schools and a feeling developed that quality was, perhaps, better pursued in private schools. This was also the time when competitive language politics led to political decision to adopt vernacular medium and postpone or withdraw the teaching of English to high school. This further quickened the exit of the middle classes from government schools (except of course the special government schools like Kendriya Vidyalaya). This movement of the children from economically better off families moving from government schools to private schools has continued to gain momentum through subsequent decades. The socially and politically significant minority, i.e., the middle classes and the rich, have more or less fully moved out of government schools. Interestingly, even those who remain in government schools go to better-endowed government schools.

Officially, in 2012, 54.8 per cent of schools were run by the education department of the government, 29 per cent run by local bodies (panchayats and municipalities), 8.9 per cent were private aided and 7.3 per cent were private unaided. The distribution changes quite dramatically when we look at secondary and higher secondary schools: 31.3 per cent by government, 8.5 per cent by local bodies, 24 per cent are private aided and 36.2 per cent private unaided (School Education Statistics, GOI, 2012). If we look at the above distribution of schools alongside dropout rates, it is noteworthy that 27 per cent of children dropout by the end of Class 5 (28.7 boys and 25.1 girls). Further 40.6 per cent dropout by Class 8 (40.3 boys, 41 girls). It is worrying that government data does not tell us who (meaning by location, income group, family education status, type of school they attend) drops out. Micro studies and field-based studies point to the very poor, among them socially disadvantaged groups like SC, ST and Muslim and within them first generation school goers are the ones who dropout.

In the 1990s, data on enrolment and retention took precedence over the painstaking process of monitoring the functioning of schools. The inspectorate system gave way to data based monitoring. As a result, as long as the local education authorities could show high enrolment rates, the work was seen as having been done. Even though the dropout rates were alarming, the ability of the system to retain children was not really seen as an important indicator of achievement till almost the middle of the last decade. It is no coincidence that a majority of children from the most deprived communities attend government schools and dropout rates calculated essentially pertain to government schools.

With growing pressure to meet globally accepted levels of school enrolment India joined the great numbers race. Issues of access and quality were analytically separated and the focus shifted to somehow getting children into schools with the belief that the government could worry about quality later. Statistics acquired an unprecedented status and we started searching for simple measures like enrolment, transition and completion rates to show progress, forgetting that highly complex webs of issues are responsible for poor quality of government schools.

First: The school system is not accountable to anyone. When the government is satisfied with monitoring numbers (number of students enrolled, teachers appointed, textbooks distributed, mid-day meals supplied, buildings constructed, toilets built, etc.), there is very little motivation to do or look for anything else. Till 2012 (this may be about to change), the academic support institutions at cluster and block levels were preoccupied with gathering data from schools. Old-time inspectors no longer monitor what happens inside the schools or, for that matter, what the children are learning. Therefore, according to the old maxim, "what is monitored is what gets done." Our school system has perfected the skill of enrolling children and showing them on the rolls.

Second: Given the no-detention policy and the way it is interpreted on the ground, schools just promote children from one grade to the next without bothering to find out if they have indeed acquired the grade-specific knowledge and skills. As a result, we now have a situation where many children reach grade 5 without learning to read or write. There is another danger that looms large. The RTE Act has extended the no-detention policy right up to the eighth grade. This essentially means that we may have children who have been in school for eight years but have not learnt language or mathematics or science.

Third: The number of days the schools actually work vary across the country. According to ASER survey (2011) student attendance has been falling. For example, average attendance of students in Bihar has declined from 59 per cent in 2007 to 50 per cent in 2011, whereas in Uttar Pradesh it fell from 67 per cent to 57 per cent in the same period. Several studies have also shown high teacher absence rates (Michael Kremer *et al*, 2004; Muralidharan, 2013). In our own field studies, we found that teachers in rural schools keep an undated leave application ready and take turns to attend class. Therefore, if there are indeed five teachers appointed for a primary school, on any given day only two or maybe three are likely to be present (Ramachandran, 2004; Sharma and Ramachandran, 2009). They rotate their "French-leave" and as a result, one teacher ends up managing more than one class. Over the last ten years I have found that the actual time spent on teaching-learning in any one grade/class could be as little as 25 minutes a day. A recent study commissioned by the government's Sarva Shiksha Abhiyan also found that the actual teaching-learning time (time-on-task) was low and student attendance was also a matter of concern (SSA TSG, GOI 2010). Why then are we surprised that our children do not learn?

Fourth: The RTE has stipulated norms for basic infrastructure and facilities, for teacher-pupil ratio, and other academic matters that determine quality. The Sarva Shiksha Abhiyan of today, the District Primary Education Programme of the 1990s, Operation Black Board of the 1980s and so on also developed elaborate guidelines and notified norms. The unfortunate reality is that many of these wonderful plans remain on paper. Often lofty intentions announced through policy are not followed up with concrete action. As a result, even after three decades of government-sponsored, central sector schemes for universal elementary education, a majority of our government schools located in rural areas and also in urban areas (the abysmal state of MCD-run schools is a case in point) have crumbling infrastructure and poorly maintained facilities. If there are toilets, there is no water; if there are toilets and water facilities, cleanliness is an issue. Apart from problems of basic maintenance, quality of construction is also poor. As a result, our schools are neither attractive nor safe.

The situation is not very different at the secondary level. Government secondary schools in many educationally backward states have poor infrastructure, inadequate teachers in some subjects, extremely poor science labs, no library etc. This list is fairly long. In addition, in many schools in rural and remote areas, a large number of girls-only schools do not offer science or commerce (Kameshwari Jandhyala *et al*, forthcoming 2014). Students are left with little option and end up doing language or arts. In a study that I did in 2008-09 in New Delhi, I found that girls' schools in some of the poorer areas did not offer science. When we asked the students of Classes 9 and 10 what they would like to do, many of them wanted to enrol in ITIs or in nursing schools, but they were unable to do so as their school did not offer science.

The problem is not lack of financial resources or of lack of good policies or strategies. The basic issue is that no one really cares if government schools function or not. Our political leaders, administrators, media and the middle classes have all abandoned government schools for their own children. In a recent study, (Ramachandran, Bhattacharjea and Sheshagiri, 2009) we had an opportunity to interact with teachers across eight states of India. I was shocked to note that not one of them sent their children/grand-children to government schools. All of them said that they wanted their children to go to a functioning school that teaches English and "maintains discipline." They all wanted English medium for their own families even though they enforce vernacular medium in government schools. They want to see their own children go to schools that function, with proper classrooms and desks, with trained teachers, while at the same time they look the other way when government school children are cramped into small windowless spaces, are made to sit on the floor, have no lights or fans and, what is worse, are not sure if they will see the teacher every day.

Official numbers tell us that all is well with our education while our eyes and ears tell a different story. India has created parallel structures of education governed by different norms and playing by different rules. In the process, the education system has got more differentiated, i.e., public, aided and private; formal and alternative; permanent, transitional, pedestrian coexisting with institutions of excellence. The poorer and the more disadvantaged are pushed into schools with poor facilities, teachers and overall learning environment. This has given rise to a new trend of "hierarchies of access," whereby, paradoxically, the democratisation of access to schools is accompanied by a reaffirmation of a child's caste, community and gender in defining which school she or he attends (Ramachandran, 2004). Having pushed the socially excluded into educational ghettos, the government wants to neutralise the inequalities of past centuries through affirmative action in the form of reservation of a certain percentage of admissions of specific social groups in higher and technical education institutions. It is cruel to offer reservations at higher levels while paying little attention to education quality and learning in school. Are we not perpetuating or even deepening inequalities by not giving our children equal opportunities in school?

The economic cake is expanding fast for some people in India. New opportunities are available to those who have been able to access quality education. There is a clamour for better schools, English education and new technologies. Quality is the new battleground.

Yet we are at a loss to define what we mean by "quality." At the heart of this concern are questions related to the goal of education. Is it to enhance the capabilities of people to negotiate an increasingly unequal, divisive and polarised world from a position of strength? Is it to enable people to reflect critically on their life situation and understand the world they live in to make informed choices? Good quality education, in essence, involves creating a system that enables children to learn to know, learn to do, learn to live with others and appreciate interdependence and diversity, and above all learn to "act with ever greater autonomy, judgement and personal responsibility" (Jacques Delors *et al*, 1996).

The segregation in education with different social classes enjoying differential access to different kinds of schools cuts at the root and poses a real threat to democracy. As Joel E Cohen (Cohen and Malin, 2010) points out, "little has been done to address questions about the universality of educational content, which varies across countries and regions. Universal could mean that all children get the same education. Or it could mean that all children get some education, but the content differs by place, type of school, or technology of instruction. Or it could mean that there are universal principles that apply everywhere but that the implementation and specification of these principles in practice depend on the local context. If content differs, there may be some or no common elements for all children. Or it could mean that education is the same for everybody except for those children who are disabled, remote, rural, minority, or otherwise handicapped."

An inability to address the fundamental goals of education does not augur well for democracy. In an increasingly polarised society, caste, religion and language identities are reinforced in politics and political parties mobilise along caste and community lines, pitting one group against the other to capture votes. Schools no longer provide a common shared space for children of different backgrounds and communities. Children today are growing up without getting an opportunity to mix with children from other social groups. While children from middle class and affluent families with greater access to the world media may potentially be exposed to different viewpoints, majority of poor children not only attend school where they mix with their own kind but also have little access to the media (print and visual). They are thus doubly disadvantaged, by poverty and by poor quality education.

Given the segregation and given that those who can access reasonable quality education opt for higher end careers, teaching as a career is increasingly becoming a last resort. The last three decades have witnessed a sharp decline in the quality of teachers. The further one moves away from the metropolis and well-endowed schools, the greater the decline in educational level, skills and confidence of teachers. With the base of the educational pyramid remaining poor and the inability of our system to attract competent teachers, we are only reinforcing the quality divide.

As we peel away the layers of the education system, more contradictions reveal themselves. Larger governance issues like corruption; rent seeking and patronage make an already difficult situation even more resistant to reform. Even well meaning reformers are at a loss about where to begin. Lofty goals are set every few years, new documents are released (the most recent being the nationwide effort to draft a national curriculum framework) and institutions are revamped to regulate quality (NCTE). Yet, institutions that are expected to set standards and provide academic leadership at different levels (national, state and district) have been reduced to petty fiefdoms that are least concerned about larger issues, such as the purpose of education. And unfortunately, the larger political debate on education continues to centre primarily on writing and rewriting history and peculiar manifestations of affirmative action that only reinforce social divisions and existing inequalities.

All these questions are about quality, of learning, of environment, of relationships and of experience. Quality is the heart of the struggle for equality and justice. The unwillingness or inability to define what we really mean by quality and institutional mechanisms, necessary to realise standards of quality, is ultimately a political question. Unfortunately, the communist parties, the social democrats, the centrist liberals and the right-wing ideologues all are on the same side in the education quagmire, together contributing to the growing schism between the rhetoric and reality.

There is an urgent need to re-imagine education, overhaul the system and link education to life, livelihood, peace and social justice. While striving for equality, the education system should be able to respond to both aspirations and opportunities while enhancing choices. A farmer should be able to enhance her productivity, weigh the pros and cons of traditional and modern technologies and make informed choices. Children living in a multicultural environment should have an opportunity to learn about each other while creating bonds of shared experiences and at the same time, learning from the catastrophic consequences of racism, parochialism and communalism on humanity. Skilled and unskilled workers should be able to negotiate just wages and resist gender and age inequalities that exist. The education system should have the depth as well as the range to span different worlds that people live in and also create bridges. A child born into a community that is rooted in a traditional occupation must have the opportunity to move out if she so wishes or infuse modern technologies or marketing opportunities into a traditional occupation. This has implications for the education system. We may have to reconstruct education in such a way that it provides multiple points of entry and exit, accommodate varying paces of learning and enable people to stand tall where they are and reach out to the world with confidence. Young people who do not want to pursue formal schooling after Grade 8 or 10 should have the opportunity to pursue learning in a different stream. Equally, a young person who may have dropped out when she was just 14 should be able to pick up the threads at a later stage, if she so desires. There is a need to rethink the value of linear progression from primary right up to higher education. This can happen only if people who are committed to an alternative vision have the courage to put an end to the mindless pursuit of numbers (also known misleadingly as "goals") and call the bluff. This is the only way we can strengthen the voices clamouring for meaningful education.

What can We Do?

It is universally accepted that three factors influence the performance of a school system; namely: inputs pedagogical process employed in the classrooms and the overall governance of the school system. Research done in the last ten years does not show any positive correlation between inputs and student learning (Muralidharan, 2013).

May be we need to start with teachers. There is something fundamentally wrong with the way we have managed teachers as a cadre, teachers as professionals, teachers as individuals, teachers as experts and teachers as government servants. Some state governments/administrators thought hiring local contract teachers was the way to manage absenteeism, some others thought that this was a bad idea and that protecting teacher tenure was the key, some others thought mandatory training would do the trick..... we in India have tried many things at different points of time. Given that teachers have been seen as a powerful constituency, accountability systems were never designed or implemented seriously.

May be the best way to move forward is to announce that learning outcomes will be the primary and most important goal in elementary education. This has to be made a non-negotiable ground rule that informs the entire education system. I am arguing for an effective system that will rescue children from the cumulative burden of non-learning.

We need to evolve a system whereby the learning levels of children are ascertained at periodic intervals in the school and presented to parents and other stakeholders in the immediate environment of the school. We still may not know how to do this, but it is high time we actively involved the parents, the education community, civil society organisations, local leaders and the media to keep the spotlight on what and how much are children learning. Yes, as many educational researchers would caution, testing cannot be an end in itself and that there is no guarantee that measuring learning outcomes and presenting it would automatically lead to improvement. It is the active interaction between teachers, parents and academic support structures that might help us arrive at a balance.

We need to make sure every single school in the country comes upto a basic minimum acceptable level: one teacher for each class should be non-negotiable; the pupil-teacher ratio has to be calculated for every school (not every district); and a robust independent mechanism should be in place to audit the functioning of schools (through toll free helplines for students and parents to lodge complaints).

What and how much do our teachers know is as important a question as what and how much are our children learning. There is a lot of evidence—in India and in the region as a whole—that point to the poor subject knowledge of teachers (Kingdon and Banerji, 2009; Banerji and Kingdon, 2010). Poor teacher competencies translate into poor learning among students, and this underscores not only the importance of knowing the subject but also have the skill to teach and transmit that knowledge. This happens because of a number of reasons — one of them being the kind of people who are attracted to the teaching profession (reference). Countries that have been able to improve learning in schools have focussed on who becomes a teacher. The experience of Poland and Finland is well known. The world is gradually waking upto the far-reaching reforms that China has been attempting.

The bottom line is that the entire education system — starting from pre-school (an essential prerequisite for school readiness) to higher secondary — has to make sure children realise their right to be taught and their right to learn in a non-discriminatory environment. Like in all other sectors, governance is the key. A school-upwards governance structure is critical to make education quality the heart of our equity strategy. Political leaders and administrators need to realise that the very fabric of our democratic polity is at risk if we do not drastically reform the education system. We – meaning political parties, bureaucrats and citizens need to abandon turf battles and petty politics and rise to the challenge of making education a real equaliser – giving every child an equal opportunity regardless of where she is located, which community she belongs to or the occupation of parents.

Notes

1. This paper is based on (a) a paper that I did in 2006 titled Democratic Inequalities (Ramachandran 2009) and (b) the work that I did as a National Fellow in NUEPA from December 2011 to June of 2013. Parts of this paper was delivered as a public lecture in Nehru Memorial Museum and Library on 5 September 2013 and subsequently published as an Occasional Paper by NMML (Ramachandran 2013). A different version of this paper is included in Vimala Ramachandran, 2018, *Inside Indian Schools*, Social Science Press, New Delhi.
2. Quoted in Sunil Khilnani, 1997, page 35.

References

ASER Centre and Pratham (2005 to 2012): *Annual Status of Education Reports*. New Delhi.

Banerji, Rukmini and Kingdon, G. (2010): *How Sound are Our Mathematics Teachers? Insights from the School TELLS Survey*. Learning Curve. Azim Premji Foundation.

Beteille, Tara. (2009): Absenteeism, Transfers and Patronage: The Political Economy of Teacher Labour Markets in India." Ph.D. Thesis, Stanford University.

Bourdieu, Pierre and Passeron, Jean-Claude (1977): *Reproduction in Education, Society and Culture*. London: Sage Publications.

Chitnis, Suma (1972): Education for Equality: Case of Scheduled Castes in Higher Education. *Economic and Political Weekly*, 7 (31/33), Special Number (August 1972), pp. 1675-1681.

Cohen, Joel and Malin, Martin (Ed.) (2010): *International Perspectives on the Goals of Universal Basic Education*, American Academy of Arts and Sciences, New York: Routledge, pp 104-12.

Delors, Jacques, et al (1996): Learning: The Treasure Within: Report to UNESCO of the International Commission on Education for the Twenty-First Century. Paris: UNESCO Publishing.

Deshpande, Satish (2013): "Introduction" in Deshpande, Satish and Zacharias, Usha (2013): *Beyond Inclusion: The Practice of Equal Access in Indian Higher Education*. New Delhi: Routledge.

Dewey, John (2001): *Democracy and Education*. Penn State Electronic Classic Series. Pennsylvania. USA (re-printed).

Dreze, Jean and Sen, Amartya (2002): *India: Development and Participation*. Second Edition. Oxford: Oxford University Press,

Dundar, Halil; Beteille, Tara; Riboud, Michelle and Deolalikar, Anil (forthcoming): Improving Learning Outcomes in South Asia: Challenges, Opportunities and Policy Priorities in School Education. Directions in Development. Washington, DC: World Bank.

Government of India (2012): *School Education Statistics*. New Delhi: MHRD.

Government of India (2009): NSSO, Report Number 532 on the NSSO 64th Round. New Delhi: Ministry of Statistics and Programme Implementation.

Government of India (2011): NSSO, Report Number 537 on the NSSO 66th Round. New Delhi: Ministry of Statistics and Programme Implementation.

Government of India, Planning Commission. (2011): *Twelfth Five Year Plan 2012–17*, Volume 3 Social Sectors. New Delhi: Planning Commission (http:// planningcommission.gov.in/plans/ planrel/12thplan/welcome.html)

Government of India (2011): *Twelfth Five-Year Plan*. New Delhi: Planning Commission.

Government of India (2010): Teachers and Students Time-on-Task in Primary and Upper Primary Schools — A Synthesis Report. Research, Evaluation and Studies Unit, EdCIL. New Delhi: SSA TGS and EdCIL.

Jandhyala, Kameshwari; Mehrotra, Nishi; Patni, Rajni; Rajagopal, Shobhita; Saxena, Niti; Agarwal, Sapna; Sharma, Radheshyam and Ramachandran, Vimala (forthcoming): *Women Teachers and the Achievement of Gender and Equity Goals in Secondary Education*. New Delhi: ERU Consultants Pvt. Ltd..

Khilnani, Sunil (1997): *The Idea of India*. London: Hamish Hamilton.

Kingdon, Geeta Gandhi and Banerji, Rukmini (2009): Addressing School Quality: Some Policy Pointers for Rural North India. RECOUP Policy Brief No. 5, Faculty of Education, University of Cambridge, UK.

Kremer, Michael; Muralidharan, Karthik; Chaudhury, Nazmul; Hammer, Jeffrey and Rogers, Halsey (2005): Teacher Absence in India. *Journal of the European Economic Association*, April–May, 3(203): 658-67.

Kumar, Krishna and Sarangapani, Padma (2004): The Quality Imperative: History of the Quality Debate. Background Paper Prepared for EFA GMR 2005. Paris: UNESCO.

Mahajan, Gurpreet (2013): India: Political Ideas and the Making of a Democratic Discourse. London & New York: Zed Books.

Manabi Mazumbar (2001): Educational Opportunities in Rajasthan and Tamil Nadu: Despair and Hope. In Vaidyanathan and Nair (Ed.) (2001): Infra.

Muralidharan, Karthik (2013): *Priorities of Primary Education Policy in India's 12th Five-Year Plan*. NCAER-Brookings India Policy Forum 2013.

Nambissan, Geeta (2001): Social Diversity and Regional Disparity in Schooling: A Study of Rural Rajasthan. In Vaidyanathan and Nair (Ed.) (2001): Infra.

NCERT (2005): *National Curriculum Framework*. New Delhi: Government of India.

Ramachandran, Vimala (2009): Democratic Inequalities: The Dilemma of Elementary Education in India. In Cowen, Robert and Kazamias, Andrea M (Ed.): *International Handbook of Comparative Education,* Volume II, The Netherlands: Springer International Handbook of Education Series.

Ramachandran, Vimala and Educational Resource Unit Team. (2004): *Snakes and Ladders: Factors Influencing Successful Primary School Completion for Children in Poverty Contexts*. South Asian Human Development Sector Report No. 6, New Delhi: World Bank.

Ramachandran, Vimala and Naroem, Tara (2012): Inclusion and Exclusion of Students in Schools and Classrooms in Primary and Upper Primary Schools of India – A Synthesis of a Six State Study. Government of India: Technical Support Group of Sarva Shiksha Abhiyan (Education for All).

Ramachandran, Vimala; Bhattacharjea, Suman and Shesagiri, K M (2009): *Primary School Teachers in India: The Twists and Turns of Everyday Practice*. Azim Premji Foundation Mimeograph. Bangalore. (http://azimpremjifoundation.org/Reports_Papers_and_Articles)

Ramachandran, Vimala (2004): *Hierarchies of Access: Gender and Equity in Primary Education.* New Delhi: Sage Publications.

Ramachandran, Vimala (2007): The Great Number Race and Challenge of Education. *Economic and Political Weekly*, September 29, pp. 3917–19.

Ramachandran, Vimala (2009): Towards Gender Equality in Education: EFA Mid-Decade Assessment. New Delhi: NUEPA.

Ramachandran, Vimala (2010): Quality, The Heart of Equity. In Cohen, Joel and Malin, Martin (Ed.): Supra, pp. 104-12.

Reardon, Sean F. (2011): The Widening Academic Achievement Gap between the Rich and the

Poor: New Evidence and Possible Explanations. In Reardon (forthcoming): *Whither Opportunity? Rising Inequality, Schools and Children's Life Chances*. Russell Sage Foundation.

Ripley, Amanda. (2013): *The Smartest Kids in the World, and How They Got that Way*. New York: Simon & Schuster.

Sharma, Rashmi and Ramachandran, Vimala. (2009): The Elementary Education System in India: Exploring Institutional Structures, Processes and Dynamics. New Delhi: Routledge.

Tilak, Jandhyala B.G. (Ed). (2013): *Higher Education in India: In Search of Equality, Quality and Quantity*. New Delhi: Orient Blackswan.

Vaidyanathan, A. and Nair, P.R. Gopinathan (Ed.): *Elementary Education in Rural India – A Grassroots View*. New Delhi: Sage Publications.

Weisskopf, Thomas E. (2013): Impact of Reservations on Admissions to Higher Education. In Tilak, Jandhyala B.G. (Ed.): Supra.

World Bank (2010): Successful Education Reform: Lessons from Poland. *Knowledge Brief*, Vol. 34, November 2010.

World Bank (2012): What Matters Most in Teacher Policies: A Framework for Building a More Effective Teaching Profession. Washington DC: SABER, World Bank.

16

Politics of School Location in Post-Reform India

The Exclusion and Inequality

R. Govinda* and *A. Mathew

India embarked on the task of establishing a mass education programme with the goal of ensuring universal and compulsory education for all children in the country. The Constitution adopted in 1950 set a stiff target of reaching the goal within ten years universal education was visualised as fundamental building block for the development of the newly created democratic republic. The importance of this commitment for education for building a democratic society based on social, economic and political justice and equality of status and opportunity to all its citizens irrespective of caste, creed and belief, could hardly be overemphasised.

The situation of school education in the country at that time was quite challenging with not even one out of three children getting enrolled in school; of every 100 children enrolled only 14 were girls; adult literacy was as low as 18 per cent. In 1950-51, there were only around 210 thousand primary and 14 thousand upper primary schools to cater to around 69.4 million children in the age group 6 to 14. Considering that the schooling infrastructure was grossly inadequate in terms of numbers and sparsely located to reach education to the vast spread of rural population, large scale expansion of the system was perceived as the right response to the challenge of achieving the Constitutional mandate of universal elementary education to all children until the age of 14.

The decade of 1950-51 to 1960-61 witnessed considerable expansion bringing more children into the folds of schooling. Yet enrolment increased only from around 32 per cent to 48 per cent. This obviously raised the issue of the strategy being adopted for achieving UEE. Some studies (Sharma and Sapra, 1969) pointed out the problem of children leaving the school midway without completing even lower primary stage. However, inadequate number and spread of schools were identified as the major bottleneck for non-participation of children and expansion of the schooling network. Further, irrational location of schools and distance seemed partly to be the reasons for dropout and wastage, hindering achievement of the Constitutional mandate. In fact, the number of schools in the country has never stopped increasing. This paper explores the policies and practices adopted in expanding the school system. In particular, it attempts to critically examine the changing principles and criteria followed in locating new schools during the last several decades and analyse the impact it has made on the issues of equality and social justice in provision of public education. In doing so, the paper locates the serious aberrations that have occurred as reflected in the establishment of incomplete, single teacher unviable primary schools from the mid-1990s which tended to become a barrier to, rather an instrument, of social inclusion. Tracing the trajectory of this tendency in official policy and practice, the paper examines how it has severely affected the primary goal of educational development contributing to democratic principles of inclusion and equity. Finally, the paper indicates some possible strategies of readjusting the distribution of schooling facilities in a more equitable fashion.

Policy Framework for School Location: Education Commission 1964-66

For provision of free and universal education to every child, it is indisputable that the school should be as near the home of the child as possible. But this would normally be impractical on many counts, and this objective could be fulfilled only through a rational basis of location of schools. This rational planning is necessary to avoid overlapping and duplication in location of schools and the resultant waste and also to ensure that other deserving areas are not deprived of educational facility. Towards this end, suitable guidelines are needed to determine the location and size of each category of schools, such as primary, middle, secondary and higher secondary, etc. Such guidelines imply the availability of educational facilities to children of all caste and creed so that schooling also promotes social equality and strengthens the democratic process of equal opportunity to all.

The Education Commission, no doubt, concurred with the imperatives, as indicated in the Educational Survey, to ensure primary schools location and planning for expansion of school education in such a way as to ensure social equality of access as fundamental to all other values of egalitarian society envisioned in the Constitution. The Commission did not reject the rational basis of habitation size and distance norms determining location of school and educational expansion plan. It took cognizance of the almost universal provision of schooling facility at lower primary level in all habitations with a population of 300 and above and in fact its availability even in smaller villages at the end of the Third Plan. The Commission felt that while rational planning of location of schools at different stages needs to be upheld and adhered in location of schools and development of school education, it made a difference with respect to primary schools, by saying that "at this stage, accessibility is the overriding consideration and small schools, in spite of their heavier cost and lower efficiency, must be accepted" (NCERT, 1971: 330). It agreed with the view of the AIES (1957) that the general rule should be to establish a lower primary school within a mile or so of the home of every child and a higher primary school within 3 miles. But, while the first Educational Survey laid down a population of 300 and above should be the criterion, the Education Commission felt that villages with a population of 200-300 should have a lower primary school and those with a population of 700 or more should have a higher primary school. Its conviction was also strengthened by the size of enrolment: one-third of all primary schools were found to have an enrolment of less than 40 pupils, and about two-thirds with an enrolment of less than 100; only about one-fourth of the primary schools had an enrolment of 140 or more. Similarly, even assuming the minimum essential enrolment at higher primary level to be about 60, 40 per cent of schools were found to be lower level than this (NCERT, 1971: 304).

The Commission readily conceded the difficulty of tagging these habitations and the hardships of far larger distance that would become inevitable by following the optimum level of enrolment it advocated, viz., 160-200 students with 4-5 teachers at lower primary level and 400-500 students with 7-8 teachers at higher primary level. One option for such a desirable larger and more efficient primary school, according to the Commission, "is to persuade people to accept for mixed schools at primary stage and to induce all neighbouring villages to share a bigger school instead of insisting on their own school, however small" (NCERT, 1971: 304). This made the Education Commission to make a difference to the primary schools from the general norms of location of schools. It was convinced that "at this stage, accessibility is the overriding consideration and small schools, in spite of their heavier cost and lower efficiency, must be accepted" (NCERT, 1971: 304).

Thus, Education Commission based its observations on the findings of the First All India Education Survey done in 1957 and recommended to follow specific criteria of distance and population in establishing new schools; even while endorsing a standard policy for locating schools it recommended to provide for exceptions to ensure for remote and isolated habitations in order that no one is excluded from schooling. This recognition was accompanied by the caution that establishing such schools is likely to be economically less viable. Based on Education Commission advocacy, in respect of interior tribal habitations and such other situations of hilly and scattered areas, and depending on socio-political considerations, relaxations were made in respect of size of population and distance in opening primary schools.

Education Commission did not view establishing a new school merely as a matter of technical planning for determining the villages and habitations where a school should be located. Rather, the Commission set the underlying principle that should guide the process of expansion reiterating the vision of the Constitution makers: *".....the provision of free and universal education to every child is an educational objective of the highest priority..... on grounds of social justice and democracy."* The Education Commission was firm in its conviction that "on grounds of social and national integration, we believe that all the children of the country should study in the common school system of public education, because this experience is extremely significant for their development as citizens." It said that "the objective of educational policy should be to evolve, over next 20 years, a common school system of public education which would cover all parts of the country, provide equality of access to all children and will maintain such a standard that an average parent will not feel the need to send his child to an independent or unrecognised school" (NCERT, 1971: 496). In the Commission's view, "the present social segregation in schools should be eliminated by the adoption of the neighbourhood school concept under which all children in the neighbourhood will be required to attend the school in the locality", and this plan should be implemented in a period of 20 years....." (NCERT, 1971: 449; 487-89).

Planning for School Location: The Beginnings in Evolution of Norms

Keeping the Recommendations of the Education Commission in view the school location had to have two dimensions. On one hand, opening of new schools should be based on norms and distance and population. On the other hand, physical location of the schools within a village should also be planned carefully to ensure easy access for all with no discrimination. In fact, it is pertinent to note the implicit principle followed in physical location of the school – that it must be accessible from every point in the village. In rural areas, generally it used to be a little away, but not too far away from the village so that small children could easily walk to the school. But within this geographical location lay also the social access such that the school is above the caste/class divisions found in the social fabric of the village. The location planning of the schools seems to have been guided by these notions and there are strong evidences in its support.

In order to assess the educational needs of the country and to plan the location of primary schools so as to avoid all overlapping and duplication of effort, the then British Government, as early as in 1911, had indicated that educational surveys be made in all States according to following procedure:

> "First of all, every village or population centre should be shown on a clearly prepared map, then all the bigger villages, i.e., the villages with a population of 300 or more, which could be given an independent school, should be marked off. Then the small villages should be grouped as far as possible in such a way that each group would have a population of about 300 and a central school could be *provided for the group at the point which would be most easily accessible from every point.* When such a group could not be made, plans should to be prepared for instituting a system of travelling teachers to meet the needs of as many small villages as possible. Only when all these attempts fail could a village be left out of the programme of school provision" (emphasis added). In a properly carried out survey, it was considered possible to provide school facilities for more than 98 per cent of the total population (MOE, 1964: 4).

However, no systematic effort on these lines was made, except in Bombay, where the inadequacy of treating the village as an education unit was convincingly shown for the first time as an educational survey of Rajapur taluka of Ratnagiri district disclosed 965 hamlets in 815 revenue villages. A note on educational survey of India, prepared by J.P. Naik, a member of the Educational Panel of the Planning Commission, was placed before the CABE in its annual meeting in January 1956. The sub-committee of CABE endorsed the proposal for an immediate Educational Survey, which in turn was further recommended by the CABE. This was accepted by the Government of India (GOI) and it was decided to carry out the necessary survey with the cooperation of state governments, with the central government bearing two-thirds of the expenses. As soon as the scheme was approved by GOI, its broad features were brought to the notice of the state governments, through a semi-official communication of the Educational Adviser and Secretary, MOE, to Education Secretaries to move state governments, to participate in the Survey, by shouldering one-third of its cost (MOE, 1964: 5-6).

Unplanned Location of Schools in the Past: It is revealing and instructive to see the unwritten sanctity of the social equality considerations implicit in the rationale behind the rational norms of location of school and plans of such norms-based educational expansion. Even at the time of the first All India Educational Survey it was noticed that schools opened in the past, whether by government or local authorities or private agencies were not necessarily according to any pre-conceived state-wise plan; in many cases, these were influenced by vested interests or local pressure (MOE, 1964).

Owing to this somewhat unplanned and indiscriminate opening of schools, disparities in provision of educational facilities were almost inescapable. Though some very small habitations had schools in them, far bigger habitations in the adjoining areas had, for years, remained without educational facility even at the primary school stage. The total population that would be benefitted did not always seem to have been taken into account while locating the schools. In some cases, the habitations were so badly located as not to attract a reasonable enrolment to justify even a single-teacher school. These were but only a few possibilities of ill-conceived planning (MOE, 1964: 10).

Minimum Population to Justify a School: In a rational planning of the school education system, a school should be proposed at any place, only when there is a reasonable chance of having in the long run, adequate enrolment to justify the opening of at least a single-teacher school. The first Educational Survey was guided by well established demographic consideration about minimum population to justify a primary school: working on the basis that children of the age-group 6-11 form about 12 and a half per cent of the total population, to have about 40 children, the total population of the area must be at least about 300 (it was also already indicated in 1911, as seen earlier) based on the 1951 census. This was, therefore, adopted as the minimum requisite population to justify a school in a habitation. Wherever possible, attempt was to be made to group together small habitations roundabout a suitable central place so that the proposed school would have an adequate strength. This in its trail raised the question of the distance the children would be expected to walk (MOE, 1964: 17).

The Walkable Distance: The Survey argued that it is indisputable that the school should be as near the home of the child as possible but as this is impracticable in the conditions obtaining, the maximum distance a child in the rural areas at the age of 6 to 11 years can be expected to walk to the school needed to be fixed. From common experience and depending generally on the accepted distance limit in the Compulsory Education Acts of some of the States, the distance limit of the one mile had been accepted in the survey for tagging on the surrounding smaller habitations to the central school-habitation for the purpose of schooling facilities at the primary school stage, i.e. for standards I to IV or I to V as the case may be. This maximum distance of one mile is the actual walking distance along the road or by-path and not the shortest distance as the crow flies (MOE, 1964: 17-18). According to this distance limit of one mile a child will have to walk up to one mile each way, which means that if the school is held in one session every day a child will have to walk up to a total distance of two miles during the day and this is already a substantially long distance for the child of the tender age of 6 or 7. If the school is held in two sessions, one in the morning and the other in the afternoon, as it is in certain places, due to the local needs and climatic conditions, then the child will have to walk a total distance of about four miles a day, which is certainly heavy for that age. Hence, it was suggested that this upper limit of one mile should not be exceeded unless there were compelling reasons to the contrary (MOE, 1964: 18).

The All India Educational Surveys: Data Base for Planning School Location

As already noted, the first All India Educational Survey (AIES) was conducted in 1957 by MOE. However, with the establishment of NCERT in 1963, conduct of such surveys of school education in the country got institutionalised. The first two Educational Surveys, 1957 and the Second, 1967 concentrated on identifying and enumerating the habitations as well as the existing primary, middle and high schools and habitations served by them, and to plan school (catchment) areas for primary, middle and secondary schools in a rational manner (NCERT 1967: 8). The Second Educational Survey was initiated in order to identify every habitation, assess the schooling facilities at all school stages and plan school catchment areas for every primary, middle and secondary school in future.

The Third Survey, 1979, unlike the previous two Surveys, covered all areas of education right from pre-primary through university, including unrecognised institutions, technical and vocational education, educational administration, etc. (NCERT, 1979: v). But in respect of school education, it followed the same pattern and scope as the previous two Surveys, with one significant addition, viz., coverage of SC/ST population and habitations across primary, middle and secondary school stages. The scope of the Fourth Survey was confined to only school education, and within school education, it had undertaken to provide information on new features like availability of minimum basic facilities in schools, such as buildings, furniture, libraries, equipment, health and sanitation and incentives (NCERT, 1979: xi).

The Fifth AIES, besides all the aspects covered in earlier Surveys, also covered the availability of these facilities and other ancillary services in SC/ST habitations as well. The Sixth Survey, besides its focus on information on school facilities as well as on physical and academic facilities and also in respect of habitations of SC and ST, also covered data on teachers. Creation of an EMIS in respect of the aspects covered by the Survey emerged as a singular important item besides and beyond other aspects (NCERT, 1997: xi). The Seventh Survey also covered the number of para-teachers in recognised schools, CSWN-enrolment, and more than two-thirds focus on physical and academic and other ancillary facilities.

Each subsequent Survey report took pride in the new educational parameters about which data have been collected and included for the benefit of educational planners and in preparation of plans of educational development. Initiated by the central government and undertaken collaboratively with the state governments, the AIESs were intended to identify all the rural and urban habitations with and without educational facilities and to plan location of schools in a rational basis *so that existing educational imbalances could be narrowed down.* The First All India Educational Survey drew satisfaction from the fact that the objectives of presenting the school location picture had been achieved. In the same vein, it went on "The gratification lies in the fact that the results of the Survey, as soon as they were ready, began immediately to be utilised by the states in the planning of the new schools. It is hoped that the data collected would continue to assist in the objective and realistic planning of educational development in future at the primary, middle and high school stages according to a properly-phased economical programme, so as to reach, at an early date, the cherished goal of universal free education enunciated in Article 45 of the Constitution" (MOE, 1964: 499).

The Second Survey undertaken in 1965 was seen necessary because the data of the first Survey, based on 1957 situation, became dated for utilising it in planning schools for the Fourth Five Year Plan. In fact, the Advisory Committee appointed for the Second Educational Survey recommended an Educational Survey at an interval of five years, preferably during the fourth year of the Plan so that the data of the Survey could be fruitfully utilised in formulating the next Five Year Plan (NCERT, 1979: 1).

The Fourth Survey in 1979 admitted the specific purpose, viz., "This information was expected to be of help in formulating the Sixth Five-Year Plan" (NCERT, 1979: 2). The rationale and purpose of the Fifth Survey and its utility was explicitly stated in the very prefatory pages of its report: "Information provided by the All-India Educational Surveys.... have been widely utilised for the formulation of policies for educational development... the findings of this Survey, conducted with 30 September 1986, as the date, have been utilised in the formulation of the National Policy on Education (1986)." It went on to premise that "the survey data are likely to be of immediate use in the formulation of the Eight Five Year Plan for educational development", besides also for implementation of NPE (NCERT, 1986: v).

As the report itself made clear the Sixth Survey which began with 30 September 1993 as the reference date, and published in 1996 was meant to meet the requirements of the MHRD in connection with the discussions on the Ninth Five Year Plan, and had also helped many state governments to formulate their Ninth Five Year Plan on education (NCERT, 1997: v). The Seventh Survey that covered many new features hoped that its report would help in "providing a reliable picture of the school education system so that India's attempts to reform the system can succeed" (NCERT, 2006: iii).

Educational Surveys and Five Year Plans: Survey Norms Guide School Location

One could clearly recognise that the first AIES carried in 1957 provided the basis for expansion of the school system under the Third Five Year Plan by indicating the complexity and magnitude of the task involved for reaching the goal of providing schools for all. The Fourth and Fifth Plans went more or less along the educational expansion plan perspective chartered by the Third Plan (which in turn was influenced by the first Educational Survey), viz., greater focus on providing schooling facilities for universalising coverage of 6-11 year age children in Third Plan and coverage of 11-14 year age children in Fourth and Fifth Plans. For example, the Working Group for Education in the Fourth Plan said that before the end of Fourth Plan, priority will be given in opening of primary schools in about 16,000 rural school-less habitations with 300 population, and steps should be taken during Fourth and Fifth Plans to expand facilities in such a manner that by the end of the Fifth Plan, "a middle school should be within a walking distance of three miles of every pupil in the country (GOI, 1968: 21, 43).

Thus, while setting up targets at primary and upper primary levels, the Fourth Plan declared its intention to lay particular emphasis in backward areas and communities. And, as if pricked by the slow pace, the Mid-Term Appraisal of Fourth Plan concluded "states should be requested to formulate district plans for expansion and improvement of education particularly at the school stage. Education of girls and children of backward communities should receive the highest priority" (GOI, 1971: 208). The clear message of the slow pace vis-à-vis that suggested by first and the Second Educational Surveys stand out clear.

In the context of the position portrayed by the second to fifth AIESs, the Five Year Plans proceeded to set up enrolment targets and exhort the States to achieve it with central funding in respect of schemes that were more critical and catalytic to the target achievement. AIESs – Second 1968, Third, 1979, Fourth, 1983 and Fifth, 1986 went by, but the Five Year Plans knew that India was falling short of the targets it set in reference to the position portrayed in the Educational Surveys, in provision of educational facilities to reach all children as per the constitutional mandate, and more importantly, in providing educational facilities to bridge the spatial, regional, social and gender disparities that could guarantee the democratic principle of equal opportunities to all. It is quite evident that the Eighth Plan and even for preparing the 9th Five Year Plan proposals followed the well established norms for expansion of schooling facilities except in respect of the tribal areas in the State of Andhra Pradesh (Sujatha, 1996; 2000).

Unplanned Expansion and Irrational Location: Evolving Story of Post-Reform Period

Starting from the mid-90s, and with the launch of the externally funded District Primary Education Programme, and as part of the expansion drive, small schools with an unviable enrolment of 10-20 children, began to emerge in rural habitations in the name of reaching the unreached. There were no serious thinking and plans of integrating them into the larger mainstream of schooling with carefully crafted enabling arrangements. But, instead, so intense has been the perceived compulsion of the State to show results that it did not examine the possible serious damage to the larger social objectives of social inclusion and education of unequal quality which these small and unviable schools were bound up with. After all, these small single teacher schools served as a cheap economic option, much in line with the requirements of State withdrawal from direct economic burden, much as the Structural Adjustment Programme (SAP) compulsions camouflaged under the sweet rhetoric of taking education to the doorstep of the people, community involvement and ownership, school/teacher accountability to the community, decentralisation, etc.

More specifically, starting with the Education Guarantee Scheme (EGS) schools in Madhya Pradesh (Gopalakrishnan and Sharma, 1998; 1999; and Sharma and Gopalakrishnan,2003) and the Rajiv Gandhi Swarna Jayanti Patshalas in Rajasthan (RGSJY), single teacher schools in rural habitations and urban slums began to be established on a fairly large scale by state governments, under funding from the Central Government. The NFE scheme, meant for out of school and working children, which followed an alternative approach and method was merged with the EGS and RGSJY and with a variety of Alternative and Innovative Education (AIE) programmes, such that the poor quality rudimentary level of education became the fate of rural and remote small habitations and urban slums. In quick succession states like as Andhra Pradesh, Bihar, Gujarat, Himachal Pradesh, Jharkhand, Maharasthra, Odisha, Rajasthan, Uttar Pradesh, etc., started recruiting para teachers, initially for remote rural single teacher primary schools, for small schools without regular teachers, and later in place of regular teachers. These were cases in point of such unviable schools, started for the poorer sections of small habitations, while well-endowed primary and elementary schools in bigger villages continued to exist side by side. But, far being criticised for the abysmally rudimentary facilities it offers, it has been praised for reaching the unreached. So successful has been the public promotion that the abrogation of recruitment norms, the poor quality of teacher training and the exploitative cycle in which it places primary-level teachers were completely overlooked (Kumar *et al*, 2001). The combination of small schools and para-teachers became a popular response, but its effect on perpetuating poor quality education to the poor in urban slums and rural small habitations was totally ignored.

A few pointers about how this changed the school educational landscape in rural India from the latter part of the 1990s, as a sequel to the DPEP initiative could be noted. EGS schools and AIE centres were started in rural locations not necessarily in due regard to the school catchment area consideration or minimum viable enrolment for a primary school. Many of these were established in smaller hamlets adjoining bigger habitations which together formed a village. These EGS schools which became an all India model from 2000 ended up as single teacher schools with 1-2 grades, with abysmally low level of educational facilities, and the teachers being inadequately qualified and trained.

When the Report Card of the RTE implementation – its third year report (MHRD, 2014) is examined, many pointers are clearly discernible regarding the probability of the socio-economically disadvantaged poor and marginalised sections in remote and rural small habitations becoming worse off in the all round increase registered in primary schooling facilities, especially after the SSA introduction.

(i) *Availability of Primary Schooling Facility:* At the all-India level as well as in some selected states, availability of schooling facilities at primary stage within the habitation nearly doubled, from 425,244 to 762,984 between 1993 and 2009, and registered nearly a three-fold increase in the category of "upto 1 km". It represented an impressive 22.37 per cent increase in primary schools within the habitations, and 13.64 per cent increase in the of "upto 1 km" category. This was also evident in the 24.94 per cent decline noticed in the beyond 1 km category; this must have been accounted for by the increase of schooling facilities in the former two categories of "within the habitation" and "up to 1 km." Probably, most of these were single teacher schools with remote rural small habitations, with very unsustainable enrolment, ostensibly with the "reaching the unreached" objective. This gets corroborated, as would be evident later, by the increase in the number of primary schools with less than 50 enrolment, along <10, 11-19, 20-29, 30-39, 40-49 enrolment slabs.

(ii) *Building Facilities for Primary Schooling:* The incidence of primary schooling in open space and tents (implying schools without building) in 2009 at 11,996 was significantly less than the position in 2002, viz., 17,748. Bihar alone accounted for more than half of the number of primary schools in open space and tents in 2009 (8th All India School Education Survey).

(iii) *Para-Teachers:* There was a steep increase of 29.28 per cent over the Seventh AIES in the number of teachers in rural primary schools in 2009. Against 1,457,788 full time teachers including Principal/Headmaster, para/contract teachers at 489,961 in 2009 were still a significant proportion.

Obviously, the double and triple increase in the number of schools between the Sixth and Ninth AIESs would have been entrusted to them, because more and more states started recruiting para and contract teachers in place of regular teachers from first decade of this century (Kumar, *et al*). There were in 2010, about 637 thousand contractual-teachers, constituting 10.97 per cent of the total number of teachers.

(iv) There were also 10,947 urban primary schools with no teachers or with zero teachers in 2009. It is really surprising to see its steep increase, viz., 4373 since 1993 even though teacher recruitment was the litmus test of EFA in DPEP and SSA. This was only in urban Indian primary schools. Its prevalence in rural areas must have been severe. It is surprising that rather than decreasing since 2002, the number of schools without buildings in fact increased in 2009 in some states like Odisha, Maharashtra and Bihar.

It is true that more than 1,00,000 lower primary schools/sections (1,32,209 to be precise) and 58,720 upper primary schools/sections were opened between 2002-03 and 2009-10. But, the enrolment at primary level actually declined from 134,132,183 in 2009-08 to 133,405,581 in 2009-10, while it increased from 50,011,110 to 54,467,415 at upper primary level in the same period (NUEPA, 2011-DISE 2009-10).

The percentage of enrolment in government schools at primary level stood at 72.13 in 2009-10 as against 21.38 per cent in un-aided private schools. At upper primary level, it was 36.83 as against 21.24 per cent under unaided private schools. But, as against an all India average of about 20 per cent, at primary and upper primary levels, in some of the educationally backward states and those taking greater recourse to appointment of para/contract teachers such as Andhra Pradesh, Madhya Pradesh, Rajasthan and UP, the average proportion of enrolment in un-aided private schools, that wean away government school students, has been more than 30 per cent at primary level and more than 33 per cent at upper primary level (NUEPA, 2011-DISE 2009-10). These also were the states which launched massive recruitment of para/contract teachers, as well as are states leading in schools with single teacher, zero enrolment and zero teachers, zero classroom for primary, and in many respects, even for upper primary schools.

The trend in enrolment slab of 10, 11-19, 20-29, 30-39, 40-49 and 1-49, i.e., <50 between 2005-06 and 2011-12 bring out certain revealing picture. The increase in the number of primary schools in the enrolment brackets at 2005-06 and 2011-12, abstracted from the Tables 5 -7, could be seen below.

Table 16.1: Increase in Schools in Lower Enrolment Slabs

Year	*1-10*	*11-19*	*20-29*	*30-39*	*40-49*	*1-49, i.e., <50*
2005-06	8870 4.28%	24910 8.14%	49450	59913	64227	207370
2011-12	19462 5.96%	50911 10.78%	85286	88573	82136	326368

Source: compiled from DISE data for 2005-06 and 2011-13

Undoubtedly, number of primary schools increased. But the point to note is that all the problems of inequity also seem to have increased. After all, as late as 2010, there were, as seen above, about 637 thousand contract teachers, constituting 10.97 per cent of the total number of teachers. There has been a consistent increase of small schools over the years, compounding the problem of social equity and inclusion.

Concluding Observations and the Way Forward

There is no doubt about the expansion in the size of elementary education system in terms of actual number of schools, teachers, physical and other ancillary facilities, and coverage of habitations, including even the smaller ones. Thus, with respect to social, spatial, regional and gender equity, the expansion would seem to be meeting the rights perspective as explicitly stipulated in the RTE. But where and what exactly are the hurdles and barriers to these equities is in respect of the smaller schools, in smaller habitations both in rural and urban areas. This is evident from the differences between smaller schools in smaller habitations and bigger schools in bigger habitations. What appears to exacerbate the widening differences within the primary and elementary education in the government system is the dwindling enrolment in small schools with abysmal lack of facilities, and increase in conversion and upgradation of incomplete schools into full primary schools, incidence of single teachers, and replacement of regular teachers with para/contract teachers.

Over the last two decades, the principle of rational norms-based school location has been sidelined with deleterious effect on educational and social equity. This initially happened by opening incomplete primary schools by way of EGS and AIE centres/ programmes, under the guise of promoting community involvement. The approach continued later on in a camouflaged fashion by renaming them, *en* bloc, as regular primary schools, doing away with the community contribution component. Establishment of incomplete small schools in smaller habitations, with abysmally inadequate physical and academic facilities with para/contract single teachers became the norm in State after State since 1997-98, even while full-fledged schools existed in adjoining or nearby bigger villages. The move was invariably sugar-coated under the banner of decentralisation, community involvement, participation and ownership, school/teacher accountability to the community and community managing teacher appointment, etc. The very rationale and basis of regular primary education with regular full time teacher, backed by teacher education and curriculum planning came to be questioned and replaced by para/contract teachers, with inadequate training and grossly reduced remuneration. All of this left a crippling effect on the quality of education of children living in smaller rural locations and urban slums, inhabited by the socio-economically disadvantaged sections. The government sector which accounts for a major part of the elementary schools/education also witnessed increasing decline in enrolment, most of which was the result of a shift away government to unaided private schools. This phenomenon, indeed, portends double disadvantage for the marginalised both educationally and economically as they migrate to so-called budget schools which themselves are invariably ill-equipped to provide quality education. Besides depriving the poor and the marginalised opportunities for quality education, this trend has also seriously dented the vision of creating schools as common public spaces which bring together children without discrimination in terms of caste, class, ethnicity and religion.

As highlighted by the Education Commission (1964-66), rational location of schools and desirability of creating relatively larger schools, if necessary, by clustering neighbouring habitations as the combined catchment area for a school is based on several considerations. The first and most explicit is that of economy of scale. Too many small schools are not economically viable. But there are other fundamental considerations also. Arising out of economic non-viability, small schools are likely to compromise on the vital academic support systems such as library, science laboratories/equipment, arts and crafts equipment, and facilities for sports. In fact, the schools are also likely to be ill-equipped to address the need for subject specialist teachers which is a mandatory requirement according to the RTE Act. They will definitely be unable to support inclusive education accommodating of differentially abled children. It is needless to mention that this suboptimal academic support in the school will directly impact learning. Besides jeopardising quality of teaching-learning process, small schools created for small habitations also tend to be socially undesirable. It should be noted that small habitations are invariably inhabited by socially marginalised groups, whether they are located in the margins of bigger habitations or in remote and tribal and forest belts with poor levels of physical infrastructure and communication facilities. While establishing schools within every habitation looks attractive in physical terms, such schools tend to create psychological distance among different groups and perpetuate social isolation and discrimination. These targeted small schools for the marginalised groups also have the potential to further disadvantage the already marginalised.

What led to this radical shift in the school location policy perspective of the State? This is important issue to be addressed as for many decades the policies in this regard had been guided by the observations of the Education Commission which advocated for adopting rational norms-based approach as the general rule while recommending a nuanced adaptation of the norm for reaching education to children from remotely located smaller habitations. Was this major change in policy prompted by political expediency of gaining short-term public approval and support, playing on the emotions of the poor? Was it due to short-sighted actions of ill-informed bureaucracy who failed to see the downstream impact of the approach by creating economically unsustainable and educationally unviable schools? Did they fail to see the socially divisive nature of this policy? Or, was it deliberately crafted as part of the post-liberalisation economic agenda? It is difficult to give a categorical answer to this. Perhaps, it would require in depth ethnographic studies engaging in dialogic explorations with the main actors who fashioned and rolled out these policy measures in the last two decades. Nevertheless, the resultant actions and strategies have the unmistakable imprint of the dominant narratives of the economic liberalisation rhetoric as they have in effect promoted privatisation of services and cost saving measures in provision of public services in social sector operations. It is difficult to assume that these measures were mere unintended and unanticipated consequences as they were indeed part of a national flagship programme designed after due deliberations at highest policy making levels.

What is the way ahead? How could the situation be rectified such that the marginalised are not further disadvantaged in terms of the quality of service they receive? In sum, how could the system be made fair and socially just? These are questions that need to be addressed urgently. It is not easy to argue that providing schools closer to the poorer habitat by itself is socially unjust and unfair to the poor. However, it is necessary to recognise that any benefit that could have accrued by saturating the field with schools, even unviable small schools, has been exhausted. One may concede that this has almost wholly settled the issue of lack of demand for schooling. Everyone, rich and poor, today want schools for their children. But they are not ready to accept any kind of school. This is evident from parents' readiness to bear with the problem of distances and even personal comfort to get their children admitted to schools with better facilities and those that ensure better quality learning for their children. It is necessary to build on this changing sentiment. There is an urgent need to move for consolidation of schooling facilities through a process of selective merging after optimally working out distance and population factors combined with educational viability in terms of quality of academic facilities and human resources made available to each school. This may even require re-examining the minimum benchmarks indicated in the RTE Act.

These measures of consolidation have to be adopted in a contextualised fashion after examining the local conditions, particularly in terms of terrain conditions and physical infrastructure. It may never be possible, as highlighted by the Education Commission, to completely disband small single or two teacher schools, even though one has to recognise the situation is vastly different with respect to perceived or real barriers of physical access and social and cultural inhibitions. But, situations even in this regard vary very widely and more creative solutions have to be chalked out in a differential manner. There cannot be a standard solution. However, it should be possible to find certain broad parameters for facilitating children in such schools access good quality education. First, it has to be recognised that per capita and per school expenditure in such situations cannot follow the norms followed for bigger schools. As pointed out these would work out to be more expensive. But it is necessary in order to meet the even higher social cost or increasing inequality. This could be addressed through a specially designed development programme to address the needs of small schools within major national initiatives such as SSA. It is also desirable to officially link the functioning of such small lower primary schools to larger schools in the neighbourhood to ensure smooth and seamless transition of all children to next stage of education. Such measures should also be complemented as needed with specially chartered transport services for younger age children and improved residential facilities in central locations for children of higher age groups.

To sum up, the way forward is to initiate efforts that are based on a rights perspective and by implication socially just and fair to the poor and the rich alike without any discrimination irrespective of their location and social extraction. It would be necessary to move on two tracks. One track is that of consolidating the existing facilities to make them more economically and educationally viable through a scientific process of school mapping. The second track is to look for creative local solutions rather than imposing pan-national standards for improving the quality and functional efficiency of small schools working in isolated locations. Such measures may prove to be politically uncomfortable and economically expensive in the short run. But there is no option as the long term educational and social costs involved outweigh the short term benefits of continuing with the current policy and practice.

References

Aggarwal, Yash (1997): Small Schools: Issues in Policy and Planning, Occasional Papers 23, New Delhi: NIEPA.

Aggarwal, Yash (2001): Progress towards Universal Access and Retention: Analytical Report, New Delhi: NIEPA.

Diwan, Rashmi (2012): Indian Small Schools: A Review of Issues and Related Concerns, NUEPA Occasional Paper 40, New Delhi: NUEPA.

Dyer, Caroline (2000): Operation Blackboard: Policy Implementation in Indian Elementary Education, Symposium Books, UK.

GOI (Govrnment of India) (1996): Report of the Working Group on Early Childhood Education, Elementary Education, Non-Formal Education and Teacher Education for the Ninth Five Year Plan, New Delhi: MHRD.

GOI (1971): The Fourth Plan Mid-Term Appraisal: Education and Manpower, New Delhi: Planning Commission.

GOI (1961): *Third Five Year Plan*, New Delhi: Planning Commission.

GOI (1968): Educational Development in the Fourth Plan (1969-74): Report of the Planning Group on Education, GOI, New Delhi: Planning Commission.

GOI (2008): Eleventh Five Year Plan (2007-2012), Social Sector, New Delhi: Planning Commission.

GOI (n.d.): Report of the Working Group on Elementary Education and Literacy for the 11th Five Year Plan, New Delhi: Planning Commission.

Gopalakrishnan, R. and Sharma, Amita (1998): Education Guarantee Scheme in Madhya Pradesh: Innovative Step to Universalise Education, *Economic and Political Weekly (EPW)*, September 26, pp. 2546-50.

Gopalakrishnan, R. and Sharma, Amita (1999): Education Guarantee Scheme: What Does It Claim?, *EPW*, March 20, pp. 726-28.

Govinda, R. and Josephine, Y (2004): *Para-Teachers in India: A Review*, Paris: IIEP, UNESCO.

Kumar, Krishna, *et al* (2001): The Trouble with 'Para-Teachers,' *Frontline,* 18 (22), October 27-November 09.

Kumar, Krishna, *et al* (2001): Looking beyond the Smokescreen: DPEP and Primary Education in India, *EPW,* 36 (7), February 17-23, pp. 560-68.

Ministry of Education (Reprint Edition, 1966): *Report of the All-India Educational Survey*, New Delhi: GOI.

MHRD (2014): The Right of Children to Free and Compulsory Education Act 2009: The Third Year, New Delhi: Department of School Education and Literacy.

NCERT (1967): Second All-India Educational Survey, New Delhi.

NCERT (1971): Education and National Development: Report of the Education Commission 1964-66, New Delhi.

NCERT (1979): Third All-India Educational Survey, New Delhi.

NCERT (n.d.): Fourth All India Educational Survey: Some Statistics on School Education, New Delhi.

NCERT,(1989): Fifth All-India Educational Survey, New Delhi.

NCERT (1997): Sixth All-India Educational Survey: National Tables, Vol. I, New Delhi.

NUEPA (2011): Elementary Education in India: Progress towards UEE – Flash Statistics - DISE 2009-10, New Delhi.

NUEPA (2013): Elementary Education in India: Progress towards UEE. Flash Statistics, DISE, 2012-13, New Delhi.

Sharma, Amita and Gopalakrishnan, R (2003): Opinion or Facts? EGS in Madhya Pradesh, *EPW*, December 6, pp. 5210-15.

Sharma, R.C. and Sapra, C.L. (1967): *Wastage and Stagnation in Primary and Middle Schools in India*, Project Report, National Institute of Education, New Delhi.

Sujatha, K. (1996): *Single Teacher Schools in Tribal Areas*, New Delhi: NIEPA.

Sujatha, K. (2000): Education of Indian Scheduled Tribes: A Study of Community Schools in the District of Vishakhapatnam, Andhra Pradesh, Paris: UNESCO, IIEP.

Online Resources

8th All India School Education Survey (8th AISES) as on 2009; Table 1(FS)

http://aises.nic.in/downloadFlash/FS/National/FS1__Rural.pdf

8th All India School Education Survey (8th AISES); Primary - Table 22(FS); Urban - Table 22 (PS); Total - Table 24 (FS)

http://aises.nic.in/downloadFlash/FS/National/FS22_Primary_Rural.pdf - Rural; http://aises.nic.in/downloadFlash/PS/National/PS22_Primary_.pdf - Urban; http://aises.nic.in/downloadFlash/FS/National/FS24_Primary_Total.pdf

8th All India School Education Survey (8th AISES) Rural - Table 65 (FS);

http://aises.nic.in/downloadFlash/FS/National/FS65_Primary_Rural.pdf -Rural

8th All India School Edn., Survey (8th AISES) Urban - Table 78 (FS); Total- Table 79 (FS)\aises.nic.in/downloadFlash/FS/National/FS78__.pdf – Urban; http://aises.nic.in/downloadFlash/FS/National/FS79__Total.pdf - Total.

17

Equity, Access and Quality in Basic Education

A Review

Shireen Motala

The democratic government which came into being in South Africa in 1994 has shown its commitment to Education for All, by ensuring equitable and universal access to meaningful learning opportunities. The government between 1994 and 2007 brought out seven White Papers, three Green Papers, 26 Bills (of which 17 were amendment bills), 35 Acts (of which 22 were amendments to existing laws), 11 regulations, 52 government notices and 26 calls for comments have been published.

There has been significant progress towards equity, equality and redress in post-apartheid South Africa, and yet a sobering reality, noted by the National Planning Commission, is that an estimated 48 per cent of the population live on less than 2 dollars a day, and, at 0.67, the Gini coefficient is the highest in the world (National Planning Commission, 2011). In the second quarter of 2013, while the overall 'strict' unemployment rate was 25.6 per cent (32.9 per cent of youth ages 15-24 were not in employment) education or training in the country as a whole. If the expanded unemployment rate is taken, which includes 'discouraged work-seekers', it is much higher in both categories (Statistics South Africa 2013: xvi).

In recent years, key education indicators have shown that mastery of basic competencies is at a very low level, leading to much policy and research Notable research produced in this period included that of the Consortium for Research on Equity, Access and Transitions in Education (CREATE), which formulated the notion of meaningful access to schooling (Lewin & Wang 2011).

This chapter deals with the issues of access, equity and quality as key indicators of progress towards achieving the goals of post-apartheid education reform. It begins with a critical overview of the major trends in policy since 1994.

The Policy Context: South Africa has a quasi-federal system, with nine provinces. The provincial governments have legislative responsibility for schooling. The country has a population of 47.9 million of whom 79.6 per cent are black African. Just over 15 million children are of school going age; 12 million learners between the ages of 5 and 19, of whom 49.8 per cent are girls, are at school. Education is compulsory from 7 to 16 or to the end of Grade 9. The schooling system is divided into the primary (Grades 1 to 7), junior secondary (Grades 8 and 9) and senior secondary (Grades 10 to 12) sectors. In 2010 there were, including 1,086 independent schools, 26,065 ordinary schools (as distinct from schools for learners with special needs) in South Africa. There were about 12 million learners in public ordinary schools, 352 thousand learners in independent ordinary schools and a total of 394 thousand teachers (Department of Education 2009: 3).

The attendance of children aged 5 increased from 40 per cent to 62 per cent and of children aged 6 from 70 per cent to 84 per cent (Government Gazette 2010). The percentage of 7-15 year olds attending schools improved to 98 per cent by 2011, and participation by 16 to 18 year olds has also increased steadily, to 85 per cent by 2011. The government aims to achieve full participation of 5 year olds in Grade R pre-school education by 2014. However, while preschool coverage has improved, good quality provision is uneven, with a lack of qualified teachers in grade R classes. The independent or private schooling system, which incorporates institutions charging a very wide range of fees, comprises about 2.8 per cent of the overall schooling system. Its coverage extends to poorer learners in areas where there is insufficient state provision (National Planning Commission 2011).

Education ministers since 1994 have contributed to education reform, each with a distinct emphasis. Minister Bhengu (1994–1998) focussed on developing frameworks to address the inequalities inherited from apartheid, at the same time creating a broad based vision for the education system. The second period, overseen by Minister Kader Asmal (1999-2004), broadened policy to include areas not previously focussed on, such as equality and social justice, and inclusive education with a specific focus on early childhood and special needs education. The third phase, under Minister Naledi Pandor (2004-2008), marked a distinct departure from previous initiatives. With questions of access on the way to solution, attention turned to quality. Continued underperformance in basic literacy and numeracy led to the Foundations of Learning campaign (2008–2011), emphasising a back to basics approach.

Since 2009, a fourth phase has been under way, with new policies emerging and significant changes in how the education system is managed on a national scale. The national Department of Education has been reorganised into two departments:

The Department of Basic Education (DBE) (headed by former Gauteng Executive Council Member for Education, Angie Motshekga) with responsibility for primary and secondary education as well as early childhood development centres.

The Department of Higher Education and Training (DHET), under Blade Nzimande, which oversees technical and vocational training, adult education and tertiary education.

Reforms to Improve Learning

During this fourth phase, several trends can be identified (Sayed and Motala 2012). These include:

- *Setting output targets: The action plan 2014*: Towards the Realisation of Schooling 2025 established key output goals, supported by guidelines which advocated a more utilitarian approach to education. Ten of its output goals focussed on improving numeracy and literacy, in a clear response to poor ongoing learner performance in the Grade Three and Grade Six national assessments and in the regional SACMEQ and international TIMSS and PIRLS surveys. There is also a strong focus on regular testing, in the form of Annual

National Assessments (ANAs) which test the quality of language and mathematics learning in all public and government-subsidised independent schools.

- *Introduction of curriculum and assessment policy*: The outcomes-based education (OBE) system, introduced incrementally since the late 1990s, has come under critical scrutiny. In 2009, the outcomes-based Revised National Curriculum Statement was reviewed by a ministerial committee, and a new curriculum document, the Curriculum and Assessment Policy (CAPS), came into effect in January 2011, signalling the end of a 14-years attempt to focus teaching and learning primarily around outcomes rather than processes or inputs. Teachers as agents of change: Policy has begun to give systematic attention to the notion of teachers as agents of change. On 5 April 2011 the national departments of education jointly launched the Integrated Strategic Planning Framework for Teacher Education and Development in South Africa, which aimed to improve both initial teacher education and continuing professional teacher development, with training for CAPS a specific priority. The establishment of the National Education Evaluation and Development Unit in 2011 indicated a more dedicated focus on the monitoring and supervision of teachers.
- *Focus on skill development*: The separation of basic education and higher education at national departmental level has led to more focussed attention to skills development as evidenced in the National Skills Development Strategy III 2011-2016 and the Green Paper for Post-School Education and Training. The SETAs were transferred by Presidential Proclamation 56 of 2009 (Department of Higher Education and Training 2011) from the Department of Labour to the DHET, a move intended to improve coherence across the university and college systems (Department of Education 2010).
- *Establishing norms and standard for funding*: Finally, a number of amendments have been made to the National Norms and Standards for School Funding (NNSSF), allowing for an expansion in the number of no-fee schools to 60 per cent of all schools and for the widening of school feeding schemes. The most recent NNSSF amendment came in 2011, allowing schools to apply for compensation for fee exemptions each year, based on a formula determined by the DBE. This is a clear pro-poor development, though even more substantial adjustments will be required if current inequities are to be fully addressed. Currently close to 20,000 schools benefit from the no–fee policy. Another important pro-poor initiative is the National School Nutrition Programme (NSNP), which by 2012 provided a total of 8,756,893 learners in 20,905 primary and secondary schools with a funded lunch (Stats SA 2013).

In 2012, around R61 billion was spent on education. From a high point of 6.8 per cent of GDP in 1998, education spending now comprises 5.3 per cent of the GDP and about 18 per cent of consolidated government expenditure, making education the largest category of government disbursement. In comparison to other developing countries, education spending in South Africa as a proportion of GDP is high although it is less than the UNESCO benchmark of 6 per cent. It has been noted that these relatively high levels mainly reflect expenditure on educator salaries with spending on other inputs being below international norms (Department of Basic Education, 2010:28; Department of Basic Education, 2012). Education expenditure takes place at both provincial and national levels. In 2010, 86.5 per cent of education expenditure was on public school education, although it is a declining proportion of GDP. Capacitating governance at provincial, district and school levels continues to receive much attention as poor service delivery continues to hamper the provision of quality education (*Times*, 11 June 2012). It continues to be unclear who safeguards constitutionally-guaranteed basic rights in terms of provincial delivery on national mandates.

The OECD report on South Africa (2008:143) identifies a number of trends in education spending. It notes that real spending has escalated rapidly in recent years and will continue to do so in the medium term; that, positively, expenditure on personnel has declined from over 89 per cent in the late 1990's to below 80 per cent in 2008, and that there have been improvements in funding equity between provinces and between schools as subventions were impacted by pro-poor funding norms. However questions continue about the impact of this funding shift, with some arguing that the impact has been less marked than expected in terms of real education opportunities and education quality. In particular the quintile system has come under scrutiny, with evidence that the ranking system is not an adequate measure of the socio-economic status of learners in schools, often disadvantaging the funding base of schools in which there are a larger proportion of poor learners (Wildeman 2008; Sayed and Motala 2012). Moreover, while schools may be ranked on an equitable basis, uneven capacity among schools and school governing bodies have meant that funds are not spent effectively and efficiently (Mestry 2012). Kanjee and Chudgar (2009), using empirical evidence, show that the quintile system is not an effective benchmarking measure, and that schools in the middle quintiles (Q3 and Q4), are often worse off than quintile 1 schools.

South Africa's commitment to the Millennium Development Goals is premised on the right to basic education enshrined in its Constitution (RSA 1996: Section 29(1)). Unlike a number of other developing countries, in South Africa there is near universal access to formal public schooling to the end of the compulsory phase (Perry and Arends 2003; Stats SA 2006; Chisholm 2011). Estimates of a gross enrolment ratio of 99 per cent in primary grades and 87 per cent in secondary grades place South Africa above what are seen to be feasible targets for middle-income countries (Lewin 2011). However, while South Africans enjoy substantial physical and structural access to schooling, this does not guarantee that learners have equal experience of or access to quality education. The specific policy challenge for meaningful access in South Africa is less one of enrolment in formal public schooling and more one of retention, attendance, achievement and completion on schedule for age, all of which contribute to quality outcomes.

How Much Child Learns

In the Department of Education's systemic evaluation of Grade 6 in 2005, learners obtained a national mean score of 38 per cent in Language, 27 per cent in Mathematics, and 41 per cent in Natural Science (Department of Education, 2008). Six years later, the results of the 2011 Annual National Assessments show little improvement. In the latest assessment of almost 6 million primary school learners in February 2011, Grade 3 learners achieved an average of only 35 per cent for literacy and 28 per cent for numeracy, while Grade 6 learners managed 28 per cent for languages and 30 per cent for Mathematics (Department of Basic Education 2011: 20). International tests such as Monitoring Learning and Achievement (MLA) administered to Grade 4 in 1999, the Southern and Eastern African Consortium for Monitoring Education Quality (SAQMEC) written by Grade 6 learners in 2005, the TIMMS administered to Grade 8 learners in 2003 and 2009, and the Progress in International Reading Literacy Study (PIRLS) conducted with Grade 5 learners in 2006, suggest that South African schools are among the worst performers in Mathematics and Literacy in comparison to their southern and eastern African counterparts (Bloch, 2009: 60-68). In the 2011 PIRLS test, 43 per cent of South African learners were not able to reach the low international benchmark (Howie *et al.* 2012). SAQMEC III (2011) focussed on education inequality, and noted that the poorest 20 per cent of learners in South Africa perform far worse than their peers in other African countries. In the fifteen countries in the region, the poorest learners in South Africa are at 12th place for reading, and 14th for reading.

The Diagnostic Report (National Planning Commission, 2011) notes that apart from a small minority of learners who attend former-white schools and a small minority of schools performing well in largely black areas, the quality of public education remains poor. Learners in historically white schools perform better, and their scores improve with successive years of schooling. In contrast, in the majority of schools with black learners, learner scores start lower, and show little improvement between Grades 3 and 5. Where there has been some improvement as measured by the pass rate — 70 per cent — of those who sat the 2011 matriculation examination, only 23 per cent achieved a university entrance pass (Department of Basic Education in National Planning Commission, 2011). Sayed and Badat (forthcoming) note that in 2007, 80 per cent of university entrance passes were produced by 20 per cent of secondary schools.

Inequalities in Learner Achievements

Disaggregated, results of 2005 assessment varied markedly between provinces and among quintiles. Across Grades 1 to 6, learners in quintile five schools received scores 10-15 per cent higher than their counterparts in other quintiles. Van der Berg (2010) has argued that inequalities in schooling outcomes are manifest in subsequent incomes, perpetuating current patterns of inequality. While poverty is often related to education outcomes, and achievement is strongly correlated with learner socio-economic status, recent research indicates that the effectiveness of the schools in which the learners are located is an important factor (Spaull 2011). Other research also shows that high performing schools can contribute significantly to learning opportunities for poor learners. Taylor and Yu (2009), controlling for learner and school socio-economic status, demonstrate that African language learners in historically white schools out-perform those in historically black schools. The achievement of equity has to be qualified since there are limits to how far education expenditure can be redistributive, since teacher salaries are based on qualifications and experience, and better qualified and more experienced teachers tend to be present in the better off schools. Sayed and Ahmed (2011) suggest that while for the state, equity/quality is conceptualised in a simple input-output model, it is in reality far from clear how these processes converge and diverge at the policy level and whether both are being addressed. The failure to come to a clear conclusion on the development of infrastructure and on minimum norms and standards for schools illustrates that much greater investment is required if the state's equity interventions are to be meaningful. Moreover, social equity and education equity need to be addressed simultaneously, so that the low quality of education offered in poor communities does not continue to perpetuate their exclusion. Important progress is being made through the delivery of social grants (Bhorat and Cassim 2013), which address poverty and inequality: Patel (2013) argues that there are real long term benefits to this social investment. There should be an attempt to treat educational and social provision as an integrated platform for an assault on poverty and underdevelopment.

The delivery of quality education has also been affected by the constitutional provision which allows for considerable decision making and diversity of approach at provincial and local levels. The failure to ensure textbook delivery to schools has been the subject of a court battle in Limpopo and Eastern Cape provinces in 2012. Decentralisation policies have sharply affected the historical legacy of poor and better off provinces and this has affected their ability to deliver quality education, contributing to both inter and intra provincial inequities.

Curriculum 2005, which fundamentally shifted the content and pedagogy of the old syllabus-based system and introduced outcomes-based education, required substantial adaptation by role players, not least by the government officials implementing it and the teachers teaching it. However, its complex terminology, its lack of alignment with the orientation of learners and skills of teachers and its poor implementation support required a decade of revision and gradual introduction into all phases of schooling. The new Revised National Curriculum Statements (RNCS) give more emphasis to basic skills, content knowledge and grade progression, and combine a learner-centred curriculum requiring critical thought and emphasising democratic values with an appreciation of the importance of content and support for teachers (Motala and Dieltiens 2011). It also aims to reduce the administrative load on teachers, and to provide guidance and consistency of approach for teachers.

The NEEDU report (2013) notes that the problems of absenteeism, late-coming and disruption to the time table still persist, and that the role of school leadership is critical for efficient time management and supporting a culture of teaching and learning. There has also been a more distinct focus on assessment in Curriculum 2005. Quality assurance, certification and exit points, and control over norms and standards for curriculum and assessment, were important measures that complemented curriculum changes. Chisholm and Chilisa (2012) note that while Botswana and South Africa both adopted outcomes based curricula, they differ considerably in the content and results of the change. The biggest contrast between the two systems was that while in the curriculum model in Botswana learning and assessment were heavily aligned, in South Africa there was great emphasis on various forms of continuous assessment to support a relatively underspecified curriculum. Since 2008, the South African government has focussed more systematically on national tests, aligning curriculum and assessment more carefully.

Recent research has focussed more sharply on classroom practice. In the CREATE numeracy tests, learners performed way below the levels expected of them (Pereira, 2010). Prior learning for the majority of learners was poor, i.e., they were not on the expected level for their grade, and specific numeracy outcomes which required deeper analytical skills were poor. There are serious gaps in the pedagogical content knowledge related to many learning areas including Mathematics in primary schools. Attention has increasingly turned to teacher skills and pedagogy. The content knowledge of teachers, in particular in Mathematics and English, tested in SAQMEQ111 showed low levels of achievement particularly in more complex topics in Mathematics which had higher cognitive demands (Taylor, 2011). Chisholm and Carnoy (2012) identify a complex set of interrelated variables related to a teachers knowledge and ability to teach as contributing to differences in learner performance across Botswana and South Africa.

Other research notes that very little actual teaching and learning taking place: lessons often start late, much time is spent maintaining order, teachers do most of the talking, and learners are passive and contribute little (Dieltiens and Motala, 2011). Many Foundation Phase (Grades 1-3) teachers are unable to teach learners adequately how to read and write (Taylor *et al.,* 2010). SACMEQ research concludes that the subject knowledge base in both language and Mathematics of the majority of Grade 6 learners is inadequate to provide them with an understanding of these foundation disciplines (Spaull, 2011).

The absence of written work in classrooms, rote learning and chorusing of lessons is common, and coverage of the curriculum very uneven (Dieltiens, Letsatsi & Ngwenya 2012). The use of workbooks varies widely between schools, and there are significant differences in the breadth of coverage across learning outcomes and in how specific content is covered. Findings suggest that more attention needs to be paid to investigating differences within and between schools in terms of opportunities to learn and how this may play itself out in terms of learner performance (Venkat, 2012; Reeves, Carnoy and Addy, 2013). The language of learning and teaching contributes to the low levels of learner achievement; yet many parents choose to have their children taught in English by teachers who are themselves second-language speakers of the language (Lafon, 2009; Alexander, 2010).

Home support for learning reflects the racially divided and class stratified nature of South African society, with poorer parents lacking the time and cultural capital to support their children's education adequately and middle class parents more likely to encourage learning and to send their children to higher performing schools. And yet school-going is highly valued by parents, to the extent of making the best of what one has, or keeping one's child in a school one does not like but which is better than no school at all (Luxomo & Motala, 2012).

Most learners in South Africa enrol in and complete primary education, despite numerous barriers to success, and even though substantial early childhood education and pre-schooling provision remain to be achieved. A negligible percentage of children of school-going age have never been to school, approximately 4 per cent of learners dropout before completing primary school (Grade 7), and 92 per cent of learners finish basic education (Grade 9) (Department of Education 2008). Girls also persist longer through the higher grades, unlike in a number of other developing countries. However, net enrolment rates drop significantly after Grade 3, suggesting that many learners fall behind age-grade norms. In addition, significant numbers of children take more than nine years to complete Grade 9 (Deacon and Dieltiens, 2007). Distinctive features of the South African context are 'school delays' (Hallman and Grant 2004), slow progression (Anderson, 2005) and differential and inequitable access to public schooling (Motala, 2006). What is clear is that patterns of progression are an increasingly important predictor of learning outcomes.

As in a number of other developing countries, massification of education has not led to an improvement in education quality. While it is true that fiscal resource inputs are not the only means to achieve the desired educational outcomes, but they do, however, have an effect on learner performance. Fiscal resources do not necessarily translate into scarce real resources (qualified teachers and school management) required to improve school performance, and even where resources are available, their effective utilisation is not guaranteed. Nonetheless, according to Van der Berg (2007: 851), equity of educational outcomes requires both well-targeted fiscal expenditure and efficient schools.

Concluding Comments

This chapter shows that a number of strategies have been put in place to address the many intractable problems in education reform and the delivery of quality education. As always, policy is one thing: implementation another, and it is apparent that necessary conditions of the delivery of quality education are adequate finance and human resources, involvement and a sense of ownership by role-players, regular monitoring and evaluation and sustained effort. At school level, institutional functionality, a focus on instructional leadership, a clear-sighted emphasis on reading, writing and professional development and professionalising the divisions of the civil service dealing with education are critical to success. Above all, it is essential to embed the notion of education as a public good, and foreground the view that equality and social justice must drive educational reform. Widespread community mobilisation is required to ensure that the undoubted gains in terms of education access and participation in schooling become the foundation for meaningful learning which offer real life chances for our young people in further and higher education and in the labour market.

References

Ahmed, R & Sayed, Y (2009): Promoting Access and Enhancing Education Opportunities? The Case of "No-Fees" Schools in South Africa. *Compare: A Journal of Comparative and International Education*, 39, pp. 203-18.

Anderson, K G (2005): Relatedness and Investment in Children in South Africa. *Human Nature*, 16 (1), pp. 3-25.

Chisholm, L (2011): Institute of Justice and Reconciliation. University of Cape Town.
Department of Education (1998): *National Norms and Standards for School Funding.* Pretoria.
Department of Education (2008): *Foundations for Learning Campaign.* Pretoria.
Department of Education (2010): Action Plan to 2014: Towards the Realisation of Schooling 2025—The Shorter Version. Pretoria.
Department of Basic Education in National Planning Commission (2011): Government Policies. Pretoria.
Department of Basic Education (2012): Education Equity: Fiscal Incidence and Socio-Economic Gradients. Pretoria.
Dieltiens, V; Letsatsi, S & Ngwenya, E (2012): Inside the School Gates: What do Learners Have Access to? In Motala, S; Dieltiens, V & Sayed, Y (Ed.): Finding Place and Keeping Pace: Exploring Meaningful and Equitable Learning in South African Schools: Cape Town: HSRC Press.
HSRC (2005): Educator Workload in South Africa. Report for the Education Labour Relations Council. Pretoria: HSRC.
Kanjee, A and Chudgar, A (2009): School Money, Funding Flames. *HSRC Review*, 7(4), December: HSRC Press.
Lafon, M (2009): *The Impact of Language on Educational Access, CREATE Pathways to Access Series*, Brighton: Consortium for Research on Educational Access, Transitions and Equity, University of Sussex.
Lewin, K M and Wang, L (2011): *Education and Change in Rich, Poor and National Minority Areas in China: Two Decades of Transition.* Pathways to Access Research Monographs, No 61. Brighton: University of Sussex.
Little, A (2008): *EFA Politics, Policies and Progress*. Pathways to Access Research Monographs, No 13. London: Institute of Education.
Luxomo, G & Motala, S (2012): The Return Home: Parental Involvement in Children's Education. In Finding Place and Keeping Pace: Exploring Meaningful and Equitable Learning in South African Schools. Pretoria.
Medium Term Expenditure Framework (2012): Pretoria: Government Press.
Mestry, R (2012): A Critical Analysis of the National Norm and Standards for School Funding Policy: Implication for Social Justice and Equities. Pretoria: Professorial Inauguration, 12 June 2012.
Morrow, W (2007): *Learning to Teach in South Africa*, Cape Town: HSRC Press.
Motala, S & Dieltiens, V (2011): *Educational Access in South Africa*, Country Brief, 2008, Johannesburg and Brighton: University of Sussex.
Motala, S; Dieltiens, V & Sayed, Y (Ed.) (2012): *Finding Place and Keeping Pace.* South Africa: HSRC Press.
Motala, S (2006): Education Resourcing in Post Apartheid South Africa. The Impact of Finance Equity Reforms in Public Schooling. *Perspectives in Education*, 24 (2), pp 79-94.
Motala, S & Sayed, Y (2009): *'No-Fee' Schools in South Africa*, Policy Brief Number 7, August. CREATE, Centre for International Education, Brighton: University of Sussex.
Motala, S; Dieltiens, V; Carrim, N; Kgobe, P; Moyo, G and Rembe, S (2007): *Educational Access in South Africa: Country Analytic Review*. Available at www.create-rpc.org.
Sayed, Y and Motala, S (2012): Getting in and Staying There: Exclusion and Inclusion in South African Schools. *Southern Africa Review of Education*, 18 (2), pp 105-18
National Planning Commission (2011): *Diagnostic Report*. Pretoria: Government Printers.
Ndimande, B (2006): Parental Choice: The Liberty Principle in Education Finance. *Perspectives in Education*, 24 (2), pp 143-56.
OECD (2008): Review of National Policies for Education. South Africa. Brussels: OECD

Shindler, J (2012): *The Contours of Access: An Aerial Perspective on Access in Two Districts*. In Motala, S; Dieltiens, V & Sayed, Y (Ed.): Supra.

Spaull, N (2011): Primary School Performance in Botswana, Mozambique, Namibia and South Africa: A Comparative Analysis of SACMEQ III Working Paper No. 8. http://www.sacmeq.org/reports.htm#working_papers 4 April 2013.

Statistics South Africa (2013). *Quarterly Labour Force Survey*. Quarter 2, 2013, Pretoria: StatsSA.

Taylor, N (2009): *Knowledge and Teachers's Work*. Keynote Address to the Conference of the Southern African Association for Reseach in Science, Mathematics and Technology Education.

Taylor, N; Mabogoane, T; Shidler, J and Akoobhai, B (2010): *'Seeds of Their Struggle': The Features of Under- and Over-Age Enrolment among Grade 4 Learners in South Africa*. CREATE Pathways to Access Series. Brighton: University of Sussex.

Van den Berg, S (2005): Enduring Inequality: An Economic Perspective on Public School Education in South Africa, with Special Focus on the Western Cape. *Africa Insight*, 34 (2/3), pp 73-81.

Van Den Berg, S (2010): *Low Quality Education as a Poverty Trap*. University of Stellenbosch. PSPPD/EU/Presidency.

Venkat, H (2012): Reading between the Lines: Examining "Opportunity to Learn" in a Sample of Eastern Cape Workbooks. In Motala, S; Dieltiens, V & Sayed, Y (Ed): Supra.

Wilderman, R A (2008): Reviewing Eight Years of the Implementation of the School Funding Norms, 2000 to 2008. Research Report: Idasa Economic Governance Programme.

18

Comparative Analysis of Large-Scale Policies on Universalisation of Elementary Education

Case Studies on Conditional Grants Scheme, Nigeria and Sarva Shiksha Abhiyan, India

Radhika Iyengar*, *Angelique R. Mahal* and *Fatima Ahmad

India and Nigeria, apart from being among the world's most populated countries, share many other common attributes. Both were once British colonies and thus share the English language inheritance. India and Nigeria are multi-ethnic and many local dialects are spoken in each country. Both countries have large and diverse populations with wide economic disparities between and within regions, and high adult illiteracy and poverty levels. Both countries have burgeoning economies and the governing structures are decentralised with authority at the state, district and local government levels. Challenges related to religious education, opportunities for marginalised children, child labour and nomadic groups are prevalent in both countries and contribute to India and Nigeria having among the highest numbers of out-of-school children and illiterate populations in the world. Accordingly, a comparative analysis of specific policy frameworks using context-specific but common parameters will help flash out important lessons on sustainability and local-level participatory planning processes to engender inclusiveness in development and, in particular, provision of educational opportunities to all.

High demographic pressure creates opportunities and challenges for education in both countries. As a fundamental human right, education is a priority focus area in the development process that is being implemented through an integrated approach within the framework for achieving the Millennium Development Goals (MDGs); education is intended to serve as a foundation for sustainable development. Achievement of universal primary education, Millennium Development Goal 2, is being actualised in India through the Sarva Shiksha Abhiyan (SSA) and in Nigeria through the Conditional Grants Scheme to Local Government Areas (CGS-LGA) that complements the Universal Basic Education (UBE) programme. In both India and Nigeria, strategic initiatives aim for local inclusion in the education planning process. Policy measures arising from the Right to Free and Compulsory Education Act (2009) in India and the UBE Act (2004) in Nigeria have contributed immensely by translating policy frameworks into concrete achievements in both countries. Essential to both SSA and CGS-LGA is inclusion and local direction of programmes through participatory approaches. This paper describes and compares the policy objectives and achievements of the SSA and CGS-LGA, with focus on the roles and responsibilities of stakeholders and how these large-scale policies address access to schools, gender and equity, inclusiveness through reaching marginalised children, role of the community, learning focus, improving school financing, local agency involvement, budgeting and planning, and sustainability.

Description of the SSA and CGS-LGA Policies

Vision and Objectives of CGS-LGA: The CGS is a large-scale investment in terms of monetary, technical and professional support at state and local government levels. "It aims to develop capacity for improved delivery of services in the public sector, with focus on public sector financing reform and development of stronger linkages and partnerships between the national, state and local government levels for better and cohesive planning" (The Office of the Senior Special Assistant to the President of Nigeria on MDGs & The Earth Institute, 2011). "The CGS is a programme initiated by the federal government to specifically target activities and investments at state and LGA levels that could enhance living standards and facilitate and accelerate achievement of the MDGs" (The Office of the Senior Special Assistant to the President of Nigeria on MDGs & The Earth Institute, 2010).

To access federal funds, the states and LGAs are expected to provide matching funds (30 per cent from the state and 20 per cent from local government). In order to receive this funding, the LGAs are required to submit written proposals that are locally developed through a participatory approach involving the LGA planning team, LGA technical team, relevant community members, and a Technical Assistant, who serves as facilitator and liaison between the LGA and the OSSAP-MDGs.

At the inception of the programme, a baseline facility inventory was conducted from 2009-2011 with data captured on education, health and water facilities throughout Nigeria. These data serves as the benchmark for measuring progress after the CGS-LGA intervention. The data is hosted on the Nigeria MDG Information System (NMIS) portal, managed by OSSAP-MDGs. Training on credible proposal development on education and health programme planning using the benchmark data on NMIS and within the context of the national governance reform (i.e., budgeting, procurement) with accompanying tools were provided by OSSAP-MDGs with technical support from The Earth Institute. A critical requirement in this process is that each proposal must be empirically derived and indicate that needs assessment was carried out and data analysis undertaken to inform the proposed project as priority within the locality. This constitutes the first section of the proposal submission; the subsequent request for interventions section is then justified by the rationale provided in the first section. Examples of intervention requests in education included school furniture, boreholes for water supply, first aid kits, teaching materials, and chalkboards. Ground rules for proposal acceptance include the indication of participatory approach/inclusiveness with inputs from local, national, and international agencies, and incorporating funds expected or received for the same projects from these agencies in ways that ensure transparency and reduce leakages. When a proposal is approved for CGS-LGA funding by OSSAP-MDGs, the DRG funds appropriated to each LGA are transferred into the state and LGA joint account, which is a statutory provision. The LGA then becomes responsible and accountable for use of these funds and completion of the approved projects to standard.

Thus, the CGS-LGA exemplifies a bottom-up approach to planning with local stakeholders strategically involved as planners, decision-makers, and leaders from initiation to completion. Emphasis is on local data collection, local data analysis, local planning, community involvement, and appropriate local interventions to enable ownership and sustainability on completion of the projects. The federal government allocates 50 per cent of the required funds but it is the sole responsibility of the LGAs to identify and prioritise local needs and come up with appropriate programmes and projects to address empirically derived needs. The Scheme exemplifies an inclusive governance structure under a democratic government with inbuilt mechanisms for accountability and transparency while addressing observed priority development challenges in a systematic manner. CGS is an example of an elaborate and dynamic policy framework that Nigeria applies to address the needs of the states and LGAs in a decentralised way, while simultaneously enhancing partnership between all three levels of government for effective and efficient public service delivery.

Vision and Objectives of SSA: The vision of SSA was to have a bottom-up approach to education in school by 2003 (later revised to 2007); and to ensure that by 2007 all children were enrolled (Department of Elementary Education and Literacy, 2004). "The SSA was launched in 2001 in partnership with the state governments and local self-governments" (Department of Elementary Education and Literacy, 2004). "The main objectives of SSA were to (a) ensure that all children are on track to complete five years of primary schooling; (b) ensure that by 2010 children are on track to complete eight years of elementary/basic schooling; (c) focus on quality of education; (d) ensure that by 2007 girls and boys alike attend school; and (e) ensure universal retention by 2010" (Department of Elementary Education and Literacy, 2004; Kainth, 2006).

"After, September 2009 meeting on the linkages between SSA and the Right To Education (RTE) Act, SSA as a policy was revised to provide a much more holistic view of education that includes equity, access, gender, and teacher motivation" (Department of School Education and Literacy, 2011). "For the first time, SSA also included Early Childhood Care and Education and looked at education with the lens of 0-14 years of age as a continuum" (Department of School Education and Literacy, 2011). In compliance with the RTE Act, SSA also changed its timeframes, activities, and approaches. Like RTE, SSA now mandated the establishment of neighbourhood schools to have the following criteria: provision of school infrastructure, all-weather school buildings, one classroom one teacher, office/store/head teacher room, toilets and drinking water facilities, barrier free access, library, playground, and fencing/ boundary walls. The timeline was adjusted to 31 March 2013. Also, provision of teachers to ensure the required PTR was listed to be completed by March 2013. "Training of untrained teachers was required by March 2015" (Department of School Education and Literacy, 2011). "SSA primarily focussed on inclusion of out-of-school children into formal schools by using alternative strategies for mainstreaming children and also improving existing school infrastructure" (Kainth, 2006).

"Assistance under the SSA programme involved a sharing arrangement between the central and the state governments; specifically, 85:15 during the Ninth Plan; 75:25 during the Tenth Plan; and 50:50 thereafter" (Kainth, 2006). "Three external partners (the World Bank, the United Kingdom, and the European Commission) contributed $1.05 billion to the Union Government′s share" (Wu, Kaul & Sankar, 2005). "At the national level, the implementing agency is the Department of Elementary Education and Literacy (DEE&L), Ministry of Human Resource Development, Government of India" (Department of Elementary Education and Literacy, 2004). "At the national level, there is a General Council, an Executive Committee, and a Project Approval Board that works at the policy level. DEE&L approves all plans at the national level and releases funds to the states, and is also responsible for research and evaluation" (Department of Elementary Education and Literacy, 2004). "At the district level, the District Collector convenes all other bodies such as the Zilla Parishad,[1] the Block Development Committee, and the Village Panchayats"[2] (Department of Elementary Education and Literacy, 2004). "At the village level, the Village Education Committees are assisted by the school-based management committees such as parent-teacher associations (PTAs) to form the SSA plans" (Department of Elementary Education and Literacy, 2004). "Many School Education Management Committees (SEMCs)[3] were instituted under SSA" (Rao, 2009).

The key feature of SSA is the local level planning process: "habitation level educational plans through community participation" (Rao, 2009: 62). SSA should aim for Universalisation of Elementary Education (UEE), which makes it mandatory to track the progress of all children in the age group of 0-14 years. "This needs to be essentially implemented by community leaders and school-based management committees" (Rao, 2009). SEMCs are responsible for developing the village education plan and school improvement plans. Under SSA, these plans are linked to specific education work plans and annual budgets. The role of the community groups is to ensure that the local needs of the community are taken into account in these plans and budgets. "The SEMCs are the mechanism through which the education funds reach the schools" (Rao, 2009).

Comparisons between CGS-LGA and SSA

Access to Schools: "The net enrollment rate in primary education was 59 per cent for Nigeria in 2010, while the number of out-of-school children was 41 per cent in 2010" (UNESCO Institute for Statistics, 2014). However, commitment to achieving the MDGs remains a critical focus in Nigeria, particularly MDGs 2 and 3, as evidenced in the advocacy, activities, and initiatives under UBEC, CGS-LGA, and federal, state, and local government programmes including those supported by international agencies.

"The CGS-LGA, which commenced in 2012 in 113 LGAs, has completed more than 5,000 projects in 36 states and the Federal Capital Territory to date, which indicates a huge success and reporting indicates that the education sector accounted for 34.7 per cent of total projects undertaken to accelerate achieving the MDGs" (The Office of the Senior Special Assistant to the President of Nigeria on the MDGs, 2013a). In 2013, the second phase of the CGS-LGA included an increase to 148 additional LGAs, and education remained a priority focus.

Complementing the CGS-LGA funds with education projects, the State Universal Basic Education Board (SUBEB), an agency responsible for managing basic education within each state in partnership with the LGAs, also supplies instructional materials to schools, supports teacher trainings, provides infrastructure and related items, and coordinates and manages school funds. The Local Government Education Authority (LGEA) manages schools and teachers in collaboration with SUBEB and pays teacher salaries. Additional funds for education at the local level are also available from the Local Government Council. Overall, the UBE programme as the overarching basic education framework in Nigeria supports enrolment in primary and junior secondary schools across the country. School meal programmes, although introduced in some states, were not sustainable and are therefore not a focus yet under the CGS-LGA in Nigeria due to enormous cost implications. A conditional cash transfer scheme under the main CGS programme to states aims to address issues of gender, poverty, inclusion, and food security. This programme is also a local level DRG intervention through a participatory approach coordinated by states, rather than LGAs.

In India, SSA focussed on access by constructing schools on a mass scale. "Approximately 160,000 new primary schools and 650,000 additional classrooms have been constructed" (Jhingran & Sankar, 2010). "Following the drive towards mainstreaming out-of-school children into schools to improve enrolment, the number of out-of-school children in India declined from 32 million to 13 million between 2001 and 2005" (Jhingran & Sankar, 2010). Special educational programmes were put in place to prepare out-of-school children to go back to school. "Concurrently, there was strong emphasis on addressing the infrastructural needs of existing schools to provide a safe learning environment" (Kainth, 2006). "Another development is that SSA now supports early childhood care in pre-school centres because the expanded outreach of the continuum approach covers children ages 0 to 14 years, whereas the previous approach covered one year of pre-school for 5-year-olds, primary schooling for children aged 6 to 11 year, and junior secondary schooling for children aged 12 to 14 year" (Department of School Education and Literacy, 2011).

Gender and Equity: Education campaigns advocating for girl enrolment, attendance, and completion were mentioned to some degree within the 148 groups of proposal requests and required monitoring plans, and the recruitment of female teachers has been a priority. "There was mention in some proposals from the March 2013 148 LGA group about collaboration with the Nigeria Girls Education Initiative, while some proposals from the Eastern part of Nigeria also intend to address the challenge of male student dropouts, which occurs mainly due to economic reasons" (The Office of the Senior Special Assistant to the President of Nigeria on the MDGs, 2013c). A national gender policy exists and gender is a focus of basic education policy, as well, to address issues of gender inequality. Context-specific strategies are applied to address inequality issues across the nation. Construction of school latrines was a popular request in previous rounds of proposals from the Northern part of Nigeria to retain girls in school. The standing recommendation is that construction of latrines in all proposals must be gender-separated to increase girls' comfort and privacy in the school environment.

"In India, SSA was envisioned to "bridge social and gender gaps" with active participation from the community (Department of Elementary Education and Literacy, 2004). Under SSA, the Government of India has launched the National Programme for Education of Girls at Elementary Level (NPEGEL) as an additional component under SSA for education of girls at the elementary school level. "State-level bodies (e.g., Mahila Samkhya programme) were responsible for implementing this policy" (Department of Elementary Education and Literacy, 2004). "Apart from NPEGEL, another initiative called the Kasturba Gandhi Balika Vidyalayas was approved in 2004-05 for establishing 750 residential elementary schools with boarding facilities for girls belonging to minorities in different areas" (Kainth, 2006).

Reaching the Marginalised: In Nigeria, policies to reach marginalised groups target out-of-school children, including pastoral nomads; the Almajiri (accessing only Quranic instruction); migrant farmers; fisher folks; those engaged in small street commerce/hawkers; girl children; and physically handicapped children. The UBE programme provides a platform for inclusion of these marginalised groups in education and national development. It enables provision of free textbooks and other instructional materials. UBE and CGS-LGA are some of the mechanisms that exist within the education system in Nigeria to support these categories of children via policy implementation. Improving the quality of teachers and establishing bridge or transition schools to help out-of-school children catch up are strategies being used to meet the needs of marginalised children.

Almajiri children constitute the largest out-of-school group in Nigeria and mostly reside in the northern zones. The March 2013 LGA group proposals included interventions to be funded by non-CGS sources for provision of Almajiri integrated schools and construction of Almajiri schools. "Support for integrating elements of Western education into Islamiya, Quranic, and Tsangaya education comes via some of the inclusion/equity programmes funded by federal and state agencies"(The Office of the Senior Special Assistant to the President of Nigeria on the MDGs, 2013c).

To support the cause of social inclusion throughout India, SSA promotes special training for out-of-school children to aid in age appropriate admission and coping in regular schools. SSA also focusses on "Child Entitlements" that include textbooks, uniforms, meals from the Mid-Day Meals Scheme, and other entitlements from state government departments. SSA supports community campaigns to raise awareness around education. "SSA also supports the RTE mandate that 25 per cent of school admissions are reserved for the marginalised in all private un-aided schools" (Department of School Education and Literacy, 2011).

Role of the Community: The community is a key stakeholder in the CGS-LGA programme. The role of the community is to effectively participate in identifying and prioritising local needs, contribute towards developing appropriate strategies to address identified needs, and monitor implementation to ensure adherence to set standards. Community representatives participate in the needs assessment that provides the foundation for carrying out the CGS-LGA programme. "The community is also a member of the partnership/cross-collaboration formed within and among the three levels of government, and with civic groups/community based organisations" (The Office of the Senior Special Assistant to the President of Nigeria on MDGs, 2013b). CGS-LGA provides an example of decentralised service delivery with substantial federal level financing and matching grants from state and local contributions to address locally identified needs with technical support. "The framework serves as a viable alternative to the traditional top-down approach to development planning and tends to accelerate achieving the MDGs, including education MDGs, in Nigeria" (The Office of the Senior Special Assistant to the President of Nigeria on MDGs, 2013b). Beyond proposal development, the community retains a pivotal role as many of its members serve on the teams managing the outputs after the requested interventions are completed, mostly as PTA and school-based management committee members.

The SSA mandate is to involve multiple stakeholder groups that represent the community at the village and the district level for the planning process. However, studies point to a disconnect between the mandate and the reality. "A survey on the knowledge of the SSA in Andhra Pradesh revealed that a majority (87.2 per cent) of the school teachers were aware of SSA" (Rao, 2009). "However, only 61 per cent of the Panchayati Raj Institutions (PRIs[4]) and only 52 per cent of the parents of school-going children were aware of SSA" (Rao, 2009). "A majority (90.4 per cent, i.e. 113 out of 125 respondents) of stakeholders (teachers, PRIs, and parents of school-going children) were neither aware of micro level planning, nor were over 87 per cent of the school teachers (41 out of 47) aware of this component" (Rao, 2009). "When respondents were asked to comment on whether there was any SEMC in the village to deal with issues related to education, nearly 50 per cent (63 out of 125) of the respondents reported that this committee was absent in their villages" (Rao, 2009). "In the case of school teachers/headmasters, 25 out of 47 (more than 53 per cent) were unaware that they were the convenors in SEMC" (Rao, 2009).

Focus on Learning: Focus on effective learning is sustained through the implementation of the UBE Act (2004) and quality assurance at all levels of government in partnership with community members. Core subjects at the basic education level, are Mathematics, English, Basic Science & Technology, French, trade subject, and Social Studies. In-service teachers are trained occasionally at the National Teachers Institute and unemployed teachers trained with the Nigeria Certificate in Education (NCE) qualification can be enlisted to teach in schools for two years on a stipend of about N18000 as interns, under the DRG-funded Federal Teachers" Scheme to fill existing teacher gaps. CGS-LGA proposals often focus on the supply side, with regular requests for funding of textbooks, NCE-qualified teachers, instructional materials, teacher training, and construction and renovation of classroom blocks. An education quality assurance framework developed and adopted for evaluating educational processes below the tertiary level gives states and LGAs an instrument for improving teaching/learning processes in line with national norms.

The official language of instruction in Nigeria is English but the National Policy on Education stipulates that pupils are to be taught in the language of locality from pre-primary to primary Grade 3, with the English language taught as a subject during this period. However, instruction must be in English from primary Grade 4 until tertiary education. Continuous assessments for remediation, along with tests and terminal examinations, abound to check levels of learning in schools. Bridge programmes are not common in Nigeria but the Almajiri Education programme launched in 2012 with a view to integrating elements of Western education into Quranic schools could fall within such programmes. The students of such schools could be mainstreamed into existing schools and to appropriate classes, but the programme is still at a take-off stage.

Since SSA closely follows RTE norms, its framework has also shifted from access to learning. India's RTE Act stipulated age appropriate admission and mandates special training for out-of-school children before their enrolment into the age appropriate grade. "The Act also requires that teachers be trained to be sensitive towards children with special needs" (Department of School Education and Literacy, 2011). RTE promotes child-centred curricular policy and directs that the teaching should be more aligned to each child's learning needs. "SSA also has funds for textbook supply. About 60 million students received free textbooks under SSA" (Jhingran & Sankar, 2010). The RTE Act mentions that the states should prepare the textbooks in line with the National Curriculum Framework 2005 (NCF 2005) principles. "The textbooks should encourage creativity and inquiry-based learning rather than relying on factual information" (Department of School Education and Literacy, 2011). In terms of pedagogy, a constructivist approach to teaching and learning is emphasised using the National Curricular Framework 2005.

Improving School Financing: Education financing in Nigeria has been a primary responsibility of government at all levels, with primary education financing being a constitutional responsibility of LGAs. However, over the years several interventions were made by the states and federal government to improve learning, including the use of the DRGs to fund education under the CGS-LGA. The education sector under the CGS-LGA programme receives substantial requests spanning investments in infrastructure, school furniture, instructional materials, teachers, and teacher training. "LGAs are accountable for all funds received and for implementation and completion of projects. As a part of the CGS-LGA operations, technical assistants, zonal technical officers, and state and LGA personnel received financial management training; an implementation manual and training material were also provided to guide implementation" (The Office of the Senior Special Assistant to the President of Nigeria on MDGs, 2013b). The matching grants expected from the states and LGAs double the federal funding available for implementation and the requisite transparency and accountability requirements embedded in the memorandum of understanding endorsed by the state and local governments further enhance school financing efforts in Nigeria.

"SSA supports the comprehensive School Development Plan focussing on all aspects of school (e.g., protection of children's rights, infrastructure, classroom processes, inclusiveness, and continuous evaluation)" (Department of School Education and Literacy, 2011). "SSA funds support infrastructure needs such as construction of the Block Resource Centres, Cluster Resource Centres, school building construction and repair, boundary walls, toilets, playgrounds, kitchen sheds, and other related needs" (Department of School Education and Literacy, 2011).

Local Agency Involvement: Local agencies involved in the CGS-LGA programme include the LGEA, Local Government Council, LGA planning team, LGA technical team, and school committees. The LGA technical team engages with the community and selects interventions for CGS-LGA funding. The LGA planning team reviews and approves/disapproves the selected interventions. "Public sector reform in Nigeria is dependent upon the state and LGAs taking constitutional responsibility for improvement of the social and economic sectors in their geographical areas" (The Office of the Senior Special Assistant to the President of Nigeria on MDGs, 2012). CGS-LGA, in addition to making available additional funds for critical social sector development including education, also aims to reform the local level governance structures for a more effective role in development within the localities. With a mandate for coordination, implementation, and logistics at the state and LGA levels, local agencies are involved from the onset. Local level accountability is inherent in the CGS-LGA mechanism. Decentralisation of management decisions such as identification and implementation of programmes to local-level agencies and community representatives is a step in the right direction for development to reach the grassroots across the nation. The capacity development opportunities that local-level stakeholders are exposed to during the design and implementation processes help to ensure sustainability of service delivery when projects are eventually handed over for community use.

As previously mentioned, the SSA mandate stipulates the involvement of multiple stakeholder groups that represent the community at the village and the district level in the planning process. The planning is done at the habitation level and needs to involve the PRIs, Village Education Councils, community leaders, teachers, and parents. SSA also has some funds allocated for voluntary agencies. At the block level there is a core planning team that is supported by an advisory body at the district level. "The advisory body includes NGOs as well as the Departments of Education, Health, Public Works, Social Welfare, Women and Child Development, Tribal Welfare, and Public Health Engineering, among other possible stakeholders" (Department of Elementary Education and Literacy, 2004). The idea is to have as many stakeholders involved in the planning process as is necessary to ensure ownership and sustainability.

Budgeting and Planning: Facilitated by the technical assistant, the LGA technical team conducts a community needs assessment and analyses NMIS data and education gap sheets to prepare education project plans, using education policy packages for guidance. Education gap sheets, generated from NMIS data, contain indicators on infrastructure repairs, water and sanitation facilities, school furniture, teaching materials, and teaching staff. Education gap sheets highlight measurable indicators and allow for visualisation of status and targets. Appropriate interventions are requested in order to meet the needs and fill the gaps through collaborative funding partnerships with local, state, national, and international agencies. The results of a well-developed planning process are presented in the proposal, coupled with itemised budgets including monitoring and sustainability plans. The CGS-LGA grants are made on the basis of valid comprehensive proposals submitted to OSSAP-MDGs through the state project support office. The planning process has to be completed within a timeframe set by OSSAP-MDGs and in relation to the set deadline for submission of proposals. Thereafter, proposals are reviewed by a technical committee. During the proposal review sessions, sections outlining technical capability, procurement procedures, budget, and monitoring are thoroughly analysed; if necessary, clarifications are sought from the technical assistant before final approval. Proposals that are aligned with CGS-LGA objectives and provided a rational basis for the requested interventions are then approved for funding and a no-objection letter is prepared at the federal level to enable transfer of funds to the LGA through the joint state/LGA account.

"The main objective of SSA is district-based, decentralised, context-specific planning and implementation strategies" (Department of Elementary Education and Literacy, 2004). "It requires states to put in place an appropriate financial management system and procurement procedures for the proper implementation and management of the programme" (Department of Elementary Education and Literacy, 2004). "Each school is entitled to SSA grants for school development" (Rao, 2009). The funds are spent on innovations, teaching/learning materials (TLM), and school development. "TLM are prepared and managed by individual teachers, while the headmaster manages the funds for the entire school after the SEMC members approve the utilisation of the funds" (Rao, 2009). However, as mentioned previously, Rao's study reveals that most community members were not aware of the financial resources the school receives and that these funds were disbursed without their knowledge. "As required under the national guidelines, the financial management system should include the following components: planning, budgeting, accounting, funds flow arrangements, internal control, external audit, procurement, financial procedures manual, and financial management staffing" (Department of Elementary Education and Literacy, 2004). These requirements for transparent use of public funds and accountability for actions/inactions with regards to project implementation are similar to the due process procedures that beneficiary LGAs and states must adopt in project implementation under the CGS-LGA in Nigeria. The Public Procurement Act (2007), as amended, entrenches the values of transparency and accountability in the execution of government projects with federal components. Not all states are using The Public Procurement Act (2007) for state projects but it is a major requirement under the CGS-LGA that also aims to reform the system at the local level for better service delivery.

The planning process for SSA is very detailed and requires an assessment of the educational needs both at the household and at the school level. At the school level, the District Information System for Education (DISE) database is used to understand the gaps. At the household level, the national census, National Family Health Survey, and other household surveys complement the school database. The household data give estimates of monitories[5] and the out-of-school population in the 6 to 11 and 12 to 14 year age groups. "The household data is also helpful in getting the gross enrolment rate, net enrolment rates, and dropout rates" (Department of Elementary Education and Literacy, 2004). The planning process involves selecting a core team of people at the district, block, and cluster levels to lead this initiative. A detailed assessment of educational needs is done in conjunction with various government and not-for-profit agencies. The planning team visits each habitation and hold meetings with the community to prepare the plans, which include a situation analysis, socio-cultural and historical contexts, and needs at the community and school levels. "School mapping is also required at the habitation level" (Department of Elementary Education and Literacy, 2004).

"Annual work plans and budgets are prepared based on the previously developed habitation level plans" (Department of Elementary Education and Literacy, 2004). These plans include both the plan for the current financial year and a progress update from the previous year including any spill over. Forecasting of funds for each activity is supported by relevant financial documents. These District Elementary Education Plans, along with the state component, are appraised based on financial, programmatic, managerial, and technical compliance with SSA norms. The appraisal also includes the commitment of the state governments to maintain their level of investments in elementary education. The plans, after being reviewed by the Appraisal Mission, are sent to the Project Approval Board at the national level. This Board is chaired by the Secretary of Elementary Education in the Ministry of Human Resource Development, with representatives from the Planning Commission, Integrated Finance Division, Ministry of Labour, Department of Women and Child Development, Ministry of Social Justice, Ministry of Tribal Affairs, National Council for Educational Research and Training, National University of Educational Planning and Administration, National Council for Teacher Education, joint secretaries, directors/deputy secretaries, representatives from the states, and members of the Appraisal Mission."Final appraisal takes into consideration the RTE norms, as well" (Department of Elementary Education and Literacy, 2004).

Sustainability: Sustainability issues are inherent in the design of CGS-LGA. Accordingly, federal commitment to the CGS-LGA programme will be of utmost importance for continued programming to occur, as operations, programme design, and a majority of the funds stem from this level of government. Beyond monetary input, local-level engagement from initiation until programme completion and handover to community users also entrenches sustainability through participation and ownership. Community buy-in from programme conception at government, school, and community levels will be central to any efforts for future local planning, implementation, and monitoring. Groups that have received previous trainings from OSSAP-MDGs are expected to support the training of new Technical Assistants to undertake the scale-up of CGS-LGA projects and proposal development processes. In essence, all current stakeholders are critical to nurture the CGS-LGA programme to stability and sustainability over time.

Educationally marginalised states will continue to receive grants mandated by the 12th Finance Commission specifically for supplementing state resources for SSA. Mukherjee, Sen, and Tapas (2007) "assert that SSA provides a lot of flexibility to improve teaching standards, reduce dropout rates, and increase student outcomes." "In terms of the sustainability of funds, the government has been able to increase the funds by pooling resources from multiple funders; the 2 per cent education cess[6] levied also contributes significantly to this pool" (Banerji & Mukherjee, 2008).

The education infrastructure projects funded by CGS-LGA require maintenance/ upkeep that will be sustainable if state and local funding is allocated and coupled with continued community surveillance and responsibility. Continued advocacy, coordination, and accountability are necessary for materials to be continually supplied to local schools as need arises. Aside from physical materials, structures, and programme design to strengthen and sustain the impact on improved and continual learning, additional interventions may be necessary and would need to be identified by the local community. A key component for both CGS-LGA and SSA to be sustainable is transparency and accountability in the management of human, financial, and material resources made available for such programmes/projects.

Policy Limitations

The CGS-LGA programme is a huge investment in various sectors of the economy that has direct bearing on achieving the MDGs in Nigeria, including the education sector. Intervention in the education sector throughout Nigeria, though mostly focussed on physical supply inputs (classroom blocks, latrines, desks, chairs, chalkboards, books), will also need an increased focus on demand side inputs through wide-spread education campaigns, teacher trainings, bridge programmes, community education workers, and early childhood development. Reaching the marginalised, focussing on learning, and sustaining quality education programmes will require strategic, directed efforts to successfully integrate this intervention with the existing wide-scale education programme in Nigeria that encompasses early childhood through junior secondary school education under the UBE programme. Though the CGS-LGA is still in infancy, the combination of enrolment, attendance, and quality learning outcomes with trained and accountable teachers, when effectively integrated with the holistic universal basic education programme, could provide a more powerful platform/tool for achieving MDGs 2 and 3. This starting point for effective partnership could provide a platform for federal government to create development policies to enable state and local levels to lead and implement through a participatory approach. Continued growth with inclusion at all three tiers of government with focus on an education programme directed at wide-ranging demand-side inputs has the potential to improve learning outcomes and strengthen schools. A larger and more holistic programme on education could be elaborated and sustained using the education component of CGS-LGA as a pilot.

Kainth (2006) "elaborates that SSA was successful in expanding the provision of education; however, there is much to be desired in terms of reaching out to the marginalised." Jhingran and Sankar (2010) also "reiterate the point that the districts that were lagging behind did not benefit from the SSA funds." The authors narrate that the proposed budgets and work plans do not reflect the actual needs in those districts. As a result, the per child allocations and per child expenditure are much lower in the marginalised districts. This situation increases the gaps between better-off districts and districts that are lagging behind. Another important aspect that Kainth (2006) "brings up is that the financial guidelines of SSA are very restrictive and not need-based." On a related note, Jhingran and Sankar (2010) "mention that the success of the districts also depends on administrative efficiency such as working in a timely manner, being results-oriented, and handling the multi-dimensional aspect of SSA." The authors suggest that even efficient districts end up working on routine activities such as distributing school level grants and textbooks, and civil works, rather than trying innovative interventions. Finally, Kainth (2006) "urges that SSA should be taken up as a People's Movement; since SSA is a programme that is primarily planned and managed by government agencies, it has failed to be a "People's Movement."

Discussion and Conclusion

The intention behind taking two large-scale government policies in two populated countries with very similar attributes was to learn from the comparative experiences of the two countries in terms of policy design and implementation. The governing structure in both India and Nigeria is decentralised, with authority at the state, district, and local government area levels. Obstacles related to religious education, marginalised children, child labour, and nomadic groups are prevalent in both countries and contribute to very high out-of-school populations. Therefore, comparative analysis of the two policies on specific parameters helps us draw important lessons on the sustainability and democracy of the planning process, especially at the local level.

CGS-LGA policies and SSA were designed to mirror global MDG targets. Nigeria has expanded its scope of coverage of MDG 2 to include three years of junior secondary education, which is a component of Nigeria's UBE programme. With RTE in India, the scope of SSA became more holistic to include a focus on learning outcomes. The programmes are designed to address issues of marginalisation occasioned by poverty, location, and other socio-economic and cultural factors. The approach under the CGS-LGA tends to support equitable resource allocation, with the initial 113 LGAs being the most challenged in terms of socio-economic development indices across the 36 states and the Federal Capital Territory. A similar approach was adopted for India; all the 640 districts will be covered under SSA and the plans created will be based on the actual educational needs. Local level planning processes are being utilised to develop the technical capacity of officers and community members so these stakeholders will be able to undertake needs assessment and drive development processes that are holistic and use a participatory approach.

The two programmes aim to increase opportunities for access and participation, and enhance quality of learning by making the school environment conducive and supportive for all learners through an inclusive approach and more equitable distribution of education inputs. Use of a flexible approach tied to identified needs in a systematic manner aims to address empirically identified challenges that contribute to educational disparities linked to languages, household income, location, and school governance issues. This approach, which complements other available resources, not only enhances partnerships but also draws additional resources for educational development while developing local capacity for planning, analysis, and proposal development and giving a voice to beneficiary communities. Concurrently, this approach enhances accountability, community ownership, effective resource utilisation, and sustainability of projects after takeover.

Both programmes, however, remain largely input-driven. Improving the learning environment of the school still remains a common framework that the two policies share. Funding is primarily used to fulfill contracts for purchasing school inputs such as blackboards, furniture and textbooks, as well as construction, repair, and maintenance of school buildings. The two policies also involve a more bottom-up approach to planning through involvement of local agencies, and creating proposals/plans that are vetted by multiple stakeholders and government agencies at the LGA/District level. Rather than creating a parallel institutional structure of its own, these policies/schemes work with the existing government bodies at the local level. Local plans and proposals do not replace any existing plans; rather, they try to fill the existing funding gap at the school level. Funds are mainly for making schools functional and constructing new schools where there is identified need based on secondary and primary sources of data (mainly DISE for India and NMIS for Nigeria). The proposals and the action plans are thus data-driven. For each of the needs identified, a full justification based on the data is mandatory under both policies. These plans and proposals are then scrutinised thoroughly at the state and the national levels. In both cases, proposals pass through sector technical reviews and financial reviews before they are finally approved at the national level.

The main difference between the programmes is the fact that the CGS-LGA uses an inter-sectoral approach involving education, health, and water and sanitation, whereas the SSA in India is purely focused on the education sector. In terms of structure, Nigeria created a special office, OSSAP-MDGs, under the President of Nigeria. Not many countries have set up a separate office to meet the MDGs. In India, the line ministries in education are mandated to manage SSA. One might conclude that this makes it harder to undertake inter-sectoral work and have implementation synergies between the sectors in India.

To mention some of the missed opportunities regarding the two policies, the first would be that the extent of outreach and inclusion of the marginalised still remains a challenge in both countries. Even though funds are often meant to construct schools, this may not automatically improve the enrolment rate. Activities such as community campaigns, although necessary, are largely missing from these funding opportunities. Funding still remains school-based, with the dilemma that community members involved in the planning process through implementation and monitoring do not have access to funds to undertake community-based education initiatives. The funding is meant to improve school functioning, exclusively. In this regard, older girls whose parents ask them to miss school and do household chores, children with physical challenges, adolescent boys who tend to work on farms, and children who attend religious non-formal schools are not adequately provided for in these plans. These large-scale policies help to equip schools with basic educational inputs and construct new schools to increase access, but have no medium to reach out to the hardest to reach populations; these policies thus cater mainly to the median school-going population who are most likely to attend school. Another aspect that the policies miss out on is making their presence felt in the community. Communities, by and large, are consulted when the funding proposal is being created and community members are called for meetings to contribute to and assess community educational needs. However, when funds are released for operational purposes, community presence is either limited to PTAs or non-existent. Therefore, rather than being a people's movement, both CGS-LGA and SSA become government-run policies with less direct community involvement in the school-based projects.

Finally, a few considerations need to be kept in mind regarding designing and planning large-scale policies. Should implementing education interventions accompany a focus on strengthening government systems that may end up being a more time consuming activity? How much attention should be given to local empowerment as a sustainable approach to meeting the local, national, and global education goals? What is the appropriate scope of a participatory approach to meet these inter-sectoral goals?

"Is it possible to rely on local level education planning agencies to create robust action plans to meet the goals" (Iyengar & Ifeyinwa, 2014)? There may be certain trade-offs in meeting the education goals versus long-term gains in terms of empowering local communities and administrations to design the plan and follow-up, as well. Local administration may be efficient in making plans, but if this is not a people's movement it will be impossible to cover the last mile to meet the goals. Policies such as the CGS-LGA and SSA are definitely steps in the right direction; however, it is time we review these policies from a comparative perspective to ensure that education gaps are filled.

Notes

1. Zilla Parishad is at the district level.
2. Panchayat works at the hamlet level; it is the government body that operates closest to the village level.
3. The SEMC in Andhra Pradesh consists of seven members: four parents of school-going children, one panchayat ward member, the school headmaster as convener, and the panchayat president as chairman (Rao, 2009).
4. PRIs or Panchayati Raj Institutions: Panchayat Raj is a system of governance in which gram panchayats are the basic units of administration. It has 3 levels: Gram (village, though it can comprise more than one village), Janpad (taluka or block) and Zilla (district).
5. As per Article 29 of the Indian Constitution, the term "minorities" is generally defined as "any section of citizens having a distinct language script and culture." Source: http://archive.indianexpress.com/news/minorities-not-defined-in-constitution-govt/1154635/. Please read http://www.hindu.com/2007/07/14/stories/2007071461651500.htm for more details.
6. In order to raise the outlay for education closer to the goal of 6 per cent of GDP, the finance minister has imposed a 2 per cent education cess on income tax, corporation tax, excise and customs duties, and service tax since April 1, 2004. Source: http://articles.economictimes.indiatimes.com/2006-04-08/news/27454253_1_education-cess-duties-and-service-tax-elementary-education

References

Banerji, R. & Mukherjee, A. (2008): Achieving Universal Elementary Education in India: Future Strategies for Ensuring Access, Quality and Finance. *Margin. The Journal of Applied Economic Research*, 2. 213.

GOI (2014): Sarva Shiksha Abhiyan a Programme for Universal Elementary Education: Manual on Financial Management and Procurement. New Delhi: MHRD.

GOI (2011): Sarva Shiksha Abhiyan: Framework for Implementation Based on the Right of Children to Free and Compulsory Education Act, 2009. New Delhi: MHRD.

Iyengar, R. & Ifeyinwa, N. (2014): Accelerating the Progress towards Universal Primary Education by Empowering Local Level Agencies and Strengthening Government Systems: A Case from Nigeria. *COMPARE*. Retrieved March 2014 from http://baice.ac.uk/2014/accelerating-the-progress-towards-universal-primary-education-by-empowering-local-level-agencies-and-strengthening-government-systems-a-case-from-nigeria/

Jhingram, D. & Sankar, D. (2010): Orienting Outlays toward Needs: An Evidence-Based, Equity-Focussed Approach for Sarva Shiksha Abhiyan. Retrieved March 2014 from http://

documents.worldbank.org/curated/en/2007/01/8933905/orienting-outlays-toward-needs-evidence-based-equity-focused-approach-sarva-shiksha-abhiyan

Kainth, G.S. (2006): A Mission Approach to Sarva Shikhsa Abhiyan. *Economic and Political Weekly*, July, 3288-3290.

Mukherjee, A.; Sen, N. & Tapas, K. (2007): Universalising Elementary Education: An Assessment of the Role of the Sarva Shiksha Abhiyan. *Financing Human Development Policy*. National Institute of Public Finance and Policy, 2.

National Bureau of Statistics (2013): *Millennium Development Goals Performance Tracking Survey Report 2012.* Abuja: Federal Republic of Nigeria.

The Office of the Senior Special Assistant to the President of Nigeria on MDGs (n.d.): Compendium of Photos, Success Stories, and Comments on Flagship Projects Implemented under the 2011 Round of the MDGs Conditional Grants Scheme. Abuja: Federal Republic of Nigeria.

The Office of the Senior Special Assistant to the President of Nigeria on MDGs (2010): *Partnering to Achieve the MDGs: The Story of Nigeria's MDGs Conditional Grants Scheme 2007-2010.* Abuja: Federal Republic of Nigeria.

The Office of the Senior Special Assistant to the President of Nigeria on MDGs (2011): *Conditional Grants Scheme to Local Governments. Training Manual.* Abuja: Federal Republic of Nigeria, and New York: The Earth Institute of Columbia University.

The Office of the Senior Special Assistant to the President of Nigeria on MDGs (2012): *The OSSAP-MDGs Conditional Grants Scheme: Home Grown Strategy for Accelerating MDGs in Nigeria.* Abuja: Federal Republic of Nigeria.

The Office of the Senior Special Assistant to the President of Nigeria on MDGs (2013a): The 2011 CGS to 113 LGAs Comprehensive Project Implementation Report: Joint Report on the Independent Monitors of 2011 MDGS conditional Grant Schemes to Local Governments in Nigeria. Abuja: Federal Republic of Nigeria.

The Office of the Senior Special Assistant to the President of Nigeria on MDGs (2013b): *Partnering to Achieve the MDGs: The Story of Nigerias MDGs Conditional Grants Scheme 2011-2012.*Abuja: Federal Republic of Nigeria.

The Office of the Senior Special Assistant to the President of Nigeria on MDGs (2013c): *CGS-LGA March 2013 Programme Proposals.* Abuja: Federal Republic of Nigeria.

Rao, V.S. (2009): Lack of Community Participation in the Sarva Shiksha Abhiyan: A Case Study. *Economic and Political Weekly,* XLIV (8).

UNESCO Institute for Statistics (UIS). *Welcome to UIS.Stat.* Retrieved January 2014 from http://data.uis.unesco.org/

Wu, B.K.; Kaul, V. & Sankar, D. (2005): The Quiet Revolution: How India is Achieving Universal Primary Education. *Finance and Development,* 42 (2).

19

Contemplating Democratic Education in a Migratory World

Sandra J. Schmidt

We live in a world defined by its interconnectivity, mobility, and change. The human world has long been defined by these elements, but the reach of digital technologies has increased the pace of change and allowed ordinary citizens to enter the global exchange. With all this seeming change, some things remain stubbornly constant. The rejection of colonial power occurred alongside Cold War discourse linking capitalism and democracy with "First World." New nation-states were instructed to adopt these systems as they sought to "progress" from the label of "underdeveloped" to "developed." The pressure facing states to adopt these institutions may be even more requisite today. Hence, proceedings such as this iterate the connectivity of *development* and *democracy*, presuming that *education* is vital to *sustaining* both.

The pressure to democratise is hegemonic and rhetorical. Attaining the label "developed" provides access to global networks while lack of development justifies military and economic intervention. Looking across the globe, there are recognizable standards of democracy – free markets, elections, laws that promote equality, and access to public institutions. But with the widespread implementation of the concept, the actual institutions and practices of democracy vary widely across the globe. Citizens of one democratic state may struggle to see their democratic values reflected in another. These proceedings host scholars from Canada, England, India, South Africa, and the United States who hold rather different senses of the foundational concepts represented herein. The title directs attention to ideas we should value in building education systems that sustain democracy. These terms, though, also overemphasise concepts that have been criticised by participants as insufficient. Critiques have centered on the problematic assumption that the purpose of schooling in a democracy is economic stability and that equal access to schooling does not produce quality schooling. It is important to get kids to school, but what happens therein? What is the democratic education they are afforded therein? In this paper, I explore the possibilities for rigorous attention to the education necessary to sustain (or develop) strong, accessible, and equitable civic and political democratic institutions.

The world order privileges the nation-state. Education plays a role in developing the national imagination of democracy (Anderson, 1991). Democracy rests on having people trust in and share the value of that system and way of organising society. Schools accomplish this by teaching civic skills/capacities and a shared (local) understanding of the construct. As national education systems contemplate how to carry out this mission, they (and the national imaginations of which they are part) face external and internal threats. Although nationalist leaders and citizens continue to "sing the nation-state" (Butler & Spivak, 2010), corporations, transnational economic and political communities, global NGOs, trade cooperatives, and supranational territories threaten state sovereignty, particularly of economically, geographically, or militarily small states. These transnational entities and identities promote the fluidity of movement and location that produce internal threats to democracy. The countries represented here share pluralistic populations and a history of racial/ethnic oppression. Each is exploring paths to redress this past and its influence of contemporary social structures. This pluralistic tension is further challenged by a migratory world. A people move between places, they bring experiences afar to bare on political actions and investments locally. I am interested in how those who re-locate expand the civic base being educated within/for democracy. Immigrants relocate for many reasons – political distress, new/different opportunities, global flow of labour/capital, proximity to family – reflecting difficulties at home and/or the promise of a new place. When people settle in new places, they do not leave behind their home languages, practices, and identities. The demand for recognition of these diverse needs and identities places pressure upon democratic societies that rest upon a belief that there is a common or collective populace. The unity of democracy has always been mythology, but the unity is further disrupted in this global era where people move more freely across space and time and less often belong to one place. How do we continue to develop sustainable education systems amidst migration and change?

Theorising Democracy for and in Pluralist Nations

Before examining what it means to educate in these systems, it is worth exploring how nations contemplate democratic possibilities and where immigrants might fit within that structure. I explore three theorists who take up different ways to consider the relationship of a pluralistic nation and democratic state. These theorists write from three of the countries represented in these proceedings. While the particular democracy and demography are significant, the theorising resonates beyond the particular.

Constitutional Patriotism

Some South African philosophers question whether South Africa should strive to create a nation, and conclude "no" (Boyce, 1999; Brown, 2001; Degenaar, 1994; Moodley & Adam, 2000; Pieterse, 2002). They note that the modernist nation is outdated for the contemporary (African) context. The concept of nation developed in Europe when ethnic groups formed states and identities that differentiated groups and land on the continent (Anderson, 1991; Boyce, 1999; Connor, 1978; Moodley & Adam, 2000). When African "nations" were born under colonial rule, numerous ethnic groups were forced together through land-based claims. Colonial regimes intentionally divided people to increase dependency (Brown, 2001). When Africans removed colonial governance, they transitioned into states the ruled people without a national sensibility (Brown, 2001; Degenaar, 1994).

These nay-saying theorists are dubious that the national concept can account for the racial complexity of South Africa. They purport to build a democratic culture and sense of "constitutional patriotism" without a nation (Degenaar, 2000; Pieterse, 2002). Rather than belonging through shared national identity, constitutional patriotism measures belongingness through the realisation of full citizenship rights and responsibilities (Boyce, 1999). These activities transcend cultural and ethnic identity (Degenaar, 1994; Pieterse, 2007). The release of culture from the political domain allows people to respect cultural co-existence. It rejects both a racial/cultural hierarchy and forced assimilation of groups into the national mould (Pieterse, 2007). It relieves pressure on whites to submit to calls for unity and immigrants to leave behind their national heritage. Civic belonging would be recognised by the adoption of civic behaviours regardless of cultural ethos. Although rarely referenced beyond this context, if able to be actualised would be a remedy for any nation unable to cohere and yet ruled.

Multicultural Democracy

Will Kymlicka is a Canadian political philosopher who explores how democratic societies should incorporate national minorities. He would agree with the previous philosophers that assimilation into a single national cultural ethos is dangerous for pluralistic democracies. His solution for retaining a multicultural democracy rests upon understanding that liberalism and collective rights are not oppositional. He distinguishes between group claims (collective or cultural rights) and communitarianism. While he tries to resolve the liberal dismissal of culture, he does not turn toward communitarianism as the solution. He argues that political rights have been distributed based upon group affiliation in democratic societies. The ability of women, indigenous groups, blacks to acquire political rights – voting, school attendance – requires that they assert membership in the group. Often critical of this group recognition is the liberal ideology that individuals should have the right to make decisions and advocate for themselves. Kymlicka contends that individual decisions are ultimately contained within collective value systems. People do not ultimately choose alone; they are informed by shared group values. Hence, in their argument for freedom, Kymlicka concludes that liberals should value collective rights:

The freedom which liberals demand for individuals is not primarily the freedom to go beyond one's language and history, but rather the freedom to move around within one's societal culture, to distance oneself from particular cultural roles, to choose which features of the culture are most worth developing, and which are without value.

In practice, this means that minority groups should have rights that protect the language, territory, and institutions that allow the values to be shared and used in deliberation. He ends his thesis with the abstract ideal that just societies can determine reasonable group claims for rights.

Nancy Fraser's justice framework may offer help and critique of this thesis. Fraser (1995, 2003) captures the tensions amidst and arising from multicultural solutions. Fraser argues that justice requires both group recognition and redistribution of political and economic resources. She also distinguishes between affirmative strategies which reify existing categories and transformative strategies that reshape oppressive structures. She argues that only transformative strategies are truly just, but states more commonly implement affirmative strategies. She agrees that societies have historically recognised that groups – Blacks, immigrant, women, Native Americans, gays and lesbians – are denied rights. The redress is to recognise them by creating laws that grant suffrage or enable access to education. These policies increase justice, but tend toward backlash and stigmatisation and risk assimilation. What is not addressed by Kymlicka that concerns Fraser is how the lack of transformation forces groups to mandate particular rights valued in the dominant political culture (consider contemporary claims for same-sex marriage) even if they retain linguistic or other cultural tools. The group I consider in this paper – African immigrant – youth face this. Even if afforded legal rights, the multiple layers of identities they carry in space make them targets for mistreatment lest they reject their African-ness. Fraser contends that societies must re-evaluate the stigmatised placement of immigrants.

Destabilising Assimilation

Stuart Hall went to England as a Rhodes Scholar after growing up in colonial Jamaica. His dark skin and cultural identity led him to participate in political critique of culturally-based social structures and in the intellectual growth of cultural studies as a field which explores how cultures are coded as a means of social control. His writing destabilises how we accept and recognise culture, limiting the strength of narrative and boundaries that distinguish cultures from one another rather than contemplating how and why they are represented within and across societies. In speaking about the multicultural question, he similarly destabilised the language associated with cultural interaction in pluralistic societies. He demonstrates like others in this section that multicultural must be discussed but extracted from traditionally rigid boundaries. Critiqued from all sides, multiculturalism is not a means of fixing the meaning of culture and difference, but a discourse that draws our attention to the function of culture and difference in society. He argues that there is no such thing as a pure culture. He also disrupts the overreliance on hybridity as the combining of cultures into a newly recognised category/form.

It is not about the literal mixing of racial categories. It's not about a question of the pure races as opposed to the hybridised ones. It is not about hybrid individuals.... Hybridity describes the inevitable process of cultural translation which is inevitable in a world where communities, people, cultures, tribes, ethnicities are no longer homogeneous, self-sufficient autochthonous entities, tightly bound within by kinship and tradition and sternly boundaried in relation to the outside world (Hall, 2000: 6).

Thus, it is insufficient to think of assimilation. Cultures and people rarely assimilate into something or somewhere else. The process of belonging in a nation does (should) not require loss of referent social structures. He states, "Race of course is not a scientific category. It's a political and social construct. It is the organising discursive category at the centre of a system of practices of socio-economic power, exclusion and exploitation" (Hall, 2000: 7). Race is not bound in or dependent upon community (the failure of traditional multiculturalism). Difference and its construction are social practices that require critique. Hall offers implications for multiculturalism and democracy. Consistent with theories that destabilise culture, he argues that in a pluralistic society, democracy and difference need to remain regularly contested and rarely contained. The process of good democracy is a disposition that questions how and where people are located within the democracy.

Immigrant Youth Negotiate Belonging

Each theory references immigration, at least implicitly, but none thoroughly explores the realities of immigrant identity and belonging that complicate the multicultural nature of contemporary democracies. This paper seeks to use the above theorising to contemplate elements of democratic education in this migratory world. Some discussion of the issues raised in migratory ideologies is necessary before proceeding in this deliberation. For this I turn to lessons learned from my research with three male African newcomer youth in New York City. African youth diversify the discussion of immigration in the United States. First, many of these youth do not physically travel between homes in the US and homes in Africa. They may desire to return to Africa (and many state they will when they have the means and are older), but cost and visas prevent this from being realised. African immigrants do not need to travel to the continent to "return" to Africa. They encounter Africa on billboards, in curriculum, in popular media, etc. In NYC, they enter African neighbourhoods, stores, churches, community centers, and homes. The narratives the encounter of themselves in US society are some of the harshest faced by any immigrant group, producing further attention to the tension of belonging. I want to summarise how three youth in the study negotiated belonging in three different spaces – school, home, and Little Senegal.

School was a place of struggle. The three boys left traditional middle schools and chose an international high school because of the lack of fit they felt. In the traditional school, they faced harassment. They embodied Africa and the labels of the continent were used to taunt the boys. Being socially successful would have required abandoning their African sensibilities and identities and transforming into "African American." Changing schools allowed them to remain as outsiders. The international high school was not utopian. They struggled with the undisciplined nature of US schools. Sana noted that discipline by teachers in schools did not facilitate good learning (students struggle to learn well when they fear the teacher), but it did keep classrooms orderly so that teachers could teach, a concern that arose from watching US teachers struggle to maintain order and get students to do their homework. They were astute enough to realise that they should not talk of this difference. The choice of schools put them on a path to value their language and national identity, but adopt the educational and civic values of America writ large.

Home was the space of the greatest comfort and belonging. In personal photo assignments, two boys chose to highlight family and family at church. Certain cultural practices followed the families but others were disrupted. Whereas the boys lived with extended families in Guinea and Senegal, they lived with only parents and siblings in the US. This was due to who travelled to the US and the small size of apartments in NYC. One of the struggles regularly discussed was the disjuncture between African and American values and how to protect these in the home. It was common in Senegal for parents or older siblings to discipline younger children. Bringing this discipline to the US put Senegalese families at risk for "discipline" from US authorities. This limited who was invited into the home and personal conversations. They recognised from watching others that to be vocal about these practices (and others) around authorities in the US endangered the family in the US. They quickly learned that social services could separate parents and children and that the family and home did not exist merely in the private sphere. They remained distant and protective in order to hold onto values and family. This moment of navigating home and public authorities was one of the many moments these youth experienced simultaneously and yet differentiated social rules.

Little Senegal is a relatively large and robust centre of African life in Manhattan, containing shops, mosques, residences, and service centers. It is different from other ethnically labelled areas in the city such as Chinatown in that it is less homogeneous and contained. Little Senegal is not congruous; it is a set of shops, markets, mosques, salons, and restaurants intermingled with buildings that do not belong to Little Senegal. People can walk through without entering and experiencing the space. The boys used cameras to capture the African-ness and relationships that defined this area. The photographs emphasised "services" that Africans cannot obtain/attain in other parts of the city. The services reflect an interaction of culture and business and the suggestion that the two cannot be differentiated. A significant set of photos came inside a grocery store where they caught couscous, milk, meat, beans, and spices that were unlabelled and yet familiar. The attention to local food was furthered in the photographing of the exterior and interior of two African restaurants and street stalls that sold juices, beans, and other West African prepared food. They captured *hijabs* in store windows and accessories such as calling cards that allowed them to communicate with home. They also spent a bit of time in a Senegalese barbershop and a West African braiding salon where owners understood cultural aesthetic. The boys choose to highlight the positive images to offset the negativity images typically encountered.

The visual projects in Little Senegal proved uncomfortable because the boys perceived the activity as a potential intrusion to the community. Discussions about the process of becoming comfortable revealed an increased awareness of and respect for the social networks of the community. White visitors and Africans negotiated these markets differently. As insiders, the boys had to rely on African relational understanding. This included first accessing people they already knew. When they encountered new people, they needed to establish a relationship first and then discuss consent. This meant that the boys regularly visited the shops and people to secure photos for their projects. Further, the negotiation of these relationships required that the boys assess the longer terms outcomes. Some people might report to parents or require an exchange of service. Thus, the relationship must be understood in advance of contemplating the photo. They turned to a few elders in the area to help learn the people and hierarchy. This was a place the boys wanted to belong and to belong meant to learn the local rules, rules that were carried from Senegal into Little Senegal. The forms of exchange and social standing maintained themselves across the Atlantic and within New York City. They functioned beneath a set of networks and exchange that locals used to navigate the same area.

Critical Multiculturalism and Democratic Education

A common convening of the words democracy, education, and development connotes that we adopt democratic principles of equity and inclusivity to ensure all students are educated as a means of economic development. This study and these proceedings draw increased attention to needed dialogue about constructing an education system that is not merely situated in democratic culture, but fundamentally wrestles with the nature of that democratic society. As the US and other countries contemplate the purpose and substance of education in this migratory era, we need to allow schools to change much in the way cultures do. This section explores three ideas that we should wrestle with as we incorporate migratory experiences into the fabric of democratic society. Students should not be forced to be absorbed, assimilate, or avoid as educative practices.

A Democratic State Needs Nations

Degenaar (1994) and Pieterse (2007) make compelling arguments about the need to invest in constitutional patriotism rather than nation-building. Consistent with the other authors, they struggle with the idea of uniformity they see as requisite for cohering a nation. They want people to honour the constitution but maintain their community belonging rather than national identity. The argument rests upon a belief in the stability and strength of the constitution (and resultant state) as something that reflects the entirety of the citizenry. Minority groups in any country, particularly those whose constitutions were not written with broad equity clauses, contend the reach of a constitution. Immigrant groups and migratory individuals further challenge this claim as they become subjected to a constitution that may not reflect them. Further, constitutional language and concepts are necessarily contested and changing in signification. Thus, the constitution/state needs substantive spaces for citizens to query the basis of the state and democracy. While nationalism may preach "blind" allegiance to the state, some shared identity sustains a democracy that contains voices of the people (Dewey, 1927). I do not mean to make a public and a nation synonymous, but to suggest that a sense of belonging socially and civically with others and not just the state, is foundational to the construction of a public.

The concern that Degenaar (1994) and Pieterse (2007) express is about the modern connotation of the nation as singular and uniform. In South Africa, the ANC advocates for a single nation unified by a narrative of diversity. Kymlicka (1995) and Fraser (1990) contemplate a multiplicity of nations. Fraser (1990) contends that counter publics provide a multiplicity of substantive spaces wherein people can collect their voices and resist dominant power structures. Kymlicka illuminates multinational states which states have groups who want to retain their institutions not only their heritage. Thinking about the nation rather than cultural community provides a more rigorous standard of what is to be maintained and addressed by the state.

The language and policies of multiculturalism, responding to an historical multiplicity of states, position Canada and South Africa to envision this system. The US is less equipped to handle this. US policies have largely reduced thinking about difference to the distinct identities of cultures, but whose practices are absorbed into the state and potentially some sense of the nation. Consider the institutions in Little

Senegal. Little Senegal was heterotropic because it allowed people to move simultaneously while employing different cultural and institutional practices. Americans and Senegalese had distinct social practices for interacting and initiating the purchase, but they also used distinct economic institutions to exchange goods.

Degenaar (1994) is right to suggest that the nation is a problematic modernist notion still being advocated in a postmodern world. But the postmodern world has not yet removed its dependence on institutions such as a public that can prevent states and democracies from becoming sedentary and cliché. The nation may be an imaginative space for producing public ideologies. The public should not allow itself to become irrelevant lest democracies fundamentally fail to enact their promise to be of the people. Deliberations about education are one arena that could be lost without an active public to organise and speak in the formation of this public good. Turned over to the state or wrested loose by private organisations, the public could lose control over the education system. While imperfect, education needs to be a public good if we are to preserve the virtues of equity and inclusivity.

Expand the Imagination of Who the Citizens are in Schools and Society

A primary function of education in the US and elsewhere is to produce citizens. But who are these citizens? Are young people citizens prior to their arrival in school or is this the end result? Are we willing to use the concept of citizen in schooling because we presume that the people who walk through the doors are on a journey toward citizenship? What then is a citizen? Is this an earned title or categorically applied to encourage people within a place to "act appropriately"? Although citizenship may be formally assigned through adult actions, the training in proper behaviour begins at a young age. What of the youth in this study who may never seek US citizenship? They represent many newcomer youth today. Their allegiance to rules of US schools societies are quickly disrupted if they do not match their home culture. We experience this in the study when these young people knew the formal rules of discipline but ignored them or avoided them. When moving in Little Senegal, even with the regulatory gaze of police nearby, their behaviour was not shaped by the threat of being stopped and frisked by police, but the threat of being caught in mis behaviour by elders. The elder system with close ties to the home did far more to surveill the youth. In a story not told above, we travelled to Central Park to interview West African pedicab drivers. One young man noticed Diallo's sagging pants and ranted at him, criticising how African youth Americanise rather than respect their home. This appearance would never be allowed in Guinea. Although the pants-up was a school rule that Diallo ignored, following this experience his pants were pulled high for the next three weeks.

Degenaar (1994) notes that people can belong in multiple ways. Citizenship need not merely be about belonging to the state; citizens may also belong to cultural communities. The reason for this belonging is not that suggested by Degenaar and Pieterse. Young citizens do not belong to other communities for the sake of allowing recognition and standing of their cultural group. As Kymlicka (1995) contends, it is within the values of these groups that people learn to make decisions and function in relation to the state. Rather than turning to the state as a uniform ideological framework within which to make decisions, people look to their national or ethnic communities for latitude in making this decision. In advocating, as schools often do in the US, consideration of a single constitutional basis upon which to make decisions, people must relinquish influential factors and structures that act upon and shape young citizens. The boys were taught how to gain consent for taking photos from two white researchers and then from a Senegalese man. It was the words of the latter who affected them. The Senegalese elder could reference and evoked acting relational while we talked through our university language of consent. The boys were able to reconsider their actions within an ethical framework that they understood. Hall (2000) warns against generating new universals associated with group boundaries and norms. Using familiar language and decision frames is not to assign these two students because of a group identity they share, but to create the inquisitive disposition with students to discuss and contemplate decisions in ways that articulate, use, and critique the rules and social institutions that guide them beyond school. As young people walk through the doors of school and are labelled as citizens, schools need to provide language and space to unpack the decisions and actions of these young citizens within ways of being that make individual/group rather than universal sense.

Develop Democratic Dispositions through Structure and Substance

Developing a society is not simply an economic matter even though strong neoliberal rhetoric tries to compel us that the reason for security and strong education is economic growth. One struggle produced by the overemphasis on neoliberal economic growth is that certain sectors become more valuable. But the sustainability of a place relies on its ability to feed, educate, and care for its people, sectors not attended to enough in development discourse. Revaluing and redistributing resources can only occur when people and the state are invested in a solid democratic society. Ideologies of equity, inclusivity, and humanity should not merely provide access to public resources but be carried out between people. The US and other countries wherein diversity has resulted in conflict and uneven-ness require an education system that actively engages with inequities. The movement of people into and across the country further burdens efforts toward equity and justice. Deliberating upon society, not preaching obedience and responsibility should be the essence of democratic education and education for democracy.

The first section advocated for retaining public(s) and the second the diverse needs to citizens. Inherent to both was a rejection of uniformity, universality, and singularity. Needs vary across national and ethnic groups. The youth in this study remain in the US, but other immigrant youth are more mobile and are punished and retained as the result of long absences due to family work or trips home. These proceedings contain reports on nomadic and rural youth in India who are similarly underserved in the one-way model of education. Two of the boys in the study had numerous afterschool obligations that constrained the time allocated to homework and their ability to participate in extracurricular activities. Creating different types of school and choice among them will always have critics. The critics worry less about the choices and more about the limitations or realness of options. Are students tracked out of certain opportunities? How can one have choice and not use it to perpetuate inequity? Often research and educational models are developed for and by those with power and access. Others are assessed by their ability to achieve in these frameworks and when they do not, changes are mandated to them. This perpetuates the uneven view of power and knowledge. Rather than ask how we can expand existing models of civic/democratic education to account for immigrant youth, I look to these youth and their social navigations to explore the possibilities for using that experience to rethink inclusivity.

Aside from structure, we need to examine the democratic content of schools. Perhaps there is value in knowing government structures, even for immigrant youth. But this is merely a beginning point. Producing a sustainable democracy requires creating a democratic society versed and practiced in the dispositions of voice and equity. As students in this study wandered school and Harlem, they felt and heard the language and gaze of discrimination. They did not need to cite moments of being prevented from entering a space or being denied a right to understand that living in America does not make one an American. They can pass through a US school and learn the necessary actions of good citizens, perform those acts, and be called good citizens. Allowing citizenship to be a set of actions or collection of knowledge does not address the foundations of inequity and exclusion that tug at pluralistic democracies. The theoretical authors that frame this paper would all be dissatisfied with democratic education that focusses on the state. They look to the language and possibilities in a critical multiculturalism to advocate for allowing tension and understanding as central dispositions needed to address the social complexities of democracy. The theorists that opened this piece give us much to contemplate. No matter the language we choose, the ideas of critical multiculturalism and addressing tensions are central to an education that helps people value and engage with the diversity of their democratic society. Kymlicka (1995: 191) contends that it is requisite that people value the type of society in which they live: "A society founded on "deep diversity" is unlikely to stay together unless people value deep diversity itself, and want to live in a country with diverse forms of cultural and political membership." Hall (2000) and Degenaar articulate what this might mean in practice. Degenaar (2000: 27) writes, "We should not romanticise too easily about reconciliation between conflicting communal cultures, but accept the challenge of continuing tension as part and parcel of a pluralist world and of the tension-generating and enriching diversity of a post-modern culture." Citizens must wrestle with race and discrimination, practices that do and have divided these pluralistic societies.

Danielle Allen's (2004) theory of political friendship provides a model for a curriculum of interaction in and out of school. Her claims for political friendship derive philosophically from the work of Ralph Ellison, Hannah Arendt and Aristotle. With justice as requisite yet not assumed, friendship requires equitable self-interest, a desire to maintain relationship with others, and trust (including rebuilding it when it collapses). At the core of these friendships – the habit upon which relationship and trust are maintained – is talking. Her argument includes that both the speaker and listener contribute important habits of evaluation and persuasion to conversation. In the end, the equitable society is not maintained by talking to in-group members, but to strangers.

Political friendship cultivates habits of imagination that generate politically transformative experiences out of ordinary interactions among strangers. Herein lies its power. To be a good rhetorician, one must see oneself as strangers so. The effort to do so entails understanding how one is implicated in strangers' lives, and how calculi of goods and ills look different from other experiential positions (Allen, 2004: 171).

Ultimately political friends enhance trust and cohesion because they are on the lookout for one another. Their shared interest in self-preservation against the power of the state means they will be vigilant about others and selves in the world.

When schools in the US centre one way of knowing, being and thinking about democratic education, they mould people in a single idea. This does not help citizens engage with the difference around them. Further, it stabilises their thinking in an era that is unstable. The boys in Little Senegal were well-versed in moving between two worlds. Good democratic education would help them talk about and explore what it means to move between these worlds. It would allow them to engage with the bully rather than to avoid. It would help them understand how to use relational understanding in the markets to build relations and navigate American institutions as well.

Conclusions

This paper draws from across contexts and in the end is situated in a specific context. Because of its presence alongside papers of similar notions written from and of different places and because it was further developed while presenting at a conference in India, it is suggested that some ways of thinking about democratic education and educating for democracy might resonate across national boundaries. The theoretical paradigms arise from outside the United States to suggest there are other places more rigorously pursuing what it means to sustain democracy in increasing diverse places. But none of these is directly and immediately applicable, but put into conversation with one another and with the experience in Little Senegal, we certainly learn some implications for conceiving of the function and design of education in the US, lessons that might offer insight to my colleagues at these proceedings.

These proceedings come dialogue across academics from at least five countries who draw upon experience in many more. Importantly, this was not and should not be a comparative space. There were certainly commonalities – like the threats to public education – that were similarly felt. What we resisted and is important to resist in general is the exporting of education and democracy. These institutions are and need to be situated in specific socio-cultural, geographic, and historical contexts. One of the struggles many places face in developing and education system that suits that political setting is the external production and maintenance of the institution.

The luxury and bane of a migratory world is the reach and pace of connecting ideas and communicating across space. Some transnational patterns draw us closer together and make the world feel smaller, but we are still organised around in the everyday around national or local ideologies that shape how we make choices and understand the worlds and places through which we move — physically and intellectually. While it may look different across the world, we need to have the institutional nimbleness and individual dispositions that are open to engaging with others.

References

Allen, D. (2004): *Talking to Strangers: Anxieties of Citizenship since Brown v. Board of Education*. Chicago: University of Chicago Press.

Anderson, B.R.O. (1991): *Imagined Communities: Reflections on the Origin and Spread of Nationalism*. New York: Verso.

Boyce, B.P. (1999): Nation-Building Discourse in a Democracy. In Palmberg, M. (Ed.), *National Identity and Democracy in Africa*, South Africa: Capture Press, pp. 231-43.

Brown, D. (2001): National Belonging and Cultural Difference: South Africa and the Global Imaginary. *Journal of Southern African Studies,* 27 (1): 757-69.

Butler, J. & Spivak, G.C. (2010): *Who Sings the Nation-State? Language, Politics, Belonging.* London: Seagull Books.

Connor, W. (1978): A Nation is a Nation, is a State, is an Ethnic Group, is a….., *Ethnic and Racial Studies,* 1: 377-00.

Degenaar, J. (1994): Beware of Nation-Building Discourse. In Rhoodie, N. & Liebenberg, I. (Ed.), *Democratic Nation-Building in South Africa*. Pretoria: HSRC Publishers, pp. 23-30.

Degenaar, J. (2000): Multiculturalism: How can the Human World Live Its Difference? In Vugt, W.E.V. & Cloete, G.D. (Ed.), *Race and Reconstruction in South Africa.* Lanham, MD: Lexington Books, pp. 155-70.

Dewey, John. (1927): *The Public and Its Problems*. New York: Holt.

Fraser, N. (1995). From Redistribution to Recognition? Dilemmas of Justice in a 'Post-Socialist' Age. *New Left Review,* 212: 68-93.

Fraser, N. (1990): Rethinking the Public Sphere: A Contribution to the Critique of Actually Existing Democracy. *Social Text*, 25 (26): 56–80

Fraser, N. & Honneth, A. (2003): *Redistribution or Recognition?: A Political-Philosophical Exchange.* Trans.: J. Golb, J. Ingram & C. Wilke. New York: Verso.

Hall, S. (2000): *The Multicultural Question.* The Political Economy Research Centre Annual Lecture: Firth Hall Sheffield.

Kymlicka, W. (1995): *Multicultural Citizenship: A Liberal Theory of Minority Rights.* Oxford: Oxford University Press.

Moodley, K. & Adam, H. (2000): Race and Nation in Post-Apartheid South Africa. *Current Sociology*, 48 (3): 51-69.

Pieterse, H. (2002): In Search of a Nation. *Safundi: The Journal of South African and American Studies,* 3 (1): 1-18.

20

Rights, Entitlements and Education Inclusion for Mobile Pastoralist Children in India

Caroline Dyer

Despite India's relatively recent rights legislation and long-standing policy commitments to the notion of universal education inclusion, children from nomadic communities still routinely face discriminatory denial of access (Tomasevski, 2003, 2004; Theis, 2004) to appropriate institutional arrangements for formal education. This chapter reflects on some of the demands of education "inclusion" and dimensions of discrimination against one particular "nomadic" group — mobile pastoralists.

Looking backwards, briefly, we are reminded that in 1990, the World Declaration on Education for All (EFA) identified nomads as one of several groups who are discriminated against in access to education services (WDEFA, 1990). The 2000 Dakar declaration called for increasing systemic flexibility to accommodate such groups, recognising that they may never be able to participate in formal schooling. In 2010, five years before the 2015 EFA deadline, UNESCO's 2010 Global Monitoring Report (GMR) *Reaching the Marginalised* (UNESCO, 2010) called for "urgent action" to be taken on mobile pastoralist groups' extensive, but generally poorly evidenced, education deprivation.

While Indian EFA policy discourse does not focus specifically on nomads, SSA's identification of children of migrating families as educationally deprived (SSA, 2005b) opens a policy space for action in redress (Sen, 1999). I explore dimensions of this space in this chapter, to show that despite increasing systemic flexibility under SSA it remains a space that is restricted for certain "nomadic" children; and one that has then been constrained rather than expanded by parameters of the 2009 Right to Education Act. The (re)production of mobile pastoralists' education exclusion is illustrated with reference to Gujarat, home to an estimated 600,000 mobile pastoralists, and exploration of the views of duty bearers to the right to education, and how this has translated into positive action in relation to mobile pastoralists' entitlement.

Mobility and the "Other" Indians

To preface discussion focussing on mobile pastoralists, it is fitting to begin by setting out some particularities about their livelihoods that normally evade consideration by education planners (Dyer, 2014). This illustrates a fundamental disjuncture between what pastoralists need to do to sustain their livelihoods and the norms and normative intentions of the post-colonial model of education (Kumar, 2005) – a disjuncture that is reflected in official views of the challenges of pastoralists' inclusion, and how it is attended to within the SSA framework and under the 2009 RTE.

All the nomads use spatial mobility strategically to access the natural resources on which their livelihoods depend. This shared characteristic belies the high heterogeneity of their livelihoods – as foragers, or hunter-gatherers; or "peripatetics" (Casimir and Rao, 2003) who offer specialised services to sedentary, or indeed other nomadic people; or sea nomads and fisher folk; or mobile pastoralists. Turning specifically to pastoralists as one of many "nomadic" groups, we are immediately confronted with further difficulties of definition. Pastoralism is itself is a "fuzzy" category (cf. Casimir and Rao, 2003), at once a livelihood and a social identity, so that those who no longer work with animals or migrate still self-describe as a pastoralist. This chapter focusses on mobile animal husbandry men who raise livestock and move them to pastures, relying on the domestic consumption or sale/exchange of animals, and/or their products to sustain themselves (Fratkin and Mearns, 2003: 112).

There is a global absence of accurate data on mobile pastoralist populations (Carr-Hill, 2012; UNESCO, 2010). This absence reflects both the kind of terminological ambiguity I have touched above; and the fact that counting the people who are marginalised is a political task, susceptible to bias towards either under- or over-claiming totals. There is no accurate count in India, but a 2003 scoping study (Sharma *et al.*, 2003) suggested that they comprise about 6 per cent of the national population (*ibid*, citing Khurana, 1999).

India's mobile pastoralists are distributed across a range of ecological zones virtually all over the country (Joshi, 2008). In mountainous regions, herders move yaks, cattle, sheep and goats up and down between summer and winter pastures; throughout the western dry land and the Deccan Plateau. In the south they move sheep, cattle, goats and camels (Casimir and Rao, 2003: 1); and in Karnataka, ducks too are "herded" (Nambi, 2001). Yet despite this obvious presence in the landscape, and the fact that in all but the most arid or mountainous areas, agrarian and pastoral activities are closely integrated (Casimir and Rao, 2003; Ikeya and Fratkin, 2005; Kavoori, 2005), regional scholarship has been surprisingly neglectful of mobile groups (Agrawal and Saberwal, 2004: 37). Ratnagar (2004) has termed them "other Indians" while Berland (2003: 108) described them as the "tenebrous others" in the body of anthropological work on South Asian rural village life.

Mobility is intrinsic to a pastoralist livelihood. Pastoralists in India's mountainous northern States practise "vertical" migration between winter and summer pastures: those in the semi-arid North Western region and the Central Deccan plateau practise "horizontal" migration. Such migration takes the form of an annual cycle of transhumance to and from a fixed location, rather than the permanent movement of a nomad. But if the broad direction of migration *per se* is fairly fixed, mobility within it remains flexible; for mobility is strategic, a means by which skilled herders ensure that their animals access, from sporadically available resources (Blench, 2001), those that best enable optimal health and reproduction. In India, this includes use of agricultural residues to supplement increasingly constrained commons grazing.

Important though it is, mobility should not be reified (Dyson-Hudson and Dyson-Hudson, 1980); optimal animal and household welfare also depend on carefully nurtured and deployed labour organisation. Children engage in situated, social apprenticeship learning, learning from adults through "legitimate peripheral participation" (Lave and Wenger, 1991) the skills they need to live well. This form of labour organisation is open to interpretation as a form of child labour that interferes with the expectation that childhood is devoted in large part to attending school, intrinsic in the state's usual offer of formal education as schooling. An alternative perspective, with more to say to challenges of education inclusion, is that these children are apprentices learning how to live as socially competent, successful pastoralists. This kind of education is not—and never will be—available in schools. From this perspective, formal education is a risk rather than the intrinsic good that policy and much public discourse presuppose.

Pastoralism is not among the policy preoccupations of national Ministries of Agriculture, and of Environment and Forest: official discourses of its assumed low productivity and backwardness (Köhler-Rollefson and the LIFE Network 2007; Sharma *et al*, 2003) reflect the lens of deficit through which pastoralism is often viewed by government actors (Agrawal and Sabarwal, 2004; Sharma *et al*, 2003; Bharwada and Mahajan, 2006) – a stance that is unfortunately not unique to India (cf. AUC 2010; Dyer 2014; Krätli 2001). In the social service sector, extensive discrimination and negative "governmentality" (Foucault, 1994) towards mobile pastoralists (Morton, 2010) have moved Agrawal and Sabarwal (2004, 37) to argue that the sedentary bias of services has "facilitated high levels of illiteracy, malnutrition and medical neglect" among them. As I shall go on to show, ten years since these authors thus remarked, there is little evidence of any significant shift in the awareness of policy actors that pastoralism is a sustainable livelihood with a place in modern India, or of how education inclusion can be perceived in ways that do not presuppose the desirability of mobile pastoralists becoming sedentary (cf. also Danaher *et al.*, 2007) — and no longer so clearly those "other" Indians.

Habitation, Neighbourhood and the Sedentary Bias of Education Provision

I move now to examining the exclusionary provisions of the two most significant current politico-legal frameworks governing universal "inclusion": Sarva Shiksha Abhiyan and the 2009 Right to Education.

Sarva Shiksha Abhiyan and the Discriminatory Notion of Habitation

With the goal of universal education inclusion long espoused in national plans and policy narratives (MHRD, 1986/92; HDR, 2012) the Sarva Shiksha Abhiyan (SSA) was conceived as "an effort to universalise elementary education by community-ownership of the school system" (SSA, 2005b: 1.1) in "response to the demand for quality basic education all over the country" (*ibid.*). It highlights the importance of focusing on "the inclusion and participation" in "the educational process" of children from the range of disadvantaged groups it specifies (SSA, 2005b: 1.7.10). Nomadic communities are not among them, although mobility finds cursory mention in the requirement of "specific strategies for special groups like [...] children of migrating families" (SSA, 2005b: 5.1.1.iii). While the national framework documentation reflects an expanding policy awareness of who is educationally "unincluded," the nature of the scheme requires individual states to develop local strategies to fit the specifics of their context.

In practice, since access has long been equated all across India with provision of a physical facility (Kumar, 2005, Dyer, 2000), expansion of the school network remained a priority. The parameters of what comprised a school have undergone change, however, in recognition of a planning norm — "Provision of primary schools in all habitations having a population of 300 persons within a walking distance of 1 km for children of 6-11 years age group" (EFA India, 2000) — that failed to make a facility universally available. The Education Guarantee Scheme in Madhya Pradesh (Gopalakrishnan and Verma, 1998) focussed on the habitation (which, as Mehrotra (2002) points out may be significantly smaller than a village, and/or multiple habitations may constitute a single village) as the unit of planning. It sets a precedent requiring the state to respond to community demand for formal education provision (within 90 days) in a habitation with no schooling facility within a kilometre (Mehrotra, 2002), providing the facility will serve a minimum of 25 learners in a tribal area, and 40 in a non-tribal area. SSA then adopted a "community based approach to planning with habitation as a unit of planning" (SSA, 2005b: 1.7.7), which paved the way for the subsequent opening of thousands of very small schools in habitations lacking schooling facilities — an approach to enabling access that raises significant concerns over social fragmentation and quality.

For mobile pastoralist children, however, this kind of broad brush change has made little difference to their difficulties in accessing provision. Despite SSA's changes in specifying the norm of accessibility, the norm is still framed entirely within sedentarist notions of geographical proximity and habitation. According to these parameters, a community that can ensure economy of scale (a minimum, and constant, number of learners) and permanently resides in a habitation (i.e. in sedentary) are reasonable prerequisites for education inclusion. This approach undermines the right to education of any child who cannot meet these prerequisites, denying them the opportunity to participate that is now increasingly available to their sedentary peers. The SSA is right, then, to call for "specific strategies" for including un(der) served groups, and I will shortly examine what those have been in Gujarat.

The 2009 RTE Act and the Discriminatory Notion of Neighbourhood

Similar difficulties arise in the discursive representations of facilitating education inclusion in the Right to Education (RTE) Act (RTE, 2009). The RTE provides the legal basis for the right of every Indian child between the ages of 6-14 year to demand eight years of quality education: specifically, the legislated right is to "free and compulsory education in a neighbourhood school till completion of elementary education" (RTE, 2009: 3) (its failure to attend to early childhood education is a keenly commented upon limitation, cf. Niranjanaradhya and Kashyap, 2006). The Act itself infringes the intention of the 1948 Declaration by collapsing the right to education specified in those Articles to a right to schooling, although they are not the same thing. The Convention on the Rights of the Child (1990), to which India is a signatory, makes this perfectly clear: it refers to education throughout and has a single reference to schools – as a place where violence against children should not be tolerated (UNICEF,

1990) (the latter is a prominent theme in both the RTE and revised SSA framework, which calls for education that is "free from fear, stress and anxiety" (SSA, 2011: 3).

The RTE Act, then makes explicit reference to schools only as the object of both duty and entitlement, going beyond this to clarify that ""school" means any recognised school imparting elementary education" (RTE, 2009: 2). It also establishes it as the duty of local state authorities to provide such a school, within "limits of neighbourhood..... as prescribed" within three years (*ibid*: 3); and emphasises that children should be able to transfer from one such school to another as necessary. Just as habitation emerges as a problematic concepts in the SSA, so does the concept of "neighbourhood" in the RTE Act. For children of pastoralist families who undertake transhumance, neighbourhoods are likely to be both numerous and transient, making the concept of neighbourhood in the Act somewhat meaningless for them.

From Reservations to Entitlements

The revised framework for the SSA (SSA, 2005b) seeks to put SSA on a rights footing, highlighting the need for a paradigm shift from an "incentive based approach" to an "entitlements perspective" not only in SSA, but also in "all [state government] interventions, programmes and schemes for elementary education" as well "in the mindset of all the agencies involved in the implementation of the SSA" (SSA, 2005b: 4). I turn now to set out something of why a pre-existing approach to entitlement for the disadvantaged communities SSA focusses on represents another obstacle to a fully realised rights-based education entitlement for mobile pastoralists.

Millions of Indians are entitled to the protection of the state, triggered by inclusion in official categories of Scheduled Tribe, Scheduled Caste or one of numerous OBCs. Affirmative action for groups thus recognised entails positive discrimination in relation to education and employment – and to fierce, occasionally bloody – battles in the politics of recognition that surround accessing the privileges that accrue from these classifications. This politics is, further, biased against "nomadic" groups, rooted in a particular historical interpretation which finds contemporary echoes in unsympathetic "governmentality" towards them (Morton, 2010). In colonial India, nomadism was conflated with criminality (Kasturi, 2007; Panda, 2008): groups living in forests and leading a "wandering" life, who included nomadic cattle grazers, were notified under the 1871 Criminal Tribes Act. The Act underwent further amendments up until 1944, but repealed after Independence, in 1952. Although previously notified communities were then re-categorised as Denotified and Nomadic Tribes (DNTs), the subsequent passing of the Habitual Offenders Act in 1959, which required police to investigate a suspect's criminal tendencies and whether his occupation is "conducive to settled way of life," continued by then well established official stigmatisation of mobility (Panda, 2008).

Although a 2007 UN Committee on the Elimination of Racial Discrimination (CERD) request that India repeal the Act and rehabilitate DNT communities was not granted, a National Commission for Denotified, Nomadic and Semi-Nomadic Tribes (NCDNSNT) was established to examine the condition of these approximately 110 million people. In 2008 the Commission recommended a Constitutional amendment to create a new scheduled community, entitled to a 10 per cent reservations quota, and deleting them from inclusion in existing ST/SC/OBC lists (Renake, 2008; ToI, 2008). Although the Registrar General strongly supported quantifying their population, the Commission's calls were rejected and, given that 97 per cent of DNTs and 84 per cent of nomadic groups were thought to be already listed in existing categories, preference was expressed for focusing instead on removing obstacles to their progress (ToI, 2008). The full report of the Commission is unavailable in the public domain.[1]

Whether universal rights-based entitlement approaches are able to upset the well established (and unconsitutional) use of disprivilege as a trigger for (affirmative) action remains to be seen. Meanwhile, the scramble for disprivilege marked by acquisition of exogenous identity labels (Tapper 2008) continues. The legacy of the old entitlement approach shapes how duty bearers to the right to education approach their responsibilities, as we shall shortly see in Gujarat.

Pastoralists and Education Inclusion in Gujarat

Pastoralists have been active in the arid and semi-arid western region for millennia – archaeologists have found evidence of their presence in Harappan times (Choksi, 1991; Ratnagar, 2004). In contemporary Gujarat, mobile pastoralists have been estimated to comprise about one tenth of the 60.30 million total state population (Census of India, 2011) – some 600,000 people (MARAG, 2012).

I draw here on field work conducted in Gujarat in 2009 with Archana Choksi, investigating aspirations for social inclusion and formal education participation among one major pastoralist group, the Rabaris of Kachchh. Using qualitative methods, including open-ended and semi-structured interviews and focus groups (conducted in Gujarati, then translated into English and thematically analysed) we held "purposive conversations" with seven senior State Education Department officials and five junior education officials at the district level in Kachchh. We held four gender-segregated focus groups, each comprising 12 boys/girls of years 10 and 12 attending the LD Rabari boarding school in Anjar; and we interviewed the Principal and Chair of the Board of Trustees of that school and nine of its teachers; and talked with parents of children using this and Rabari-only habitations and villages in Kachchh (see Dyer, 2014, for detail on the methodological approach).

Gujarat is one of India's fastest growing states: it is a strategic economic power within the national economy, with annual growth rates consistently above the national average (IHDR, 2011). The Bharatiya Janata Party (BJP)-led government has energetically promoted "Garvi (vibrant) Gujarat" as a national /global investment destination. This ambition can only be realised by widespread land acquisition: and while defective land acquisition practices are not particular to Gujarat, its "murky" deals (Sud, 2008: 11-12) raise many questions over the powers of the state-corporate alliance so prominent in Gujarat"s development. Industrial land acquisitions show disturbing disregard for traditional land users coping with the disappearing commons (and curtailed access to natural resources that results); or the impact of industrial activity on the natural resource base (Bharwada and Mahajan, 2006; GSHDR, 2004; Iyengar, 2001). These, along with encroachment and population expansion, are cumulatively limiting the possibilities for pastoralist transhumance, making a mobile pastoralist livelihood increasingly difficult to sustain.

Despite a steady overall decline in income poverty, Gujarat's record of human development is uneven and inequitable, and the aftermath of violent communal tensions in 2002 casts a persistent shadow (Simpson, 2006; Varadarajan, 2002). Regional disparities have accompanied growth, seeing a rise rather than fall in inequalities (IHDR, 2011; Thaker and Shiyani, 2008): the first State Human Development report reflected on how "distortions" of unsustainable growth had failed to "translate positive outcomes of growth into appropriate benefits for everyone, and particularly the poor" (GSHDR, 2004: 31). Gujarat's underperformance in relation to its comparative wealth on indicators of human development was remarked upon in the national 2011 Human Development Report which, like its earlier state counterpart, remarks critically: "the high growth rate achieved by the state over the years has not percolated down to the marginalised sections of society" (IHDR, 2011: 50).

In the education sector, despite comparatively high standards of physical infrastructure (ASER 2012), public education provision in relation to conventional quality indicators clearly remains problematic. In the 2011 Education Development Index (EDI)[2] Gujarat was placed 15th nationally, with a score of 0.657 (IHDR, 2011). ASER (2013) showed that in rural Gujarat fewer than 5 per cent of children aged 7-10 years have been out of school since 2006, but the trend of reducing out of school numbers has flattened and fluctuates within that band, and an increase in unenrolled girls clearly emerged in 2013 (ASER, 2013: 103) (the same is found with both sexes aged 11-14, where the out of school ratio is higher, at approximately 7 per cent for girls but consistently below 5 per cent since 2011 for boys, cf. ASER 2013, 103). ASER's 2013 figures for children's achievements in reading and arithmetic make for miserable reading[3], and official figures, available for 2010-11, showed a *declining* retention rate (down from 83.66 per cent in 2006-7 to 80.83 per cent) with an "apparent survival rate" up to Standard 5 of 88 per cent in 2010-11 (DISE, 2010).[4]

Gujarat was late to pass its own RTE rules, requiring (along with West Bengal and Karnataka) a central reminder in January 2012 to do so. It complied the following month[5] and its attention to learning outcomes has been hailed as an innovative interpretation (Counterview, *ibid*). As the broader critique above showed, however, such concerns focus on children who are able to access formal provision in the first place, and mobile pastoralist children can only do so with difficulty. SSA has, however, prompted attention to mobility, particularly since achievement of MDG/EFA targets enforces concern over how to cater to Gujarat's well established status as a "receiving" state for migrant labourers from outside its boundaries, and extensive labour mobility within the state. Such mobility is a common response to addressing income and food insecurities in contexts of rural poverty and landlessness (Chatterjee, 2006). SSA's focus on flexible strategies of service delivery has provided a policy space for districts to submit projects that respond to local needs. In Gujarat — as elsewhere — such projects have included residential and non-residential bridge courses, back to school camps and seasonal hostels (Patra/SSA, 2007): the aim of such provision is to facilitate access and retention in mainstream education. Education Department officers interviewed in 2009 in Kachchh, a district with a high concentration of mobile pastoralists, reported for example on the establishment under SSA, and in collaboration with NGOs, of seasonal hostels and four boarding schools serving children of salt workers, fishermen and agricultural labourers. Yet there was nothing to report from this district on initiatives for mobile pastoralists or of the challenges of their mobility in and out of Kachchh during the school year.

In focus group discussion, state-level SSA officers recognised the challenge of learner mobility in relation to one particular form of it – seasonal labour migration, and that "Migrants should get a schooling facility, which hasn't happened till now". In keeping with the state's e-governance strategy, SSA had made significant effort to use telecommunications to develop a predictive/tracking system for seasonal labour migrants via Block and Cluster Resource Centres. This system was intended to enable responsible authorities to ensure that children could access provision as required throughout the year. Officers reported that in 2011, they had tracked some 13,000 children of families working in sugar cane, salt pans, and construction (and remarked on this being "a lot of work") but were unable to report on how whether/well this had worked on the ground for the children using the schooling system. Questions as to how receiving schools might view "floating" learners of this kind, and how their learning would be monitored, were met with assurances that there would be no issue for intra-state migrants at least, as the curriculum and books are in the same language, and pacing of delivery across the year is uniform in all schools. Such perceptions of schooling processes bear little relation to well established empirical realities in Gujarat (cf. Dyer, 2008).

In relation to entitlements, it was evident that State officers understood mobility in terms of migrant labour, and that attending to the disadvantages experienced by ST and SC groups was a well established priority. The need to demonstrate progress against "targets" also lends itself to prioritising opportunities for success, which further undermines rights-based strategies. In the case of mobile pastoralists, these perspectives come together with traditions of negative "governmentality" and misrecognition of a mobile pastoralist livelihood as an anachronism that education can cure. This is amply demonstrated in how officers constructed the issue of education inclusion for all mobile people: "First priority is the seasonal ones because that can be thrashed out quickly. They [pastoralists] change from season to season so it is very difficult to trace them. If they are seasonal you can work out where they go, for the irregular ones they are here one night and somewhere else the next" (Gujarat State Education Officer Focus Group, December 2012).

Mobile pastoralists contradict state assumptions of governability, posing not just a mere challenge to bureaucratic operations, but a more profound challenge to the normative framework of sedentary human-being on which governance depends. Despite the physical proximity of schools, formal education remains inaccessible to pastoralists who seek to remain within their traditional livelihood. Officials, however, did not see pastoralism as a respectable contemporary livelihood: rather, they misrecognised it as a wilful way of life, and transferred to mobile pastoralists the responsibility for non-use of education services: "Often the parents resist so they don't easily send them so if they send them they will get all the facilities" (State Education Officer Focus Group, December 2012).

Exiting Pastoralism

Globalisation and land pressures are making life as a pastoralist very difficult to sustain. Formal education provision has shown no capacity to be sufficiently adaptable to allow households who pursue mobile livelihood to combine doing this with formal education for their children. Yet pastoralists widely acknowledge there are advantages of owing basic skills of reading, writing, numeracy, and having the confidence to speak which they associate with schooling. It is also apparent from many discussions with Rabaris that the social status inequality of being "uneducated" (unschooled, in popular imagination) is a stigma that they construct as an inherent part of a socio-economic identity as a pastoralist in contemporary India (Dyer, 2014). Provision of formal education has lent itself only to being a route *out* of mobile pastoralism, making it difficult to know what difference more flexible arrangements might have made to practices of contemporary pastoralism, or indeed in defending this livelihood from the onslaught of "development" as envisaged by powerful others.

Conclusion

This chapter has raised many areas of general concern in relation to ideas of education, democratic plurality and sustainable living. Despite the passing of the Right to Education Act and growing systemic flexibility under Sarva Shiksha Abhiyan, the two instruments promoting the right to education have identifiable flaws in relation to mobile groups. Action in redress requires looking again at relations of community and place: SSA's community- and habitation-based strategy, and the notion of neighbourhood school espoused in the 2009 RTE Act, clearly make assumptions about the notion of community, habitation and neighbourhood that discriminate against those who have "multiple residences and different sets of neighbours at different times of year" (Barfield, 2004: iii).

To some extent, the Alternative and Innovative Education strand of SSA can help – and supports the possibility of making education provision at least to some extent flexible, or even mobile. The Gujarat case has shown, however, that local perceptions of priorities – which SSA's policy parameters rely on to shape contextual responsiveness – may also reflect pre-existing patterns of discriminatory governmentality. State actors' legitimate non-rights based notions of entitlement, particularly in a target-orientated EFA era (Jansen, 2005), combine to dictate priorities that undermine the universal basis of the right to education and foreclose the policy space. Initiatives under SSA's AIE reflect the contradictory nature of education "inclusion": they are at once individually valuable in expanding the options for (some) mobile learners to access at least basic skills; yet they are too isolated and small in scale to mount a real challenge to the status inequality inherent in the dichotomous division of mainstream and "alternative" provision, or between sedentary and mobile people (Danaher *et al*, 2009).

The 2009 RTE Act conflates education with schooling in a narrow, legislative instrumentation of the right to education (Sen, 2006; Robeyns, 2006; McCowan, 2010; Niranjanaradhya and Kashyap, 2006). Its strict parameters, in apparent defence of quality, lend themselves to an interpretation of "inclusion" as participation in a form of education (Rao, 2006) that affirms the incompatibility of mobile pastoralism with modern society. Yet at the same time, there are growing national and global concerns about how humankind can live sustainably on the planet (IHDR, 2011; UNSTT, 2012). This is a compelling reason to reconsider the ecological and social value of situated learning, which teaches children how to do exactly that, as a valid and valuable form of education that is better nurtured and supported than abandoned.

Notes

1. The NCDNSNT website is at http://ncdnsnt.gov.in/
2. The EDI is calculated on parameters that include availability of schools per 1000 school-going children, drinking water facilities, common toilet and separate toilet for girls, teacher-student ratio, enrolment ratio, drop-out rate and also the pass percentage of students.
3. To take Standard 3 as an example, 9.1 per cent of children tested could recognize numbers 1-9, 38.5 per cent could recognise numbers up to 9 but not more; in (Gujarati) language 10.7 per cent children could not even read letters, while just 21.7 per cent could read the Standard textbook.
4. Available at http://www.dise.in/Downloads/Publications/Publications%202010-11/SRC%202010-11/STATE_REPORT-CARDS_2010-11.pdf
5. Information provided in http://counterview.org/2013/05/09/right-to-education-and-where-gujarat-stands/

References

African Union Commission (2010): Policy Framework for Pastoralism in Africa: Securing, Protecting and Improving the Lives, Livelihoods and Rights of Pastoralist Communities. African Union Commission: Department of Rural Economy and Agriculture. Available at http://au.int/en/dp/rea/sites/default/files/Policy per cent20Framework per cent20for per cent20Pastoralism.pdf. (accessed 19.10.2012).

Agrawal, A. and Saberwal, V. (2004): Whither South Asian Pastoralism? An Introduction. *Nomadic Peoples*,8 (2): 36-53.

ASER (2012): *Annual Status of Education Report*. http://www.pratham.org/file/ASER-2012report.pdf

ASER (2013): *Annual Status of Education Report*. http://www.pratham.org/file/ASER-2013report.pdf

Barfield, T. (2004): Nomadic Pastoralists in Afghanistan: The Reconstruction of the Pastoral Economy. Washington, DC: Bank Information Centre.

Berland, J. (2003): Servicing Ordinary Folk: Peripatetic Peoples and Their Niche in South Asia. In Casiminr and Rao (Ed.), *infra*, pp. 104-24.

Bharwada, C. and Mahajan, V. (2006): Lost and Forgotten: Grasslands and Pastoralists of Gujarat. In *The Forsaken Drylands: A Symposium on Some of India's Most Invisible People, Seminar* #564. http://www.india-seminar.com/2006/564/564_a_agrawal_&_v_ saberwal.htm.

Blench, R. (2001*): You can't Go Home Again: Pastoralism in the New Millennium.* London: ODI. Available at http://www.odi.org.uk/sites/odi.org.uk/files/odi-assets/publications-opinion-files/6329.pdf

Carr-Hill, R. (2006): Educational Services and Nomadic Groups in Djibouti, Eritrea, Ethiopia, Kenya, Tanzania and Uganda. In Dyer, C. (Ed.) (2006): infra, pp. 35–52.

Carr-Hill, R. (2012): Finding and Then Counting Out-of-School Children. *Compare* 4 (2): 187-212.

Casimir, M. and A. Rao (2003). The Historical Framework of Nomadism in South Asia: A Brief Overview. In Rao, A. and Casimir, M. (Ed.), infra, pp. 43-72.

Census of India (2011): Available: http://censusindia.gov.in/.

Chatterjee, C. (2006): *Identities in Motion: Migration and Health in India.* Mumbai: Centre for Enquiry into Health and Allied Themes.

Choksi, A. (1991): Pastoral Adaptation in the Late Harappan Tradition of Gujarat: An Ethno-Archaeological Approach. Unpublished Ph.D. thesis. Maharaja Sayajirao University, Vadodara.

Constitution of India (CoI). (1950): Available: http://india.gov.in/govt/constitutions_india.php.

Danaher, P., Kenny, M. and Leder, J. (Ed.) (2009): *Traveller, Nomadic and Migrant Education.* London: Routledge.

Dyer, C. (2000): *Operation Blackboard: Policy Implementation in Indian Elementary Education.* Oxford: Symposium Books.

Dyer, C., (Ed.) (2006): *The Education of Nomadic Peoples: Current Issues, Future Prospects.* Oxford: Berghahn Books.

Dyer, C. (2008): Early Years Literacy in Indian Urban Schools: Structural, Social and Pedagogical Issues. *Language in Education*, 22 (5): 237-53.

Dyer, C. (2014): *Livelihoods and Learning: Education for All and the Marginalisation of Mobile Pastoralists*. London: Routledge.

Dyson-Hudson, R. and Dyson-Hudson, N. (1980): Nomadic Pastoralism. *Annual Review of Anthropology*, 9: 15-61.

EFA India. (2000): *Education for All. The Year 2000 Assessment Report India.* New Delhi: Ministry of Human Resource Development, Government of India. http://www.unesco.org/education/wef/countryreports/india/contents.html.

Fratkin, E. and Mearns, R. (Ed.). (2003): Sustainability and Pastoral Livelihoods: Lessons from East African Maasai and Mongolia. *Human Organisation* 62 (2).

Gopalakrishnan, R. and Sharma, A. (1998): Education Guarantee Scheme in Madhya Pradesh: Innovative Step to Universalise Education. *Economic and Political Weekly,* September 26, p. 2546.

GSHDR (2004): Gujarat State Human Development Report. New York: UNDP.

Ikeya, K. and Fratkin, E. (2005): Introduction: Pastoralists and Their Neighbours: Perspectives from Asia and Africa. *SENRI Ethnological Studies* 69: 1-14.

IHDR (2011): Indian Human Development Report: Towards Social Inclusion. New Delhi: Oxford University Press.

International Institute for Environment and Development, and SOS Sahel (IIED/SOS Sahel). (2009): *Modern and Mobile. The Future of Livestock Production in Africa's Drylands,* Ed: H. de Jode. London: IIED/SOS Sahel.

Iyengar, S. (2001): The Gujarat Experience. In: Wastelands: A Symposium on Regenerating Our Degraded Land Resources. *Seminar* #499. Available. http://www.india-seminar.com/2001/499/499 per cent20sudarshan per cent20iyengar.htm

Jansen, J. (2005): Targeting Education: The Politics of Performance and the Prospects of "Education for All." *International Journal of Educational Development*, 25 (4): 361-476.

Jeffrey, C.; Jefferym, R. and Jeffery, P. (2004): Degrees without Freedom: The Impact of Formal Education on Dalit Young Men in North India. *Development and Change*, 35 (5): 963–86.

Jha, J. and Jhingran, D. (2002): *Elementary Education for the Poor and Other Deprived Groups.* New Delhi: Centre for Policy Research.

Joshi, A. (2008): *The DNT-NTs: Some Fundamentals, Some Reflections*. MUKT – SAAD, October, pp. 49-55. Available at: www.indianfolklore.org/journals/index.php/Mukt/article/view/133

Lave, J. and Wenger, E. (1991): *Situated Learning: Legitimate Peripheral Participation.* Cambridge: Cambridge University Press.

Kasturi, K. (2007): Presumed Guilty: India's Denotified Tribes. http://infochangeindia.org/index2.php?option=com_content&do_pdf=1&id=6677.

Kavoori, P. (2005): Environmentalism, Development and the Crisis of Pastoral Legitimacy: Rajasthan's Nomadic Pastoralists and the Forests of Madhya Pradesh. *SENRI Ethnological Studies*, 69: 215-26.

Köhler-Rollefson, I. and the LIFE Network (2007): Keepers of Genes. The Interdependence between Pastoralists, Breeds, Access to the Commons, and Livelihoods. Rajasthan: LIFE Network.

Krätli S. (2001): *Education Provision to Nomadic Pastoralists,* IDS Working Paper #126. Brighton: Institute of Development Studies.

Krätli, S. and Dyer, C. (2009): *Educating Mobile Pastoralists: A Strategic Review of Literature.* Education for Nomads Issues Paper #1. London: IIED.

Kumar, K. (2005): *Political Agenda of Education: A Study of Colonialist and Nationalist Ideas.* Second edtion, New Delhi: Sage Publications.

MARAG (2012): Personal Communication to Caroline Dyer, Ahmedabad: Maldhari Research and Action Group.

McCowan, T. (2010): Reframing the universal right to education. *Comparative Education*, 46 (4): 509-25.

Mehrotra, S. (2002): *Basic Social Services for All? Ensuring Accountability through Deep Democratic Decentralisation.* Background Paper to Human Development Report 2002, Innocenti Research Centre. Florence: UNICEF.

Minister of State for Development of Northern Kenya and Other Arid Lands (MDNKOAL). (2010): *Getting to the Hardest to Reach: A Strategy to Provide Education to Nomadic Communities in Kenya through Distance Learning.* Nairobi: MDNKOAL (Office of the Prime Minister) and Education for Nomads Programme.

Morpeth, R. and Creed, C. (2012): Reframing Basic Education to Deliver Education for All: Flexible Provision and Enabling Frameworks. *Open Learning*, 27 (3): 201-14.

Mortimore, M., with contributions from S. Anderson, L. Cotula, J. Davies, K. Faccer, C. Hesse, J. Morton, W. Nyangena, J. Skinner and C. Wolfangel. (2009): *Dryland Opportunities: A New Paradigm for People, Ecosystems and Development.* London: IUCN, IIED and UNDP/DDC.

Morton, J. (2010): Why Should Governmentality Matter for the Study of Pastoral Development? *Nomadic Peoples*, 14 (1): 6-30.

Nambi, A. (2001): Modern Technology and New Forms of Nomadism: Duck Herders in Southern India. *Nomadic Peoples,* 5 (1).

Niranjanaradhya and Kashyap, A. (2006): The "Fundamentals" of the Fundamental Right to Education in India. Bangalore: Centre for Child and the Law, National Law School of India University, and UNESCO. Available: http://www.ncpcr.gov.in/Acts/Fundamental_Right_to_Education_Dr_Niranjan_Aradhya_ ArunaKashyap.pdf.

Panda, S. (2008): Redressing the Stigma of "Nomadism" and "Criminality": Underpinnings of Its Omission and Incorporation in Indian Reservation Policy. http://www.indianfolklore.org/journals/index.php/Mukt/article/viewFile/131/140.

Pennells, J. and Ezeomah, C. (2000): Basic Education for Refugees and Nomads. In Yates, C. and Bradley, J. (Ed.): *Basic Education at a Distance: World Review of Distance Education and Open Learning.* Vancouver, BC: Commonwealth of Learning. pp. 173-91.

Rao, A. (2006): The Acquisition of Manners, Morals and Knowledge. In Dyer, C. (Ed.): supra, 53–76.

Rao, A. and Casimir, M. (2003): Nomadism in South Asia: An Introduction. In Rao, A. and Casimir, M. (Ed.) *Nomadism in South Asia.* New Delhi: Oxford University Press, pp. 1-38.

Ratnagar, S. (2004): The Other Indians. Essays on Pastoralists and Prehistoric Tribal People. New Delhi: Three Essays Collective.

Renake, M. (Chairman of the National Commission on De-Notified and Nomadic Tribes) (2008): Personal Communication to Caroline Dyer, New Delhi, May.

Robeyns, I. (2006): Three Models of Education: Rights, Capabilities and Human Capital. *Theory and Research in Education*, 4 (1): 69-84.

Robinson, B. (1999): Open and Distance Learning in the Gobi Desert: Non-Formal Education for Nomadic Women. *Distance Education*, 20 (2): 81–204.

RTE (2009): *Right To Education Act*. Available: www.education.nic.in/Elementary/free per cent20and per cent20compulsory.pdf.

Sarva Shiksha Abhiyan (SSA). (2005a): *A Programme for the Universalisation of Primary Education, India*. Department of School Education and Literacy, Ministry of Human Resource and Development, Government of India. http://ssa.nic.in/.

Sarva Shiksha Abhiyan (SSA). (2005b): *A Programme for the Universalisation of Primary Education, India. Framework (Revised)*. Department of School Education and Literacy, Ministry of Human Resource and Development, Government of India.

Sen, A. (2006): Human Rights and the Limits of Law. *Cardozo Legal Review*, (27): 2913-2927.

Sharma, P.V., Koller-Rollefson, I. and Morton, J. (2003): *Pastoralism in India: A Scoping Study*. New Delhi: DFID. Available at: http://uploads.vli.co.uk/lpp/disseminations/ZC0181/ZC0181ScopingStudyRollefsonSharmaMortonJun03.pdf.

Simpson, E. (2006): The State of Gujarat and the Men without Souls. *Critique of Anthropology*, 26 (3): 331-48.

SSA (2011): *Sarva Shiksha Abhiyan. Framework for implementation. Based on the Right of Children to Free and Compulsory Education Act, 2009*. Department of School Education and Literacy, Ministry of Human Resource and Development, Government of India. Available: http://mhrd.gov.in/sites/upload_files/mhrd/files/upload_document/SSA-Framework.pdf.

Sud, N. (2008): *Narrowing Possibilities of Stateness: The Case of Land in Gujarat*. Working Paper Number 163, Oxford: Queen Elizabeth House. http://www3.qeh.ox.ac.uk/pdf/qehwp/qehwps163.pdf. 7.7.2011.

Tapper, R. (2008): Who are the Kuchi? Nomad Self-Identities in Afghanistan. *Journal of the Royal Anthropological Institute (NS)*, 14: 97–116.

Thaker, H. and Shiyani, R. (2008): Socio-Economic Development in Gujarat: Rosy Picture with Concerns. *Journal of Rural Development*, 28 (4), 515-28.

Theis, J. (2004): Promoting Rights-Based Approaches. Experiences and Ideas from Asia and the Pacific. Sweden: Save the Children. http://www.equalinrights.org/fileadmin/filelist/documenten/Guides and Manuals/2._Human_rightsbased_development_programmoming/theis_-_promoting_rights-based_approaches.pdf.

Times of India (ToI). (2008): Quota for Denotified Tribes Impractical. *23* September. http://timesofindia.indiatimes.com/india/Quota-for-denotified-tribes-impractical/articleshow/3515570.cms.

Tomasevski, K. (2003): *Education Denied: Costs and Remedies*. London: Zed Books.

Tomasevski, K. (2004): *Economic, Social and Cultural Rights: The Right to Education*. New York: United Nations Economic and Social Council, Commission on Human Rights.

UIS (2013): *Schooling for Millions of Children Jeopardised by Reductions in Aid*. UNESCO Institute of Statistics Factsheet. Available http://www.uis.unesco.org/Education/Documents/fs-25-out-of-school-children-en.pdf

UN-DHR (1948): *The Universal Declaration of Human Rights*. United Nations. http://www.un.org/Overview/rights.html

UNESCO. (2010): Reaching the Marginalised. Education For All Global Monitoring Report 2010. Paris: UNESCO.

UNICEF (1990): Convention on the Rights of the Child. http://www.unicef.org/crc/.

UNSTT (2012): *Building on the MDGs to Bring Sustainable Development to the Post-2015 Development Agenda. Thematic Think Piece.* UN System Task Team on the post 2015 UN Development Agenda. Available at: http://www.un.org/millenniumgoals/pdf/Think per cent20Pieces/17_sustainable_development.pdf. Last accessed 2.11.2012.

Varadarajan, S. (Ed.) (2002): *Gujarat: The Making of a Tragedy*. New Delhi: Penguin Books.

21

An Invisible Presence "On the Move"

The Subjective Constructions of High School Youth in a South African City

Aslam Fataar

IN Africa, young people constitute the majority of the population and are at the centre of societal interactions and transformations. Yet children and youth are often placed at the margins of the public sphere and major political, socio-economic, and cultural processes. This challenging situation on the African continent today makes young people particularly vulnerable. Many have little or no access to education, employment, healthcare and basic nutrition. Over the past two decades, political conflict, armed violence, and the HIV/AIDS pandemic created a crisis of unprecedented proportions for younger generations of Africans.

This paper is a conceptual account of how within these stressful environments, such as now found in African cities such as Cape Town, school students as young people organise and make sense of their daily lives, and how they negotiate their private and public roles and envision their futures (Fataar, 2013). This paper argues that mobility is central to their youthful mediations. I advance the view that a consideration of the nature and extent of their struggles, which involve the cultivation of survivalist epistemologies, "on the move," can explain how marginal urban youth go about establishing their survivalist subjectivities in light of rapidly reconfiguring urban terrains.

This paper is based on a number of ethnographic studies on high-school students in various spaces of the city. The paper uses the lenses of space, mobility, and embodiment in order to understand the relationship between young people's socialising contexts in and across their neighbourhood and their school going in city spaces. My point of departure is that there is a specifiable interactive relationship between students' living contexts and how they construct and position their educational subjectivities within these contexts. I suggest that qualitative work enables us to provide acute understandings of how students go about developing interactive, spatially inscribed, everyday practices, relations and interactions in terms of which they shape their livelihoods. They work to keep their aspirant constructions relatively parallel with their everyday peer and neighbourhood engagements, in effect managing to accumulate their "schooled" dispositions mostly out of sight, on the move, spectrally, while engaging in urban peer discourses as "spectacle," show and bravado, in effect establishing street credibility that secures them space for their parallel survivalist navigations.

Poor black children are the focus of this account; specifically their ability to navigate rewired urban space and, in the process, transacting feasible lives in the light of desperate urban living. As suggested above, the argument I offer is that they do so largely in parallel to the normative school choice discourses — unrecognised and undervalued by their urban schools. The notion "bodies in space" is apposite to capture the complex ways in which these children go about accessing the city and its schools. However, in spite of these precarious bodily adaptations, the extant formal discourses of the city are oblivious to the ontological presence of the black. Other, in the form of these school-going children. Their mobile subject making in the city remains an invisible presence, with consequences for what the city is able to recognise and the schools' (in)ability to offer genuinely inclusive institutional cultures. I suggest that these children carve out aspirant bodily dispositions while actively engaging their city's social and educational infrastructures.

Puncturing Functionalist Readings of Schooling in the Elusive African Metropolis

This paper contributes to a nascent body of work that attempts to bring the submerged worlds of the black urban under-classes in the South African city to academic consciousness. Nuttall and Mbembe's (2008) edited a collection on the city of Johannesburg, which they conceptualise as an "elusive metropolis," does much to recuperate a form of scholarship that punctures functionalist readings of cities. Their work sets out an interrogation of Africa as a sign of modern social formation, based on a gesture of defamiliarisation, and a commitment to providing a sense of the worldliness of contemporary African life forms. Life forms in the "Afropolitan" city, they suggest, involving connections among various forms of circulation – people, capital, finance, images—and overlapping spaces and times. Writing about the worldliness of the contemporary African city requires a profound interrogation of Africa in general and as a sign in modern formulations of knowledge.

The elusive metropolis is juxtaposed with the global city paradigm's (*See* Sassen, 2001) emphasis on economic and technological global integration. The global city paradigm could be viewed as a highly functionalist reading of the city, as well as ignoring the specificity of cities of the global south. An analytically richer notion of the global city would account for what Appadurai (1996: 32) describes as urban life that are now constituted by "complex, over lapping, disjunctive, order of multiple centres, peripheries, and scapes of various scales, moving at various speeds." Mbembe & Nuttall (2008: 3) point out that the major cities of the global South share many of the characteristics of northern cities but that ways of seeing and reading African cities, for example, are still dominated by the metanarratives of urbanisation, modernisation, and crisis. They call for an analytical frame that captures the "fracturing, colliding and splintered orders of urban life" (2008: 5), in other words, views that move beyond the misery associated with urban poverty, to richer, more nuanced accounts of the uncertain, spectral and informal quality of life, understood as elusive yet momentarily "mappable."

Beyond the fact of urban poverty, this type of analysis is interested in the complex ways the "terms of recognition" – the ability and capacity of the poor to exercise their voice is pursued and substantiated (*see* Appadurai, 2004). The elusive African metropolis exists beyond its architecture where, Simple material infrastructures and technologies, as well as their dysfunction and breakdown, thus create, define and transform new sites of transportation, new configurations of entangled spatialities, new public spaces of work and relaxation, new itinerancies and clusters of relations. The main infrastructural unit or building block is the human body (Nuttall & Mbembe, 2008: 71).

Similarly, the position I develop here is contrasted with predominant accounts of a sociology of education and knowledge that is inscribed with functionalist epistemologies. The analytical task is to present a view of the socialities associated with schools in the post-apartheid city, founded on a complex reading of urban subject making. My focus is on what Appadurai refers to as a "cultural economy" (1996: 37) associated with unfolding urban spaces and the formative role of schooling processes in them.

Mine is an attempt to bring those urban post-apartheid citizens into view, who live below the city's normative lines, planned pathways and built architectures. They live in the city's shadows, as old and newer urban residents in sprawling urban townships and shacklands, and some as refugees in squalid infrastructures in run-down parts of the inner city. They are mostly out of sight of the city's planning intent and normative consciousness. The children of the black working classes and unemployed poor go to great lengths to access what they perceive as better schools across the city, where they end up receiving a modernist curriculum that strips them of their access to their cultural knowledge and social survival epistemologies, on the assumption that modern middle-class education is what will emancipate them from their parochial cultural identifications. The assumption of cultural assimilation is hard at work in the urban post-apartheid school, albeit with multicultural genuflection to the newer incoming kids' backgrounds. Assimilationist curriculum practices are alive in the city's classrooms, which ostensibly provide the vehicle for their induction into modern life.

My focus is on the subjective processes of kids and families who make their school choices in the light of their physical extensions across the city, how they live their choices and how their subjectivities are formed. Such a defamiliarising view is interested in understanding how they work with their extant knowledge as they access the formal codes of the school, and how they work with their cooptation and assimilation into the formal registers of their schools.

My research indicates that schools deny them any recognition of their physical and ontological worlds and their epistemic forms, instead inducting them into a one-dimensional modern racial-colonial canon (*See* Fataar 2007, 2009, 2010). This leads these young people to encounter a around a narrow functional institutional culture at their schools that focusses primarily on what"s wrong with the learning of poor black kids, which translates into unproblematised pedagogical approaches that conceptualise student learning as a problem in isolation, understood apart from the reconfiguring social forms that swirl around it. The socio-cultural forms of the black working and urban poor, coupled with the everyday deployment of their cultural knowledge, what I call the counter-normative epistemic forms of the urban underside, are not given curricular currency.

Such a deficit approach to curriculum and knowledge embeds a modernist colonial and racial teleology. It embellishes the city's colonial, racial modernist form, while simultaneously hiding its productive capacity, making race continue to live an unseemly life, invisible to the eye, but operating beneath the surface. Commenting on the pervasiveness of race as productive social articulator, Goldberg (2009: 311) suggests that "Much like a shroud in its ghostly appearance, race still exercises a magnetism, modes of referentiality and divisive effects, if now informalised and sublimated into the body politic, just as it is shrugged off." Goldberg argues that with the secularisation of race, the language of racial order disappears even if its outlines and impressions, its structural imprint and threats continue to have social force.

The structural informalities of society continue to embed its racial legacy. I would suggest that the changing schooling landscape in the post-apartheid city provides a key articulating platform for the ways in which these continuing informalities, in "post-racial" context, play out. My key argument is the suggestion that these informalities work way beyond what a racial or modernist trope can recognise or make visible. It is in the interstices of the cracks, fissures and leaks of urban textualities that newer referential modes are productive, made up of urban self-writing governmental processes, which I will later suggest are brought about by young people who put their bodies on the line as they access the city's schools.

The "Visibly Invisible" Mobile School Subject

Making visible the mobile school-going subject that moves below the city's radar is meant as a challenge to the one-dimensional understandings of schooling and its subjective entailments. The dominant version of the educational subject in the city and its attendant knowledge form is not seen in the light of a radically altered social form, whose grasping requires one to see the link between the social unfolding and the curricular and knowledge forms. Two tropes reflect this dominant view: those that advocate fixing schools as transmitters of formal knowledge codes and those that advocate for an equity-informed schooling policy reform platform. Both leave the hegemonic knowledge and curriculum code untroubled. Induction into formal school knowledge is presented as a kind of moral commitment to providing kids access to middle-class knowledge and upward mobility. For both of these tropes the radically transforming social (and epistemological) form of schooling and education more generally are swept off the table. Both suffer from a kind of historical evisceration, in support of a forward-looking teleological commitment to functional educational and social improvement.

As Archer (2007) suggests, such a view embeds an entirely modernist view of the world. As a social realist and pragmatist philosopher, he (2007: 17) suggests that "courses of (human) action are produced through the *reflexive deliberations* of subjects who *subjectively* determine their practical projects in relation to their *objective* circumstances". It is the relationship between the subjective and objective that is important for my argument here. Archer's work opens out the possibility of viewing the imbrications of the educational, curricular and epistemological terrain of subject formation, in my case in a post-racial urban context. Archer provides for an understanding of the emergence of an architectonic map of those for whom access to the city's commercial and educational landscape remains formally closed, and for whom the city's schools represent a chimera, where, in their exercise of school choice, they put body and soul on the line to access its empty and emptying promises, on an empty promissory note, based on the "politics of aspiration." This happens in urban spaces that are being worked over by a neoliberal reconfiguration, where state withdrawal from social welfare provision and from acting as a buffer, has pitted the bodies of people in the direct firing line of an exclusionary school choice market, which is an example of "individual responsiblisation" in contingent neoliberal city space (Gulson & Fataar, 2011). Gulson (2011: 99) explains, "Aspirations and responsibilities circulate as part of education markets in inner city areas; and the racialisation of desires and concerns can be diluted to, for example, discourses of responsible, rational parenting." In other words, the responsibility for social and welfare related services, including education, are transferred onto the individual, families and communities. Young people have to figure out their aspirational maps based on what neoliberal discourses make available as knowable and possible, allowing "desiring neo-liberal subjects to gloss over race and racism, by recourse to the realm of personal preference."

The focus is on those city kids who cultivate their aspirations in the thickness of social life that is variously described as "bare" (Comaroff, 2007: 12), and "miserable urban life" or "intensifying immiseration" (Simone, 2008: 89), where cities no longer offer poor people the prospect of improving their livelihoods or modern ways of life. The growing distance that emerges between how urban Africans actually live, on the one hand, and the normative trajectories of urbanisation and public life, on the other, can constitute new fields of economic action (2008: 89). This distancing can lead to the disarticulation of coherent urban space, where people have to make what they can out of bare life. Simone describes this as a situation where people throw "their intensifying particularisms – of identity, location, destination and livelihood – into the fray, (and) urban residents generate a sense of unaccountable movement that might remain geographically circumscribed or travel great distances" (Simone, 2008: 89).

In other words, what is crucial to understand is the performance of subjectivity on the move, as I argue, on the basis of navigational maps that are constructed "as you go," based on formal destinations somewhat in sight, only somewhat, but with end destinies largely unknown, even unknowable. Clarity of end goals is not the key to subjective construction. It is not the clarity about where one ends up that motivates school aspirants, but the reaching out for a destination whose route remains unclear and tenuous. Investing in the "destination," however tenuous, serves as a motivation for remaining en route and it is the remaining en route that matters. Herein resides the "banality" and utter hopefulness of the investment. The hope invested in becoming a recognised urban citizen – children are "on the move," across borders, bridges, and highways, under subways, on trains, taxis, and busses – provide the motive force for investments in these children's urban making.

This brings the theorisation of space, or "lived space" (*See* Lefebvre, 1991), into view. People"s subjectivities are shaped in dynamic interaction with the reconfiguring physical landscape. This can be understood analytically as the outcome of a spatial dialectic: the imbrications of physical or material space, representational space, and spatial representation (or lived space). "Lived space" (or social space, relational space, or spatiality) refers to how people live in particular sites, how they are wired into their geography, and how they transcend this geography. Lived space focusses on what people become when engaging their geographies, appropriating space and inventing new practices. In their book, *Mapping the Subject,* Pile & Thrift (1995) explain that mappings of subjectivity or "subject becoming" need to be drawn in ways that are capable of elucidating the fixity and fluidity, the ambivalence and ambiguity, the transparency and opacity, and the surface and the depth of the mapped subject. It is out of a complex, fluid, open and layered lived experience that these school-going kids encounter their subjection and subject becoming. People's educational choices, for example, are invested with readings that draw on notions of the rapidly changing city and the spatial provenance they expect their choices to provide. What one wants to capture is the splintering quality of the metropolitan experience itself. Schooling subjectivities, constructed in motion, involve complex readings and navigations of the city's environs, often by children who have to travel long distances in precarious transport arrangements.

With regard to the structural outlines of the subjective formations associated with school life in the post-apartheid city, I argue that lived space has been the key articulator or organiser of these newer school subjectivities in the city. The rigid, racialised apartheid city grid has been fundamentally rearranged by families and increasingly mostly children, who make decisions on their own over their schools of choice. While school kids by and large still live in racialised pockets in the city, their school choices have increasingly been transacted across the city. Students have either burst out of racialised township spaces to attend remoter schools in adjacent townships, suburbs or the inner city, or they have moved to schools on the other side of the township. They have been developing a sense of citizenship rooted in the space of the city on the move, while becoming affectively distanced from their place of living to which they return every day.

Students have moved across the apartheid-generated city grid to access schools elsewhere, away from their homes. They do this on the basis of careful readings of the social-spatial attributions of the schools close by. The empirical evidence suggests that close to 50 per cent of school children in cities choose to go to schools in remoter locations (*See* Lemon & Battersby-Lennard, 2010). They have come to understand that the school close by has to be avoided, trapped as it is in place and devoid of aspirational capital.

Facilitated by a decentralised state governance model, schools have developed methods to preserve and induct their students into their hegemonic identities. Examples of such exclusionary school practices are: (1) the non-racism by stealth at the former coloured middle-class schools, involving, for example, discriminatory social practices among different black groups; (2) the linguistic apartheid at working-class schools in coloured townships; (3) the assimilation of incoming children into the hegemonic cultures of suburban schools; and (4) the exclusion practices that confront the recalcitrant children at the functional black township schools (*See* Soudien 2004, Fataar, 2009). What is apparent is that the city's schools, their different identification articulations notwithstanding, have evolved cultures of inclusion and exclusion, buttressed by their specific hegemonic ways of being.

Given this structurally rearranged city school landscape, what is important to consider is how these aspirational students construct their subjectivities as they move across the city to access their schooling. How do they come into subjective consciousness? How do they comport themselves as they burst out of their immediate surrounds and move into an unknown metropolitan order, with far-off hopes and dreams? How do they embody the routes, routines, repertoires and performances of their becoming as they access their education? How do they become city subjects as they emerge from their informalised, anti-aspirational, traumatised spatialities? And what can we learn about the way the city and its schools now work to include these newer "bodies on the move and on the make," while simultaneously blocking off the ontologies of these subjective flows from emerging out of the shadows and co-constructing the post-apartheid city's metropolitan imagination?

School Students' Subjectivities Articulated in Space

Articulated in space, youth bodies are carved out of complex processes that involve their physical mobility as they move across the city in search of functioning modern schooling, the embodiments they take on in their uneven spatial terrains, and their classification struggles (working with their uneven knowledge dispositions) as they open a path into their urban becoming. They adopt a type of multi-sited adaptive literacy as they daily navigate various spatialities — surviving in their ephemeral and impoverished domestic spaces, the mobile and unsafe spaces of their travel and transport arrangements, and the dissonant spatiality of their assimilation-orientated schools that fail to recognise their complex subjective dynamics.

They use their bodies as a kind of human infrastructure as they establish their presence in the city. Simone (2008: 68) explains that the notion of "people as infrastructure" captures the idea of "incessantly flexible, mobile, and provisional intersections of residents that operate without clearly delineated notions of how the city is to be inhabited and used." These intersections or conjunctions become a kind of infrastructure, a platform for reproducing life in the city out of "complex combinations of objects, spaces, people and practices" (p. 69). Out of these types of social practices emerge a kind of regularity capable of anchoring these mobile students" lives. While radically open, these practices are transacted in the light of various threats of physical violence, especially for girls (*See* Lancaster, 2011). These children nonetheless succeed in opening a viable path into their schooling careers.

Their spatial consciousness is based on acute readings of what type of behaviour is expected of them in each space. They adapt to these expectations, sometimes with great difficulty, on an understanding of the type of bodily comportment required. They take on a type of dual identity based on the desire to fit into their shifting environments. In their township spaces they try to live below the radar by fitting in with peer-group activity, which works against their appearing too strange, thereby avoiding verbal or physical recrimination. In the taxi, train and/or bus on the way to school they adopt an appropriate body language that aids their safe travel, and they work hard to fit into the culture of assimilation of their schools.

Bodily discipline and appropriate comporting seem to characterise their successful navigation across these different worlds. Based on interviews and observing them in these spaces, I deduced that they have an acute understanding of the dominant discourses of each space. They figure out the appropriate behaviour that would enable them to survive in these spaces. For example, feigning obliviousness to the exclusionary discourses at their school is adopted as a bodily tactic deployed to access the school's formal educational goods. Similarly, smoking or flirting on a taxi or adopting a specific bodily style over the weekend in the township is used as a means of fitting into the expectations of those spaces. Strategic readings, street-smart literacies and tactical deployment of appropriate behaviour constitute the lineaments of their subject making, in effect securing them access to the city. This notion of tactics operating at the interstices of strategic constraints is a recurring theme in the work of Michael de Certeau (1984: 29-44). His work allows one to understand how these children's subject making arises from everyday practices and tactics based on improvisation and opportunism that combine disparate resources and material to gain momentary advantage. It is the daily accumulation and repetition of such practices that secure them viable school going experiences in the post-apartheid city.

Conclusion

The children's active bodily adaptations are thus central to their urban subject making. They carve out complex bodily orientations to navigate materially deprived urban spaces by adopting a range of tactics, including resistance, strategic compliance, acting tough, and dressing and behaving with calculated sensibility. They establish their everyday bodily practices on the move across the city, developing acute readings of the expectations of each space that they enter and exit daily, including their schools. They acquire highly sophisticated street literacies that inform their readings of these spaces, enabling them to survive, adapt, and access the requisite cultural capital to get on.

It is important to note that these flexible and disciplining configurations are pursued not in some essential contrast to more formal priorities and routines in the city, although they perceptibly are, but as specific routes to a kind of stability and regularity that poor urbanites have always attempted to realise (*See* Simone, 2008). This brings me back to the link between the cityscape and the dominant discourses of the school. There seems to be a widely unacknowledged formative relationship between different urban discourses: the planned and the providential, the informal routes of the urban poor and the formal accessibilities of the middle classes, the exclusions of the discourses of the urban underside and the predominance of middle class "ways of knowing." These operate in parallel. The extant formal discourses of the city are oblivious to the ontological presence of the black other. The latter's precarious subjections in the city remain an invisible presence. Schooling in the city plays a largely reproductive role in circulating this parallel message — that is, it circulates an exclusive focus on the narrow epistemological code that prevents the ontologies and knowledges of the city's poor and black majority from entering the formal public domain. Despite the complex subject-making processes at play, a narrow epistemological orientation remains the hegemonic trope in the post-apartheid city and its schools.

References

Archer, M. (2007): *Structure, Agency and the Internal Conversation.* Cambridge: Cambridge University Press.

Appadurai, A. (1996): *Modernity at large: Cultural dimensions of globalisation.* Minneapolis: University of Minnesota Press.

Appadurai, A. (2004): The Capacity to Aspire: Culture and the Terms of Recognition. In Rao, V. and Walton, M. (Ed.): *Culture and Public Action.* California: Stanford University Press.

Comaroff, J. (2007): Beyond Bare Life: AIDS, (Bio)Politics, and the Neo-Liberal Order. *Public Culture*. 19 (1): 197-219.

De Certeau, M. (1984): *The Practice of Everyday Life.* Berkeley: University of California Press.

Fataar, A. (2007): Schooling, Youth Adaptation and Translocal Citizenship across the Post-Apartheid City. *Journal of Education*, 42: 9-32.

Fataar, A. (2009): Schooling across the Post-Apartheid City. *African Education Review*. 6 (1): 1-18.

Fataar, A. (2010): Youth Self-Formation and the "Capacity to Aspire": The Itinerant "Schooled" Career of Fuzile Ali across Post-Apartheid Space. *Perspectives in Education*, 28 (3): 34-45.

Goldberg, D. (2009): The Threat of Race: Reflections on Racial Neo-Liberalism. Oxford: Blackwell.

Gulson. K. (2011): *Education Policy, Space and the City*. New York: Routledge.

Gulson, K. and Fataar, A. (2011): Neo-Liberal Governmentality, Schooling, and the City: Conceptual and Empirical Notes on and from the Global South. *Discourse: Studies in the Cultural Politics of Education.* 32(2), 269-83.

Lancaster, I. (2011): Modalities of Mobility: Johannesburg Learners' Daily Negotiations of the Uneven Terrain of the City. *Southern African Review of Education.*17(1): 49-64.

Lefebvre, H. (1991): *The Production of Space.* Oxford: Blackwell.

Lemon, A., & Battersby-Lennard, J. (2010): Studying Together, Living Apart: Emerging Geographies of School Attendance in Post-Apartheid Cape Town. *African Affairs*. 110/438: 97-120.

Mbembe, A. (2006): What is Postcolonial Thinking? Retrieved on 30 March, 2011, from http://www.eurozine.com/articles/2008-01-09-mbembe-en.html

Nuttall, S. & Mbembe, A. (2008): *Johannesburg the Elusive Metropolis.* Johannesburg: Wits University Press.

Pile, S. & Thrift, N. (1995): Mapping the Subject: Geographies of Cultural Transformation. London: Routledge.

Sassen, S. (2001): *The Global City.* Princeton: Princeton University Press.

Simone, A. (2008): People as Infrastructure. In Nuttall, S and Mbembe, A. (Ed.); supra.

Soudien, C. (2004): "Constituting the class"; An Analysis of the Process of "Integration" In South African Schools. In Chisholm, L. (Ed.) *Changing Class: Education and Social Change in a Post-Apartheid South Africa.* Cape Town: HSRC Press, pp. 89-113.

Soudien, C. (2011): "What to Teach the Natives: A Historiography of the Curriculum Dilemma in South Africa. In Pinar, W. (Ed.) *Curriculum Studies in South Africa: Intellectual Histories & Present Circumstances.* Hampshire: Palgrave Macmillan.

Contributors

Dr. Fatima Jiddum Ahmad is a Nigerian Education Specialist with 35 years of public service and development practice experiences. She is an experienced Director of Education with a demonstrated history of working in the education management industry. She has skilled in Policy Analysis, Strategic Planning, System Monitoring, Public Administration, and Work under Minimal Supervision. Strong education professional with a Certificate focused in Advanced Training Program in Educational Planning and Analysis from UNESCO-IIEP.

Prof. Madhumita Bandyopadhyay is a Professor at the Department of School and Non-formal Education in National Institute of Educational Planning and Administration (Deemed to be University), New Delhi. She is currently engaged in research, teaching and training programmes of the University. Her research interests include education of disadvantaged groups, decentralization of educational governance and the education of women.

Prof. H.S Bhola is a Professor (Emeritus), Indiana University, USA. He is a widely published author in the areas of policy analysis and evaluation, focused on adult education for development in the Third World. Research and consultations have taken him to Asia, Africa, and Latin America on behalf of multiple bilateral and multilateral agencies, among them, UNESCO, UNICEF, and USAID.

Prof. Caroline Dyer is a Professor of Education and International Development at the University of Leeds, UK. She co-directs the University's Centre for Global Development and is Chair of the World Universities Network Global Challenge of Higher Education and Research. She has researched education inclusion among mobile pastoralists in Africa, South Asia and Mongolia. Her publications include a 2014 Routledge monograph, numerous academic papers, reports, and policy reviews for governments and development partners.

Prof. Aslam Fataar is a Professor in the Department of Education Policy Studies at Stellenbosch University in Cape Town. He specializes in the areas of Sociology of Education and Education Policy. He has published three books: Education Policy Development in South Africa's Democratic Transition, 1994-1997 (2011) 'Engaging Schooling Subjectivities across the Post-Apartheid City' (2015), and 'The education practices and pathways of South African students across power-marginalised regions (2018). He is the outgoing President of the South African Education Research Association and the former Editor-in-Chief of the journal, *Southern African Education Review,* Fataar has won three research awards and three prizes for his published articles.

Prof. R. Govinda is currently Distinguished Professor in Council for Social Development, New Delhi. He has been a former Vice Chancellor of National University of Educational Planning and Administration, New Delhi which has recently become National Institute of Educational

Planning and Administration (Deemed to be University), New Delhi. He headed the Department of School and Non-formal Education at NIEPA, New Delhi for many years and guided a DFID funded international Collaborative Research on Educational Access, Transition and Equity (CREATE) along with University of Sussex, UK. He was the J.P. Naik National Fellow for Studies in Education and Culture, Indian Council for Social Relations. His career highlights include Visiting Professor at Institute of Education, University of London. He has taught at the M.S. University of Baroda and at the International Institute of Educational Planning, UNESCO, Paris. He is member of several national and international bodies such the Council of Consultant Fellows of International Institute of Educational Planning and the International Advisory Group of the Global Monitoring Report, UNESCO.

Prof. S. Irfan Habib is a Historian of science and of modern political history. Besides a large number of papers, he has also edited and authored and co-authored several books. Till recently, he held Maulana Azad Chair at the National Institute of Educational Planning and Administration, New Delhi.

Dr. Radhika Iyengar has a Ph.D. (with distinction) in Economics of Education from Teachers College at Columbia University in 2011. She holds an Associate Research Scholar's position at the Center for Sustainable Development at the Earth Institute, Columbia University. She also oversees multi-country research projects on language literacy, promoting and implementing the Sustainable Development Goals for Education and Gender. Her research interests are in conducting evaluation of educational programs and international educational development which is in line with her role and responsibilities at the Earth Institute

Prof. Roger Jeffery has been Professor of Sociology of South Asia, University of Edinburgh, since 1997. His research has been largely based in Pakistan, Delhi and Uttar Pradesh (UP), involving extended periods of time resident in village and small-town western UP. His work has focused on public health and health policy, especially maternal and reproductive health, access to medicines, medical education and secondary schooling in the context of socio-economic development and social change in South Asia.

Prof. Praveen Jha is a Professor of Economics at the Centre for Economic Studies and Planning (CESP) and Adjunct Professor at the Centre for Informal Sector and Labour Studies (CISLS), is with the School of Social Sciences, Jawaharlal Nehru University, New Delhi, India. He has been a Visiting Fellow to several Institutions/Universities, including University of Bremen, Germany; Tianjin University of Finance and Economics, Tianjin, China, Rhodes University, Grahamstown, South Africa and Sam Moyo African Institute for Agrarian Studies (SMAIAS), Harare, Zimbabwe, International Labour Organisation (ILO), Geneva and Kassel University, Germany. He has also been associated with several research studies with the UN institutions such as the ILO, the UNICEF, the UNDP, the FAO etc. His major areas of research and teaching include: Political Economy of Development, with particular reference to Labour, Agriculture, Natural Resources, Public Finance, Education, and History of Economic Thought.

Prof. Kenneth King was Director of the Centre of African Studies and Professor of International and Comparative Education at Edinburgh University for many years. He is now Emeritus Professor in its Schools of Education and of Social and Political Studies. His research focuses on international education, aid policy, and skills development, especially in the informal sector. He edited *NORRAG News* for 30 years until 2017. Since 2016, he has been researching, with Pravina King, India's Human Development Cooperation in Africa.

Prof. Keith Lewin is Emeritus Professor of International Development and Education at the University of Sussex. He was formerly the Director of the DFID funded Consortium for Research on Educational Access, Transitions and Equity (CREATE) and was Director of the Centre for International Education at Sussex for 17 years. He was Founding Director of the Sussex International Masters programme in Education (1979). He is a Fellow of the UK Academy of Social Sciences and a Chartered Physicist. He chairs the Trustees of the UK Forum for International Education and Training. His publications include more than 15 books on education and development, over 100 refereed journal articles and book chapters, 60 commissioned policy reviews and substantial consultancy reports, and a wide variety of occasional papers and working documents for research projects.

Prof. Thomas F. Luschei is a Professor of Education at Claremont Graduate University. The primary focus of his research is the impact and availability of educational resources—particularly high-quality teachers—among marginalized children and youth.

Dr. Angelique R. Mahal is an Education Technical Advisor at Nigeria Scale-up Project. She is responsible for providing technical education services through analysis, strategy, knowledge transfer, literature review, tool development, and proposal review to the Conditional Grants Scheme of the Office of the Senior Special Assistant to the President of Nigeria on the Millennium Development Goals while also developing concept notes, communications, and managing education project functions.

Prof. A. Mathew, ICSSR Senior Fellow earlier is currently In-charge of Digital Archives of Education Documents, NIEPA. He has a doctorate in educational studies from Jawaharlal Nehru University and has worked in NIEPA, National Literacy Mission; UNESCO/UNDP as Resource Person of Education Community in Solution Exchange - Knowledge Management Project and as NIEPA's National Fellow since 2011. He has published many books and Monographs, Working Papers, etc. in areas of adult, primary and higher education, history of education, and education policies.

Prof. Santosh Mehrotra is a Professor of Economics at Centre for Informal Sector and Labour Studies, School of Social Sciences, Jawaharlal Nehru University. He has been a former Director-General of Institute of Applied Manpower Research, Planning Commission from 2009 to 2014. He is a human development economist, whose research and writings have had most influence in the areas of labour/ employment, skill development, child poverty, and the economics of education. From 1991 to 2006, he worked for two UN agencies – UNICEF and UNDP as Chief economist of UNDP's global Human Development Report (2002-05), New York. He also headed the Rural Development Division, and then Development Policy Division, Planning Commission (till August 2009). He is an author of several chapters in India's 11th Five Year Plan (2007-2012), and the 12th Five Year Plan.

Prof. Teboho Moja is the Director and Professor of Higher Education at New York University, an Extraordinary Professor at the University of the Western Cape, and a Visiting Research Fellow at the Centre for the Advancement of Scholarship at the University of Pretoria. She has published extensively on higher education, presented numerous keynote addresses at international conferences on higher education issues, and her research has focused on higher education policy. In 1993, she was appointed to the Centre for Educational Policy Development (CEPD) as a policy analyst for higher education. The Centre produced policy documents and also proposed implementation strategies for hand-over to the new Minister of Education after South Africa's first democratic elections. Following the elections, she served as a Special Advisor to two Ministers of Education and was appointed as Executive Director and Commissioner of the National Commission on Higher Education. She has served on numerous committees and boards of international bodies such as UNESCO and Councils of Universities in South Africa. She has served as Chair on the Boards and continues as a member for the Center for Higher Education Trust and University World News – Africa edition.

Prof. Shireen Motala is the Senior Director of the Postgraduate School: Research and Innovation Division, and Professor in the Faculty of Education, the University of Johannesburg. She has worked extensively in research and research management and has provided leadership for regional and international partnerships. These have led to collaborations with universities across Africa, Asia and with northern partners. Her research record is substantial and includes books, editorship of local and international journals and chapters in books. Her research interests and expertise are in education financing, internationalisation, postgraduate pedagogies, decolonisation and globalisation. She has provided leadership in education, including serving on the Council of Higher Education (CHE), the Ministerial Task Team to review the national Senior Certificate examination and the SA UNESCO Commission. She was the first inaugural president of the South African Education Research Association and is currently on the executive.

Prof. Badri Narayan is a Professor of Social Historian and Cultural Anthropologist in Centre for the Study of Discrimination and Exclusion at Jawaharlal Nehru University, New Delhi. Earlier, he worked at the G.B. Pant Social Science Institute, Allahabad. His wide-ranging interests cover culture, memory and politics, contemporary histories, Ethnography of marginalized politics, social and anthropological history, Dalit and subaltern issues and Identity formation and the question of power. He has been a fellow at the Indian Institute of Advanced Study, Shimla (1998-99), and Visiting Fellow at the International Institute of Asian Studies, University of Leiden, The Netherlands (2002) and HGIS Fellow at the Royal Tropical Institute, Amsterdam (2001). He is a recipient of the Fulbright Senior Fellowship (September 2005-April 2006) and the Smuts Fellowship, University of Cambridge (February 2007-October 2007). Besides having written a number of research articles both in English and Hindi for national and international Journals, he has authored many books.

Dr. Judith E. Parker is an Adjunct Assistant Professor in the Department of Organization and Leadership at Teachers College/Columbia University in New York, USA. She has over 20 years of experience working for 3M Company in Minnesota in the research and development area and then designing and delivering leadership development training programs for the global technical community in Europe and Asia. She has taught physics in college and has been elected a Fellow of the American Association for the Advancement of Science and a member of Sigma Pi Sigma (Physics Honor Society). She has been awarded the National Association of Academies of Science Distinguished Service Award, the 3M Technical Circle of Excellence Award, and the American Association of Physics Teachers Innovative Teaching Award. Her professional interests have focused on the effective use of technology in teaching and learning and resulted in numerous publications and presentations globally.

Ms. Pooja Parvati is associated with Tata Trusts, which is amongst India's oldest, non-sectarian philanthropic organisations since 2016. A development practitioner with 17 years of progressive work experience, she has studied at Indian Institute of Technology Bombay and Delhi School of Economics. Before joining Tata Trusts, she has worked in Oxfam India, Centre for Budget and Governance Accountability and Centre for Social Research. Key areas of interest include public provisioning for education; understanding inequality and its correlation to basic essential services such as education, health, social norms etc.

Prof. Vimala Ramachandran is the Director of ERU Consultants Pvt. Ltd., has been working on elementary education, girls' education, women's empowerment and the intersection between health, nutrition, education and childcare practices in children. She was involved in the conceptualization of Mahila Samakhya (Education for Women's Equality) and served as the first National Project Director from 1988-93 in MHRD, GOI. She established Educational Resource Unit (now known as ERU Consultants Private Limited) in 1998 as a network of researchers and practitioners working on education. From 2011 to mid-2015, she was a National Fellow and Professor of Teacher Management and Development in NIEPA. She has published extensively on the various issues in the field of school and teacher education.

Dr. Sandra Schmidt works as the Associate Professor and Program Director of Social Studies at Teachers College. Her research interests include geography education, critical social theory in geography, civic education, social studies education, postcolonial theory, and gender and queer theory. In the past, she has worked on education initiatives in Malawi, South Sudan and Ethiopia, and taught secondary social studies within the United States. Schmidt's recent publications have been focused on queer theory and global social studies education. Schmidt received her B.A. from Swarthmore College, a M.A. from the University of Michigan, and a Ph.D. from Michigan State University.

Dr. Satadru Sikdar is currently working as Assistant Professor at National Institute of Public Finance and Policy, New Delhi. He is with NIPFP, New Delhi, since 2006. He was also Visiting Scientist at ICDD, University of Kassel, Germany under DAAD fellowships during November-December 2018. He did his Ph.D. from Centre for Economic Studies and Planning (CESP/SSS), Jawaharlal Nehru University, New Delhi. Title of his Ph.D. thesis is "School Education in India: An Assessment of Public Provisioning since the Early 1990s". He has been associated with several research studies in NIPFP, including preparation of Medium-Term Fiscal Policy for different states; effectiveness and utilization of funds for selected schemes, property taxation and urban poverty alleviation among others. His key research areas are: Public Policies, Public Finance Management, Subsidies, along with Education and Labour Economics.

Prof. Crain Soudien is the Chief Executive Officer of the Human Sciences Research Council and formerly a Deputy Vice-Chancellor at the University of Cape Town where he remains an emeritus professor in Education and African Studies. His publications in the areas of social difference, culture, education policy, comparative education, educational change, public history and popular culture include three books, four edited collections and articles, reviews, reports, and book chapters. He is involved in a number of local, national and international social and cultural organisations and is the Chairperson of the Independent Examinations Board, the former Chairperson of the District Six Museum Foundation, a former President of the World Council of Comparative Education Societies and had been the chair of the Ministerial Committee on Transformation in Higher Education and is currently the chair of the Ministerial Committee to evaluate textbooks for discrimination. He is a fellow of a number of local and international academies and serves on the boards of a number of cultural, heritage, education and civil society structures.

Prof. N.V. Varghese is currently the Vice-Chancellor of National Institute of Educational Planning and Administration (NIEPA) and Director of the Centre for Policy Research in Higher Education

(CPRHE), New Delhi. He holds a doctoral degree in Economics with specialisation in educational planning. He was Head of Governance and Management in Education at the International Institute for Educational Planning (IIEP/UNESCO), Paris, until October 2013 and Head of its Training and Education Programmes from 2001 to 2006. In the 1990s, he was a Professor and Head of the Educational Planning Unit at NIEPA, New Delhi. While in NIEPA, he was responsible for managing the Asian Network of Training and Research Institutions in Educational Planning (ANTRIEP) and was editor of its Newsletter. He has directed several research projects and has published around 25 books and research reports, research papers and articles in areas related to educational planning, financing, and higher education.

Dr. Volker Wedekind is an Associate Professor in Vocational Education and Deputy Head of the School of Education at the University of Nottingham, UK. He is Coordinator of UNESCO's Nottingham UNEVOC Centre. Previously, he held the research chair in Vocational Education and Pedagogy at the University of Witwatersrand, South Africa, and remains an Honorary Associate Professor linked to the Wits Centre for Researching Education and Labour (REAL). His major research interest focuses on the intersection between policy reform and how these affect the people and institutions working in the system. He has been involved in policy processes at national level and served on a number of ministerial committees, government task teams, and statutory committees in South Africa.

Index